Manny Shinwell

Manny Shinwell:

An Authorised Biography

Peter Slowe

Pluto  Press

LONDON • BOULDER, COLORADO

First published 1993 by
Pluto Press
345 Archway Road
London N6 5AA
and 5500 Central Avenue
Boulder, Colorado 80301, USA

British Library Cataloguing in Publication Data
A catalogue record for this book is available from the British Library

ISBN 0 7453 0736 1 hb
ISBN 0 7453 0737 X pb

Library of Congress Cataloging in Publication Data
applied for

Designed and produced for Pluto Press by
Chase Production Services, Chipping Norton
Typeset from author's disks by
Stanford Desktop Publishing Services, Milton Keynes
Printed in Finland by WSOY

This book is dedicated to
Alistair Slowe

Contents

Acknowledgements

This biography has been quite a project and there are many people who have helped me complete it.

Outstanding among them has been Manny Shinwell's nephew, the distinguished writer Alan Shinwell. In a number of interviews with his uncle and with others, many of whom are now dead, he provided the framework for a television biography which, owing to misjudgements on the part of the television companies, was never made. It was extremely kind of him to have me as his house-guest and to take time to go through whole cupboards full of material with me. I particularly appreciate the sacrifice of so much time in his busy life. I hope that he feels the material has been well used.

Manny Shinwell's son, Ernie, and his wife Netta, have also been unstinting in their help and generous with their time. Ernie has provided me with information and insight which only a favourite son can have.

Another of Manny Shinwell's nephews, Roger Robinson, and his wife Maureen, have been kind and hospitable and full of ideas. In his later years, Manny was probably closer to Roger than anybody else. I am very grateful to him for material, ideas and – again – his time.

Among those who have helped with my research, I would like first and foremost to thank my mother, especially for her work at the National Newspaper Library. And I am also very grateful to Ian Harris, Viv Harris, Ross Moody, Ian Nurse, Daniel Powell, Paul Rodaway and Mark Williams.

I am especially grateful to the following interviewees: Julia Robinson, Ernest Shinwell, Sam Shinwell, Nina Davis, Lord Dormand, Sir Arthur Drew, Lord Glenamara, Asher Grossman, Lord Healey, Lord Jenkins of Hillhead, the late Ian Mikardo, Paddy Kavanagh, Reny McManners, Lord Oram, Ernest Shinwell Snr, Netta Shinwell, Charlie Short, Bob Taylor and Lord Underhill. And I also appreciate the time and trouble taken by the many others whom I interviewed, who wrote to me or who spoke to me on the telephone.

I am very grateful for helpful ideas and insights from discussions with members of Easington Constituency Labour Party, and others whom I have interviewed in Glasgow, the North-East, Tower Hamlets and Westminster, as well as others members of the Shinwell family.

I have particularly appreciated the help of the staff in the following libraries: Churchill College (Cambridge) library, Durham County libraries, the Gallacher Memorial Library, Linlithgow Library, the Mitchell Library, the National Museum of Labour History archives, Nuffield College (Oxford) library, the University of Sussex Library, the University of Warwick Library and the West Sussex Institute of Higher Education Library. Staff at the National Newspaper Library and at the Public Record Office were also very helpful.

The excellent typist was Jenny McAlear.

Finally, my son Alistair, to whom this book is rightly dedicated, was a joy throughout.

Peter M. Slowe

FOREWORD

The Rt Hon. Lord Wilson
of Rievaulx

Manny Shinwell told me that Nye and I were wrong to resign in 1951. I told Manny that in my view, as President of the Board of Trade, the country could not afford what he was proposing as Minister of Defence. It was our most public disagreement. In private he admitted I might well be right, but told me firmly that I was recklessly throwing away any chance of high office in the future!

Thirteen years later, as Prime Minister, I suggested Manny should chair the Parliamentary Labour Party. It was a job he did superbly, and it is much to his credit (and to Ted Short's as Chief Whip) that the 1964–66 government survived its crucial eighteen months – with a tiny parliamentary majority – until we felt it was right to go to the country for a clearer mandate. Manny was eighty-three when he finally resigned as chairman – in a characteristic rage after a row with Dick Crossman – and he was eighty-six when he left the Commons. He was an astonishing one hundred and one when he made his last speech in the Lords!

When I first met Manny, he was virtually the Leader of the Opposition to Churchill in the war, a role he filled with dignity and without losing public support. He had a reputation as a fighter. Born into poverty in the London slums, he received his political training in the Glasgow shipyards and tried to start a revolution there in 1919. He went on to serve as a member of both pre-war Labour governments under Ramsay MacDonald. After the war, in Attlee's Cabinet, he had a disaster at Fuel and Power when the winter of 1946–47 turned bitter and the country nearly ran out of coal, but he came back with flying colours a few years later as Minister of Defence.

Manny had a great love of boxing and had been a good amateur in his day. On one famous occasion, he applied his skills in the Commons, crossing the floor of the House to box the ears of a Tory MP who had made an anti-semitic remark. It was typical of the man captured most vividly in Peter Slowe's biography.

This welcome account deals fairly with Manny's tenacity and raw ability and also with his many political failings which kept him from ever reaching the very top. It is an honest assessment of the one hundred and one years of a man who could be on one day infuriating, unreliable and ungracious, yet the next day competent, loyal and charming. This is the biography of a man who was pivotal in the Labour movement for seventy years. It is an important story of an extraordinary life.

Part 1

CHAPTER 1

Ghetto Child

'Y'varekh-o adonoi v-yish marekho ...'

These are the first words an Orthodox Jewish boy hears. Manny Shinwell was blessed on the Sabbath day, 18 October 1884. The English version of the ancient Jewish benediction by his father on the new-born boy is simple and direct: 'May the Lord bless you and keep you; may the Lord cause his face to shine upon you, and be gracious unto you; the Lord lift up his countenance towards you and give you peace.'[1]

Eight days later, like every male Jewish baby, Manny was circumcised. There were only two rooms in the Shinwell lodgings at 17 Freeman Street, Spitalfields; but, no matter how cramped, the circumcision ceremony still had to be performed there. Sam, Manny's father, was a Polish immigrant and belonged to a small Yiddish-speaking Orthodox synagogue, whereas his mother, Rose, came from a Dutch Jewish family which was more well-to-do and held liberal views on religion. No other home or synagogue was acceptable to both sides and so, on Sunday 26 October, a crowd of relatives and a few neighbours and friends squeezed into the two upstairs rooms which made up Manny's first home in the back streets of Spitalfields. There they admitted Manny, Emanuel ben Pesach in Hebrew, to: 'the covenant of Abraham, so may he enter into the study of Jewish law, the blessing of marriage and the practice of goodness.'[2]

The covenant of Abraham was no easy option. Manny Shinwell, the first of thirteen, was born into poverty in London's East End 'ghetto', an impoverished world unto itself. The people living in Freeman Street, in the heart of it were nearly all Jewish and generally poor.[3] By no means everybody was equally poor but, as Manny wrote many years later, the area had an 'atmosphere of poverty'.[4] Terraces of houses were let by the room, and there was no water boiler, no bath and just one squalid shared lavatory in the yard. Meagre sticks of furniture in dingy rooms with linoleum floors and whitewashed walls lacked even the comfort of a carpet or a single armchair. And there were the bedbugs. Rose laundered and cleaned but nowhere, however clean, was immune; now and again the Shinwell lodgings, like their neighbours', were fumigated with sulphur – and when they were allowed back, there would be hundreds of dead bedbugs, on the walls, around the beds and under the windowsills.[5]

The poverty of the ghetto was not noble but dirty, noisome and miserable. Even in the nostalgia of his nineties Manny remembered mainly grimness and squalor from those early years. There does not appear to have been much of a sense of community:

> Times were hard and distressing. I remember scores of beggars searching the dustbins. I thought they looked like clowns in the grotesque garments they wore ... Children and many adults went barefoot. There was much drunkenness ... Apart from family gatherings I do not remember much association with neighbours. Families kept mainly to themselves.[6]

Like all children, however, Manny knew no other life and found plenty of time and places for games and mischief. The streets at least were safe from cars if not from drunks, and the backyards with their chickens and rabbits were exciting places for small explorers. Life was often bleak, but at least it was interspersed with thrilling visits to Petticoat Lane market on a Sunday. Then there was the annual Purim festival with its flour-throwing and dressing up, and the mystery of the blessings and candles on Friday nights, the Jewish Sabbath Eve. Then, the family portraits on the white-washed walls of their lodgings seemed to take on new life, the photographs and paintings of mothers, fathers, grandmothers and grandfathers. Relations, living and dead, stared down on Manny from heavy oval frames. They told him a silent story of persecution, struggle and poverty.

When, years later in Parliament, Shinwell was told by a fellow MP to 'Go back to Poland', there was some slight basis in fact for the intended insult. His father and grandfather were born in the town of Augustow on the modern Polish border with Lithuania.

As far back as 1830, when the Jewish population of Poland was just starting its explosive growth, the Jewish quarter of Augustow had been uncomfortably overcrowded, and the local gentile population had felt increasingly threatened by the Jews, both a burgeoning source of cheap labour and a sharp and wealthy middle class. As for the Shinwell (then Sheinwald) family, they had a foot in both camps. Although there was a successful branch of the family that had become flour-millers, most of them, like nearly all the rest of the Jewish population, were grindingly poor. In fact, about half the family were without any regular form of income, dependent on charity.

Despite the poverty, during the 1850s life was not yet so hard for the Jews of Eastern Europe that they would willingly consider leaving. But in

1863 their plight grew worse. The Czars defeated the Polish rebellion, and the Jews were to be the scapegoat. Tight economic restrictions were imposed and insulting social and political deprivation was added to growing poverty. Worse still, in 1869 and 1870 there were serious famines in Russia and Poland; and the consequences were to be the last straw for the Sheinwalds and thousands like them. To channel the anger of the population at large, the Jews were blamed for hoarding food and were expelled from some areas and violently persecuted in others.

In Augustow there was a pogrom in December 1870. Neighbours with whom they had lived and worked for generations entered the Jewish part of the town and set fire to about half the houses; men fleeing the flames were beaten, the women raped many times over and, in some cases, their children were thrown back into the flames before their eyes.[7]

The persecution and pogroms had still not reached the terrible ferocity of the next two decades, but the wealthy flour-milling family would have been less able than ever to support its growing numbers as more and more restrictions on Jewish trade started to take effect even on them. Those most capable of making a living on their own were encouraged to move away, a few roubles in their pocket and passage paid, to England or America. Manny's grandfather was an excellent baker so he was reckoned to be capable of making a living abroad. So, in 1871, at the age of seven, Sam Shinwell went with his parents to Danzig; there they took a ship to Hull and travelled on to Leeds.

Manny's grandfather scraped a living as a baker, and eventually opened his own small shop, but the family soon needed income from little Sam. After just one year at school, barely able to read, quite unable to write but perfectly able to talk and swear in both English and Yiddish, Sam went to work as a tailor's errand boy.

When he was just twelve, Sam's father found him stealing and he beat him severely. Humiliated, Sam ran out and used all the money he had left to buy a ticket on the night train to London. At St Pancras Station he asked a policeman where he might find some Jews, and he was directed past Islington, still at that time containing a few tiny farms, to the City. Every now and again he stopped likely-looking people in the street and asked them for a job. Most children in his position joined London's vast ranks of homeless beggars and prostitutes, but he had the luck to find an elderly Jew who took pity on him, invited him home for a meal in the Moorgate area and found him a job.[8]

Sam started work at a Jewish tailoring sweatshop. After two years as an under-presser he went back to Leeds, now an arrogant fourteen-year-old. His father still treated him like an errant child, so he moved on. He shifted to Glasgow where he was involved in a strike and then back to London and to Spitalfields. One Sabbath Eve, at the end of a sixty-five-hour week

in the sweatshop, he met Rose Koenigswinter, trying to obtain some
work for her father.

Rose came from a very different family. Her parents had moved to England
not because of persecution but because by the mid-1850s London looked
as if it would overtake Amsterdam as the centre of the diamond-cutting
and polishing trade, and Rose's uncles were all in the diamond business.
Rose's father was not, but his brothers had persuaded him to move to London
to continue plying his trade as a glazier. Their judgement was bad. Old
Koenigswinter's life in London was a misery. In Amsterdam he had been
poor, but he could get by with the language and a few coins a day. In London,
even in old age, he would start out in the morning with a frame on his
back and small sheets of glass, looking for broken windows, and often return
home late at night with nothing. Rose's mother would tell him off roundly
in front of the whole family, and then borrow some more from her
brothers-in-law in the diamond trade, who by now regretted their advice
of years before. As for Koenigswinter himself, by the time Sam met him,
so long as he had tobacco to chew and bread to eat with raisins on Friday
nights, he was happy; Amsterdam was forgotten and he was used to his
brothers keeping the wolf from the door.[9]

The Koenigswinters frowned on Rose's marriage to a poor Pole. They
looked down upon an urchin who now seemed to be getting a reputation
as a rabble-rouser; they pointed out, in vain, that he rarely found work
and, when he did, he just seemed to cause trouble. The Shinwells on the
other hand, when they were eventually told of the engagement, far from
seeing the Koenigswinters as a step up for their son, looked with horror
on a marriage outside Eastern European orthodoxy; for although the
Koenigswinters would nowadays be regarded as Orthodox Jews, they
were not strict on Sabbath observance.

Rose and Sam married in 1883, with grudging blessings all round. The
following year Rose gave birth to Manny.

Sam Shinwell soon had more pressing matters to think about than his infant
son. A couple of weeks after Manny was born, his involvement with a
sweatshop strike cost him his job and therefore his home. Strikes in the
tailoring workshops were still quite rare and troublemakers, unprotected
by unions, could be sacked and effectively banned from working in the
same town. Any sympathy there might have been for people like Sam who
took direct action was dissipated by the fact that Gladstone's Liberal
government was taking a real interest in social legislation and even trying
to promote working-class candidates for Parliament in some areas. There
was also a strong movement towards legislation for a maximum eight-hour
day. Sam left London unmourned except by Rose who took Manny to
live with her parents a few streets away while Sam looked for work in Leeds.

While he was away Sam sent as much money home as he could but it was rarely enough to keep Rose and Manny; they therefore depended on the Koenigswinters. Even when he found relatively steady work, it was always in a tailor's sweatshop and the wages were meagre.

Eventually Sam found a few months' work in London, but even then he spent little of his time with Rose and Manny. The working days started early and ended late, and on the Sabbath he refused to go with the Koenigswinters to one of the larger synagogues; he went instead alone to a little 'Stiebel', a meeting room in one of the ghetto's larger lodgings, where other Polish Jews met to pray in the same traditional way.[10] Only for the Sabbath Eve meal, if he happened to be in London, would the whole family be together. He would finish work in good time on the Friday afternoon and go straight to the steam baths in Petticoat Lane, where he could relax and speak his native Yiddish, before the more Anglo-Jewish experience of Sabbath Eve with his parents-in-law.

Rose's family was slightly better off than the Shinwells, but they were still very poor. For her uncles it was one thing to support their brother but quite another to support their married niece. There was little to spare for Manny. Rose, to her husband's bitter humiliation, had to go out to work. She found a job as a cook at the Jews' Free School, which was badly paid but had the one distinct advantage that Manny could be taken along for something to eat at the school when food was short at home. Rose would dress Manny warmly in the early morning, trail him ten minutes through feebly gaslit streets to the school, where he would get a good helping of coffee and porridge before the other children arrived.[11]

At the age of five, Manny went to the Jews' infants' school but he never got into the Jews' Free School itself. The vast number of immigrants had filled the school to bursting so, at six, Manny went to the boys' elementary school in Oldcastle Street. His two years spent at that school were the only two years of Manny's life devoted entirely to education. He was luckier than some; education was not made compulsory until 1888 and became free only in 1891.

School was dull and uncivilised. Manny learnt his tables by singing them in his class of nearly a hundred boys and did long hours of dictation to learn spelling. He learned history from a book which gave him the crucial facts to recite about Henry VIII, namely that he had six wives and, in later years, became bloated, vain and selfish. In geography, he learned that the English climate was 'moist but healthy' and that the character of the English people was 'brave, intelligent and very persevering'.[12] With these kinds of 'facts' at his fingertips, it is clear that his schooling was not much use to him.

There was an emphasis on duty at the school. Children had to be silent and attentive, and they had to march in and out of class in strict order. Manny was good at marching in time but found it extremely hard not to whisper to his neighbour. At the age of seven he was caned on his left hand time and time again and then made to write seemingly endless punishment lines with his right.

The School Inspector, on whom the school's grant depended, pointed out, in Manny's second year there, that discipline was too lax. Even though there was no 'flagrant disorder', too much whispering and talking was allowed, lesson changes were chaotic and 'the system of lessons was not always such that each child knows always what he has to do and is kept fully employed'. 'Irregular habits and practices' had crept in and it was 'impossible to say how much evil may be allowed to shelter there'. The response was to impose more drill and harder caning.[13] Manny was not sorry to leave.

One evening a week, for a few months, was taken up with Hebrew classes:

My mother also sent me to learn Hebrew, so I found myself along with a few other boys attending a class run by an old man, whom I best remember not for what he taught me but because he always seemed to be having a cold. We attended twice a week and paid him sixpence every Friday … What was important was his regular gift of a farthing to each of us. For a farthing you could buy a big orange or an ice cream or a bag of nuts. After some months even sixpence became a burden to my mother, and my Hebrew learning terminated.[14]

As a troublemaker, a Pole and a 'Schnorrer' (a scrounger unable to support his wife and child), Manny's father was despised by the almost respectable Koenigswinters, but this didn't prevent them from liking young Manny who was sometimes even allowed to join his richer cousins on trips out of the ghetto. These trips always took place on the Sabbath and would certainly have been forbidden by his father, but several hundred miles usually separated father and son. Manny was taken to the Tower of London, Kensington Gardens, Westminster Abbey and the Houses of Parliament. In later years he forgot about Henry VIII, the English Character and all his Hebrew, but these early visits to another world stayed firmly in his mind.

It was on one of these trips that Manny came across anti-Semitism for the first time. On a visit to Kew Gardens with two cousins, who were Orthodox Jews and kept their heads covered, they started to play rounders when several quite well-dressed larger children came up to them and started to kick and taunt them: 'Jews!' 'Yids!' 'Shonks!' The children's respectable parents eventually called them away, remarking loudly that 'these Jew creatures should not be allowed in the gardens. If they insisted on coming, what could they expect?'[15]

The casual anti-Semitism of the world beyond the ghetto came as a shock for Manny. He was learning to be Jewish and English at the same time, but was this really possible? Manny was only seven years old when the incident happened and it would be wrong to make too much of it, but it illustrates the pressure to conform, to the point of trying to look and behave like gentile society, to which the Koenigswinters – and in a different way Manny – succumbed more and more.

The Jewish establishment wanted nothing more than conformity for the mass of Jews pouring in from the East. They had neither wanted nor helped the immigration but, now it was a fact, their main aim was to make the new arrivals stand out as little as possible. Schools had to be English through and through, and the adults had to be quiet and reliable workers in the sweatshop. In sermons, Chief Rabbi Hermann Adler (who, incidentally, dressed as much like a senior Anglican clergyman as possible, right down to his dog-collar) preached to the newcomers the dangers of rebellion; socialists and active trade unionists could not be proper Jews; Jews should work diligently and accept their allotted place in society; the way out of poverty was through hard work and education.

Just before Manny left school, Rabbi Adler made a visit to give away the prizes (although the school was not officially Jewish, 98 per cent of its pupils were).[16] In his address he acknowledged that most of the children there, clean for the occasion but many still bare-foot and very poorly clothed, would go to work in the tailoring sweatshops. Even if they were clever enough to stay on at school, in most cases their parents could not afford to sacrifice a wage-packet. 'There is much that is evil about the sweatshop system,' he declared, very much to the surprise of the assembled dignitaries who had travelled down from the West End and some of whose large incomes owed a good deal to sweatshops. To their immediate relief he added: 'it is through education that, in Heaven's own time, the evil will be removed. There is no relief in socialism. The remedy lies with the individual efforts of every man and boy.'[17]

Certainly the great Jewish families of the time, notably the Rothschilds, the Adlers and the Montagus, tried to prevent what they regarded as excessive exploitation. They also tried through well-organised charity to alleviate the worst of the poverty, in part to avoid Jewish poverty becoming a burden on the parishes, which would have encouraged anti-Semitism and threatened their own status.

The great families had only limited success. By 1888, with immigrants still flooding in, the death rate among infants in the ghetto reached 81 per cent.[18] His playmates' funerals were already familiar to Manny by the time he was three or four years old. Lord Rothschild was concerned that these were parish funerals because the families were so poor, so he arranged for the Jewish Board of Guardians to organise a system of weekly payments by ghetto parents to a funeral fund for their children – just in case.[19] Whatever she may have thought about Lord Rothschild's helpful suggestion, Rose never had enough money to contribute to a funeral fund for Manny; but neither, in her gentle and apolitical way, did she recognise what Sam saw as Lord Rothschild's hypocrisy in trying to get desperately poor parents to insure against not being able to bury their children in a way considered respectable. To Rose at least he seemed to be doing something for the poor, even if it never actually lifted them from their misery.

The Koenigswinters as a whole were much more inclined than Sam to accept life as it was. They were occasionally very poor but they were never really hungry. They worked long hours in bad conditions for low pay but at least they had work. They went to hear Rabbi Adler preach on Yom Kippur – 'Obey the law of the land! Don't stir up anti-Semitism! Cause no trouble!' – and would nod their agreement from the hard back seats of the Great Synagogue. And they occupied themselves with the diamond and tobacco trades, escaping the worst tailoring sweatshops, gradually advancing into the lower middle class and towards emancipation beyond the ghetto.

No one who knew both of them could doubt that Manny grew to be like Sam in many ways. Neither had many friends; both had devoted wives whom they were inclined to neglect, along with their children. Both men also took a similar view of right and wrong in the way in which employers treated workers, which led them into the world of trade unions and strikes; neither father nor son needed theories of revolution to understand what was going on when they encountered problems of pay, conditions, mal-treatment and so on; but the simple clarity with which they set out to achieve immediate objectives made both of them effective activists at the sharp end of trade unionism. Sam was actively – and sometimes violently – involved in labour agitation from a year or two before Manny was born until he was eight years old.

Neither father nor son had any patience with intellectuals who tried to make theories out of what they knew instinctively. This meant that both of them clashed with left-wing intellectuals and it also meant that when Sam's circumstances changed later on in his life, he carried no intellectual baggage. Without an intellectual framework it was relatively easy for him to change his views with his circumstances. Manny was also flexible in this way, but his world – with a powerful labour movement – was very different from Sam's.

Sam was a confused man, full of strong and contradictory convictions. He strongly supported the organisation of labour but opposed socialism; he was a religious Jew but rarely prayed; he was a family man but deprived Manny of an education by making him work for him as a child, away from his mother, his school and his friends. In fact, until he went away to work for him, Manny saw little of his father. From Koenigswinter family talk he was rather frightened of him.

It is not known why or exactly when Sam Shinwell came to be involved in the Jewish labour movement. He had no particular vision and certainly never wanted a revolution. He just wanted better pay and conditions for himself and the people he worked with, the 'sweaters', in the tailoring trade. He never saw himself as a crusader; but he always found it hard to understand why so few of his fellow workers were prepared to stick their necks out too.

The world of the tailoring sweatshop, which Sam first saw at the age of seven in Leeds, was dirty, impoverished and sad. By the mid-1880s conditions were deteriorating fast as waves of new Jewish immigrants, 'greeners' desperate for work, provided endless cheap labour. They were generally conned into paying their last kopeks or pawning their few pathetic possessions to be 'trained'; then, like Sam when he first came to London, they might be found a job as a buttonholer, as a learner machinist or as a presser. Four to six weeks as free labour would follow 'to learn the trade'. The trainee learned to make the fire, clean the stove, act as water-carrier and to wheel the work away on a barrow. He would soon come to hate the disgusting state of the sweatshop, the cramped conditions, the continual discomfort, the vile latrines, the stench and the filth everywhere, but he would have to get used to it. Then he would quite likely be told that he had not got on as well as the master had hoped and he could stay on only at a special low rate of pay. He might well have known he was being taken for a ride, but he would be faced with the fact that labour was plentiful and he would be in no position to argue.[20] Sam found his situation as a trainee as humiliating as the beating he had come to London to escape. He would rebel.

Sam was never a leader nor even a reliable follower in the labour movement of his time. He had become by 1883 a sort of unofficial shop steward. Sweatshop conditions, poverty wages and frequent bouts of unemployment led Sam and a few others to try to organise the workers in a handful of tailoring sweatshops in the Spitalfields area to agitate for more pay.[21] At the same time, on 16 July 1883, a Tailors' Union under the leadership of the revolutionary socialist Isaac Stone was formed and began to agitate for shorter hours, an ambitious task in an industry consisting of over nine hundred workshops employing an average of ten sweaters each.[22] There is no record of Sam being involved in it; on the contrary, he probably opposed the idea. Indeed, a month or two after the union was founded, Sam was involved in a fight outside a small workshop in Fashion Street, Spitalfields, when he and a few friends tried to stop blackleg 'greeners' from entering the workshop. To his annoyance, he received no backing at all from the new union then or a week later when he was sacked.[23]

Freelance activities of this sort happened a few times and led to all activists in the East End being effectively blacklisted. People like Sam found it more difficult than ever to find jobs for themselves. This seems to have frightened the union organisers – even though they had done practically nothing – and they quickly agreed with a proposal put forward by the local millionaire Jewish Liberal MP, Sir Samuel Montagu, to turn the Tailors' Union into a mutual contributory friendly society to provide doctors' fees, funeral expenses and a library.[24] The Union agreed to stop organising labour in any shape or form. For Sam, this confirmed the spinelessness of intellectuals, but at least the atmosphere improved and he found another job in London, this time as a machinist.

During 1884 and 1885, the Jewish socialist movement in all its various forms held no interest for Sam at all. He had nothing to do with the socialists who produced the new radical journal *Polishe Yidl* (the Polish Jew) in 1884 and then *Arbeter Fraint* (the Worker's Friend) in 1885, and of course, in common with most of his fellow-workers, he was illiterate and couldn't read them. The Jewish socialists were anti-religious and generally either anarchist or Marxists.[25] Sam found many of their ideas incomprehensible, irrelevant or shockingly atheistic. But at least agitators like him were no longer alone; the threat of workers' power, which had never troubled the East End tailors before, was in the back of their minds from now on. Sam didn't realise it but the union intellectuals like Isaac Stone had strengthened his activist hand by communicating with the world beyond the sweatshop; they had at least pointed out the problems and the threat.

Sam found himself two days before Manny was born in October 1884 in a brawl at the final meeting of the Tailors' Union. The meeting was constantly interrupted by hecklers from this or that sweatshop accusing the leaders of doing nothing to help them and of misusing union funds (confirmed a few days later when the disappearance of the treasurer coincided with the disappearance of all the funds). The atmosphere was further soured by a feeling against the Lithuanian intellectuals who had set up the union in the first place; they were known as the Litvaks, or the 'little Brille' (*Brille* was Yiddish for the glasses most of the leaders happened to wear). Sam said they were using poor Jewish workers for their own revolutionary ends and that all Jews would suffer as a result, while others, apparently mistaking their atheism for Christianity, thought they were missionaries. It took only a few minutes for mutual suspicion to develop into insults and taunts, and a few minutes more to become a brawl. The outnumbered Litvaks' glasses became a particular symbol of hate, and several men were held and made to watch while Sam and his friends ceremonially crushed their glasses underfoot.[26]

These divisions in the labour movement could only have pleased the sweatshop employers, and Sam was one of the first to suffer. Manny was just three months old when Sam got into trouble again and lost his job. This time he had no friends willing to help him and the East End employers had no intention of letting him work again in London. Rebuked by Rose, sneered at by Rose's family, he left for Leeds where he vowed to keep out of trouble and send back money regularly.

Conditions in Leeds were, if anything, worse than in London. When Sam Shinwell arrived there early in 1885, they were cutting meal breaks, increasing working hours and laying men off. Trade was bad and made worse by cut-throat competition. In May, workers met at a local synagogue and set out their demand for a reduction in the working day from fourteen to twelve hours. Sam went to the meeting but just out of curiosity and with no intention of joining any strike.

It was Joseph Finn who persuaded him to strike. Ironically, Finn was a good deal more scholarly and intellectual than Stone but he also undoubtedly had a common touch, and he was an outstanding organiser. He had shown himself capable of producing results on the ground, especially as far as the treatment of 'greeners' was concerned, in a couple of disputes earlier in the year, and now he was organising a strike to reduce the expanded working. He had carefully chosen May, the busiest season of the year when the employers had tight deadlines and the workers had a little more money in their pockets than usual. He got mass support for the strike at a meeting of over three hundred machinists, pressers and under-pressers; and he laid down firm ground rules there and then: no violence, no law-breaking and peaceful picketing to turn back scab labour at the railway station. Sam knew at this synagogue meeting that he would simply not be able to keep out of the action despite his promises to Rose, and he found himself volunteering for picketing the station.

After a fortnight of hardship they won. The employers sent to London for scabs, but Sam and his friends waited for them at the station, took them to a specially hired room, gave them 'a brotherly talk', and handed them prepaid return tickets. The whole action was a success. At a meeting at the Belgrave Street Synagogue, the employers gave in and agreed to a twelve-hour working day with no loss of pay.[27]

There was no victimisation of the strikers this time. The employers just wanted them back to work as soon as possible, for the stoppage was costing them orders. The only blacklist was Joseph Finn himself, two other organisers and the small group of railway station pickets, including Sam. Once again he was on the move.

Sam moved briefly to Manchester but tried returning to London in the slack season. A second child, Bessie, was the only fruitful outcome of that visit. He heard of opportunities in Glasgow and stayed quietly in Scotland until Manny was five. He was to make one last attempt to find work and settle down in London. But this was 1889, an inauspicious year for someone liable to get himself involved in strikes. London was seething. It was the year of the Bryant and May match girls' strike, the gas strike and the great dock strike.

National politics, full of promise a few years before, had little to offer the East End now. Lord Salisbury's Unionist government was preoccupied with Ireland and the Empire and opposed by disorganised Liberals still led by Gladstone, a failing Grand Old Man in his eightieth year. A new system of local government introduced in 1888 looked like doing nothing to help the slums. The corrupt London Board of Works had been disbanded but the ineffective vestries and district boards remained, designed to run rural villages and lacking the resources or imagination to cope with the East End. Destructive riots arising out of the frustrated expectations of the early 1880s crystallised into effective strike action in 1889, especially in the docks. The dockers won their sixpence an hour – 'the full round orb of the dockers' tanner' – and eightpence for overtime. In this atmosphere, Sam Shinwell slipped quietly back into London in February.

The family moved back into their own rooms and Sam got yet another job as a tailor's machinist. He didn't get involved with unions or strikes, satisfying himself with attending the occasional mass workers' meetings. Manny, now six, was apparently quite unimpressed when his father took him on his shoulders to hear John Burns rousing twelve thousand dockers with his oratory. But there was nothing comparable for the sweatshop workers. Sam was certainly not inclined to get involved with the London Jewish Tailors, a new and ineffective union organisation run by Lewis Lyons, an inadequate personality who always seemed to be in a financial muddle which included some of his members' funds.[28] There could have been no greater disincentive for Sam who had to support a family of four on a machinist's meagre income.

It was at Sabbath prayers that Sam first heard of Woolf Wess. Apparently a group of disaffected workers had bypassed Lyons and recruited Wess. From the description, Sam thought that Joseph Finn had returned under another name to England (he had moved to America when he had been blacklisted in Leeds). When he met Wess, Sam realised that here again was an efficient planner, organiser and communicator; he had come to recognise these skills as important and, although he never possessed them himself in large measure, he passed his appreciation of their significance on to Manny.

Led by Woolf Wess, the London Jewish Tailors struck in sympathy with the dockers and to press their own demands for reduced hours and improved conditions. Sam was swept up in the action willy-nilly, whipping up the anger of sweatshop workers against their masters at pavement meetings. For a hectic month the strike grew and Sam became more and more involved, never in running the strike – he was never on a committee in his life – but in organising groups of pickets and speaking to small groups of workers. Every evening Sam and a hard core of about sixty activists would meet in the large upstairs room at the White Hart in Greenfield Street, Whitechapel. There they would get the latest news and reports from across the whole of the Jewish East End and decide what to do that night and the next day.[29]

The strike ran from 2 September to 26 October. On that day Sam entered the White Hart for the last time and to applause heard Wess say that the employers had caved in to all their most important demands. Wess had negotiated an agreement to reduce working hours to the Leeds level of twelve hours a day with much improved break arrangements. To Sam's relief there was nothing left to chance and there was actually a 'no victimisation' clause. The strike had caused at least a hundred bankruptcies and a good deal of bitterness, but still the strike committee mostly got their old jobs back. But not Sam. His part had been too much in the open; too many people knew him as a stirrer. Despite the agreement, he never found work in London again.[30]

Rose and Sam had never argued during the strike, but now Sam had to leave her again to find work. She exploded at him for once again putting her in the position of having to rely on her family for food and money. Manny could still vaguely remember the row ninety years later as 'shouting and language which I was too young to understand'. He clung to his mother's skirts and cried.[31]

The tailoring strikes of the late 1880s led to a great deal more subcontracting as an alternative to waged labour. More and more machinists like Sam were setting up on their own, usually scraping a living from a mixture of subcontracting and retailing. Sam heard from his sister that her husband, who was a successful grocer in Newcastle, might be interested in financing a small tailoring business for him. When he had used his last few shillings getting to Newcastle, he found there was less money than he had been told. He had little choice but to do what he could. A few miles down the Tyne at South Shields, he set up a small tailor's store for seamen. His helpful next door neighbour could write, so she wrote on his behalf to Rose in London.[32] The gist of the letter was that Sam needed an assistant but he couldn't afford one. So he sent for Manny whose working life was about to begin.

CHAPTER 2

Child Labour

Manny saw his mother only once in the two years he worked with his father at South Shields.[1] Dispatched by rail to the North East at the age of eight with a label saying 'High Shields Station' round his neck, he must have felt rejected and thoroughly miserable. After all, he hardly knew his father, and he was leaving everything familiar. He would lose his friends, he would never regularly go to school again, it was an end to trips out on the Sabbath. He would never again be part of the little neighbourhood of Spitalfields which was the only place in the world he knew inside out. He was leaving his grandparents Koenigswinter who were old and, within their limited means, had indulged him. Above all, he was leaving his mother, an upsetting and unhappy experience for an eight-year-old boy who had never spent a single night away from her before.

He cared less that he was leaving his sister Bessie who was one of the causes of his distress. His father had sent for him; but it was also a fact that it was impossible for Rose's parents to keep the three of them, and her uncles were more and more reluctant to help, since it was a particularly bad time in the diamond trade. Even if Sam had not actually needed him, Manny would probably have had to go. It was a family used to uprooting itself. After all, his grandparents had left their families behind in Holland or Poland a few years before, knowing they would never see them again. Manny wasn't being asked to emigrate, just to move away for a while.

Once the parting was over, the journey was indeed quite an adventure. He was taken by Rose and both her parents to Liverpool Street Station and put in the charge of the guard on the train to York, who took him under his wing and pointed out all the great sights. Years later he still remembered the view of Lincoln Cathedral. From York he had to catch another train to Sunderland, where he unintentionally locked himself in his compartment. Released by an amazed passenger, he caught his final train for High Shields, where to his enormous relief Sam was waiting to meet him.[2]

Sam and Manny became sailors' outfitters. Their main source of income came from the sale of mattresses to sailors who had to provide their own bedding on the tramp steamers. Sam would buy several yards of canvas and sew them up; Manny then stuffed them with straw. The good ones sold for a shilling. On good days they would also dispose of a second-hand oilskin or a ditty bag in which seamen carried their belongings.[3]

The only way to make a living in this business was to go on board a ship as it docked and to grapple with pedlars, grocers, pimps, landladies, and other tailors, for the meagre business available when the sailors were paid off. While all this was going on, someone had to mind the shop, usually Manny. The shop was in an alley near the docks and consisted of half the ground floor of a narrow terraced building. It made their two rooms in Spitalfields seem large and luxuriously appointed in comparison. In the living space behind the shop, they had just a few simple cooking implements, a second-hand bed which they shared, and packing cases for tables. The shop itself contained a sewing machine and a small stock of thread and material.

Separated from the rest of his family, alone with his father who was increasingly preoccupied with making ends meet, most of Manny's time was taken up with work. He was quite typical of the shop-boys and factory children of South Shields. Children as young as five or six used to roam the streets, fetching and carrying and running errands. In fact, Manny was lucky in one respect because at that time his father always made sure that he had some kind of shoes to wear, while plenty of other little boys ran barefoot whatever the weather.[4]

Like all children, he also found time to play, and he soon found that his new home offered opportunities even more exciting than Spitalfields. In the 1890s, South Shields had its fair share of brothels and gambling dens, not least in the Holborn area where Manny and his father lived. Sam, exhausted from long hours of selling and sewing just to make ends meet, barely had the energy to feed Manny, let alone to supervise his free time. Call-girls and call-boys openly sold themselves in the nearby streets, and Manny, like the other children, probably earned a few extra pence touting for them on the quayside.

There was a constant battle for the custom of poorly paid and demanding sailors. If the bedding was not cut just so, they would refuse to pay, and Manny noticed how the sailors became more and more disinclined to pay as their ships came close to sailing. He himself was beaten and thrown off ships on a few occasions when, on behalf of his father, he demanded to be paid. The port area of South Shields was extremely rough, and a small boy known to be carrying a shilling or two was always at risk. The docks themselves were dangerous with the loading and unloading of heavy cargoes which could, and frequently did, crush grown men, let alone small boys, if they got in the way. There were plenty of accidents, as well as intentional injuries and deaths, among the quays and gantries of the Tyneside docks.

Trade was never good, and Sam was rarely able to send money back to Rose and the baby. Rose wrote to him from time to time, mostly with inquiries and instructions concerning Manny and his schooling – she was keen that Manny should go back to school, and eventually Sam sent him. But he was never in school for long, because his father could not manage without him. All Manny could later remember about school was meeting a little girl there, but she was the daughter of a prosperous ship's chandler and her parents would not allow the urchin Shinwell to play with her.[5]

After about eighteen months, Sam was at his wits' end. Fewer ships were coming in and there was growing competition from the larger tailoring workshops. He tried briefly to diversify into general tailoring but with little success. In the hot summer of 1893, Manny was part of a bizarre and wholly unsuccessful attempt at diversification:

> Our financial circumstances were most depressing and it either occurred to my father, or was suggested to him by his grocer neighbour that he should obtain some goods which we could sell on the nearby beaches during the fine weather. So my father obtained credit from someone in Shields market place, bought a number of articles – spades, buckets and a few toys – and decided that I should take some in a basket, cross by the ferry to Tynemouth and endeavour to sell them. I had not yet reached the age of nine, and this was my first experience as a petty salesman. However, I crossed by the ferry, and found myself on the amazingly spacious beach where I saw small family groups with many children, and decided to approach them. I exposed my basket of goods, but I said nothing about them, asked no one to buy, just hoped for some response. There was none. After several hours, I returned home with the same number of articles in the basket as when I left.[6]

There is no record of Sam's reaction.

Sam told Manny they were moving to Glasgow only a few hours before they were due to leave. Perhaps he was unsure how the boy would react and didn't want to give him time to argue. Manny had shown every sign of getting to like South Shields and had lots of playmates. But customers were still dropping away and father and son found themselves idle for days on end. There was no more credit and only a couple of small subcontracting jobs for local factories. One of the subcontractors, Jacob Gombenski who had a high regard for Sam's work, suggested moving to Glasgow and wrote ahead to workshops there, recommending Sam as a good tailor and a friend fallen on hard times.[7]

Sam was right to be worried about his son's reaction. He hated leaving. They were impoverished in their hovel in South Shields but at least the privy and tub were theirs. In Glasgow for the first and only time Manny knew desperate poverty. For the only time in his life he went hungry and barefoot.

For Manny, Glasgow held no attractions. At South Shields there had been the sea, the River Tyne, the docks and ships and a sandy beach. It was

> a paradise compared to the residence found for us in a grim squalid-looking building on the banks of the Clyde. We had two rooms in a tenement which must have been constructed in the eighteenth or seventeenth century. The sanitary arrangements were appalling.'

There was one disgusting toilet overrun with cockroaches for up to twenty people on each storey. Baths were unknown. There were the usual bedbugs, on a scale Manny had not experienced before, and there were the rats; huge, mangy, disease-carrying, maggot-ridden rats. Even in the daytime they scurried over the floors and stairways and scratching sounds continued throughout the night. The first time Manny played with some other children in his tenement, they played at catching and tormenting rats. One bit Manny and made him ill. He was lucky, looking back on it, to live to tell the tale.[8]

Manny was still only ten and he started to miss his mother again, but there was no prospect of seeing her. Sam had lost every penny in the South Shields venture by the time he had paid off the creditors, other than his brother-in-law, leaving himself barely enough money for the journey to Glasgow and a week's rent.

Fortunately, this disaster was short-lived. For the first time in his life Sam started to make a little money. Gombenski had been right about Glasgow: the tailoring trade was expanding and subcontracting was a popular alternative to fixed investment (which was hard to shed if the market declined). Good tailors willing to take on subcontracts at competitive rates were at a premium, and Sam was indeed a good tailor.

> He always did what he said he could do – the right quality and on time. This was more important than pure skill in those days. There were always fellows around who could do a perfect job, but never very many that could be relied upon. The thing about Sam Shinwell was that you could always rely on him.[9]

After about six months in Glasgow, Sam had enough money to rent three modest rooms in a more modern tenement in the less oppressive Candleriggs district and to send for Rose and Bessie.

It seemed like paradise. Bessie and Manny remembered the first few months of the reunion as the very best years of their childhood. Rose was happy too, reading romantic penny novelettes and singing Irish love songs.[10] For a while at least the prospect was of work and money to pay the rent. Was it too good to last?

One of the first things Rose arranged in Glasgow, a few weeks after the family were reunited, was for Manny to go back to school; but he was now a long way behind in class and he hated everything about to. Manny had seen too much to put up willingly with the routines, rituals and hierarchies of school. On his first day back, he clung ferociously to the railings outside; finally they forced him in, but he was disruptive and quite unable to settle. At twelve, Sam and Rose stopped even trying to send him, and Manny was greatly relieved.

With short spells in London, South Shields and Glasgow, Manny went to school for long enough to have reading and writing thrashed into him, but little else. He certainly showed no particular enthusiasm or aptitude for any school subject at the time, and of course there was nothing unusual about a small boy rarely attending school in the 1880s and 1890s. Many small shopkeepers like Sam Shinwell, who had never been to school themselves, could not have run their businesses with the luxury of a kept child away all day. This situation may have been undesirable but it was not out of the ordinary. Children like Manny never felt deprived at the time, as a middle-class contemporary might have done in such circumstances.

As a small boy, Manny had loved his freedom. It was only many years later that he resented his lack of education and wished he had made more of any opportunities there might have been in Glasgow. But it is extremely doubtful whether the kind of insight into political literature and highbrow speeches, which he later complained he didn't have, could have been acquired at any contemporary school with its crude discipline and endless learning by heart. It is even possible that the fact that he never really had a school's unquestioning acceptance of authority and hierarchy drilled into him made him challenge authority and hierarchy in such a naïve and effective way in later life.

Glasgow in 1896 was a bustling and exciting metropolis for an optimistic twelve year old starting to make his own way in the world. Released at last, as he saw it, from the shackles of school, Manny had no intention of volunteering for the shackles of his father's little sweatshop. A tailor's career was not what he had in mind. His first job on leaving school was as an errand boy, sometimes for his father, sometimes for other customers who paid better. He took odd jobs in a local furniture factory making glue and in a local bakery kneading dough. He acquired no formal skills but accumulated plenty of useful experience.

The early teenage years were difficult for Manny. He was still only a child in need of his mother's love and he was rather jealous of his siblings

– he had three brothers and three sisters by now – who were never taken away from his mother as he had been. At the same time he was street-wise, independent and arrogant, smoking his clay pipe while running to join the crowds at the great engineering lockout of 1897.[11]

The lockout had started as a strike at a time of growing profits in the engineering industry, as penny-pinching in the army and navy came to an abrupt end with the outbreak of the Boer War. It was also, as in the strikes of 1889, a result of frustrated expectations. Gladstone's last Liberal government, and then Lord Rosebery's, made little headway with reform and the Unionists, led by Lord Salisbury, were returned with a large majority in 1895.

Disillusion with the Liberals had helped gather support for the new Independent Labour Party – although the only labour representative, Keir Hardie, actually lost his seat in the general election. Increasing but still localised union activity and strike action, when added to the ILP on its political wing, meant that labour was emerging as a coherent independent political force for the first time, albeit still a small minority political force. In several parliamentary by-elections, the ILP did not win but did well. Everything changed with the Boer War. The country was soon in a fervour of jingoism as Kruger's Boers inflicted a series of defeats on British imperial forces. Queen Victoria furiously denied the possibility of defeat and her subjects experienced for the first time thousands of casualties in a colonial war. By 1900, the defeats had been reversed and the relief of the sieges of Ladysmith and Mafeking had brought flag-waving crowds on to the streets in the largest numbers ever seen.

Manny was completely caught up in the nationalistic atmosphere. Whenever he had the chance, he would go with a crowd of youngsters to Glasgow Green to heckle the Irish speakers who supported the Boers. He was a patriot who had no idea what patriotism meant and no concept whatever of the Irish problem on which he vociferously (but in a safe crowd) expressed his opinions.

Most of the time, though, Manny sought excitement in sport. He found that so long as he appeared regularly and worked passably for his father in return for his keep and some pocket money, his parents were hardly bothered about what he did in his free time. The teenager escaped as often as he could into the company of his own contemporaries from the neighbourhood, a gaggle of youths from barefoot urchins to the sons of almost-respectable tailors. There Manny learned to hold his own in sport – sprinting, football, weightlifting; he was well-built and fearless.

When news of the Fitzsimmons–Maher fight hit the headlines, Manny started to take a keen interest in boxing. The fight, at Langtry in Texas on 21 February 1896, was a British victory over the Irish, and the British Fitzsimmons seemed invincible. A few sharp blows to the solar plexis, some cuts worked on around the mouth and eyes, a wicked right to the jaw – was there a man in the world the great Fitzsimmons couldn't defeat?[12] Was there anyone in the world Manny would sooner copy?

In the event, he could take only an indirect interest until he became involved with a local football club a year later and gained access to a small gym set up in the corner of a furniture workshop. There he worked the punchbag and lifted weights every night. After a few months of this, he and some friends felt confident enough to take on new opponents for bets. At the age of fourteen Manny became a prizefighter. It brought in some useful pocket money and he gained a local reputation for his Fitzsimmons-type thrust to the solar plexis.

Manny's reputation soon spread beyond the immediate neighbourhood, and a gang of boys a good deal older and larger than himself were determined to defeat him. When he started to run rings round the leader of this gang, who had challenged him with gloves for a shilling, the gloves came off and Manny was knocked to the ground with a fist in the eye. The bare-knuckle fight with no holds barred that followed sent both parties home very hurt. The career of Manny the prizefighter ended at about the same time as his hero Fitzsimmons crashed to the American Jeffries in California. Manny always maintained that it was not the black eye and swollen face that made him give up, but the affront to his father's respectability:

> I was pretty good at it, and I wanted to be a professional boxer, but my father would have none of it. Oh no, it was against the dignity of the family you know, he wanted to prove how respectable he was.[13]

Whatever the precise reasons, Manny never fought again for money. But for fifty years he kept himself in good condition with weights and a punchbag, and there were a number of occasions, especially in the Glasgow docks, when his fighting skills were needed.

At fifteen Manny decided that life would be more interesting if he left home and joined the navy. He would be someone to be looked up to and admired; it suited his patriotic ideas and his self-esteem. Unfortunately he had not reckoned on needing his father's consent. He remonstrated, fought and threw a tantrum, but nothing worked. Eventually Sam beat him and tore up the paper Manny had asked him to sign.[14] It was to be the tailor's sweatshop for Manny, watched over by his father from now on, and no more wild ideas.

The only escape route he could now find from his father's workshop, and what seemed to Manny like petty tyranny, was the library. By sixteen Manny was becoming obsessed with books. On his own admission, he could barely understand the contents pages of some of the books he ploughed through at Glasgow Corporation's Miller Street Library, but gradually he started to develop specific interests and views. Science, he decided in his adolescent way, was the key to all things. He spent hours studying the pictures of dinosaurs at the Kelvingrove Art Gallery and reading about evolution. He read about everything from pharmacy to steam engines: 'I got the definite idea that scientific discovery was going to solve all our problems and I would not accept any other argument.'[15] By the time he was seventeen, Manny had become a highly argumentative bore, dissatisfied with his life and hard to live with. His father, who had probably been just as intolerable at seventeen, completely failed to understand him. His mother was more sympathetic but equally bewildered.

In the summer of 1901 Manny's life took on new purpose as a result of a chance encounter on Glasgow Green. He had been a regular visitor there since leaving school. At this time his concern was to oppose religious speakers, especially those who prophesied the imminent end of the world, with what he saw as absolutely irrefutable scientific arguments. On the day of the encounter, a Presbyterian, a regular on the Green, was talking about the fall of man and dismissing evolution as a sinful notion. This was too much for Manny. He started yelling everything he had just read about Darwin and science in general, concluding that the speaker was talking nonsense and that if he went round the corner to the library he would find out the real truth. The crowd evidently loved it and collected ten shillings for him. An elderly socialist handed him *Wage, Labour and Capital* by Karl Marx, saying: 'Read it and you'll stop talking a lot of nonsense.'[16]

Manny was ripe for socialism. He hardly understood a word of Karl Marx, but he was soon on to Robert Blatchford whose *Merrie England*[17] was a much easier proselytising read for a young man with little formal education. To a teenager frustrated at home and at work, a quiet life of modest prosperity as a successful tailor was an inadequate substitute for the rolling drums of the revolution. Manny was haunted by a yearning for something exciting, less as a reaction to his parents' poverty and constant struggle than as a reaction to their limited horizons which were increasingly those of middle-class respectability. If Manny took anything from those teenage years, above all other things it was a lifelong disdain for respectability.

Manny started listening to the émigrés (he had never bothered with all their political talk in the past) on Glasgow Green as they spoke about workers' struggles in Russia, Poland and Germany. He read and re-read Blatchford's *Merrie England* and *Not Guilty*.[18] Now almost forgotten, Blatchford's influence at the turn of the century was enormous, his clear and simple prose sold over a million copies at a penny a book. Manny read and was convinced when Blatchford told him:

> Your duty is clear enough. First of all, having seen that misery and wrong exist, it is your duty to find out why they exist. Having found out why they exist, it is your duty to seek for means to abolish them. Having found

out the means to abolish them, it is your duty to apply these means, or, if you have not yourself the power, it is your duty to persuade others to help you. Do your duty![19]

Robert Blatchford had founded the Clarion movement back in 1894 and Manny now became a Clarion Scout. The Clarion Scouts' love of the great outdoors was common to all types of scouts at that time. ('I never wander', wrote Blatchford, 'in the stuffy sordid London streets or in the squalid gruesome Northern slums, but I think of dancing sea waves, of the flower-starred meadows and the silky skies.'[20]) So was a quasi-military type of organisation; Blatchford, who had loved being a sergeant in the army, had imported a system of captains and corporals for his Clarion Scouts. The big difference between the Clarion Scouts and any other similar movement was the former's outspoken political aims. Bands of young Clarion Scouts would cycle to a country village expressly to sell Blatchford's books or his *Clarion* magazine, and to convert local people to socialism.

The Clarion Scouts, whom Manny now joined, were hard and uncompromising. He and two or three dozen other young men and women would go along to the Clarion office in Elmbank Crescent on Wednesday nights to be briefed for the following weekend. They were expected to give up whatever else they might have planned if this was to be a weekend for a 'raid'. The captain would reveal their destination and brief them about it. He would tell them what literature had to be sold, and he would remind them that it was a disciplinary matter, which could even result in expulsion, if they failed to sell their allocation. The corporal, who was usually much younger and led the troop at the weekends, would then announce individuals' responsibilities. Scouts would usually be paired, each pair consisting of one speaker and one seller; Manny always preferred to be a speaker.[21]

On the Friday night, in all weathers, they would cycle perhaps twenty or thirty miles to a Renfrewshire village:

Down to the haunts of the parson and squire
Putting opponents to rout;
Bestriding his steed with a pneumatic tyre,
Through village and hamlet thro' mud and thro' mire
Rideth the Clarion Scout.[22]

During the night they put up notices announcing that the Scouts were in the area, and urging people to gather and marvel at the message of hope the Scouts would bring them:

Nailing down lies and disposing of fables
Improving the landscape by sticking up labels

They would find a field by a stream where they could camp for the night. The corporal was then supposed to keep the sexes apart, but for the young Scouts away from home, huddled together under the stars after an invigorating cycle ride, their burgeoning sexuality undoubtedly added a good deal to the excitement of the whole weekend.

No later than six in the morning they would ride off together to the appointed village. Wherever the villagers happened to gather, by the shop, the pit-head, the pub, the village hall, at least one pair of scouts would be there, one speaking the socialist gospel, the other hawking their quota of literature:

What is the message they bring?
A gospel of Brotherhood – that's what they sing.
They say that all produce belongs to the toiler,
To sweep from old England each idler and spoiler,
Abolish the sweater, the rack-renting knave!
The land for the people, the just and the brave!

In the pit villages they were generally well received and plied with bread and broth, but elsewhere they were sometimes abused. Once in a while, the whole troop would have to stick together and sing the socialist songs they had learned at Elmbank Crescent at the tops of their voices, trying to turn a brave face to disaster. There were days when it would take until midnight to sell their quotas, and then they would go back to find their camp ruined and their canvas torn by farmers or villagers who resented their ideas. There were even one or two occasions when Manny's pugilistic skills came in useful.

It was a tough life being a Clarion Scout. Manny learned again, as he had from his father when he had talked about his militant early days, the importance of careful planning, good organisation and the effectiveness of having one clear message. He had also found a new set of ideas which made sense to him; and these ideas also seemed to address his personal dissatisfaction with life and its prospects for him at the time.

At the end of a scouting weekend, Manny would slip home exhausted. There would be a little chicken soup. And there would also be a family exasperated by this strong and determined young man who would put huge amounts of energy into boxing or science or politics, but who so hated the work that could, as they saw it, bring them all prosperity. He had grown away from them and it would soon be time to leave altogether.

One day Sam announced that the family was moving back to South Shields where he had been offered the job of manager in a tailoring business. Manny could come too or Sam would be prepared to help him set up a little business on his own in Glasgow. Manny took up neither offer, said he might follow later and found himself some digs.

Not long after his family had moved away, Manny got to know Fanny Freedman, a slight, dark and vivacious girl who wanted to be a professional singer. He had already met her through one of her brothers, Nat, now a bookie, who a few years earlier had taken small bets on prizefighting. Now Manny moved digs to be next door to Fanny. But although she was polite to him, he obviously did not interest her. As he was unable to find a good job, he reluctantly moved back to South Shields to join his family. His boyhood memories of South Shields had been quite romantic, but when he saw it now and as soon as he set foot in his father's new workshop, Manny realised his mistake. He stuck it out for just three months before he sold all his books to buy a return ticket.

Manny returned from South Shields to Glasgow in the cheapest possible way, going from Newcastle to Leith by sea: 'I shall never forget how seasick I was; the North Sea must have been at its worst. There was no cabin accommodation except for the first-class passengers, so I lay flat out on deck through the night.'[23] (Three years before, this same boy had thrown a tantrum because his father refused to let him join the navy!)

After a fair amount of searching, he found himself a job in a Jewish sweatshop as a machinist. Jewish owners preferred to employ only Jews and so Manny had been right for the job (although the religious side of his Judaism had lapsed). The factory closed on the Jewish Sabbath and operated on Sundays; otherwise it was the same as any other with bad conditions, a fifty-eight-hour week and low pay: twenty-eight shillings a week for buttonholers. Manny was urged by his workmates to join the recently formed Jewish union.

I had read enough of Blatchford to want to be part of a properly organised workforce. Even so, I could not for the life of me see how your race or religion had anything to do with getting a few bob more a week, making machinery safer or whatever. In fact, the intimacy of the relationship between master and man in the small Jewish world would, if anything, make real gains less likely. So I announced publicly that I was going to join the Amalgamated Union of Clothing Operatives and not the Jewish union. I was very brash in those days. I got the sack and most of my workmates were pleased to see the back of me![24]

His only remaining link with the Jewish community was Fanny Freedman. Now he was back, she had replied to his letter saying she was willing to see him. By now, she was singing minor parts in pantomimes and public concerts, helped along by her brother Archie, a rather more successful music hall singer. Unfortunately, Archie strongly disapproved of Manny. Indeed, none of her family thought Manny suitable for Fanny. He still earned very

little and was always having to change jobs, and now he was working on
the Sabbath as well; at nineteen he was three years younger than Fanny
and evidently irresponsible; he stirred up trouble for Jewish tailoring firms
and was getting a reputation for speaking at the street-corner meetings
organised by the Independent Labour Party or Clarion. He also got into
brawls. On one occasion Manny turned up at Fanny's with a black eye
which created a terrible impression, and he got very little sympathy even
from Fanny.

To the fury of both the Freedmans and the Shinwells, on 14 November
1903 they secretly married in their local Register Office and set up home
in a one-bedroom tenement flat at the poor end of Govanhill in the centre
of Glasgow.[25]

CHAPTER 3

Unions and Violence

Getting married was one thing. Living together afterwards was another. Two rooms soon gave way to one, then some of the furniture had to be pawned and eventually their most personal belongings had to go, even Fanny's spectacles. Manny Shinwell was unemployed and stayed that way for three months. He found it hard to take the unfairness, the degradation and the helplessness of this experience. He had nowhere to turn.

From now on he would take control of events. His maxim would be that of so many people who have climbed high in public life: 'Don't get mad; get even.'

When he got work, training girl machinists at the Co-operative factory in the Glasgow suburb of Shieldhall, Shinwell was already a member of the most militant trade union he could find, the Amalgamated Union of Clothing Operatives. The local secretary was Tom Carswell, who had been Shinwell's corporal in the Clarion Scouts, and Shinwell told him enthusiastically that he was now ready to fight the capitalists in the way he had preached to the villagers in the Clarion Scouts.[1]

Carswell seems to have set Shinwell the task of recruiting new members from the factories and workshops around Shieldhall. To Shinwell's relief, he did not suggest more Clarion weekends which would have taken him away from Fanny. He found out in fact that Carswell had stopped all that because of a racking cough and regular fevers. (These would soon kill him when he developed tuberculosis.)

Before Shinwell's 1903 recruitment drive, the Amalgamated Union of Clothing Operatives had fifteen members in Glasgow.[2] Carswell evidently no longer had the energy to organise it properly and there had been only one recent strike at a particularly cramped and dirty workshop; nothing had been achieved and twelve members had left the union. Shinwell now set about trying to recruit in the new factories. They were fertile ground. Changes in technology meant that tailoring needed fewer craftsmen but more operatives. He worked night after night and recruited over a hundred new members in three months, transforming the Glasgow branch of the union into one of the most successful in Britain.[3]

Shinwell also covered his back by joining the Scottish Co-operative Wholesale Society which actually owned the factory where he worked. He got to know the directors and ingratiated himself with the manager. He almost certainly reached an informal understanding that he would not press for industrial action in his own factory. In return, when it eventually came to a showdown with his foreman over time off for union activities, the foreman was overruled.

People who knew Shinwell at this time remembered his energy, remarkable even for a fit young man of twenty. At the end of a twelve-hour day, he would be out recruiting, speaking at street corners, attending meetings or looking after members.[4] A spate of workshop closures in 1905 led to an attempt by some of the surviving workshops, under pressure from the competition, to cut wages. Shinwell helped to organise a series of strikes, establishing himself for the first time as a good planner, timing picket duties, keeping lists of blacklegs and boycotting the suppliers of strikebound workshops.[5] He was a young man with every appearance of knowing where he was going, a straightforward trade-union organiser with vaguely Marxist views, or at least a contempt for 'the capitalists'.

A year later, Carswell's increasing ill health gave Shinwell the break he wanted. He much preferred to be his own boss and he found the sick Carswell increasingly dithering and irritating. He was pleased to see the back of him. Instead of taking over as secretary, he stayed as organiser and took over what seemed to him Carswell's more interesting post, delegate to the Glasgow Trades Council. When he walked proudly to his first meeting at Albion Hall, he felt he was entering a new and more important world. He was the youngest of more than two hundred delegates.

Never daunted by a hall full of men undoubtedly more experienced than himself and, in their opinion, much cleverer, Shinwell determined to make his mark quickly. For a young man in a hurry, the Trades Council in 1906 must have seemed a ponderous place. It was not like the Trades Council which a few years earlier had been a power-house of debate and decisions on the conduct of industrial disputes in Glasgow; on the contrary, it had become sluggish and demoralised. Unemployment was rising fast and trade-union membership was slipping for the first time since the Taff Vale judgment which, in July 1901, had made unions in dispute liable for damages.[6]

There was a split in almost every debate between the pragmatic trade unionists who wanted to use industrial pressure for a narrow range of improvements in pay and conditions and the more idealistic socialists who saw the Trades Council only in the context of the wider class struggle. It reflected the national divide between some trade-union leaders and the handful of Independent Labour Party MPs led by Keir Hardie and Ramsay MacDonald. Shinwell was one of the few delegates who felt at home in both camps, carefully balancing his contributions to debates.

He received applause from all sides when he used a debate early in 1907 on the old-age pension to attack his rival union, the Amalgamated Society of Tailors and Tailoresses, for its lack of interest in this issue. He listed the achievements of his union in pressurising ministers on pensions, despite its small size and limited resources; then he attacked on political grounds those who failed to recognise the old age pension as a vital class issue.[7] This kind of contribution, made eloquently and without too much detail, marked him out. He also had a tendency to adopt a high moral tone which, in 1907, chastising shipping lines for recruiting on the Christian Sabbath, was exactly the right way for the young Jew to impress the many devout Presbyterians among his new colleagues.[8] In general, his contributions were on the side of the pragmatists. The Liberals had just won power with an enormous landslide when he joined the Trades Council and most of his contributions could have been made by one of its more reform-minded ministers. Occasionally his choice of words marked him out as a member of the Independent Labour Party, but almost never the content.

His vigorous practical union work also attracted favourable comment. His idea of carefully organised picketing shifts was copied in disputes all over Glasgow and there was a good deal of interest in the effectiveness of the way he dealt with blacklegs. He only occasionally had them beaten up, like the dockers (although when he did, the job was usually thorough and he often joined in personally), but he had gone beyond simply trying to take their names as he had been doing before; he now had them trailed to their homes. On one occasion a blackleg member of his own union was so frightened by the appearance of Shinwell and three other men at his front door that he broke both his legs jumping from his top window into his yard at the back. A cynic commented that it 'saved Shinnie the trouble'. It may have done, but the main purpose of his feared 'home-checks' was proper identification to stop the culprits getting other jobs by warning potential employers. Sometimes, if the blackleg belonged to a rival union, the Trades Council could be called upon to intervene. When one of Shinwell's members was thought to be blacklegging on the Society of Tailors and Tailoresses, the culprit, a presser, was expelled by Shinwell just in case and never found work in Glasgow again.[9]

Shinwell also soon got the hang of self-promotion. He became good at keeping everyone informed about what he was doing and his name was kept firmly in the minds of people who mattered. People on the Trades Council, in the Independent Labour Party and in his union got to know everything that Shinwell felt they needed to know. He rarely quoted membership figures when they went down but always emphasised them when they went up, and he always stressed the significance of disputes which he had helped to resolve satisfactorily. Balanced reporting of anything involving himself was never to be one of Shinwell's strengths.

As far as the intellectual socialists were concerned, he never lost an opportunity to express Blatchford's simplified Marxism as the explanation for all kinds of events and views. He castigated fellow trade unionists, for example, for failing to take an adequate interest in the arts, quoting *Clarion* as a publication which aimed to remedy working-class exclusion not just from political power but from literature and the arts as well. He and Fanny had become lovers of literature and music.[10]

Anything he did well he drew to the Trades Council's attention at once. Usually it was union activity but it could be purely political. Shinwell was inordinately proud of having been thrown out of a Tory meeting for shouting 'What about the workers?' He brought it up at every opportunity and implied strongly that other members of the Trades Council would do well to put themselves on the political front line in the same way.[11]

Perhaps most important of all for his quick advancement on the Trades Council was the friendship he cultivated with its secretary, George Carson. Carson, who was by now in his seventies, took to the young Shinwell. He too had been a fiery youth, first organising the weavers, then as one of the founders of the Independent Labour Party. A friend of Keir Hardie, he had enlisted his help in opposing the TUC's exclusion of Trades Councils in 1893, and when this failed he had helped set up the Scottish TUC to include them. He had been secretary of the Glasgow Trades Council and the Scottish TUC since 1896 but had now rather lost his fire, becoming a rather boring, precise and bureaucratic figure with influence behind the scenes rather than any noticeable presence on the stage.

Shinwell saw at once that Carson had influence in the labour movement and especially on the Trades Council. People listened to him and it would be best if they listened to him saying nice things about Shinnie. He made a point of going to all the meetings Carson ever suggested, however out of the way and inconvenient; in Airdrie one day, at Wishaw the next. He made sure that Carson stayed impressed. Carson indeed saw a vision of his own youth in Shinwell, and Shinwell knew it:

> My style of debate was a swashbuckling one. I'd debate with anybody. And very often I'm quite sure I got up and talked about things I hadn't the faintest idea about. But you know I could impress other people by my vigour – and that was enough.[12]

Carson came to adore Shinwell. To the surprise of Trades Council members, he campaigned for Shinwell to be one of its delegates to the Scottish TUC. Then the vice-presidency of the council fell vacant. Shinwell put his name forward immediately, apparently without even discussing the matter

Manny Shinwell

with Carson who might have thought it over-ambitious.[13] He quickly gained support as a compromise candidate between the radicals and the pragmatists, at a time when trade unionism was in difficulty in a deepening recession and needed nothing so much as good organisation and unified leadership. Presumably Carson worked for him again and, to his considerable surprise and on the day his first child Sammy was born, Shinwell was elected by a narrow majority. He succeeded the elderly president a year later, in 1908, at the age of twenty-four.

The Shinwell presidency started with a bang. He organised a demonstration in Cathedral Square against unemployment, and for once his planning went awry. Perhaps it was just inexperience when he thought that some of the demonstrators were going into the Cathedral's morning service out of piety. The waiting police had no such illusions and they drew their batons and struck down everybody down within reach. Shinwell himself got a bruised arm, and they were all chased helter-skelter down the High Street.[14]

Increasing violence was the hallmark of trade-union activity in the years leading up to the First World War. In Glasgow, unfortunately, most of the violence was between rival unions. It was ironic in the light of his own problems in tailoring that Shinwell now often had to mediate between craft and general unions. Even when the opposing parties could agree at a Trades Council meeting, gangs still sought out their rivals for a beating on the shop floor or on the dockside. It was a depressing part of his job.

He was also determined to set his own agenda for his presidency. The task he set himself was to place the Trades Council firmly in the party political arena, actually playing a leading part in making Labour Party policy and helping to get Labour councillors elected. This had always been a stated aim of the Trades Council but in practice little had been done. A time of recession, when not much could be achieved industrially, was, to Shinwell's mind, a good time to make political progress. The Osborne judgment of 1909 had stopped trade unions contributing directly to getting Labour MPs and councillors elected, so the involvement of the Trades Council in helping indirectly to get ILP members elected was more than welcome; it was held up by Labour leaders as a national example and Shinwell received a personal message of support from Ramsay MacDonald.

After nearly a year of planning, on 3 November 1909, Shinwell chaired a policy-making conference of delegates from the Trades Council, the ILP and various smaller organisations in the labour and co-operative movements. This conference came up with a clear programme for Labour candidates for Glasgow City Council. When a dozen Labour councillors were later elected, the programme on which they fought was virtually unchanged from the one agreed at Shinwell's conference.

The range of policies covering every aspect of municipal life from laundries to local income tax was remarkable and shows how carefully Shinwell prepared the ground in advance. He lost his proposal for prohibition but among the many proposals accepted, he regarded as crucial a rather esoteric one on municipal contracts. The policy on contracts was a direct result of Shinwell's experience in the tailoring unions; he had been proposing for some time a rule preventing councils from placing contracts with firms that failed to provide decent wages and working conditions. The publicity arising from the conference, however, concentrated on the new housing, the construction of 'cottages' to replace the rat-infested tenements in which the working class of Glasgow, including the Shinwells, was forced to live.[15]

'Always scurrying around,' stage-whispered George Carson delightedly when Shinwell arrived to take the chair at the Trades Council with seconds to spare.[16] On this particular occasion, early in 1911, he had scurried straight from the London train. He had been carrying out a new task for his union, sitting on the new Tailoring Trade Board.

The Tailoring Trade Board and three other similar boards had been set up by Winston Churchill, the Liberal government's young President of the Board of Trade. The boards each had a cumbersome committee of forty-nine, made up of five independent members and twenty-two from each side of the industry; these were set up with the intention of avoiding industrial disputes by agreeing minimum pay and conditions.[17] Shinwell was one of the twenty-two tailoring workers.

He was not at all impressed by the first meeting in December 1910, in which most of the time was taken up in wrangles over expenses. The Board of Trade insisted that the union side should get third-class train fares and the employers first-class ones. After nearly three hours it was finally agreed that everyone should have first-class fares but nothing for accommodation.[18] Shinwell, who by now had two children (Fanny had given birth to a girl, Lucy, the previous year), a full-time job and a long list of Trades Council commitments in Glasgow, was bored stiff. But he quite enjoyed the opportunity to visit London, so he gave it another month.

The next meeting was taken up with another row but this time it was about tailoring. Shinwell gave the straight union line:

> Every employer I come across pretends to hold the opinion that sweating in the tailoring trades should be abolished, But what constitutes sweating?
>
> Employers have pointed out to me recent statements in the press showing where women have worked fourteen or fifteen hours per day for a shilling, and this is, they agree, sweating. In my opinion, the hours alone constitute sweating apart from the wage. Even if the wage stated

was doubled and the hours considerably reduced I would still contend that the worker was sweated.

The only wage that could be considered as not being a sweated wage is a 'living' wage. By that I mean that all workers should be able to earn, by working reasonable hours, at least sufficient to keep them in comfortable circumstances the whole year, and there should also be a margin so that provisions may be made for sickness and loss of employment.[19]

Several others on the union side followed in a similar vein and then came the employers talking at considerable length about the 'tyranny of the trade unions'. There seemed no chance of any agreement and Shinwell started to wonder if his time could be better spent.

Then Churchill told his civil servants to step in. From March 1911 onwards, strong Civil Service chairmen forced the board to concentrate on the issue of wages. In just one meeting agreement was reached on threepence farthing an hour minimum wage for women and twelve shillings and sixpence a week for girls under fourteen.[20] This was good for London and Leeds but not for Glasgow. Shinwell was hardly a returning hero with a proposal for minimum wages which were already paid in even the smallest sweatshop and were well below acceptable lower limits in the factories.[21]

He was soon more than happy to leave the Trade Board to face a far greater challenge. He was on his way back from the board's June meeting when he heard the seamen were on strike.

The leader of the National Sailors' and Firemen's Union (the predecessor of the National Union of Seamen), Havelock Wilson, had announced the strike, but the men on the Clyde were still working when Shinwell returned from London. This was hardly surprising as the union was almost defunct on Clydeside with no local office or secretary.[22] It was exactly this lack of activity that made the Trades Council, when approached by Wilson's representative, very unwilling to collect money and help to organise the strike.[23]

Shinwell argued on the Trades Council that they simply could not stand back and do nothing. 'Clydeside ought not to be the place where trade unionism is seen not to work,' he insisted. It is not clear whether it was with or without the Trades Council's blessing that Shinwell eventually set out for Leith to meet Havelock Wilson. It may be that George Carson backed him but not the rest of the Trades Council. Anyway, for Shinwell, bursting with self-confidence, it was to be a journey he would later often regret having made.

Wilson had been a leader in the Labour movement back in the 1880s when he became MP for Middlesbrough, and he had built a powerful national union from nothing. Unfortunately, the union had got into financial difficulties and Wilson had been made personally bankrupt as a result of legal action by a shipping company. This had changed his approach to trade unionism, for it was now generally known that he accepted the protection of some major shipping companies in return for keeping disruption to a minimum, just occasional shows of force, it seemed, and then a deal.[24] It was this union baron who shook Shinwell's hand at his union's rented office by Leith docks.

It is unlikely that Shinwell had much explaining to do as far as the situation on Clydeside was concerned. Wilson's spy network was legendary. They agreed that Shinwell should address a series of open meetings of Clyde seamen over the next two days, carrying a personal message from Wilson, urging them to join the national union and support the strike. Wilson himself would visit Clydeside at the end of two days when he had finished his business in Leith.

Just why Shinwell allowed himself to get so directly and personally involved with Havelock Wilson is not at all clear. He had undoubtedly been warned. The simple answer is that he was inexperienced and naïve, that he knew about Glasgow and tailoring but not much else; after all he was still only twenty-seven years old and his total experience of seamen was one trip on a paddle steamer; Wilson was a persuasive man and could easily have flattered Shinwell's considerable self-esteem. He certainly appears to have had Shinwell talking in terms of virtually revolutionising the Clyde seamen and putting the fear of God into the ship-owners. It would have been quite easy for Wilson to use Shinwell to stir things up on the Clyde. Wilson also offered Shinwell paid work for his union, a real possibility to get out of tailoring into full-time trade unionism. In short, he won Shinwell over. Later, when he realised what sort of man he had been dealing with, Shinwell played down the Leith meeting, but the fact was that, for a while, he quite willingly became Havelock Wilson's man on the Clyde.

The new job was good enough for Shinwell to give up his old secure job. He was sick to death of tailoring, but with two children he could only have given it up for a job that looked equally remunerative – which this was at two pounds a week – and reasonably long-term. Yet some of Shinwell's behaviour at this time is, with hindsight, quite mysterious. What could possibly have been the prospects of working for a union with a history of running out of money and closing offices, and at the beginning of a strike which, so far, was hardly taking place on the Clyde at all? Shinwell's claim, many years later, that he used up his Glasgow Fair holiday to organise the seamen and only later changed jobs must either have been a lie or a lapse of memory; the holiday that year ended two weeks before the strike was called. Did he really think that the strike would be a long one and that there would be money available for a Clyde organiser for some time to come? If so, he must have ignored a good many warnings. Certainly, in view of Wilson's use of Shinwell's enthusiasm for trade-union work and his strong desire to get out of his present job, it is unlikely that he told him very much about plans he probably already had to end the strike. He would simply have told Shinwell that negotiations would take place nationally and that he would be kept informed. For Shinwell, enthused by getting the kind of job he wanted, the shady character of his new employer and the financial uncertainties of his newly adopted union appear hardly to have mattered.

Shinwell's confidence in his new job was such that a few days later he felt able to turn down a generous offer of ten pounds a week from the dockers. Again, his explanation years later is dubious. He said that he turned them down because the Trades Council had obliged him to help the seamen and so he was duty-bound not to change. This must be nonsense. First of all, the Trades Council had always been hesitant over the seamen's dispute, although they finally endorsed it, and they certainly would not have objected to Shinwell shifting to the dockers' union which they supported more strongly than the seamen. Indeed, Joe Houghton, who went to the dockers instead of Shinwell, had also been appointed by the Trades Council to help out the seamen, and he went on to be the secretary of the Scottish Union of Dock Labourers with no record of any reproach.[25]

Whatever his motives, Shinwell set about organising the seamen with passion and skill. Wilson never made it to Clydeside as he had promised, but it was soon obvious that Shinwell didn't need him. A ship would come in and Shinwell with a small body of volunteers would be there to meet the men as they were paid off, before they had a chance to go on a spree or clear the debts accumulated by their families while they had been away. More dangerously, Shinwell and his men would picket the mercantile marine office to try to stop the men, sometimes blacklegging unwillingly because of desperate poverty, going in to sign on for a voyage; officials called in the police on several occasions and Shinwell soon found himself tailed by a plain clothes (but obvious) policeman.[26]

Wilson sent an experienced seaman from London to run the office on Clydeside – to Shinwell's surprise since he had been told to expect an assistant rather than a boss.[27] It was his first encounter with grey, dapper, Alfred French. French had been a collaborator with Wilson in the 1890s on Humberside and now helped out at the union's London headquarters. He was already in trouble with the police for threatening the lives of ministers in violent speeches in Hyde Park. Sent to Scotland by Wilson partly for his own safety, he turned out to be useless to Shinwell who mostly seems to have ignored him. There were, however, a series of warehouse fires that occurred shortly after French arrived. Shinwell suspected French and the police suspected Shinwell, but nothing was ever proved.

For two weeks Shinwell closed down the Clyde. It was a remarkable feat for an inexperienced young man in his first full-time trade-union job. Once again, his excellent organisation was the key. Shinwell identified at once the two distinct requirements of, first, raising money for relief and, second, carefully planned pickets. Money was raised from the men as they left the ships and relief was made available to the poor who tried to blackleg. (Relief had to be handled very discreetly for fear of encouraging blacklegging.) As for the meticulous timing and distribution of pickets, this was a subject for which Shinwell was getting a reputation, as he tightened the noose around the Clyde shipping lines. Then, quite suddenly, Shinwell was faced with what the Trades Council, Carson in particular, and everybody who knew Havelock Wilson had suspected might happen, a quick end to the dispute was negotiated with far fewer concessions from the employers than could reasonably have been expected for the men's sacrifices and efforts. Wilson sent his friend 'Captain' E. A. Tupper 'VC DSO', 'hon. trustee' of the union, to tell French and Shinwell the news and to explain the terms.

Shinwell was angry even before Tupper arrived and they disliked each other from the start. Tupper had somehow impressed Wilson with his story that he was a born aristocrat and Boer War hero anxious to help poor seamen as a gesture of friendship and admiration, and in return for expenses. In fact, he was originally an errand boy and a native of Worthing, and his limp had nothing to do with winning a VC but had been the result of a kick from a horse. It fell to Tupper to explain that Wilson had settled for five pounds a week, a full ten shillings short of the original aim, and had also failed to achieve various improvements in conditions.

What precisely happened on 9 August 1911 between Tupper and Shinwell, between French and Shinwell, or between Shinwell and his conscience, will never be known. What is known is the outcome. Shinwell announced that the Clyde seamen would ignore the national agreement and fight on.[28] French said the opposite. Tupper took the next train back to London to give Wilson a first-hand account of what had gone on.

Shinwell sent a message for more pickets to come to the mercantile marine office, and by seven o'clock that night there were about two thousand men milling around:

> I'm amazed to find that there are people who call themselves seamen who are prepared to settle for five pounds. You fellows in the stoke hole – are you willing to settle for five pounds? Of course not. We'll get five pounds ten.[29]

Wilson was furious. He had agreed five pounds a month and he would ensure that Shinwell would regret the day he crossed him and declared that the Clyde would fight on.

The special circumstances of the Clyde meant that Shinwell had in fact a reasonable chance of success. His negotiating position was strengthened by Glasgow's heavy dependence on transatlantic liners. At least three liners a week carrying a thousand passengers each sailed to Canada or the United States. There was cut-throat competition with narrow profit margins and the profits from a voyage could very quickly disappear altogether if a thousand people had to be fed and accommodated for extra days on the Clyde. That was not all of Shinwell's good fortune by any means. It also happened that three of the ship-owners were on his side. James Allen, chairman of the Allen Line, was a millionaire member of the Independent Labour Party; Algernon Henderson of the Anchor Line was a sympathiser; and 'Holy' Joe Mackay, who had a large cargo fleet, was interested in social reform from a Christian point of view and quite willing to pay the extra ten shillings Shinwell was demanding.

The powerful Cunard Line, on the other hand, was having none of it. For them the national agreement was all that was needed, and they recruited blacklegs for a Glasgow to New York voyage – strictly speaking not quite enough, so the ship was technically undermanned. When Shinwell heard about it, he reported the undermanning to the Board of Trade but they were determined to avoid entering the industrial dispute. Then he heard that the ship was stuck at Greenock and would have to wait for the tide. There was just time for him to get together a full crew only willing to work for the extra ten shillings and put them all on the train to Greenock. Before the police could intervene, he had hired a small boat, rowed alongside the liner and offered his services to get the blacklegs off and his replacement crew on board. He made a lot of the undermanning and lied about the intent of the Board of Trade to prosecute, and he threatened other Cunard ships. He won. Returning to shore, he jubilantly clambered up a lamp-post to give the good news to the men who had followed him that they were to be the crew and at the full new wages. Then he hurried away before the blacklegs, who were now to be forced off, could kill him. It was a major breakthrough. First Glasgow, then Southampton, and at length the rest of the country, started to pay five pounds ten. Wilson was humiliated and dangerous. Shinwell seemed momentarily unassailable.

A fortnight later Tupper was back, this time with two other Wilson 'trustees', the Irish Nationalist MP Dick McGhee and the strange 'Rev.' Charles P. Hopkins, a 'volunteer sky pilot' dressed in a black habit with a blue seaman's jersey and a gold crucifix.[30]

They sacked Shinwell at once, leaving French in charge. During the night Shinwell returned with a group of friends and took all the books. Wilson later alleged that this was because Shinwell wanted to cover up where he had cooked them. This is impossible to prove or disprove and it is really much more likely that Shinwell's version was true, that he needed the books because they had the names, addresses and payment records of all the seamen he had signed up. It is not known whether he transferred funds from the old to the new union – probably a few pounds in cash, so the new union could pay him and possibly a little relief right away. Although Shinwell eventually gave the books back, their temporary possession made all the difference in setting up a new union; he certainly needed to be quick for he himself was out of a job and had no money until the new union could employ him. At the same time, not having the books made French's job of keeping his union together very hard indeed.

Just four days later, Shinwell was secretary of the Scottish Sailors' and Firemen's Union which merged a month later with a similar breakaway in Southampton to become the grand-sounding British Seafarers' Union. His new union was not recognised by the Trades Council (nor incidentally by the TUC) and anyway Shinwell was still technically a delegate of the Amalgamated Union of Clothing Operatives, so he had to resign as president and apply to be a delegate of his new union. At the same time, French wrote to the Trades Council asking to replace Shinwell as a delegate of the National Sailors' and Firemen's Union (which Shinwell never had actually been) with a new appointment. There was no problem in accepting the new official union delegate but there was a long debate about whether Shinwell should be allowed back on to the council as a delegate from his breakaway union. With Shinwell looking on disconsolately – he had after all chaired this powerful gathering for the last three years – delegate after delegate expressed earnest doubts about the principles of breakaway unions until it looked practically certain that Shinwell would be thrown off the Trades Council altogether. The turning point was a speech by a certain Victor Miller, a boilermaker, who said that the new union had obviously done the best thing for the Glasgow seamen and, since that was the case, they should have the guts to stand up for the workers without being scared of offending 'official this or official that'. It did the trick and Shinwell stayed on the Trades Council as a delegate of the Scottish Sailors' and Firemen's Union.[31]

Relieved of the presidency and of a full-time tailoring job, Shinwell now had to make a success of his new union. By the simple expediency of transferring every name from the old union to his new one, he already had a good many members and he was inclined to be complacent in those first few months, regarding French as quite incapable of salvaging either the old union's members or its reputation.

Shinwell also went through a phase of political activity outside the unions. He was adopted as a candidate for Glasgow City Council at what was for Labour the difficult ward of Tradeston. He was a worthy but humourless candidate according to the local press.[32] His opponents, perhaps influenced by his union enemies, took him seriously enough to inveigh against Shinwell as 'an interloper' (from just outside the ward) with 'doubtful credentials' and 'unworthy to sit on the City Council'.[33] Shinwell lost by a wide enough margin in a difficult ward to suggest that nothing in the local press made any difference to the outcome.

It was also at this time that a small group of Glasgow's left-wing political activists started to meet informally. Away from the Trades Council and the Town Council, they would meet once or twice a week in a tea room or at the home of one of the members of the circle. It was not yet the regular get-together at Kate Cranston's Tea-Room – that started only towards the end of the First World War – but for Shinwell it was good to get away from the docks and meet with other socialists. It was at the same time a form of relaxation and a way in which he could re-establish his political status with an influential group now that he had lost almost all his official status, running a breakaway union which was just tolerated locally but ostracised nationally.

It was an impressive little group that met over tea. John Wheatley, later Minister of Housing, was the only businessman and he usually picked up the bill. Like Shinwell, his strength lay in organisation, but he was a councillor and his expertise was the manipulation of committees and caucuses. He regarded Shinwell as a thug. There was the young James Maxton who looked satisfyingly revolutionary with long black hair and emaciated features; at that time he assisted the communist John MacLean at his highly successful adult academy of economics (Marxist economics only), the largest in Europe. Tom Johnston was the editor of the popular radical paper *Forward*. Willie Gallacher was the other regular at that time; he was a Marxist and a personal friend and admirer of Shinwell's, the only one of the group who regularly went to the docks to see what was really going on. Although it took only a small part of his time, there is no doubt that in the autumn and winter of 1911, Cranston's was important for Shinwell. It kept his eye on the horizon when he could easily have drifted into an obsession with day-to-day tactics; he could easily have become a typical minor union boss.[34]

By spring 1912, Shinwell started to realise he had been spending too much time over tea. He had been too complacent about the threat from the official union. Wilson had quietly drafted in more men; several of them were thugs, but others were experienced seamen from other ports, and Shinwell stood to lose members and money. The atmosphere started to change. He was threatened in the streets when out with Fanny and the two children, and sinister reports of the maltreatment on board ship of some of his active members started to filter through to him.[35] Wilson was now rapidly out-manoeuvring him.

Shinwell counter-attacked the only way he knew how, by careful planning and organisation, by meeting every boat, by staging a permanent picket at the main recruiting office, and by taking every opportunity to exploit a grievance and to remind seamen how the official union had always let them down in the past. For a time he started to win again, but he could see that Wilson was never going to give up. Wilson's hired thugs kept him permanently on the defensive and his own hired thugs scared French witless but seemed to achieve little. Shinwell suggested parleying with French but got no reply. By the early summer, violence was part of the daily routine; French and Shinwell were always accompanied by bodyguards. It was a low point of trade unionism.[36]

Wilson also kept up a constant pressure of litigation in an attempt to recover papers allegedly stolen by the breakaway union, and he spread the word that Shinwell was growing rich on the earnings of poor seamen. Shinwell retorted with a recital of Havelock Wilson's misdeeds (which he now knew by heart and presumably wished he had taken into account a year before in Leith). As a precaution, however, Shinwell handed over responsibility for the union's financial affairs to his popular, church-going and transparently honest colleague, Jimmy Martin; Shinwell apparently continued to draw just two pounds a week.

The rivalry between the two unions was using all the energy and resourcefulness that should have gone into improving the pay and conditions of seamen. It was getting out of control.

One to one, Shinwell could outsmart French – both in the Trades Council and on the dockside. Also, Shinwell's thugs usually out-fought French's thugs – and had often done so in acts of violence in which three men had been killed.

Tuesday 18 June 1912, was different. French had the upper hand. The MacBrayne's ferry from Loch Fyne, *Columba*, had berthed and Shinwell's union had been made to look foolish by French's union. Shinwell should have known about *Columba* but he had overlooked it and French had got there first. Shinwell saw her from Jamaica Bridge and he was in no mood to come second to his rival. Since it was already well into a warm summer's evening, he calculated that although French seemed to have a lot of men around him, a good many would be the worse for drink, while Shinwell himself had with him only a dozen of his toughest and best.

If he had been honest with himself, as soon as he reached the dockside he realised he had got it wrong. There seemed to be as many as seventy or eighty men with French, and even if plenty of them were drunk they looked menacing as they surged towards Shinwell's little group. In fact, they looked quite capable of murder.

There was nothing for it but to outface them. In that hard world, turning back would not have been taken as common sense but as weakness.

As they advanced steadily, Shinwell briefed his men: 'Start nothing. Stay close together – so close you can touch each other. Just do what we always do. Get to the dockside. He won't make the first move ...'

Then the unexpected happened. French himself stepped out in front of his men. 'The whole situation', French was later to say at his trial for murder, 'was getting too much'. He was losing his members, his reputation and probably his job because of 'that Jew' Shinwell. Here and now, backed by an army of supporters, French would tell him.

French never got a chance to tell him anything.

The precise sequence of events during the few seconds it took for Shinwell's men to encircle French and for him to get his automatic revolver out of his hip pocket and fire is a matter for conjecture. The witnesses at his trial were unanimous only on one point: French was in fear of his life. He had heard of threats to 'corpse' him and he had twice been badly beaten by the men who surrounded him. His own crowd seemed to him to hang back when he was struck a blow to the back of the head.

Dazed, he reached for his revolver. After a moment's shocked hesitation, some of Shinwell's men started to laugh at him. No one thought for an instant that the weapon was loaded or that he would use it. They underestimated both his fear and his courage.

He took hurried aim at Shinwell, the leader of his tormentors, and fired. Just one bullet was enough to kill.[37]

The shot was fired at Shinwell. The corpse that arrived at the Infirmary half an hour later belonged to Jimmy Martin.

Part 2

CHAPTER 4

'Shinbad the Tailor' Goes into Politics

Four hundred members of Shinwell's British Seafarers' Union set off on the *Titanic* in April 1912. It was the world's newest and smartest liner on a voyage from Southampton to New York. Even for hardened seamen, this voyage was exciting. 'Forests of masts and funnels, hundreds of portholes twinkling in the dusk, the bright ribbon of light that marked the promenade deck'. [1] Five days later, the *Titanic* struck an iceberg and sank in two hours. Over two thousand drowned, including more than three hundred members of Shinwell's union.[2] Lifeboats and safety training, as well as the pay, conditions and responsibilities of seamen, were impossible for any government to ignore from that night forward.

In a unique act of solidarity, representatives of the two rival seamen's unions stood shoulder to shoulder at Plymouth to receive the returning survivors. Back in Scotland, on the other hand, Shinwell's British Seafarers and Havelock Wilson's National Sailors' and Firemen's Union glowered at each other across criminal and civil courtrooms.

It was in the criminal court that the prospect of hanging loomed over Alfred French for the shooting of James Martin. French's defence counsel set out to reduce the likelihood of the death sentence by blackening both the murdered Martin and his boss, Shinwell, as part of their case. Martin's end was violent, but he was a gangster, they said, who had died as he had lived. Certainly Martin was no saint. French had lost most of the sight of his right eye just two months before the shooting, when Martin, wearing heavy boots, and some thugs acting on Martin's payroll, had kicked him about the face while he was chalking on the pavement a notice about one of his union's meetings.[3] Shinwell in his eulogy had described Martin as 'straightforward', 'outspoken' and 'fearing no one', before turning to his 'eager eyes' and willingness to help out seamen in distress.[4]

An attempt was made to blacken Shinwell in a different way.

'Are you a Jew?'

'Yes'

45

'Are you an atheist?'

'I am by birth a Jew, but for seven or eight years I have held somewhat unorthodox views on religion. But I am a Jew. I am not an atheist.'

Prosecuting counsel protested that this line of questioning was meaningless. The elderly judge, Lord Guthrie, intervened: 'What is thought to be the significance of the witness's doubts on religious matters?'

The reply was sharp and anti-Semitic:

'A great deal rests on this gentleman's credibility. He is a Jew and may be an atheist. We are honest Scots. What faith can we put in this "gentleman's" words?'

The defence lawyers revealed a whole series of violent incidents from the gang warfare in the docks involving Shinwell with Martin. Then they asked him if he ever threatened to get French killed. 'Who can believe the denials of this Jew or atheist with a known history of violence? Some key witness for the prosecution!'[5]

This public demolition of Shinwell's character, which later in the trial included claims of violent injury by people he had never met and a robust performance by Havelock Wilson swearing that Shinwell had stolen money from the Sailors' and Firemen's Union, made him think again about the nature of the establishment, the judiciary and the police. Could socialists really ever work with these people? The trial marked the start of Shinwell's four-year shift from respectable trade-union leader to revolutionary. It also gained French his liberty.

The quick and unanimous verdict of the Glasgow jury was 'Not Guilty'. They had been treated to a history of vicious inter-union rivalry, injury and death. It must have seemed to them that they had witnessed a parade of gangsters. If any among them had been a seaman, he would at best have been very doubtful about the capacity of either the Sailors' and Firemen's or the British Seafarers' Union, utterly obsessed with mutual hatred, to look after his interests.

Yet the year between the acquittal and the outbreak of the First World War was marked by a steady rise of membership in the Glasgow branch of the Seafarers' Union and the decline to insignificance in Glasgow of the Sailors' and Firemen's Union.[6] The problem for the latter seems to have been French's flat refusal to carry on union work after the trial, probably through fear of reprisals; he left a temporary gap in organisation and recruitment which was rapidly filled by the British Seafarers'.

A further helping hand was given to Shinwell by the extraordinary ineptitude of Havelock Wilson's civil court case to recover the books and papers of the Glasgow branch of the Sailors' and Firemen's Union. By this action, which failed because Wilson had not even bothered to register his union in Scotland, Shinwell's popularity and reputation were both enhanced. His popularity increased because Wilson now went beyond the limits of decency by accusing Shinwell in a series of speeches and pamphlets of being an embezzler, a cheat and a spy for the employers' Shipping Federation. Shinwell sued him and won £50 damages in February 1914. His reputation for effective and thorough work spread as the case he had prepared in minute detail progressed. He had had every item of expenditure externally audited and withheld the revelation about Wilson's failure to register until the very last moment to make his rival liable for the highest possible costs.[7]

All in all, 1913 was not a bad year for Shinwell. He had started the year heavily involved in violent inter-union rivalry; he had a seat on the Trades Council but the long-term prospects there, as for his union and his job, were poor. He ended the year with a reputation for thoroughness and efficiency, with sympathy in the Scottish Labour movement for his stand against Havelock Wilson, and with a union which organised some 80 per cent of the seamen on the Clyde.

Before the First World War, Glasgow was a Liberal city. Labour had only nineteen out of a hundred and thirteen seats on the council in 1914. The majority of working people voted Liberal, and a handful supported the movements of the far left. Yet it was a city in which politics mattered. The eclectic left-wing weekly *Forward* sold up to thirty thousand copies and it was the new Labour Party – the Glasgow branch was formed only in 1912 out of the policy-making committee chaired by Shinwell when he was president of the Trades Council – that seemed to have the new ideas.

Labour's policies on housing, national insurance and industrial organisation were starting to translate into votes. By 1914, Labour nationally looked well placed for the following year's general election. But instead of a general election there was a world war.

Ramsay MacDonald was Labour's mercurial national leader at this time, but it was the pedestrian, hard-working organising abilities of Arthur Henderson, the party secretary, that laid the practical foundations for Labour before the First World War. Henderson visited Glasgow in August 1912 and he met Shinwell who was already back on the Trades Council's executive, and he knew right away he had found a man after his own heart.[8] Shinwell, he saw, was just the kind of well-organised bureaucrat that the party needed. Henderson was full of praise for Shinwell's work in helping to develop agreed policy for Labour in Glasgow, although he confided to him that he was very anxious as far as the breakaway Seafarers' Union was concerned; he was instinctively a mainstream union man himself and he told Shinwell that he would do well to get out of the 'entanglement'. Shinwell admired the stolid and safe figure of Henderson; he felt it was Henderson and men like him, much more than Ramsay MacDonald, Keir Hardie or any other national figure of the left, who understood the feelings and problems of ordinary working men, and could organise the new political party so they could be articulated on councils, in Parliament and eventually in government.[9]

It was also Henderson's line in the fierce war or peace debate in the Labour Party in the lead-up to the First World War that Shinwell followed. In 1913 and 1914, Henderson nationally and Shinwell in Glasgow worked at manoeuvring Labour into a position where it could be seen to have worked for peace but could also defend workers' interests in war. A series of resolutions in the Glasgow Labour Party and the Glasgow Trades Council affirmed Labour's position against opening up jobs done by time-served men to other groups of workers – even in war emergency – without a great many safeguards. To Shinwell's satisfaction they reaffirmed the importance of having ships fully manned and equipped no matter how dire the need to expand the size of the fleet. At the same time, backing Henderson's line nationally, Shinwell moved a Trades Council resolution condemning any alliance with Russia, 'the land of the knout and the blood-libel against the Jewish people', which could drag Britain into war.[10]

But when all peace efforts had failed, Shinwell followed Henderson into collaboration with the government at war and showed no interest in MacDonald's more critical position against 'the disastrous consequences of a policy of this balance of power through alliance'.[11] At that time, of course, no one anywhere realised just how disastrous the consequences of war would be.

Why then did Shinwell support the war? The simplest answer is the same for him as for Henderson and thousands of others on the left and elsewhere on the political spectrum: patriotism. Genuinely stirred by the German attack on neutral Belgium, Shinwell accepted the rationalisation of British intervention that the defence of Belgium was a matter of British national honour. Insular politicians like Henderson and Shinwell at the time could not really grasp the intricacies of the arguments about the iniquitous international alliance which persuaded MacDonald to oppose the war. Instead they were drawn into the popular feeling of support for a war which most people thought would be justified and brief. They were certainly on the side of the vast majority of Glaswegians who volunteered in droves; on Glasgow Green on Sundays, the Clarion band stopped playing the 'Red Flag' and instead struck up the Belgian national anthem, the 'Brabançonne', along with the allies' 'Marseillaise' and 'God Save the Czar'.[12]

Shinwell was patriotic but he was never jingoistic, as were some on the left such as Clarion's Robert Blatchford and a number of Labour MPs and trade unionists, and as he himself had been during the Boer War. He felt this war should now be fought and won; but it should be used to strengthen the Labour movement (and incidentally his own political career) as well. He seems to have recognised three equal causes to be served: the nation at war, the Labour movement and himself. His very first act of the war, however, appeared to belie the second and third of these causes.

To the amazement of friends, colleagues and family alike, on Tuesday 4 August, the day Britain declared war, Shinwell volunteered to join the navy. Fanny, using the Yiddish expression for 'bonkers', told Rose her son had gone 'm'shuga'. Shinwell said years later he had wanted to join the navy as a boy but his father had stopped him, so volunteering at the beginning of the war should have surprised no one.[13]

The fact is, however, that there is justified doubt about his genuine intentions when he volunteered. Certainly he was no coward and would have been keen to show that he was willing to fight for King and Country. Now he was in his thirties and had a wife and three children (the third, Rose, had been born the year before, in the middle of French's trial), he may have been reluctant to go to sea in wartime, but no doubt he would really have done if necessary. But, on 4 August 1914, no one thought it necessary.

The truth must be that he was almost sure of exemption. They would need him in a war to recruit men for the Merchant Navy, just as they had already decided they needed the Sailors' and Firemen's Union with whom they had – to Shinwell's very great chagrin – an informal agreement.[14] By putting himself forward as a volunteer, Shinwell calculated that he would force the Admiralty and the Ministry of Shipping to treat the British Seafarers' Union in the same way.

Just as he had expected, within ten days of volunteering Shinwell heard that the Admiralty required him to stay in his present job. He had calculated correctly that if the Admiralty were faced with the choice between one more sailor and the likelihood of serious recruitment problems in the towns where the breakaway union was strong, Glasgow and Southampton, they would have to opt for recruitment; and they did. A few weeks later the Admiralty and the British Seafarers' Union came to a informal understanding similar to the one they had already reached with the Sailors' and Firemen's Union.[15]

The Admiralty certainly knew nothing about Shinwell personally and knew and cared very little about the his union. All that happened was that some of the ship-owners, tipped off by Shinwell, indicated informally to the government that certain trade unionists, including Shinwell, would be helpful in recruitment at a time when labour shortages were bound to arise as men joined the forces. Exemption was granted.

On 10 September, five weeks into the war, the British Seafarers' Union and the Admiralty's National Maritime Board came to a formal agreement on recognition and recruitment. All merchant seamen serving on vessels requisitioned by the Admiralty would get an extra pound a month, the dependents of merchant seamen killed in action would get compensation from the government, and there would be no strikes but a binding Board of Arbitration for the settlement of disputes. It was an identical agreement to the one the Admiralty had made with the Sailors' and Firemen's Union a week earlier.[16]

Shinwell was allowed to carry on with his union work but it was no longer his main job. That was defined in the agreement. It was to find the men to serve at sea in ships based at Southampton and Glasgow. The immediate problem was Southampton, so Shinwell's first war work was to recruit throughout Scotland and bring the potential sailors to Southampton.

He was embarrassed for the rest of his life that he never joined up and he reacted by aggressively defending his role as a recruiting agent for the Admiralty, even saying it was 'much more difficult and dangerous than being at the front' and 'vital to the survival of the mercantile marine'. He certainly exaggerated the difficulties. At a time when the regular army was being cut to pieces at Mons, it was audacious to describe herding a hundred and fifty raw recruits, who had admittedly spent their 'advance notes' on drink, as 'dangerous'. Shinwell at this time was an abstainer and the Southampton train was undoubtedly extremely unpleasant, but hardly dangerous. It was nevertheless a task which needed to be done and the Admiralty needed a trade unionist to do it; Shinwell was quite effective in collecting what he later called 'some of the scum of the earth', getting them to Glasgow, corralling them on to trains south, marching them across London and 'dumping them in Southampton'.[17] It was this work that got him the title 'Shinbad the Tailor' which stayed with him for fifty years.

After about a dozen journeys between September 1914 and the new year, the Clyde was as critically short of labour as Southampton, and shipowners everywhere started to recruit Chinese seamen in large numbers. The demands on Shinwell as a recruiting agent within Scotland diminished with the general industrial labour shortage and a plentiful supply of Chinese, and he found himself with more time on his hands for his union, politics and party, as the war moved into its second year.

It was the women who did more than anything to turn Shinwell into a radical agitator. With many of their men away getting killed and injured in France on a shilling a day, the women of the slum tenements of Glasgow refused to pay the increased rents demanded by their landlords, who in turn threatened eviction.[18]

Shinwell was keen to play a part in this new dispute. To do so he had to start to take women seriously for the first time in his life. Suffragettes he had simply regarded as hysterical;[19] he had insisted that Fanny should be only a housewife and he had forbidden her to work even when they desperately needed the money.[20] Yet now it was the women who were politically active ahead of him.

The first that Shinwell knew about the women's intention to take action was when he was handed a pamphlet at a Trades Council meeting in February 1915, announcing a 'Meeting of Women' arranged by the Glasgow Women's Housing Association to 'protest against the increase in rents'. It quoted the 'patriotic' president of the Houseowners' Association as saying: 'This is just the time to raise rents.' Two Labour town councillors and the Scottish Engineers' leader, David Kirkwood, were speaking, and there were also to be 'musical selections, songs and readings'.[21] Shinwell realised he was getting out of touch. Before the war this kind of event would never have happened without him knowing about it and being in the thick of it.

On 21 April 1915 Shinwell proposed a resolution at the Glasgow Trades Council in support of the women and urging the Coalition government, which by now included a handful of Labour members, to act to restrict rent increases.[22] On 5 May a further resolution was passed calling on the government to prevent increases in the cost of living in general.[23] The specific issue of rents seemed to be fading in importance. The news of the British victory at Neuve-Chapelle and the holding of the German army along the whole Western Front coincided with the coming of summer and a feeling that things were going to get better.

The catalyst was the case of the McHugh family of William Street, who had a wounded father and two sons in the army when the mother fell into arrears of nineteen shillings in June 1915. When the landlord's agent came to serve the notice of eviction, a crowd of a thousand blocked his way and then marched him back to his office and burnt him in effigy. John Wheatley in what was, for him, an unusual piece of street oratory, stirred the crowd, exclaiming this was 'just the latest in a long line of cruel, crushing, insulting treatment to which the capitalist class has subjected the working class'.[24]

At this vital moment, Shinwell was called away to assist in recruitment for the Merchant Navy in Liverpool, where the British Seafarers' Union shared responsibility with the Sailors' and Firemen's Union. The problem there was that the new recruits were turning up late and drunk, and sometimes missing the deadline for sailing altogether. The competing demands of the munitions industries and the army meant that only the dregs were left for the Merchant Navy. There was little Shinwell could really do.[25] It was a maddening time for him because he was missing all the political developments in Glasgow while playing an impotent bit-part hundreds of miles away.

To get the Liverpool problem out of the way so that he could get back home, he agreed to the employment of more Chinese crews, at least avoiding the Admiralty's threat to impose strict naval discipline on union members.[26] Even so it was September before he was back in Clydeside politics.

Meanwhile, the Trades Council and Labour members of Glasgow Town Council had both appealed to Arthur Henderson, Labour's only member of the Coalition Cabinet, to get the government to act on rents; they had recommended that rents should be paid at the pre-war rates, regardless of what landlords demanded.[27] It was obvious by the autumn that Henderson could not deliver, and an all-out rent strike would be needed to get results. It was in this phase, the organisation of the strike, that Shinwell was able to become involved for the first time.

Apart from withholding his own rent, Shinwell co-ordinated support from other trade unions through the Trades Council, and used his connections to 'split the capitalists' by obtaining supportive statements for the rent strikes from ship-owners and shipyard-owners.[28] As far as organisation on the ground was concerned, he had arrived back in Glasgow too late; nowhere more so than in his own area, where he was extremely surprised to find the strike already well organised. The Shinwells now lived in the Limehouse area of Govan, in relatively good-quality tenements where better-paid draughtsmen, clerks and skilled workmen were particularly badly affected by price rises on fixed incomes; on the subject of rents these mild, almost middle-class, respectable families were militant. To his surprise, and utter disapproval, Fanny had found her old independence again while he had been away. She was on their local tenement committee planning barricades against landlords' agents. Even twelve year-old Lucy had been caught dropping flour bombs on a pair of rent collectors who had dared to enter their courtyard. All Manny could do was listen to his excited family and pretend to be amused.[29]

By November, forty thousand tenants were withholding their rents. The far left was trying to stir up a general revolt, while the jingoists were talking of sedition and treachery. Wheatley and other Labour leaders with seats on the town council were running the show, along with women who had shown little interest in politics before. Now women like Fanny went to demonstrations with banners saying 'Defeat the Hun Landlords' and 'We Want Justice'.

Shinwell, now back on its executive, did his best to persuade the Trades Council to support Wheatley's tenants' organisations, but nothing much really came of them. As news of the deaths of young Glaswegians in their thousands at the Battle of Loos poured in through the disastrous autumn and winter of 1915, the climax of the rent strike came with the summons of eighteen poor tenants to the Small Debts Court. A crowd of fifteen thousand people, including workers from five munitions factories and delegates from many others, threatened the sheriff with violence if he went ahead with the prosecution. He gave in, frantically persuading London to get on to the landlords to drop their case.

The Trades Council, the Labour members of the town council and various far left groups, all immediately claimed credit for the 'victory for working people and good sense'.[30] There may have been a grain of truth in each of the claims, but the demonstration which tipped the balance was organised only by word of mouth. Much of what had happened was the result of spontaneous anger. Even Sam Shinwell, having ordered Rose not to go, then went himself 'out of curiosity'. Fanny went round to her parents-in-law's house and cheered the men and women on their way.[31] Shinwell himself, concerned for his exemption from military service, slipped away when there was a threat of violence against the Sheriff, but until that moment he was, at last, one of the leaders.

Along with a similar strike in Birmingham, the Glasgow rent strike succeeded in bringing about the abrupt introduction of legal rent controls by the government. The new Act was rushed on to the statute book by 23 December.[32] All rents were to be frozen at their pre-war levels. When the government announced their decision, Shinwell resolved never to be on the sidelines again if he could possibly avoid it, and he hurriedly contrived to be out of Glasgow for Labour's big Christmas celebration of 'Wheatley's finest hour'.[33]

Shinwell was pleased to turn his political energies to a new cause, less likely to involve 'unpredictable' women,[34] but one which would ultimately cause a good deal more concern to Asquith's government. 'Dilution', the use of less-skilled labour to do the jobs of time-served skilled men, was the next big controversy. Shinwell had learned from the rent strike the value of illegal direct action. It brought results. The establishment, already pressed by the exigencies of war, had cracked. Could he, as an outsider from a mixed skilled and unskilled union, obtain political influence in a movement to protect the skilled worker in wartime? The answer was yes, but only with the unintentional help of the government, especially the Labour leader Arthur Henderson and the powerful political hero of the hour, the Munitions Minister, David Lloyd George.

Throughout the second half of 1915, the government stepped up the pressure on Clydeside. Lord Kitchener warned Asquith's Cabinet that a long war was inevitable and that a much larger army would be needed. Britain was experiencing previously unimaginable numbers of casualties and all possible resources were being mobilised. Shinwell was part of this mobilisation with his seamen; the seamen themselves were 'resources'.

He was soon in the thick of opposing a particularly repressive measure of 'resource' mobilisation introduced by Lloyd George; this was the Munitions of War Act passed in July 1915. The Act gave Lloyd George the power to designate any factory a 'controlled establishment' where strikes were banned and employees were forbidden to leave. It was in these 'controlled establishments' that 'dilution' would be imposed. Women or unskilled ex-soldiers would be added to the workforce to do the same jobs – on lower wages – as the skilled men, with the aim of increasing production.

On the Clyde, William Weir, head of of Weir Pumps, a large engineering works, had already tried dilution and caused a strike earlier in the war. Now the government was trying to give employers like Weir the legal authority to impose dilution on their men. They even added insult to injury by making Weir Munitions Controller for Scotland. They had understood Weir but had failed to understand the majority of employers on Clydeside, most of whom were very cautious and preferred to wait for some test cases before introducing dilution into their own factories. Many of them had long-standing agreements with their skilled men, who were scarcer than ever because of the war, and they had no wish to antagonise them.[35]

Shinwell, like many others on the Trades Council, recognised that restrictive practices in war industries would have to be diluted to some extent. The objection, as he explained it at the time, was that the way chosen to improve the efficiency of industry was not to use the war profits of the big companies more effectively nor to provide more effective incentive pay nor even to arrange to train more skilled people, but to give extra powers to employers which, from Shinwell's point of view, would simply put more money into the bosses' pockets. Dilution was all right but not dilution alone.[36]

It was the part of the Munitions of War Act to do with 'Leaving Certificates' that brought Shinwell directly into the fray. He was pleased not to have to defend every last engineer against dilution. Instead it was the consequences of two shipwrights at the huge Fairfield Shipyard being sacked for 'slacking' that came to the attention of the executive of the Trades Council in October 1915. Under the Act they had to obtain a Leaving Certificate from their 'protected' workplace and their certificates stated that they had been sacked for slacking. Seventeen of their colleagues led a walkout, only to be arrested because they were not allowed to down tools at a 'controlled establishment'; they were hauled before a General Munitions Tribunal two days later and fined £10 each.

All Shinwell could do was to volunteer to 'frame an appropriate resolution' for the next Trades Council meeting a week later. By that time three of the men had refused to pay their fines and were imprisoned, so Shinwell had to put two resolutions to the Trades Council, one deploring the Act and the other demanding that the three men be released at once. After three days of false promises and public accusations of bad faith between the Engineers' Union and the government, Shinwell on behalf of the Trades Council managed to convene a private meeting which lasted all night between David Kirkwood, the Engineers' leader, and two senior officials sent by Lloyd George. They met at first in two separate rooms with Shinwell going backwards and forwards down a corridor. By 7a.m. it was agreed that any remaining strikers would go back to work, the 'slackers' would be issued with fresh Leaving Certificates and the men in prison would 'in all probability' be released and given a long, perhaps indefinite, time to pay their fines.[37]

William Weir immediately complained to Lloyd George that the Act was unenforceable and declared that the powerful Trades Council was holding a pistol to the head of progressive employers, threatening action by one group of workmen in support of others unconnected with them.[38]

Weir's accusation was unrealistic, but Shinwell always believed that the Trades Council could do three things well. First, it could put fear into the government because it represented a great cross-section of the workforce essential to the war effort; this was the message that had undoubtedly got through to William Weir. Second, it could provide a platform for an ambitious politician; Shinwell soon realised that a move to the left would capture the mood of the time – his own preference for carefully organised action well-planned in advance would have to give way anyway under the new laws to almost spontaneous demonstrations and strikes; so he started to shift his ground. Third, it could go some way to co-ordinating its sixty affiliated organisations for action short of actual strikes; his greatest success as far as this went was in getting the Trades Council involved in the humiliation of Lloyd George on his 1915 Christmas Day visit to Glasgow.[39]

Lloyd George arrived in Glasgow on 22 December. His visit was to be Shinwell's chance to prove his radical credentials. He also needed an adversary and an event on which to build a political reputation as opposed to his trade-union activist's reputation, and Lloyd George was a mighty adversary.

Lloyd George had a plan for weaning Glasgow's munitions workforce away from militancy to patriotic fervour and active support for the Munitions of War Act. He would flatter their leaders, take with him Labour's leader, now his colleague in the Coalition Cabinet, Arthur Henderson, and even make favourable references to Ramsay MacDonald. With his unlimited self-confidence, he would talk as if in a dream of the worker-heroes of the 'socialist' munitions factories and charm his audience with a mixture of oratory and banter. Years later, he said of a political opponent's oratory 'he's not dangerous, he's too relevant'.[40] Lloyd George intended to be dangerous in Glasgow and to win hearts and minds. He had done all these things before; but he had never before come across a combination of labour organisers like Manny Shinwell and his Trades Council friend, Willie Gallacher. They were not of course his only opposition, but Shinwell's and Gallacher's great strength was organisation, and on the night, their organisation was better than Lloyd George's.

Gallacher had been a seaman and was now on the far left of Glasgow politics, the chairman of the self-styled Clyde Workers' Committee, a believer in class struggle and eventual revolution.[41] Shinwell and Gallacher, 'who was a Marxist but never talked Marxism with me', were friends and destined to be co-conspirators for the next few years. Their views on the tactics for opposing dilution and, more especially, for opposing Lloyd George were very similar. They agreed on the aim of worker involvement in running the munitions factories as a quid pro quo for some measure of dilution and they agreed on the need to organise carefully with the aim of scaring Lloyd George to make him think about repealing or drastically altering his Act. Gallacher needed Shinwell because he was on the executive of the mainstream Trades Council, a respectable Labour man. Shinwell needed Gallacher for his radical political edge.

Just before coming to Glasgow, Lloyd George made a significant tactical error. He announced without consultation a change in the date of his big speech at St Andrew's Hall from 23 December to Christmas Day, a working day at that time. He did this with only four days' warning and many trade unionists had to cancel their plans as a result. As soon as he realised that the sudden change had caused serious problems, Lloyd George agreed that every worker attending the meeting should be given seven and sixpence compensation for loss of pay; but the damage was done.

Shinwell and Gallacher worked three days and nights touring the factories and shipyards, and between them they managed to persuade the shop stewards at the munitions factories which Lloyd George planned to visit that they had been insulted by him and should have nothing to do with him. They were successful in every case except Beardmore's Engineering Works where the Engineers' Union leader David Kirkwood himself was based; Kirkwood had been flattered by a personal telegram from Lloyd George requesting a meeting, but even he delivered the bemused minister a largely incoherent lecture at the top of his voice, telling him that his Act had bound the workers 'as if their brows had been branded with the initial of their employer'.

No other Clydeside workers would see Lloyd George. Not realising that Shinwell himself was one of the instigators of the boycott, Henderson, who knew and admired Shinwell from pre-war days, tried through him to get the Trades Council to intercede.[42] Shinwell used delaying tactics rather than turning Henderson down flat, fixing a meeting time, changing it, fixing another and arriving late. By the time he told Henderson that there was no chance that either the Trades Council or the Clyde Workers' Committee would budge, it was too late for the government side to do anything about it. Instead, on the evening of 23 December, the Trades Council agreed by a large majority not to listen to Lloyd George but to turn up only to disrupt his big meeting. Shinwell said, to loud applause, that in his opinion the only way to deal with these people was to use plenty of ridicule. 'We are asked to welcome Lloyd George as a prophet and Arthur Henderson is coming to allay heavy opposition among trade unionists. I hope the trade unions will give these people exactly the welcome they deserve.'[43] Shinwell captured the mood precisely. When the time came for Lloyd George's stage-managed performance to start, Gallacher and Shinwell had made sure that the vast majority of the three thousand people in the audience in St Andrew's Hall on Christmas Day were their supporters. At the same time he made sure by playing down the seriousness of the situation in further discussions with Henderson that the whole event was not called off. Lloyd George's confidence in his own ability to turn an audience would probably have seen to that in any case.

First came a troupe of girls in khaki trying to sing patriotic songs but the audience jeered them off the stage. Apparently unaware of the mood, Lloyd George walked from his car into the hall as the band struck up 'See the Conqu'ring Hero Comes'. For once the Welsh Wizard's face fell as the audience drowned the band with the 'Red Flag' – it was surely the only time Lloyd George entered an auditorium while the audience was singing 'Raise the Scarlet Standard high!' Henderson spoke first, went on too long and he found the heckling difficult, but it was Lloyd George they were waiting for. He still calculated he could win the day by persuasion; no one could remember him ever failing. As he stood, the real uproar started, much of it the ridicule that Shinwell had wanted. When he talked about the hard life of a minister in wartime, a heckler brought the house down asking him how he could possibly manage on such a pittance as a Prime Minister's wage. Someone else yelled at him to get his hair cut. Those who dared oppose him, he said, were 'haggling with an earthquake' – it was the last simile of the day. The meeting ended in pandemonium and Lloyd George for the only time in his political life slunk away through the rear door with the little dignity he could still muster.[44]

Shinwell had made his mark. 'Every effort will now be made to crush us,' Gallacher warned the Clyde Workers Committee.[45] He was right. Within days, the radical press was censored or closed down and it was very clear there would be no concessions to workers' control. Within weeks, Gallacher, Kirkwood and other agitators were deported from Glasgow. Shinwell, Henderson's 'respectable' friend and patriotic recruiter of seamen, survived to fill the vacuum. No one could deny his credentials now as a formidable Red Clydesider.

CHAPTER 5

Bolshevik

The establishment turned on the Clydeside Reds in January 1916. It was the attention that many of them craved, but it was also a time of fear. The sinister knock on the door at three in the morning, exile and imprisonment were also part of the new reality.

Glasgow's radical paper, *Forward*, edited by Thomas Johnston (later a very respectable Secretary of State for Scotland), dared to ignore the government's official press briefing on Lloyd George's chaotic visit to Glasgow. The visit had been a disaster and that was how Johnston reported it in his New Year issue. On the grounds that to say such a thing about the Minister of Munitions was seditious, Lloyd George personally organised its suppression.[1] His stage management had failed in Glasgow, but at least the damage could be limited.

Some of Lloyd George's civil servants wanted to go even further, deporting all the troublemakers out of the Clyde region. If they stayed around, would the army get the weapons it needed? The soldiers needed howitzers on the Western Front; they needed flat-bottom barges in Mesopotamia; they would soon be launching the summer offensive on the Somme. No more delays could be tolerated.[2] The solution Lloyd George actually chose was to appoint 'Dilution Commissioners' with the power to impose unskilled workers on the munitions factories, ignoring all opposition; and they would have a brief to have new workers in place in an incredible ten to fourteen days.[3]

When they arived in Glasgow, the Commissioners made it clear that they would prefer to work by agreement with the trade unions if at all possible. They carefully negotiated an agreement with the Engineers' Union leader, David Kirkwood, that soldiers and women could 'dilute the employment' at Beardmore's Forge and Engineering Works where he was chief shop steward, provided that this 'new class of labour' would be paid according to the hours they worked without affecting the pay and conditions of the craftsmen already employed. At the same time, Lloyd George told the House

58

of Commons that there would be an Act after the war to restore pre-war practices.[4]

At five other leading munitions factories, the Clyde Workers' Committee caused a good deal more trouble for the Commissioners than Kirkwood at Beardmore's. The committee in theory accepted dilution only with the expropriation of capitalists, but in practice they simply wanted tough separate negotiations. Above all, they wanted to be recognised as a serious political force. The Commissioners were having none of it. Their circumspection came to an abrupt end. A syndicalist article, calling for a general strike, in the committee's paper *The Worker*, was just the excuse needed to arrest the committee's leaders. According to Lynden Macassey, the chief Dilution Commissioner, they were 'all pro-German agents' anyway.[5] With its leaders under threat of gaol, with its treasurer, Kirkwood, having settled on his own terms, the Clyde Workers' Committee lost much of its effectiveness. The baton of the leadership of the left was passed to the Trades Council. Shinwell, once again its rising star, was the first to seize it.

He told the Trades Council that they must seize the initiative, accept dilution and set about negotiating safeguards with vigour:

> When the lordly Commissioners have come and gone, we will still be here and the employers will still be here with us. They will have to live with us. The Trades Council will watch over the diluted factories like a hawk. We will look after the interests of the soldiers who have been drafted in to the forges and shipyards and we will even look after the interests of women brought in to do the work of men.[6]

Delegated to represent the Trades Council, he appeared to the Commissioners to be sweet reasonableness itself, a welcome contrast to the Clyde Workers' Committee. In front of Macassey, he told a seething Kirkwood that it was not the job of the Trades Council just to take up the interests of his skilled craftsmen; the general workers, the ex-soldiers, the women and the seamen were all part of the Trades Council's larger constituency. Its interest in the dilution debate was to ensure fair play all round.

Meanwhile, Kirkwood, who had isolated himself from both the remnants of the Clyde Workers' Committee and from the Trades Council by stepping out of line and reaching a separate agreement, was inevitably picked off. Shinwell had no intention of stepping in to help a man he saw as both incompetent and a rival; and Lloyd George was never likely to forgive him for introducing him to the workforce at Beardmore's as their 'enemy'.

The fall came when Kirkwood tried to persuade the newly recruited women at Beardmore's to join the Engineers' Union. The women's manageress protested at his 'impertinence' and Kirkwood found himself banned from moving around the factory and in addition banned from talking to the English ex-soldiers who also refused to join his union. A strike among the skilled men broke out on 17 March and spread to half a dozen other major munitions plants in a few days. It was the Clyde Workers' Committee's final drive for a general strike in 1916, and with little organisation it was a complete flop. By 15 April, there were only thirty strikers remaining and they were fined; the strike leaders, including Kirkwood, were roused in the small hours of the next morning and dragged off to gaol. A few hours later they were deported to Edinburgh, under the war emergency Defence of the Realm regulations, and ordered to keep out of Glasgow for the rest of the war. The Clyde Workers' Committee had disintegrated completely.[7]

Kirkwood expected Shinwell and the Trades Council to jump to his defence. But Shinwell refused to help. Denying Kirkwood's accusation of a stab in the back, his riposte was vitriolic: 'Kirkwood is too easily flattered and his opinion of his own abilities is so inflated it has to be witnessed to be believed.' As far as Shinwell was concerned: 'Kirkwood has gone his own way, he has not shown the solidarity a trade unionist ought to show and he deserves his humiliation and suffering.'[8]

Shinwell half-heartedly prepared a Trades Council resolution demanding the return of the deportees but refused to mention Kirkwood by name. He planned a demonstration which was, as he had certainly anticipated and probably arranged, banned by the magistrates.[9] He breathed a sigh of relief when the Trades Council voted to accept the ban on the demonstration, and he put his name forward for the vice-presidency of what was now the only broad-based workers' organisation left intact in Glasgow.[10]

The year 1916 was to be hard enough without any more left-wing heroics. Conscription was introduced in January. In the diminishing band of the left in Glasgow, James Maxton and John MacLean had spoken against it and were gaoled. In an atmosphere of bitterness, self-styled 'patriots' had even stoned Maxton's dog to death and Sir Edward Carson had suggested to Lloyd George that Kirkwood, MacLean and the rest should be tried for their lives for high treason.[11] And the slaughterhouse of the Somme was just around the corner.

Shinwell's view was that for the time being the conventional activities of the Trades Council were the only way of keeping up any pressure for workers' rights.[12] If there were to be any more strikes, they had to be very carefully co-ordinated; the higgledy-piggledy reaction of different committees and shop stewards to a sudden and aggressive government offensive had been disastrous. He was under no illusion, from his experience in tailoring, shipping and on the Trades Council, about the need for direct action and the reality of class conflict. But most of the leaders of the Glasgow working class were either locked up or deported and consequently useless. If they were to emerge from the war no worse off than they went into it, then thinking and planning, rather than rushing headlong into strikes, demonstrations and disaster, were urgently needed.

Meanwhile, the dropping of flour-bombs apart, Shinwell's home life became more comfortable during the war. Manny and Fanny and their three children, Lucy, coming up to thirteen, Sammy now seven, and baby Rose, suffered from the same high prices and shortages as everyone else, but his income from the Seafarers' Union seemed increasingly secure and was enough for them to live at a reasonable standard, not luxuriously but at least with enough to eat and in a tenement flat with its own lavatory and running cold water.[13]

In his long absences recruiting seamen, the children would often stay with their Shinwell grandparents. Sam was now fairly prospering in his tailoring business and lived away from his workshop in a comfortable flat in Great Hamilton Street. Rose would still help out at the workshop but spent more time at home to make her chicken soup. Everyone got on with Rose, and they were therefore inclined to put up with her morose husband. She always seemed to have a house full of friends and grandchildren, priests from across the road and 'schnorrers' taking advantage of her easy generosity. There was one big comfortable spare bed where the children all slept and ate chips together.

Sam's and Rose's home was strictly kosher; Great Hamilton Street was not in a Jewish area and Rose had to walk several miles for provisions for her family which had now grown to nine. Manny and Fanny on the other hand did not observe the Jewish festivals and certainly never thought of keeping a kosher home. In fact, one Passover, Lucy ran halfway round Glasgow to find unleavened matzos for them so they would have some at home for Sam and Rose making one of their rare visits.[14]

Manny and Fanny made very little of their Jewishness, although neither ever denied it. But when John Wheatley wrote a sickeningly anti-Semitic article in *Forward*, it stirred deep feelings in both of them and caused an irreparable rift between the two families who had been friends. Manny read the worst passage out loud to Fanny who burst into tears.

> with all the shrewdness of Abie, Isaac and Moses on his head, it is the Jew who knows that the Government is in a better position than he to make such regulations as will enforce you to pay him his pound of flesh. Please note Micky, of the £9/16/- that is debited against you (and 50 million others), £4/18/- goes to smash the Germans and £4/18/- goes to square the Jew.[15]

Wheatley never apologised. He was bullied by Thomas Johnston into hamfistedly trying to make amends by personally proposing Shinwell for Glasgow Town Council to fill the vacancy at Fairfield ward, following the death of one of the Labour councillors. Wheatley made his reluctance obvious. Shinwell accepted the chance of co-option, perhaps with a little malicious pleasure since he must have known Wheatley's views on him not just as a Jew but as a potential troublemaker and even, eventually, as a rival in the Council Chamber. He never forgave Wheatley.

The town council would now add its demands on Manny's time to his ever-growing list of councils, boards and committees, but he saw his family every day he was in town. Fanny rarely inspired quite the warmth with which Rose surrounded her later children at Great Hamilton Street, but Manny and Fanny had a home with a lot more to offer than Manny had known in his own broken childhood. His children were well-dressed, well-fed and went to school. They now learned to be proud of their father, likely to be president again of the Trades Council, and now a town councillor as well.

One place where Shinwell still had to fight physically was the Broomielaw. That was where his Seafarers' Union office was, by the docks. It was still too dangerous for him to walk alone there because of the constant physical threat from thugs hired by Havelock Wilson's rival Sailors' and Firemen's Union.[16] The risk was greatest, however, whenever he left Glasgow; his union office in Liverpool was set on fire with him inside and when he escaped into the street they first tried to push him back in, telling him 'to look after your important affairs'. Then they beat him up and left him in the gutter. They also defamed him in their magazine, *The Seaman*, calling him a 'wrecker' and 'a leech that grows fat on the blood of the working man'.[17] They constantly tried to move in on his activities and to persuade the Admiralty that he and his union were surplus to their recruitment needs.

Shinwell's most bitter opponent in the Sailors' and Firemen's Union was 'Captain' Tupper. Tupper was an altogether more unpleasant rival than David Kirkwood and far more brutal. Shinwell had seen Tupper off in the 1911 strike, but Tupper had learned a lot since then. Now, during the war, Tupper sought revenge.

Tupper immediately, for public consumption, sought the high moral ground with such ferocious jingoism and hatred of everything German that it made even patriots wince. He hated the Chinese too, almost as much as the Germans, because they were taking British seamen's jobs, albeit at a time when, as Shinwell pointed out in vain, there were no British seamen to recruit. These 'cowardly heathen yellow-heads', Tupper inveighed, were serving at sea for 'a bowl of rice and 40 per cent less pay than the civilised native of English soil'. Although Tupper and Shinwell were agreed that the Chinese would have to go at the end of the war, Tupper's ferocious line made it hard for Shinwell to appear as anything other than weak to many seamen, as Wilson put it: 'the British seaman's enemy and the Chinaman's friend.'[18]

Shinwell never actually met Havelock Wilson in the war, but he did formally meet Tupper and they were almost civil to each other. Shinwell and Tupper came together to welcome the men returning from the Glasgow-based SS *Bellaisla* which had been in Hamburg when war broke out and had been impounded by the Germans. At first they small-talked about the job they had come to do. The men of the *Bellaisla* had been treated brutally, half-starved and beaten almost as a daily routine for two years. While they were waiting together at Dover harbour for the neutral ship carrying the survivors, Shinwell and Tupper turned to politics. Did Tupper support the nationalisation of shipping? No – Shinwell, like so many of his sort 'who were always crooked, could not appreciate the property-owning rights of the freeborn Briton'. As for the ship-owners, Tupper revealed proudly that he had dined recently with the officers of the Ship-owners' Association, and found them a fine body of men whom he, Tupper, knew how to handle in negotiations if he needed to do so; this was a snippet Shinwell was later able to use when he accused the Sailors' and Firemen's Union of 'banqueting the ship-owners'.

Somehow, Shinwell and Tupper did manage to agree to co-operate in negotiations with the Admiralty and its National Maritime Board over shipwreck benefits for the dependents of seamen who were drowned or taken prisoner or had lost all their possessions in battle at sea, but they could agree on nothing else. Shinwell thought Tupper an impostor and a fool. He could understand – especially when Tupper warned him that 'his Jacks' would skin him and roast him slowly on a spit once he got away from this polite reception committee – why Wilson only ever employed Tupper by the day.[19]

Tupper wrote later that he always quite liked Shinwell, but he certainly never showed it. Within two weeks of their meeting at the Admiralty, he sent five men to Ardrossan 'to teach the Jew Shinwell one or two lessons by ducking him in the oily dock'. On this occasion Shinwell got away. Both men sabotaged each other's recruitment efforts, using hired thugs to threaten men who might have volunteered. At a difficult time, Shinwell and Tupper were experts at making things a good deal worse.

Yet, in all their antagonism, did the two rivals really hate each other? After all, every few weeks, both men had to face the truth about the dangers of the sea in wartime; both men had to face grieving relatives when they went to see them about rents and food; often Shinwell or Tupper had been the recruiting agent for the dead breadwinner, and the grieving family would attack them with their bare hands – the recruiting agents, after all, were still alive and well. Despite these bitter shared experiences, Tupper still was willing to risk getting Shinwell killed, and both men were willing to put their rivalry before the needs of the Merchant Navy in wartime. They must indeed have hated each other.[20]

Shinwell discovered one particularly bad omen for the post-war period through some correspondence leaked to him by a sympathetic ship-owner's clerk. At the beginning of March 1917, the Clyde Steamship Owners' Association apparently resolved at their monthly meeting that the Board of Trade Food Scale, the so-called 'sailor's whack', would need revision downwards after the war; it allowed more meat, vegetables and bread than necessary for the work a seaman did and all at the expense of the ship-owner, 'and this has been proved by the Chinese sailors'. This was at a time when many seamen were in fact giving up half their meat ration anyway to help bring more meat into Britain.[21] Shinwell confronted the ship-owners with the minute and they brazenly denied everything, saying no such cuts had ever been planned. Shinwell believed none of the denials and said so.[22]

Then he raised the matter of the brothels and opium dens being set up near his office on the Broomielaw. The reply was that nothing could be done. The Chinese were needed and if it meant having a few seedy brothels, so be it. In the opinion of the ship-owners, this was the Chinese way, innocent fun. In any case, a number of his own members were not averse to occasional visits – although no one accused Shinwell himself, a genuine innocent in such matters, of going anywhere near them.

No matter what the rebuffs, Shinwell realised that progress would have to be made with the ship-owners during the war because there would certainly be no chance after it. The ship-owners had made enormous profits out of trade in war conditions and would be able to withstand strike action far better than the unions. Shinwell set about exposing 'profiteering' and by September 1916 he had moved to a position where only out-and-out nationalisation of ships and shipping would save the wages and conditions of the British seaman. In an article in his union's paper, he laid out for the first time a socialist political line in relation to two Clyde ship-owners he had found particularly difficult in negotiations, F. W. Lewis and Sir Alfred Booth:

> Some of the ship-owners are greedier than others, for while Lewis does not appear to object to wartime profits tax (knowing, of course, that he is still doing excellently after paying it), Booth, the Chairman of the Anchor Line, thinks that the tax is a 'blunder for which the country will have to pay sooner or later'.
> He wants the whole blessed lot.
> He says: 'The money taken by the Exchequer ought to be turned into new ships if we are to maintain the size and efficiency of our mercantile marine.'

I agree, if he means that the Government should build the ships, and own and control them. But the ship-owners who have already put by reserves for this very purpose, after paying huge dividends and making themselves as rich as emperors, want to use the new ships for the purpose of making yet more profits.

For colossal impudence Booth's suggestion would be difficult to beat. He was careful to add that he does not object to the excess profit tax from the point of view of his own pocket – 'quite the contrary.' Just so! His heart no doubt is bleeding on account of the sufferings and hunger of the people but he takes his profits just the same.

The ship-owners, merchants, and all the trading interests that are making money out of the war have a very large number of 'Pals' in the House of Commons, and the hungry people have but very few. As a consequence the laws are made in the interests of the rich people, and if for the purpose of making a show they levy taxes on themselves they very soon find ways and means of recouping themselves.

Ownership by the state for the state's purposes is the only way forward.[23]

It was after a dreadful day visiting the relatives of the crew of a coaster lost in the Irish sea,[24] and dodging the hirelings of the Sailors' and Firemen's Union, that Shinwell went to the Trades Council executive meeting, only to hear of the dismissal of the 'gentle revolutionary' John MacLean, from his job as a schoolteacher. An out-and-out revolutionary, he had been arrested for seditious behaviour in the dilution struggle, but he had not yet been convicted. The *Glasgow Herald* was already screaming that it was high time that men like MacLean were locked up or shot.[25] Now the School Board had twisted the knife.

The School Board, Shinwell declared angrily, was filled with Liberals who had not surprisingly behaved disgracefully. He himself had no time for MacLean's strong anti-war views but experience was teaching him to be increasingly sympathetic towards MacLean's perception of society in terms of class struggle.[26]

It was one more perceptible shuffle to the left. Shinwell's contacts with the far left on Clydeside had been sporadic but never antagonistic. Recently he had actually worked quite successfully with MacLean during some further agitation over rents.[27] He thought MacLean paranoid but harmless, a supporter of working class causes, sometimes eccentric but never dangerous. In his peroration at the Trades Council he said he would be 'proud and happy' to have his children taught by John MacLean.[28] He won over the meeting, but the protest was in vain. MacLean's dismissal was not reversed and he went to prison, which all but killed him.

This kind of free association within the left, where the Trades Council would appear to be supporting a self-confessed revolutionary, was characteristic of the relatively confined and isolated world of Clydeside politics. It had the undoubted effect of encouraging the establishment to see all left politics there as potentially revolutionary. This was of course a mistake. Shinwell, whatever he thought of MacLean personally and however far left he shifted, went on thinking of the Marxist doctrine of inevitable revolution led by a vanguard industrial proletariat as a mere pipedream.

Nevertheless, Shinwell's leftward moves were not restricted to industrial matters. The events of 1916 also moved him from an uncritically pro-war stance to sympathy for the ILP demand for a negotiated peace. In all these matters, throughout that dangerous year, he was extremely cautious of what he said in public; deportation, conscription or imprisonment, he could see perfectly well, meant temporary heroism but long-term obscurity. He wanted to be in the middle of the fray, not forced out of it.

By the time he went to Leeds for the ILP Annual Conference in April 1917, the whole international scene had changed dramatically. Russia had experienced her first revolution of that year, the Battle of the Somme had been a costly disaster and Shinwell was using all his influence on Glasgow Town Council as well as the Trades Council – of which he had now been elected president again with a record number of votes – to ensure a hearing in Glasgow for Ramsay MacDonald.[29]

Shinwell by now completely shared MacDonald's view of the war as a foreign policy disaster. He had always had difficulty in seeing the war as purely 'capitalist', because he had recognised the injustice of German militarism overrunning Belgium, but persistent jingoistic feelings did not come naturally to a Jew born in London and living in Scotland. He managed to put the weight of the Trades Council behind the Glasgow branch of the National Council for Civil Liberties who finally invited MacDonald to Glasgow in May.[30] Shinwell took the chair: 'We welcome him and we welcome his search for peace ... labour must regain the initiative from the capitalists who have brought us this calamity.' Simple enough sentiments for a man beginning to believe the fundamentals of socialism.

MacDonald greeted the first Russian revolution as the 'springtide of joy' which brought new hope to the international scene. He warned:

> It is the Red Flag that flies over the Imperial Palace at Petrograd. If the allies insist on the Russians staying in total war, they can only expect the extremists [the Bolsheviks led by Lenin] to take power. Then Russia will be in anarchy and will hand the Germans victory on a plate.[31]

Meanwhile, a threatening crowd of 'patriots' had gathered outside the all-ticket meeting at Charing Cross Halls. MacDonald, Shinwell and Mrs Pethick-Lawrence, the second speaker, were all too professional and too experienced to be concerned about some booing and hissing from the corridor leading to the street. But Shinwell, who knew the hall better than his guests, was at first irritated and then, as the three-hour meeting went on and the stewards were unable to gain control, increasingly alarmed by the obvious and sinister fact that the stewards were getting no help from the police.

All of a sudden there was a loud commotion from behind a door at the side of the stage where the speakers were seated. MacDonald nervously asked Shinwell if there was an escape route to the rear and quickly shied away when a burly six-footer wielding a heavy piece of lead pipe jumped up next to him.

'Who's this?' MacDonald stammered.

'Oh, you've no need to worry about him,' replied Shinwell. 'It's only McGovern. He's a pacifist.'

'He's the sort of pacifist I much prefer on my side,' declared MacDonald, much relieved.

Meanwhile, Neil Jamieson, the leader of the jingoists had broken through the side door and loudly demanded a place on the platform as a citizen's right. He confronted Shinwell who agreed: 'All right then! Let's be having you in!' Perhaps it was the threatening tone in Shinwell's voice or perhaps it was the obvious hostility in the audience; whatever the cause, Jamieson lost his nerve. Shinwell and several others, including the pacifist with the lead pipe, tried to haul him up on to the platform. Jamieson yelled for help and made a heroic and eventually successful effort to get out of the hall.

Thirty men were arrested in the brawl that followed the meeting as the audience tried to leave, but where had the police been earlier? Shinwell waited behind with MacDonald and Mrs Pethick-Lawrence in a stuffy box-like office backstage for nearly an hour until they got the all-clear from two stewards, 'one with a black eye and a bruise from a truncheon on his arm and the other barely able to walk'.[32]

It turned out that the police had actually been present at an earlier open-air meeting of Jamieson's Scottish Patriotic Federation, when he had announced his intention of breaking into 'the traitors' gathering in the Charing Cross Halls'. They had then done nothing whatsoever to prevent it. To cap it all, not a single 'patriot' had been arrested and only stewards and ticket-holders trying to fight their way home had been charged.[33] Shinwell himself received a summons a week later for a breach of the peace and assault before he had even finished writing a formal letter of complaint to the Lord Advocate. He went to court on 21 May 1917. His accuser, Jamieson, was cross-examined:

'Did you see Mr Shinwell raise the piece of metal?'

'Yes.'

'But there were three men between you and Mr Shinwell?'

'Well, just two men and a part of one.'
'Who took the piece of metal from Mr Shinwell?'
'I don't know.'
'Do you know Shinwell?'
'Er … I know him by repute.' (Laughter in court.)

P C Duncan M'Lean swore Shinwell was bareheaded. A Sergeant Melvin then swore Shinwell was wearing a black felt hat. P C Macintosh swore he took a weapon from a very small dark man but could not say if it was Shinwell or not. A dozen unimpeachable witnesses then swore Shinwell never left the chair during the meeting and also swore that he cowered backstage with Ramsay MacDonald during the brawl afterwards.

The magistrate declared finally that he understood the 'natural feelings' of the police, which would be shared by 'all true Scots', but he had 'listened to the evidence with something of wonder that ever a prosecution was undertaken under such circumstances, not against the invading body, but against the chair of the invaded meeting'.[34] The 'Not Guilty' verdict was greeted with cheers in court. But the majority feeling in the street and even in the factories was still fiercely 'patriotic' and totally against negotiated peace while Germany was undefeated. The demoralisation of Passchendaele and the German Spring Offensive of 1918 was yet to come.

Shinwell complained about the lack of protection at the meeting and the attempt to frame him to the Lord Advocate but to no avail.[35] Jamieson even turned out to be a special constable, and his views were really only an extreme version of those of the full-time police, the Lord Advocate, the magistrate and most of the establishment. For all his indignation, Shinwell might as well have saved his ink.

He was interested enough in MacDonald's line to follow up the Glasgow meeting with a visit to the conference of the new United Socialist Council at Leeds in June. Ever the sceptic, he wrote afterwards:

The conference congratulated the Russians on their revolution and passed airy resolutions about establishing workmen's and soldiers' councils in every town and village in Britain. By implication MacDonald was expected to organise this essay into revolution, and the picture of MacDonald manning the barricades was probably absurd enough even to reassure Lloyd George that there was no need to ban the meeting.[36]

MacDonald spoke eloquently of the need for peace without annexation or indemnities, whereupon, to Shinwell's immense surprise, Tupper, now plain Mr instead of the earlier Captain, and without his medals, got up and demanded indemnities for merchant seamen: 'Never mind all this talk of Germany, what about the sufferings of my Jacks?' There followed a list of atrocities, men deliberately left to drown, men tied to trees and beaten, men flogged to death at sea. Then he attacked the Seafarers' Union: 'there are some who purport to speak for the seamen who are little better than the Huns; there are some who for all we know are in league with the devil-Kaiser himself ...' They stopped him there.

Shinwell who had not originally intended to speak retorted that seamen should indeed be indemnified but at the expense of the ship-owners and not at the expense of the future peace of Europe. It was not a great speech but it made its simple points about the profits of ship-owners in the war and the need for nationalisation. Then with a touch of theatre, Shinwell raised his voice: 'Can we stand by and allow brother to call brother such damnable names and can we tolerate such groundless accusation? I ask Edward Tupper to leave the hall. If he does not go, I shall move his forceable removal.' It went down so well that the audience jeered till Tupper finally stormed out of his own accord, yelling abuse at all and sundry, especially Shinwell and MacDonald.[37]

Only ten days later Tupper had his revenge. Grateful to find an alternative to the barricades, MacDonald decided to go to Russia himself, following Henderson who had already been sent secretly by Lloyd George (who had succeeded Asquith as Prime Minister). His brief was to stiffen the resolve of the revolutionary premier, Kerensky, leader of the Russian government of the democratic left that preceded the Bolshevik revolution. Lloyd George felt that MacDonald might have a stronger influence, being more sympathetic towards the new Petrograd government; he could discuss the role that socialists from Russia could have in a meaningless international peace meeting going on in Stockholm, while at the same time warning of the awful consequences of separate negotiations.[38]

MacDonald arrived in Aberdeen on 10 June to board SS *Vulture* to Bergen, whence he would travel to Stockholm and then Petrograd. Using information leaked to him from the Admiralty, Tupper had got there first. Physically barring MacDonald's way on the quayside, the egregious Tupper pushed his face against MacDonald's and yelled the statement he had prepared on the long train journey (it included a pun): 'Stockholm, eh? Stop home – MacDonald! Unless you can take on a damned long swim!' After a good deal of undignified pushing and shoving, a burly member of the crew from MacDonald's home town, thoroughly briefed by Tupper, threatened to throw MacDonald into the harbour: 'We'll no' carry such traitors as ye on this ship.'[39]

Closely followed by Tupper, MacDonald returned to his hotel and spoke at once on the telephone to Shinwell in Glasgow to ask him for a crew from the British Seafarers' Union. Shinwell said he could do it in Glasgow. MacDonald hesitated and said he would ring him back. When he did so the next day, he had, infuriatingly for Shinwell, changed his mind.[40]

MacDonald decided to wait for reports back from Henderson and from some of the other socialists Tupper and his crew had allowed on board.

The whole incident was forgotten as the papers filled up with the explosion of the great land-mines of Messines and the gradual decline of the first Russian revolution into the second more uncompromising Bolshevik revolution. Shinwell was also soon too busy to worry about it; the entry of the Americans into the war increased the demand for seamen and Shinwell found himself once again scouring Scotland on behalf of an increasingly frantic Admiralty for likely 'Jacks'.[41]

The burst of recruiting activity was a godsend; for Tupper and Wilson had been working behind the scenes to end Shinwell's exemption from military service. They collected anti-war quotes from his speeches since he started backing MacDonald and they claimed he was using his exemption to cause revolution, to stop workers working and to help the Germans. At one point, they very nearly did get him called up. He was brought before a military tribunal where he was interviewed by the Sheriff about his views on the war, 'not proper for a person enjoying exemption'.

Shinwell admitted he deplored the war and claimed that if 'the people been consulted on 4th August 1914 there would have been no war'. The furious chairman told him he was unpatriotic and talking rubbish. 'You have stated views which simply amount to a denial of the National Conscience. That is something approaching anarchy. Do you still advance these views?' Shinwell replied that his work and his opinions were two separate things:

> As far as my work is concerned I am doing everything all my working days for the national interest. The Admiralty and the Ministry of Shipping could not complain about me. I sweat for them. I think I should be permitted to express my views apart from my profession.

They disagreed with him and told him he was abusing their trust. He was given a date to report for the army which meant he would have arrived in Flanders just in time for Passchendaele. He appealed to the Glasgow local tribunal against the decision. In a frenetic week between the military tribunal and the civilian appeal, Shinwell hurried to London with several members of the Trades Council, which had passed an emergency resolution supporting his continued exemption, to lobby the government. Only the intervention of several Labour MPs, and Arthur Henderson personally, saved him. Henderson enlisted the support of the Admiralty who wrote a decisive letter to the appeal admitting that Shinwell's record, as far as getting men on to ships was concerned, was very good, however misguided he might be in his opinions. His exemption was reinstated.[42]

Shinwell decided to lie low for a while and not make too many public speeches and statements, using the lull to also start a series of meetings with Clyde ship-owners aimed at improving conditions for crewmen at sea. The problems were most acute on the great liners, now used as troop ships, where the men were crammed into shared bunks three or four abreast, so they had to crawl over each other to get to them. There were no mess rooms so they had to eat their food where they slept and the food itself was sometimes contaminated and always very poor. Very few ships had baths, wash-basins or even make-shift latrines for the crew. Even the better-paid firemen had to perform all their ablutions in a bucket in the stokehold.[43]

Shinwell's aim was gradually to improve conditions on the liners by negotiation, while at the same time pressing through the Trades Council and the British Seafarers' Union proposals for amendments to the Merchant Shipping Acts to try to force improvements. Wages had nearly doubled since the outbreak of war (sailors and firemen got eight pounds ten shillings and leading stokers got £10 a month), but barely kept pace with the cost of living. By comparison, ship-owners' profits had increased by some 500 per cent since the outbreak of war. Shinwell had already decided that the only way of overcoming this 'obscene contrast' was nationalisation. But he was starting to feel he was hitting his head against a brick wall. There was really very little prospect of improving seamen's conditions by industrial or legal processes; so he started to take an interest in new forms of political organisation as well. With events in Russia gathering pace, he was tempted by the idea of the 'Soviet'.

Shinwell was elated when Lenin's Bolshevik revolution succeeded. He started to believe in the possibility of destroying the centres of state power in Britain and replacing them too with soviets. After three years of war and oppression, sheer frustration with the authorities – ship-owners, police, the Admiralty and the rest – Shinwell started to contemplate a world without any of them:

> I was looking for something new but I didn't know what. And this used to madden people. I would hold everyone up on the Town Council before they even got a chance to read out the minutes, complaining about the excess profits of ship-owners one day or the insufficiency of compensation rights on another. I could also do what I liked on the Trades Council. But was it enough or was it just tinkering? I was still a relatively young man and I felt sure we could learn something from Lenin and the revolutionaries.[44]

Was Shinwell a Bolshevik? For a short time the answer must be yes. If there had been a more effective revolutionary movement in Scotland in late 1917 and early 1918, Shinwell would probably have joined it. By the time there was such a movement, he was less sure. He certainly remained in favour of the removal of capitalists from economic power and the elevation of workers' committees to take over units of production, and workers' committees were basically soviets. 'Running industry is not so hard that only capitalists can do it. Fifty members of Glasgow Trades Council could make as good a fist at it as fifty capitalists.'[45]

In the end he was pragmatic. The conventional organisations he was now so good at manipulating looked as secure as ever and the soviet idea seemed very remote. Shinwell was not one to allow himself to be marginalised for an unattainable idea.

Then, suddenly, in the autumn of 1918, the war was over and the nation was plunged into the 'Coupon' election.

Shinwell's selection as Labour candidate for the parliamentary seat of 'Linlithgowshire' (West Lothian) had surprised him as much as anyone back in March 1915. He heard from Thomas Johnston of *Forward* that they were selecting a candidate and wrote off almost casually to the constituency secretary. He was shortlisted and with a swashbuckling speech to the selection committee beat the local miners' union leader.[46]

Even as an officially adopted candidate, the prospect of election to Parliament never seems to have been very high on Shinwell's agenda at that time. There was plenty else to think about and no prospect of an election until after the war. He did manage an occasional visit to the main towns of Bathgate and Linlithgow on his recruiting journeys,[47] but he did no serious campaigning at all until the election was called two weeks after the Armistice was signed.

It was a lack of interest typical of the Clydeside left at the time. Municipal politics seemed far more important. Johnston himself had gone so far as saying: 'Our Town and City Councils have as large, if not a far larger, part to play in the building of the Socialist Commonwealth than huge Imperial Governments.'[48] Shinwell's and Johnston's commitment to home rule for Ireland and greater self-government for Scotland were extensions of the same idea. It was a commitment to a scale of authority where they knew meaningful changes could be brought about in areas such as housing, sanitation, transport and leisure facilities which affected everyone's day-to-day life. Parliament seemed very remote.

As soon as he had called the 1918 election, Lloyd George endorsed a 'coupon' candidate in each constituency in a sloganising 'Hang the Kaiser' and 'A Land Fit for Heroes' atmosphere. In his candidates' speeches, including those of James Kidd, Shinwell's Coalition Conservative opponent in Linlithgowshire, it was hard to find an actual policy:

> What is to come in the future? The country stands on the borders of a new era and what is it to bring forth? It has come to me with great and overwhelming force that the same courage and the same faith which has carried the nation through the last four years so triumphantly would carry us through in the future if we keep to the same high ideals – the pursuit of truth, honour, righteousness, mercy and justice. But these high ideals by themselves will not win victory; we must use the means which lie in

our hands to have those ideals realised. The great instruments for bringing our ideals to victory will be the personality and genius of Mr Lloyd George, and the unanimity which exists between him and Mr Bonar Law.[49]

There was no answer to these generalities, but 'Making the Germans Pay' was a real issue. Kidd insisted that he would see to it that 'Germany paid and paid sweetly for her extraordinary crime. She might be excused by long-haired high-browed gentlemen of the type of Ramsay MacDonald and crazed socialists such as Emanuel Shinwell.'[50]

When Shinwell first argued back, he tended to sound quite convoluted: 'Can Germany pay? To whom will she pay? To the State, to the capitalists or to those who have directly suffered? That is the question for the International Commission to resolve in due course.'[51] At meeting after meeting, Shinwell was hounded by the indemnity argument. Towards the end of the campaign he was starting to sound more convincing:

> Mr Kidd says Germany must provide us with ships for every ship we have lost. What about the men who produce the ships? Hundreds of men have been dismissed from the shipbuilding yards, and hundreds are going on short time. There is not sufficient work to go round. And yet they say we must get ships from Germany! Who is at the back of a policy of that kind? Why, the people who are going to get the ships. If Mr Kidd were going to do with the ships what is happening now with the munitions factories and the workshops, to hand them over to the private interests, then I am having none of that.[52]

How to treat the Germans, Kidd's 'whining beaten bully' and Shinwell's 'wretched defeated race', was the most important but not the only issue of the campaign. Shinwell was also committed to prohibition: 'I am in favour of prohibition. I'll be sorry to interfere with the glass of beer of the working man, but I'm sure in your hearts you do not want your children to love a glass of beer.'[53]

Shinwell declared himself in hour-long speeches three times a night throughout the two weeks of the campaign to be in favour of the rights of farm-workers, miners and foundry-workers and against protectionism ('Look how the capitalists profited from it in the war'), and he was against the boycott of German seamen: 'Does your hate make your spirits any brighter?'[54] In a battered motor car he rattled through a hundred villages. On 14 December 1918, it was not enough to win:

James Kidd (Coalition)	12,898 (60%)
Emanuel Shinwell (Labour)	8,723 (40%)
Majority	4,175

Only fifty-nine Labour seats nationally, on defective registers with inadequate voting arrangements for servicemen, scarcely reflected the increase in Labour's popular strength. There would be four years to wait for that. Still, Shinwell had achieved the biggest Labour swing in Scotland.

The *West Lothian Courier* in an editorial headed 'A Splendid Result' declared: 'No Bolshevism in Linlithgow.' It went on to publish some verses by an anonymous local poet:

There's joy to-day in ha' and bield,
And loud huzzas ring far a'field,
Where Victory's sun illumes the shield
    Of Coalition in West Lothian!
And just as Kidd, like Whittington,
To London town goes marching on,
Emanuel quits the battle zone,
    And treks him back to Glasgow.[55]

His first general election campaign had given Shinwell new dreams and new ambitions. After the result was announced, he declared to his supporters that he would nurse Linlithgowshire. There was plenty of work to be done to persuade the voters. 'I'm not downhearted ... from this day we must start and maintain a vigorous and strenuous effort to bring to Linlithgowshire the day of victory for our Party.'[56]

For the time being, however, there were other matters needing his urgent attention back in Glasgow.

CHAPTER 6

Bloody Friday

Labour's heavy defeat in the 1918 general election was something of an illusion. Although three hundred and thirty-nine Coalition Conservatives and one hundred and thirty-six Coalition Liberals faced a mere fifty-nine Labour men and 30 Independents, the gigantic Coalition majority concealed an inability among the 'coupon' MPs to agree among themselves. Labour had increased its share of the vote from 8 per cent to almost 24 per cent, and party membership had doubled during the war.

Revolution was in the air and not just in Russia. In Germany, a republic had been proclaimed in November 1918 and a socialist government had taken office; the Bolshevik 'Spartacus' League had threatened revolution only to be put down by the Free Corps controlled by officers of the former Imperial Army. In Britain, Ramsay MacDonald feared that anti-parliamentary revolutionary tendencies would now threaten the Labour movement. In the Glasgow *Forward* he wrote:

> Our own people go mad. We have dreams of a better world – calm dreams they ought to be … But after war these dreams become frenzied. The furious violence of hate takes possession of them. The ruling classes have drenched Europe in blood. The slaves now rise to make more blood flow.[1]

Despite his fear of violence, not even Ramsay MacDonald was a consistent democrat in the bitterness of the aftermath of the 1918 defeat. At a meeting in Glasgow, Shinwell, Maxton and Wheatley sat astounded while he proposed a Soviet Bolshevik as possibly the best solution to Britain's problems.[2]

Within days of that aberrant speech, Shinwell was at the head of a revolutionary riot in Glasgow. The Cabinet was talking of Bolshevism on Clydeside, and Lloyd George's government was sending tanks into Glasgow's Cattlemarket. Shinwell led the nearest Britain came to a Bolshevik uprising without ever apparently being clear whether he was organising a revolution or a strike. His real view of what was going on probably lay between the two, not a settled mid-point but a constant wavering, a tension between a desire to make modest changes and the realisation that violent revolution might be the only way to achieve them.

Without any doubt, Shinwell had become one of the leading figures on the left in Clydeside during the last couple of years of the war. He claimed later, only slightly tongue-in-cheek, that this was because he was a good deal cleverer than any of the possible competition,[3] but the truth is more mundane. The expulsions in 1916 had removed some of his rivals, and his dogged hard work on the town council and on numerous boards and committees from the Blind Asylum to the Widows of War Pensioners, evening after evening, combined with a knack of organising the disparate groups from the left and right on the Trades Council, had brought him into prominence. Nevertheless, by the end of the war, he was thoroughly frustrated.

Like many others in similar positions in politics on the left, Shinwell was in a state of contradiction with himself. What he believed and what he did were based on two very different sets of ideas. If things were to change, if Labour were really to be effective, if there were to be anything like a socialist state, then it had been obvious that the way the city and the country were governed would have to change. The people in charge at the moment and the system they operated, he realised, would have to go. Yet, here he was, starting to enjoy the fruits of that very system he knew he should destroy; he was respectable, his activities were regularly reported in the newspapers and sometimes even looked upon with favour by the establishment, and he was a well-known voice – albeit usually of protest – in the City Chambers.

In short, Shinwell felt like countless democratic socialists down the years, confused, approaching middle age, beset by worries about his job, with no real prospect of significant progress beyond his present platform of modest achievements. His talents for oratory and organisation, he felt, were not being used to the full; there was so much more he could do if he could just find himself the right opportunity. What was it to be? His trade-union activity was limited by constant opposition from Havelock Wilson. Parliament and national government seemed unrealistically remote, so what were the possibilities for revolution?

On 7 January 1919, he heard from his friend Willie Gallacher that the revived Clyde Workers' Committee would be approaching the executive of the Trades Council the next day for help with the organisation of demonstrations and strikes in support of a thirty-hour week. The principle was to shorten the week for all workers – for no less pay, of course – to make way for the thousands of demobilised soldiers who were starting to look for jobs. The Clyde Workers' Committee's main supporter on the executive, as Shinwell knew, was the treasurer, a fiery twenty-nine year-old woman called Edith Hughes. She herself was a Marxist and shared many of her far left views with the Clyde Workers' Committee.

Shinwell glimpsed an opportunity for glory. The committee needed him because he was recognisable, a pillar of the Labour establishment. He needed the committee to find new political ground and to prove, if to no one but himself, his socialist credentials.

Gallacher, Hughes and Shinwell hatched a plot that evening and carried it out the next day when the executive met. The fourth item on the agenda was the committee's request. Hughes, whom everybody knew was on the left, was called first from the chair by Shinwell, and of course she advocated the fullest co-operation. The next speaker, McGovern of the Municipal Workers, predictably opposed Hughes. Eventually, Shinwell 'allowed himself to be persuaded to enter discussions'[4] with the Clyde Workers' Committee and to make his recommendation to the full meeting of the Trades Council – which was to the left of the executive – on 15 January.

When Shinwell met with Gallacher and Hughes later the same evening to start formal discussions with the committee, it must have been obvious that the aims of the committee were not 'purely industrial'[5] as Hughes later claimed, and it could not possibly be true that it never had occurred to Shinwell that he would be drawn into the agitation, as Shinwell claimed many years later.[6] On the contrary, he must have known all about the committee and its members, many of whom were openly in favour of violent revolution. The truth of the matter was that instead of getting out as soon as the talk turned to blowing up canal bridges and sabotaging power stations,[7] Shinwell stayed on, hoping to take the lead in a general strike which would paralyse Clydeside, achieve some of its objectives – whatever they might turn out to be – and turn him from a successful trade union official and a municipal agitator into a working-class hero.

To be fair, he himself rarely encouraged violence and also insisted on the lowering of the aims to a forty-hour week from a thirty-hour week. Hughes and Shinwell both felt they could sell this more modest objective to the whole Trades Council, and it also meant they would be able to bring on board the Scottish TUC which, partly at Shinwell's own instigation, had had a policy for a forty-hour week since the previous August.[8]

At its full meeting on 15 January, the Trades Council predictably gave a campaign for a forty-hour week its full backing, and Shinwell, Hughes and Pat Dollan, a fellow town councillor and one of the Shinwells' few personal friends in Glasgow politics, were all appointed to the new strike committee. The Scottish TUC still dithered but gave its backing 'in principle'. Shinwell was elected chairman of the strike committee that evening at its first meeting and Gallacher was put in charge of 'tactical organisation'. One hundred and sixty thousand pamphlets were circulated from the 'Committee representing the official and unofficial sections of the industrial movement', declaring a general strike on Monday 27 January.[9]

One of these pamphlets reached Sam Shinwell at his workshop in Candleriggs. 'The boy's taken leave of his senses,' he muttered.[10]

Secret agents sent Lloyd George messages about 'revolutionary gangs' making 'a determined effort to emulate the Russian Bolshevik movement by intending to set up Soviets on the Clyde'.[11] Shinwell and Gallacher, he realised, the pair who sabotaged his visit to Glasgow in 1915, were now preparing to sabotage the first month of his new Coalition government.

Lloyd George started to prepare for a fight. At least in Glasgow, the police force, made up mainly of highlanders, had a reputation for brutal effectiveness and loyalty to authority. They could be depended upon. Troops would be kept only as a last resort. Whatever happened, it was essential that no revolutionary movement got much beyond the talk stage. Short-lived army mutinies at Dover and Shorncliffe as well as mutiny also brewing in the Metropolitan Police made Lloyd George and his government jumpier than ever about losing control altogether if there was unrest in several different parts of the country at the same time.

Meanwhile, Shinwell, supposedly at the very heart of Glasgow's dangerous revolutionary brew, was getting more and more pessimistic about anything much happening at all. The big meeting called for 18 January to plan the general strike turned into a damp squib when just eight hundred people attended rather than the hoped-for two thousand. More seriously, nearly all those who attended were Clydeside engineering and shipbuilding workers rather than the variety of workers invited from all over Scotland. Shinwell noticed in particular that there were no seamen and hardly any dockers. Worse was to come when, the next day, the dockers concluded separate negotiations for a forty-four-hour week. The carters also withdrew, and the municipal employees refused to come out at all even though George Kerr, their local organiser, was on the strike committee.[12]

The more the conventional trade unionists quit, the more the strike committee came to be dominated by the left. Shinwell, perhaps willingly, became a prisoner of the left. It was an odd situation in which the Trades Council, a pillar of respectable trade unionism, was manoeuvred – or had manoeuvred itself – into calling a general strike from which most of the individual unions which made up its membership were rapidly withdrawing. Even the engineers who had started the ball rolling agreed nationally to a forty-seven-hour week, leaving David Kirkwood, back from his Edinburgh exile, and Harry Hopkins, the hot-headed local union secretary, out on a limb; Hopkins was actually sacked and evicted from his union house for publicly disagreeing with the forty-seven-hour week.

When Shinwell went home in those first days of planning the strike – sometimes for as little as five hours out of twenty-four – Fanny or Lucy, who would always wait up for him and cook for him, found him increasingly short-tempered and noticed that he was starting to look ill. He had trapped himself into an obligation to lead an unrepresentative far left group into a hopeless strike. Even the few followers he had left hardly trusted him, Dollan had warned him about that. And he was also starting to suffer from flu or an appalling cold in the head.

Around 22 and 23 January, just a few days before the strike was due to begin, rather different messages about the amount of support it enjoyed started to reach the strike committee, not from union officials but from shop stewards and works organisers. Employers had responded with crass insensitivity to the nationally agreed reduction of the engineering working day by cutting out the breakfast break. At the same time unemployment was rising and there was an atmosphere of political frustration; in the euphoria of the armistice, the electorate felt it had been conned into supporting coupon candidates who were really Conservatives. This 'atmosphere for action', encouraged by Pat Dollan's widely circulated *Strike Bulletin*, started to make it look as though there might just be enough unofficial and official support to make a real impression.[13]

As Shinwell wheezed and coughed his way through the last few days of preparation, the prospects really did seem to be improving. In a moment of self-delusion, after an encouraging visit to Greenock, he even declared: 'The greatest strike that has ever taken place in the industrial world has begun.'[14] In his official report from the strike committee to the Trades Council, he soberly played down expectations, stating that 'the strike will not be revolutionary in character' and was motivated merely by 'the desire of the workers generally to make room for demobilised servicemen'.[15]

What was really in Shinwell's mind? He certainly knew that the only way the forty-hour objective on Clydeside could succeed was if workers in other areas also stopped work. Messages of support from Tyneside and Manchester suggested that if Clydeside made an impressive show then action could well spread, although none of these other industrial centres was as badly hit by the post-war slump as Clydeside.[16] Only Belfast planned action at the same time. So if the strike did not spread, what were its real aims? In Shinwell's aching head at least, the aims were confused.

If he had really believed that a reduction of hours was the main objective, he would never have endorsed the use of such a blunt weapon as a general strike. From all that Shinwell had done in both tailoring and shipping, this was evidently not his style; his way of doing things was by exhaustive negotiation, the isolation of employers and detailed planning, and none of these characterised the preparations for the coming strike.

John Wheatley's opinion, typically jaundiced, was that by going for a stoppage on a scale never so far attempted, the action itself became Shinwell's objective. He wanted to put the Trades Council, the one place where he had real authority, on the map as the single organisation which could bring Clydeside to a standstill. Wheatley had of course reluctantly supported Shinwell's co-option on to the town council a couple of years before to make amends for his outburst of anti-Semitism, but he had kept him sidelined there so he served on no important committees and was mainly known as a protester in the council chamber. Fresh from irrelevance in the council and failure in the general election, and already embroiled in a new round of infighting with the Sailors' and Firemen's Union, Wheatley's argument was that Shinwell simply wanted to prove that he was a force to be reckoned with.[17] Organising a general strike was a way in which this 'excellent chairman with support from all quarters, hardworking and well credited'[18] could prove his political virility.

Wheatley's idea of his younger rival's motives accords with his original reasons for getting involved with the Clyde Workers' Committee, the proving of his political virility. The mood of discontent on Clydeside, he judged, was such that a total protest lasting a few days, extracting enough concessions to claim a victory, was just possible. And he would emerge as the strongman who organised it all.

What about the wider, even revolutionary, objectives? Shinwell must have known that there was a possibility of the strike developing from the industrial to the political, although this mainly depended on similar action occurring in other industrial centres. The only formal co-ordination was with Protestant workers in Belfast; otherwise there were no other deals.

Shinwell guessed that if the strike did happen to spread beyond Clydeside for whatever reasons, the government would have to react by sending in troops. So he allowed the strike committee, urged on by its revolutionary members from the Clyde Workers' Committee, to prepare a list of strategic points in Glasgow with notes on how they might be occupied by the workers or sabotaged. The exact nature of this material will never be known because all the incriminating material was burned when the strike was collapsing, but the fact is that Shinwell chaired a committee which, in preparing the general strike of 27 January, also discussed contingency plans for bloody revolution. If there were to be a revolution, it seems, he had decided that he was going to be one of its leaders.

Riding two horses at once, industrial action and Bolshevik revolution, Shinwell kept repeating at the strike committee's final meeting before the strike was due to begin the need to stay 'for the time being' within the law and 'then let us see what answers we get'.[19] On Monday 27 January some forty thousand workers joined the strike, on the Tuesday sixty thousand and on the Wednesday seventy thousand. Was the revolutionary bandwagon starting to roll?

On the Wednesday afternoon, Shinwell addressed a crowd of six thousand packed into George Square in the heart of Glasgow. Forbidden by the police to talk from the steps of the City Chambers, he made his way to the Gladstone Monument in the middle of the square. He announced in a rousing, swashbuckling speech that he would lead a delegation to see the Lord Provost in the City Chambers 'so the just demands of the workers of Clydeside could be put before the government'.

In the crowd they were waving the Red Flag, a band played and relations with the police were almost cordial. Indeed, Shinwell referred in his speech to the police as fellow workers, though Gallacher, who was in a froth of excitement, did clash with them. Despite a sense of forboding, this was not really a menacing event.

The nastiest incident of the morning was when a tram had driven through the marchers, slightly injuring some miners from Cambuslang. The police did nothing as some of the crowd, angered by the tram driver's strikebreaking as well as his bad driving, accused the police of encouraging him and not caring for the life and limb of the marchers. Apparently the sergeant in charge merely smiled. It was a bad omen for the bigger demonstration two days later.

The working tram-drivers were indeed a potent symbol of what the strike had not yet achieved. At least thirty thousand trade unionists were still at work on Clydeside, among them the tram drivers, fearful for their secure jobs and their pensions, and the workers at the electricity generating plant at Pinkston where the power for much of Glasgow's streetlighting and all of its trams was generated. There the workers were being given board and lodging on site to avoid intimidation and picketing.

After the speeches, Shinwell collected a delegation to see the Lord Provost, a Liberal, and a supporter of Lloyd George, Jamie Stewart, in the City Chambers. It was not, as it happened, the delegation agreed on the night before. Several Clyde Workers' Committee men were left out and representatives from other groups, such as the miners and railwaymen who were playing only lesser roles in the strike itself, pushed in. Even if he had wanted to, on the spur of the moment there was little Shinwell could do; so a dozen men, about half of them quite unknown to their supposed leader, entered the Chambers to be duly received by the Lord Provost.[20] The Lord Provost knew only Shinwell, although David Kirkwood and Neil MacLean MP for Govan (Labour's only Glasgow seat), were vaguely familiar.[21] Shinwell introduced Kirkwood out of politeness and realised his mistake when he got no further.

Kirkwood took over while Shinwell seethed and 'wished he had been exiled to St Helena or Tristan da Cunha and not just Edinburgh, since he might then have been swallowed by a whale on the way back'.[22] Kirkwood, now and again backed up by an excitable miner, would talk only about the trams, suggesting how the Lord Provost should call a special meeting of the Tramcars Committee to get them stopped. The dimmer members of the delegation looked impressed. The brighter ones, including Shinwell, just looked embarrassed as Kirkwood droned on and on.

After a quarter of an hour, Shinwell half-expected that the Lord Provost would say it was all very interesting but he really must get going before he, the 'spokesman', could get a word in edgeways. He tried to start off a couple of times when Kirkwood paused for breath, which was hardly ever at the end of a sentence, but Kirkwood just raised his voice and boomed over him.[23] At last Kirkwood really did run out of steam and Shinwell decided not to risk introducing anyone else. The strike's main aim was a forty-hour week, he explained. The Lord Provost should send a telegram to Lloyd George – or his stand-in while he was at the Peace Conference in Paris, the Conservative leader Andrew Bonar Law – to pass on the strikers' demands that the government should persuade employers to introduce a forty-hour week which would make way for the employment of demobilised soldiers.

After a fair amount of discussion and drafting by committee, in which Kirkwood played a major part, a telegram over the signature of the Lord Provost, was agreed. This opened with an explanation of the demand for a forty-hour week and went on to report a new threat that Shinwell introduced:

> It was further stated that the strikers had hitherto adopted constitutional methods in urging their demands, but that failing consideration being given to their request by the Government, they would adopt any other methods which they might consider to be likely to advance their cause. They have however agreed to delay taking any such action until Friday.

To this, the Lord Provost added a sentence of his own after the delegation had left: 'I have just learned from the manager of the electricity department that all men in generating stations have been compelled today to join the strike.'[24] In fact, the vital Pinkston power station remained open.

Outside in the square again at last, Shinwell reported to the crowd what had happened in the last hour and a half, clambering back on to the plinth of the Gladstone Monument. With a painfully sore throat from what seemed more and more like flu, he somehow managed to shout:

> We have advocated constitutional action all along the line. The newspapers have now charged us with a crime of intimidation. Whether they charge us with that crime or any other, we are going to see to it that every class of worker in the city is out. [Applause] When we leave this hall we are

going to take a walk – an orderly walk [Laughter] – with bands heading the procession – to the power station [Applause] – at Pinkston – for the purpose of holding a meeting ... If as a result of our meeting today there is no change in the situation other events will rapidly follow.[25]

Following the plan agreed the night before, the procession, swollen to over eight thousand, marched to Pinkston power station. What the men inside, locked in for three days and nights, were thinking can only be imagined. The band outside struck up the blood-curdling 'Scots W'hae Wh' Wallace Bled' as Shinwell organised Britain's first ever mass picket.

Kirkwood asked the pickets not to rush the gates, just yet, but their time for revenge would come. The police reaction to Kirkwood's threats was to baton the front row of the pickets, forcing them several yards back. One man's nose was broken. From nowhere broken glass crashed into a policeman's ear, nearly severing it from his head. This time Shinwell appealed for order and calm.

When the exhausted members of the strike committee met on Thursday 30th, they faced a decision. The Lord Provost's clerk had delivered Bonar Law's brief reply, summarised by his first few words: 'The Government cannot entertain the request for intervention in the strike ...'[26]

It was the moment of reckoning and Shinwell and his committee proved themselves not up to it. For one thing it was far too late for action elsewhere to be co-ordinated with the planned demonstration in George Square the next day. Invitations had already gone out to trades councils and shop stewards in other cities to organise some sympathy action, but as yet there were no signs of success. They agreed to send delegates to Tyneside, Edinburgh, Aberdeen, Leeds and Manchester, but they also realised that it was something they should have been doing weeks before, and Shinwell must have cursed this uncharacteristic lack of thoroughness on his part. Incredibly, the strike committee's meeting broke up without taking any further decisions.

Twenty thousand *Strike Bulletins* summoned strikers and unemployed to George Square at noon the next day. Shinwell, Gallacher, Hopkins, Kirkwood and Edith Hughes were left to plan the next day's events independently of the strike committee. When the square was full, they decided to try to see the Lord Provost again and receive formally the government's rejection. They would then return to the crowd which would by now be angry with the government's sharp rebuff. The scene would be set for action and set too for Shinwell to use the full powers of his oratory. He would let rip. He would rouse the assembled masses ...

The third item in the otherwise dull Cabinet meeting, which took place about the same time as the meeting of Shinwell's strike committee on 30 January, was the telegram from the Lord Provost. It livened the meeting considerably. Bonar Law who was in the chair reported on his telephone call on the subject with Lloyd George. The Prime Minister had apparently considered coming to London specially to take charge of the Clydeside situation. It was the only time Lloyd George seriously contemplated such a sudden return and Bonar Law had had to persuade him that it would give Shinwell and the rest an exaggerated opinion of their own importance and also undermine his own authority.

The Secretary of State for Scotland, Robert Munro, came up with a request for special protection for public utilities apparently openly threatened by the strike committee, and it was agreed to send in the army.[27] The Cabinet also decided to send John Lamb, a senior civil servant at the Scottish Office to 'acquaint the Lord Provost and the Sheriff of the Government's policy and keep the Government informed of any development in this direction'. Finally, the Lord Advocate was asked to find grounds for arresting the ringleaders.

What else were the Cabinet told? Or, at least, what else did Bonar Law and Lloyd George know? The series of coincidences that followed suggest that an informer, possibly Edith Hughes, had been at the meetings of the strike committee or even in Shinwell's inner circle and was supplying information to the authorities. The government knew that there were moves to raise the stakes when the inevitable negative reply was received from the Lord Provost. The police knew exactly what to expect and when to act, while Shinwell was in the City Chambers and before he would have a chance to speak to the crowd after emerging empty-handed.

Another twenty thousand joined the strike on Friday 31 January, bringing the total to a hundred thousand,[28] and between twenty and twenty five thousand took part in a giant demonstration which overflowed George Square. Shinwell, Kirkwood, Gallacher, Hopkins and all the others must have felt their pulses quicken. The day would begin with the entry into the City Chambers, the formal rejection of the strikers' demands and then, surely, insurrection by the strikers, the unemployed, the demobbed soldiers and – who knows – maybe the police as well. Shinwell had warned of the consequences of the strikers' demands being ignored. Who could tell where it would all end?

Shinwell and his deputation entered the City Chambers just before noon. It was the sign for action. Not by the demonstrators; their action had been planned for later when the leaders were out of the Chambers. It was the sign for the police to move.

At almost the exact moment when the doors of the City Chambers closed behind Shinwell and his delegation, the first serious trouble started. A tram provocatively advanced on the south-east corner of the square. The demonstrators in the area closed in on it. The driver jumped out and disappeared – no one ever found out who he was. The police were ordered to use any means to clear the way for the driverless tram which had also by now been cut from its overhead wires. With great relish, they used batons and boots with crushing force.

Barely two minutes later, the police in front of the City Chambers were ordered 'to push the crowd back a few yards'. It was an order which was carried out with the utmost violence; with this baton charge 'Bloody Friday' really began. As the police hacked their way into the crowd, Gallacher, who had been left behind again by the deputation to 'keep an eye on things', shouted hopelessly that police and workers were on the same side. Within thirty seconds, when he saw what was happening, his tone changed completely and he was encouraging the strikers to 'Rush them up behind!' He was too late; the police had rushed first and the men at the front were falling and bleeding under flailing batons. Further back in the crowd they were frantically looking for missiles. At first, they threw clods of earth, but soon they found pieces of railing and a ripped-up 'Keep off the grass' sign which destroyed the sight in one young policeman's eye.

In nearby North Frederick Street, lemonade bottles were taken from a hijacked lorry and hurled at the advancing police. When they crashed to the ground not only did splinters of glass fly everywhere but anyone standing nearby was immediately covered with sticky lemonade. The battle of the flying bottles was finally enough for the Sheriff to come out of the back of the City Chambers to read the Riot Act, the legal signal for a police charge, avoiding Shinwell who was still waiting to be received and had not yet quite grasped what was going on.

The Sheriff got only halfway through when the text was torn from his hand and he fled. It was enough for the police to redouble their fury. Within seconds there were more baton charges and an eruption of chaos as the mounted police tried to enter the square. Two horses were pulled over crushing their riders and whoever else failed to get out of the way. The square and all the streets around exploded with fighting, the hurling of missiles, shouting and screams of agony, excitement and terror.[29]

Inside the City Chambers, Shinwell sat quietly listening to the battle outside, realising the certainty of defeat. The government had acted first. He slipped quietly away from the delegation without seeing the Lord Provost, left the City Chambers by the same back entrance as the Sheriff and headed for the strike committee's office, finding to his immense relief that the police had not got there before him. He set about burning any materials or plans for the acts of sabotage the committee had discussed. Into the fire went maps and notes, names and designs. When it was done, Hopkins of the Engineers, who had turned up with the same idea, thought it best Shinwell should be disguised when he left, to avoid the prying eyes of the people who habitually watched their office on behalf of the police. He slunk home wearing a false beard made from a broom, with no idea of what to expect next.[30]

Davie Kirkwood reacted somewhat differently to the disaster. He broke a pane of glass, cutting his hand, and tried to shout from the City Chambers to both the crowd and the police to stop misbehaving. This time his booming voice let him down and all that came out was a strangled croak. He had caught Shinwell's cold. He ran downstairs into the street waving his arms around. A moment later, he provided the anti-police lobby with ammunition for a decade; he stumbled into a constable who hit him squarely on the back of the head, felling him with one blow, at the exact moment a press photographer was pushing the button on his camera. His arms and legs twitched. The police kicked him hard a couple of times, which made another good photograph, and Kirkwood was out cold for an hour. The riot intensified as resentful crowds, forced away from George Square, heard the rumour that Kirkwood had been killed. Someone even rushed to tell his wife and it was nearly two hours before she knew she was not a widow.

Gallacher, watching all his plans crumble around him, rushed up to the Chief Constable who ignored him. He pulled at his arm as he remonstrated, and a sergeant felled him instantly, knocking him out. For one ferocious hour, the Battle of George Square raged between the police and a leaderless crowd. Incredibly there were no immediate fatalities, but sixty rioters and police were seriously injured with batons, sharpened metal or broken glass. The cracked heads, the broken bones and puddles of blood on the pavement marked the end of Britain's only serious attempt at Bolshevik revolution.

Gangs of rioters, forcibly dispersed, charged around the city centre for several hours, breaking windows and looting. There were several more pitched battles, and the police came off worst in some of them. Harry McShane, a Marxist and one of the strikers, described the Battle of Cathedral Street:

> First the workers rushed and the police retreated, then the police rushed and the workers retreated. This happened two or three times, until the police didn't know what to do. Then one old policeman rushed forward with his baton drawn to lead the others — but they didn't follow, and he landed in the strikers. Finally the police ran for it, and we ran after them. They rushed up the Cathedral Street closes and tried to go over the back walls, but the strikers got them by the legs and pulled them back; some of them got a terrible hiding. I'm sure that the best fight of the riot took place in Cathedral street.

And there was the Battle of the Saltmarket:

Strikers went about cutting the trolley ropes and hundreds of immo-bilised trams blocked every route. Two policemen tried to intervene at the Saltmarket; the strikers stripped their uniforms off them and they had to run off naked. The demonstrators were on their way back to their own areas, cutting more trolley ropes on the way. In some places jewellers' shops were looted.[31]

By the late afternoon, gangs had arrived in the well-to-do suburbs for an orgy of aimless destruction, terrifying the residents and doing thousands of pounds' worth of damage to houses and gardens. It was here that the only two deaths occurred: a maid who was burned to death in an upstairs room and a policeman who was shot in the stomach by an angry house-holder who mistook him for a demonstrator.[32]

At the same time, twelve thousand troops, six tanks and an uneasy calm descended on the city centre. More than anything else it was the sinister sight of the tanks, designed for the battlefields of Flanders, which told anyone who needed telling that the revolution had failed. With it also went any hope of a forty-hour week and even the chance of satisfaction of that most feeble and reasonable demand, an extra break for breakfast.

Shinwell was taken into custody at midnight. Up to the time of his arrest he was frenziedly preparing a pamphlet to get Gallacher and Kirkwood released – they had not even got home. Now whoever took over from him would have to add Shinwell's name too. Glasgow, though, was no place for any kind of activist now the army had arrived: 'They were recruits with no experience, and they were very aggressive ... those young ones would have shot us down.'[33]

The strike finally petered out on 10 February, and it was left to history to decide what it had been and what had gone wrong. In November 1918 the *Glasgow Herald* had wondered out loud whether the 'plague of Bolshevism' would spread to Glasgow.[34] Red flames had indeed flickered briefly, but they were snuffed out quickly and brutally. One of the reasons why it was done so easily was that the man who lit the flame never had a clear revolutionary objective, just a vague desire for glory and a possible contingency plan for success.

What would have been in the speech Shinwell never made? In later years he claimed that he was interested only in the forty-hour week, but by then he was elderly and respectable. What did Bell, Hopkins and Shinwell burn when they reached the strike committee's office? There remain only snippets in Bell's and Gallacher's memoirs, and a notebook that was used in the trial, to suggest that at least acts of sabotage to disrupt transport and electricity were planned. But if it had come to real revolutionary violence, it is hard to imagine that Shinwell would have lasted very long as its leader. Lloyd George never thought Shinwell or any of the others had a real chance of defeating the government, but he was writing with the wisdom of hindsight after the defeat of the strike:

> I know Shinwell, who is a Jew, and the other men in Glasgow who are at the head of the movement there, and I know that in normal times they carry no weight. They have a little fictitious importance now because of the confusion consequent upon demobilisation and the number of unemployed.[35]

When the Cabinet met again on the afternoon of the riot, Munro reported that 'foot and mounted police had charged the crowd in order to quell a riot' and said that it was 'more than ever a misnomer to call the situation in Glasgow a strike – it had been a Bolshevist uprising'.[36] The Cabinet decided that no further action on its part was needed.

The ambiguous nature of Bloody Friday and the violence with which the George Square demonstration was put down lent a heroism to the day, remembered by activists for half a century. The fact that no one was killed in the main demonstration turned the arrested and gaoled ringleader into the next best martyr. For the rest of his life, no matter how much his actions belied it, Shinwell's reputation was above all that of the Red Clydesider who led the strikers on Bloody Friday.

The morning after, Shinwell did not yet know he was a hero. Taken from his home and family at midnight, Shinwell was locked in a freezing police cell. There was not even a bench, just the icy tiled floor. It was now 1 February 1919. What dreams he had had for this day!

A sleepless few hours later, he saw Willie Gallacher. He, it turned out, had not even reached home before he was arrested. But he was relishing the martyrdom, the blood-red flag, the dungeons grim.

'We'll not be forgotten,' said Gallacher. 'Did you ever read Olive Schreiner's story of the ants?'

'No. What about the ants?'

'It's really inspiring. When an army of ants, millions of them, goes on the march and come to a shallow stream, the foremost ones go fearlessly into the water, fill it up and make a bridge, across which the workers march to victory.'

'I'm no bloody ant.'

Shoved into a bare and also freezing interview room, Shinwell was kept waiting the best part of an hour for the detective in charge of his case. He came in slowly, looked his prisoner over, grinned and said that he was going for his breakfast. Shinwell was given nothing to eat or drink. This time he was forced to wait twice as long. At least there was a chair in the interview room, but by eleven o'clock in the morning he felt like hurling it at the walls. It was probably just the way the detective wanted him to feel.

'You're in for trouble, my lad.'

'What trouble?'

'Rioting.'

'What are you talking about? We weren't rioting.   Nonsense.'

'You'll get five years for this.'

The detective then told Shinwell how his first fortnight of five years' hard labour would begin: there would be no bed, just a plank – yes – they'd make him sleep on bare boards, if he could sleep at all... And there'd be the silence rule very strictly enforced... And no possibility of escape - ever.[37]

Part 3

CHAPTER 7

Political Prisoner

One fearful image haunted Shinwell in custody in Glasgow's Duke Street prison. He could see himself walking out of a distant prison gate, years later, jobless, friendless and forgotten. Many a political career had been badly damaged by one miscalculation and his had been serious enough to destroy him. There was suddenly no future except a trial, a sentence and prison. True, others on the Glasgow left had been gaoled in the war, but Maxton and MacLean had opposed conscription; like the conscientious objectors, they had had a specific moral cause. His 'crime' was vaguer yet more serious. His punishment would probably be to miss the years of rebuilding which would shape the political world – and political careers – for decades.

Fanny visited Duke Street prison every day of those four long weeks in custody, bringing food and warm clothes. As the February temperature dropped below freezing, twenty-three hours a day of confinement in a barely heated cell started to wear Shinwell down. Even Gallacher, hardly a sensitive observer, noticed that all Shinwell's resilience seemed to have ebbed away into depression.[1] When Wheatley heard it, he laughed that Shinwell was tough enough to take almost anything; what really mattered was getting 'poor innocent Davie' Kirkwood out.[2]

Manny's face started to swell horribly with toothache but that was bad enough! A few days later there was no choice. The prison dentist, who always operated without chloroform ('Anaesthetics are only for cissies,' the prison governor insisted, 'and for free men.'), had failed in private practice back in Victorian days and had long since sought refuge in the prison service where his victims could not complain. His advanced years made his hands distinctly shaky. When his blood formed a puddle on the floor of the icy cell and the torture of the extraction was at its height, Shinwell grasped the real meaning of imprisonment: being at the mercy of men who despise you and want you to suffer.[3]

93

While he was out of the way in his prison cell, long before his trial, Wheatley and some of the other Labour councillors were already talking about a replacement for him on the town council. The Trades Council was more loyal but even they, Shinwell reflected gloomily, could hardly be expected to wait for more than a few months. Worst of all, he heard that Havelock Wilson had chosen this moment to send Tupper with a 'delegation' to Glasgow to poach members from the British Seafarers' Union.

Soon the union started to lose members in substantial numbers, but not to Tupper. It was simply the general crumbling of support that many trade-union leaders, including Shinwell, had feared would happen after the war. Shipping was a typical case in point; the ship-owners had made vast fortunes and could cope quite easily with the reduction in demand brought about by a temporary post-war depression. The unions, on the other hand, unable to solve the problem of cheap Chinese labour, and threatened by mass unemployment, were suddenly weaker than they had been since the beginning of the century.

When he finally got bail, Shinwell went straight back to the union office at Broomielaw to inspect the membership books and hear the latest reports. The union's position was indeed gloomy. Members were simply not renewing their subscriptions and, contrary to what they had promised, the ship-owners were recruiting still more Chinese labour. Even the men of the Clyde ferries, one of the Seafarers' closed shops since 1911, were interested only in keeping their jobs at any cost and were not at all interested in the Union.

With support slipping away, Shinwell was gripped by an urge to 'do something'. He persuaded his local committee to join with the dockers who were planning a strike over hours and conditions; it was an extraordinary miscalculation, presumably arising from his isolation in custody and his preoccupation in the weeks leading up to Bloody Friday with the organisation of the forty-hour strike. Whatever the reason for his mistake, the seamen were not in any mood for militancy, least of all in support of other workers. There could not have been a worse time to try to organise secondary action. Only a handful of his members struck. A number of others tore up their union cards.

The inevitable result was a lowering of the status of the union in the eyes of the employers. When Shinwell turned up at the Anchor Line offices to discuss the grievances of two of his members who had been sacked as stokers on a transatlantic voyage, he found he could no longer stride into the chairman's office. In fact, he was at first barred entry altogether, nearly coming to blows with a young security guard who told him that 'the likes o' you are no' welcome here'. Only when he threatened pickets and publicity did he eventually get to see – after an insultingly long wait in a corridor – a junior official who 'took notes in a disinterested fashion.'[4]

Even the press were losing interest. A Bolshevik revolution in the making was one thing; a failed Bolshevik and a failing trade-union leader awaiting trial was another. In February 1919 the Russian Bolsheviks shot the Czar and his family in cold blood and Béla Kun in Hungary established communist revolutionary control within a stone's throw of Vienna. The attempted insurrection in Glasgow seemed small fry indeed. The mountain had rumbled and brought forth a mouse.

It was much the same with Glasgow Town Council and the ILP. Bloody Friday was history. Now was the time to plan progress in the city and in parliamentary seats. The Trades Council organised a defence fund for Shinwell and some of the others awaiting trial and raised over a thousand pounds,[5] but it was really only his immediate supporters, such as Pat Dollan and Willie Shaw, Carson's replacement as secretary, who were close to Shinwell at this miserable time for him. His fellow conspirators found themselves in the same boat. The Clyde Workers' Committee had disintegrated around Gallacher, Kirkwood and Hopkins.[6] Right across the country there was a marked shift away from militancy towards constitutional means. The martyrs of Bloody Friday and of lesser insurrections in Belfast and Manchester would perhaps be heroes in years to come, but for now they were embarrassing reminders of post-war euphoria, a foolish revolutionary moment.

Shinwell's depression deepened considerably when he walked with Fanny on the Sunday after his release to the scene of much of the trouble, George Square. Outside the City Chambers was a machine gun post, manned by recruits newly arrived from Devon. To them Glasgow was as foreign as Flanders, and at first they had thought it would be just as dangerous, having been warned by their officers to expect armed resistance from a sullen and warlike people who despised them. Instead, they found a city bewildered by the overreaction of the government in London and hardly able to believe that there were still soldiers guarding its public buildings nearly a month after Bloody Friday. But the soldiers were deadly serious. When Manny and Fanny tried to approach the machine-gunners, they were told 'fraternisation' was not allowed. It was like an enemy front line. The officers, terrified of mutiny, had forbidden any contact with civilians, let alone Manny Shinwell.

With three days to go before his trial, as his world crumbled around him, Manny took what was probably the best option open to him: he decided on a weekend's holiday alone with Fanny. The children went to his parents and the couple took the train to Girvan.[7] There, in a boarding house, they conceived their fourth child.

The trial opened at the High Court in Edinburgh on 7 April. Shinwell was one of a dozen accused of incitement or rioting on Bloody Friday. The prospect of a full five years in prison, the enforced separation from Fanny and his worries about the future of the British Seafarers' Union, all combined to shift his mood from one of depression to despair.

In court, he sat, eyes glazed, through long hours of evidence in the ten-day trial, rarely changing his expression and rarely even glancing around him. He had fought and lost. He was now unwilling putty in the hands of his establishment enemies – Lloyd George, the judge, the baton-wielding police. In fact, the whole system had closed in on him. He was respectful to the court; he had no wish at that moment to antagonise anyone further. Unlike Gallacher who defended himself with great vigour, Shinwell sat back and let his KC, shared with Harry Hopkins and paid for by the Trades Council, do the thinking for him. 'He just sat there like a sack of potatoes,' said Gallacher later, rather uncharitably. 'It was as if he now wished to dissociate himself from our great enterprise.' Shinwell fervently wished he could.[8]

The trial soon got down to details of who exactly had said what to whom and when. Shinwell's speeches were taken apart, 'a salutory exercise since long passages turned out to be gibberish when they were written out.' Did they or did they not amount to incitement to riot or revolution? By the fourth day of the trial, Shinwell was thinking that the whole case against him might be lost in the detail. Then Detective Constable Coulter, one of the policemen who arrested him, read out resounding and damning extracts from Shinwell's own notebook:

> The creation of a Labour Party is not an end in itself; it is the means to an end, the creation of a Socialist Republic. The opportunity of a Labour majority in Parliament may not come for two years, perhaps five years. Are we to remain quiet during that period to be the victims of the capitalists? There is only one way to compel the government to grant our demands – the fear of industrial strife or revolution.
>
> The House of Commons is an illegal assembly. It does not represent the electorate. Workers' and Soldiers' Councils, Soviets, are needed as a first stage in the establishment of a true democracy. The workers will not be granted power. They will have to use every means to seize it. We must use every ounce of energy to smash the government.[9]

To avoid upsetting him while he was freezing and having his tooth pulled in Duke Street prison, Fanny had decided not to mention the police search of their home. She thought they had found nothing, but they had found the notebook.

The judge, Lord Scott Dickson, pointed out that while this gave the jury 'a good account of Shinwell's deficiencies of character' it was not in itself evidence of incitement to riot. Nevertheless, a good deal of damage had been done. In Shinwell's prospective parliamentary constituency, the local paper screamed:

> 'Shinwellism' does not spell 'Labour' in the sound and sane meaning which the vast majority of working-men attach to the term. On the contrary, it is very clear now that it spells 'Revolution' and 'Bolshevism' – two ugly monsters which the people of this constituency rightly abhor. This kind of thing reared its head in Glasgow for a few exciting days. The movement, led by Shinwell, was intended to take the community by the throat and establish a Labour tyranny after the model of ignorant, misgoverned, unhappy Russia – a model, by the way, which even Germany has most sedulously shunned in spite of the fact that Socialism is so strong in that country. It was unthinkable that the Second City of the British Empire would allow itself to suffer under such a tyranny for however short a time; but the attempt to foist Bolshevism in Glasgow was deliberately made, and we now know the man, Shinwell, who was the inspirer of this ugly movement.[10]

Other papers joined gleefully in the attack on the seditious Bolsheviks in the dock. For a couple of days of the trial, the atmosphere became much the worse for all the defendants. Then revelations of police brutality restored a good deal of public sympathy for them. After a week or so, though, public and press interest declined sharply.

Witnesses for the defence described everything that had been carefully omitted by the police witnesses. In the case of David Kirkwood, Pat Dollan arranged for the production of the 'coup de grâce' (in both senses), with the photographs of a policeman clubbing Kirkwood who then lay crumpled on the ground where he was kicked. Discomfited police witnesses started to seem less reliable and convincing. A Sergeant Beaton swore that Shinwell threatened tram-drivers with violence, but an Inspector Gillies had no such recollection. Inspector Gillies, on the other hand, saw a civilian fall after being hit on the neck by a broken bottle, but a Sergeant Wark who was standing in exactly the same place at the same time said it was a policeman who was hit and, as far as he was concerned, Shinwell had threatened the 'greasy and oily magnates' in the North British Hotel with violence but had never mentioned the tram-drivers.[11]

At the end of ten days, the detailed indictments were looking like flights of imagination. The idea of inciting rioters to take forcible possession of the City Chambers or the North British Hotel plainly could not be proven. On the other hand, the judge said in his summing up: 'A riotous mob of more than twenty thousand evil-disposed persons did without doubt conduct itself in a violent and tumultuous manner.' The leaders were now in the dock. One of them, Shinwell, had shown his true character in his notebook and in violent speeches. The question for the jury was whether these had amounted to incitement to riot. It was a serious charge: 'Nothing more grave at such times as they were now living in could be brought against Shinwell and Gallacher than they deliberately incited their fellow workers, their fellow trade unionists, to take part in serious rioting.'

To underline the gravity of the case, the judge reminded the jury of the injuries of a fifteen-year-old boy whose head had been cracked open and of three young policemen left unconscious in the street, and he referred to the 'frightening collection of missiles' paraded before them in court, 'spectres of Bolshevism'. How much blame could be laid on Shinwell and the others for these 'wild and disgraceful excesses'?[12]

The jury found all the defendants 'Not Guilty' of incitement, except for Gallacher and Shinwell. In Gallacher's case only, the jury recommended leniency, because he had appealed to the crowd to leave the square at the request of the police after he had been arrested. Standing in the dock, Shinwell heard Gallacher sentenced to three months and himself to five years. He was close to collapse when he was told of his mistake. It was to be five months. Gallacher was so thrilled at the lightness of his own sentence that he declared he could do it 'standing on his head'.[13]

They were led away as prisoners. The sentences were relatively short and they had already served a month in custody, so now they had only two months and four months to run respectively. But for four months Shinwell was to be at the mercy of the establishment he detested. It would not be pleasant.

Lloyd George in Paris was told of the verdicts but made no recorded comment on them. The Secretary of State for Scotland thought the sentences very lenient and referred to the paltry nature of the demonstration outside the court held to protest in favour of these 'forgotten men'.[14] Only *Forward* publicly complained that the verdict and sentences were unfair. The Trades Council paid to launch a formal and unsuccessful appeal but soon got on with pressing business with a temporary chairman.[15]

The warders laughed, as they always made a point of doing at this humiliating moment for new prisoners, when the once-powerful leader of Glasgow's 'revolution' was forced to strip and take a cold bath on arrival at Edinburgh's Calton gaol. He was scarcely dry before he had to put on an ill-fitting uniform decorated with arrows and stripes, made of rough 'remnant' material – and well used by other prisoners before him – and some old boots a few sizes too large. He exchanged his name for a number and his hair was cropped before he was marched through the dark corridors to a small cold cell with a slit for a window. They slammed the door and he was left for seven hours wondering what his new masters had lined up for him.[16]

Shinwell was deemed to be a dangerous prisoner, capable of persuading his fellow prisoners to rise against the warders and take over the gaol. He was to be kept under the strictest supervision and allowed only the bare minimum of association with other prisoners. The silence rule, then in force in most British prisons, was to be especially strictly observed and he was to receive no privileges.

Two warders came in the evening and explained that the cell he was in was too good for him, too comfortable, it was only a temporary cell. As a new prisoner, he was not allowed even the scant comfort of a standard straw mattress for the first two weeks of the sentence, just bare boards. 'The prisoner will sleep on a plank,' the regulations said. So Shinwell was marched to an even colder and darker part of the gaol, a converted castle, and made to remove a few comforts from a tiny cell; out went half a mattress and a chamber pot; in exchange he was made to take in a large plank of rough wood and a foul-smelling bucket. This, along with an uncomfortable wooden upright chair, was to be the extent of his home comforts for a fortnight. For a full month, he was curtly told, there would be no visits from outside and no access to the small prison library.[17]

Then it was time for Shinwell's first prison meal. Since his last meal had been breakfast in his Edinburgh lodgings, he was ravenous, but he could not force himself to swallow the adulterated swill described as 'porridge'. He was left with it all night, and the next morning the same meal was served again:

> The large stone jar was nearly full of a greyish-looking thickened liquid which was identical to the previous evening ... Along with it came a small canister of milk. As soon as the door closed, I tried the milk. It was sour, I could not drink it. Though I tried the porridge again, my stomach would have nothing to do with it.[18]

He was given the job of sewing horses' nosebags in his cell, but he was soon faint with hunger. He complained to the prison doctor about the food only to be told brusquely that it was in fact both appetising and nutritious. Shinwell's 'Then eat it yourself,' terminated the consultation. On his way back to the cell, the head warder smiled and told him how unpleasant it would be if he were to be force-fed – it had nearly killed John MacLean:

> Nevertheless, I suspect that it was the Head Warder's action that produced a huge jar of tea and a lump of bread the following evening. There were quite two pints of warm and sweet liquid and I drank it all. During the period of four months and ten days I was in prison my diet consisted solely of that tea and two pieces of bread morning and evening. On some Fridays potatoes were served at the mid-day meal in place of the soup ... all frost-bitten and uneatable. Other prisoners somehow managed to

swallow that awful concoction of soup, but even they could not eat the blackened pulp of the potatoes boiled in their skins to prevent them disintegrating.[19]

Fanny visited after five weeks. She was coping, but only just. In the early stages of pregnancy she was not well and for the first time in their marriage she had taken a job, part-time for a hatter in Govan. The British Seafarers' Union were giving her a pound a week, compared with Shinwell's two pounds a week when he was working, yet inflation had doubled the cost of living since the end of the war.

There was of course nothing her husband could do; but there was one very useful thing she could do for him. She passed on complaints to one of the Scottish Prisons Commissioners whom he had known slightly through the town council. The prison governor treated Shinwell in those first five weeks as a political prisoner, refusing to allow him to associate with other inmates for fear that he would 'stir up trouble'. Fanny's intervention with the commissioner was surprisingly quick and successful. An angry governor was forced to concede 'association' but vowed to make Shinwell pay for it by tough and unpleasant labour.[20]

At last out of his cell, Shinwell's first job was shovelling coal in the prison cellars. Ironically, the first person he met there had an even better claim than Shinwell to be a political prisoner. He was a conscientious objector, an ex-miner, serving his statutory two-year sentence with hard labour. In this case, 'association' was the wrong word to use because the silence rule still applied and was most rigorously enforced. A bread and water diet or loss of remission were the usual punishments for breaking it. Occasionally Shinwell and the conscientious objector risked talking in whispers, but most communication was between cells using tapping, one tap for A, two for B and so on; locked in cells for fourteen hours at a stretch, twenty-one hours on Sundays, prisoners held surprisingly long conversations by tapping.

Exhausted each night, Shinwell soon protested against the hard labour in the cellars. He had, after all, not been sentenced to hard labour. So he was transferred to the prison ashpit where his job was in daylight. It was just when he started this new work that Fanny visited again with Lucy and Sammy. Fanny told him that the union was now under more serious attack from the Sailors' and Firemen's Union which were threatening his colleagues and recruiting vigorously.

Shinwell found himself simply unable to cope all at once with his visitors, the complicated news from outside, his first days in daylight and his new job in the prison. As he had in court, he glazed over. He had reached a stage that everyone within an institution almost inevitably reaches, be it a prison, an army camp or even a hospital; he had become institutionalised and found it difficult to think beyond the four walls which enclosed him.

His concern was with his own survival; he tried to show concern for the union, for Fanny and the family, and for the Trades Council which had re-elected him president in his absence, but he found it a great effort. Secretly, like many prisoners, he was quite glad when his visitors had gone.

Shinwell's overriding concern now was with the prison ashpit, where his job was to shovel out reusable pieces of coke. The dirt and monotony of this new work were a new low-point of his time in prison. His mate there was a stocky character with a 'frightening face which dripped brutality'; but despite unpromising appearances, in the ashpit something more like a conversation was occasionally possible:

'What are you in for?' asked the frightening face.

'None of your business,' Shinwell replied, keeping his distance.

'I'm in for burglary. C'mon. Tell us. What you in for?'

'Rioting,' said Shinwell, through his teeth.

'Rioting? Anybody hurt?' the face asked hopefully.

'One policeman killed,' Shinwell lied.

'What did you get?'

'Five months.'

'Five months,' he dropped his shovel, 'five bloody months, and I got twelve years for burglary.'[21]

His time in Calton gaol profoundly affected Manny Shinwell's life. Talking about it afterwards he tended to play it down. He would deprecate the old socialist campaigner Tom Mann's often-quoted view that 'Unless a Socialist leader has been in prison his education has been neglected'. Mann after all, although he had actually shared a platform with Shinwell before the war, had been sent to prison at a very different time, fighting for unskilled workers in the 1880s. Shinwell always thought his view of prisons romantic and highly personal.

Yet in many ways his prison experience did make Shinwell a better socialist. True, he did not, as Mann would have expected, commit himself more strongly than ever to the revolutionary cause, vowing to bring about the destruction of authority and all its agents. This was the reaction of people like John MacLean, Gramsci and even Stalin. Shinwell was never a revolutionary thinker on their scale and so his reaction was the only real alternative – to deal with the established authority on its own terms, to become a part of it and to change it from within. To that extent Thomas Mann was right. Shinwell's prison experience turned him into a better socialist, at one and the same time conniving with the establishment and seeking to destroy or radically alter it.

Witnessing at first hand, as every prisoner does, the most direct and simple examples of the abuse of power, Shinwell came to appreciate more than ever before the potential for power to corrupt. Before he went to prison he had a reputation for double-dealing; even friends who admired him never quite trusted him. Once out of prison, his reputation, even among his enemies changed. At worst, he was accused of pig-headedness. He would change his mind, he would be uncompromising and he would be intolerably difficult as a colleague; but at least in the political field, if not so much in the union field, he exchanged the style of the gangster who steals and abuses power for the style of the politician who gains power and tries to use it for a purpose. The abuse of power in Calton gaol had a lot to do with this improvement in Shinwell's character.

Prison was also a reminder to him of that grim poverty he had known so long ago in South Shields and in his early days in Glasgow. The majority of his companions in prison were the real losers in life. They were the ones whose fathers had not even made a modest success of a small tailoring business, and they were not looking to him for favours, like the seamen's families or the women on rent strike. On the contrary, he was sharing their fate, learning again to understand it. It was not, of course, that Shinwell had led a sheltered life, far from it. But in some areas his memory now needed jogging.

A further very important reminder provided by prison life was of the significance of the lumpenproletariat, the right-wing or apolitical working class. Prison warders and prisoners were generally both in that category. Shinwell always liked to tell the story of the warder who befriended him shortly before he was due to be released and allowed him to work with him in the prison garden. He had a great love of roses and would talk about them with obvious joy. How could such a man tolerate being a prison warder? One day this warder confided that he hoped to be leaving soon. Shinwell was hardly surprised, assuming he was going to be a park-keeper or maybe a gamekeeper in the Highlands. Not a bit of it. He had put in for the job of hangman because the piece-work was better and the hours less arduous. In future this kind of attitude – although the warder was a rather extreme example – would come as no surprise. The instinct to accept as God-given their role in life comes more naturally to most people than the desire to work long hours to change their lives. Shinwell the activist, like many before and after him, had been in danger of forgetting this iron rule of human nature. Shinwell the trade unionist, Shinwell the Labour town councillor, Shinwell the president of the Trades Council, had worked every day in Glasgow with people with views similar to his own; others had been his opponents. Here, on the other hand, was a section of the very working class Labour needed to support it, but holding views and values opposite to his own. These were voters whom Shinwell would go out of his way to attract in future.

In Calton gaol, Shinwell also learned hard facts about himself. He was horrified afterwards by the ease with which he had adapted to a new institution with a new set of rules. He had often noticed at the Blind Asylum where he sat on the board of governors, how the inmates, no matter how extensive their general knowledge, talked of their institutional life and little else. It was a trait he had tended to despise, but now it had happened to him in a big way. The prison routine became his life, and his release when it came was disorientating. When he first got home, he even found himself whispering and preferring to drink from a jar. He was no different from most prisoners recently released, but it was a valuable lesson on the power of institutions which he never forgot. He would learn all the rules of the establishment, the conventions of the House of Commons, of being a minister, even of being a Cabinet minister, but no institution, however attractive the security of its rules might seem, would ever quite capture him again. He had lost his individuality in prison and in future he would choose be the oddball or loner, rather than being enmeshed again.

The professional organisations of the law and religion were two establishment systems which Shinwell suspected before he was sent to prison and utterly despised when he came out. Probably wrongly, he always regarded his imprisonment as Lloyd George's revenge on Gallacher and himself for the embarrassment they caused him in 1915.[22] Lloyd George certainly bore grudges but not badly enough for that, and there is really no evidence of him taking much interest once the revolution had failed. But the fact that Shinwell believed this to be so for the rest of his life is reflected in his developing view of the whole legal process as part and parcel of the establishment. Up to 1919, he had seen the law as being for the present in the hands of wealthy and powerful men, but also having a certain standing in its own right. From then on he despised most lawyers and saw the legal system simply as an instrument of power.

As for organised religion, prison changed his views from indifference to contempt. The religious services in prison and the uncritical collaboration of organised religion with a system of obvious cruelty and brutality provided him with an eye-opening experience of hypocrisy – particularly for a man who had not witnessed priests parading as Christians at the battles of Ypres or the Somme. The Jews were just as bad. In prison, a rabbi visited once and advised him to be a good citizen in future. Shinwell got him out of his cell as soon as he could, and had almost nothing to do with organised Judaism for the next thirty years.

Shinwell was released at the end of July. They took him in a Black Maria back to Duke Street for his last night in prison. A small reception from the Trades Council had meanwhile gone to Edinburgh but the prison governor, who had got wind of it, feared a demonstration. So no one was there to greet him when he finally emerged. He took his ten-shilling gratuity and exchanged his prison uniform for the clothes he had worn in court. He caught a tram to Govan, startling Fanny on the doorstep as she was leaving to take Sammy to school.

There was a big party at the Trades Council and Shinwell was presented with a gold watch. He thanked them and told them that for seven gruelling months his life had been dominated by the events surounding Bloody Friday and the forty-hour strike. He had neglected the Trades Council, his union, the town council and his prospective parliamentary seat. He had a lot of catching up to do.

Fanny made it clear she was right behind him. Maddening though his political life had always been, she wanted nothing more than for him to be his old self again and to sink his teeth into the Conservatives, the Liberals, Havelock Wilson, John Wheatley and anybody else who was wrong and stood in his way. There was nothing she feared more than his demor-alisation. She stiffened his resolve.[23]

CHAPTER 8

Moving Forward

Labour in Parliament in 1919 and 1920 had been badly weakened by the loss of MacDonald and Henderson in the 'coupon' election. Even in Glasgow, Labour was still a dozen years away from a majority on the council. The unions had been helped by new laws on strikes overturning the Taff Vale decision, but post-war unemployment made them generally ineffective again. Years of liberal reform before the war had limited the appeal of socialism. The labour movement in Britain was altogether one of the least impressive in Europe.

It turned out, nevertheless, to be an auspicious time for Shinwell to shift decisively from revolutionary to parliamentary politics. Revolution had in fact failed everywhere except in Russia (even Béla Kun in Hungary had been ousted), and voters were soon disillusioned with the Liberals who were dominated by the Conservatives in Lloyd George's Coalition government. The only real alternative, the constitutional labour movement, was expanding fast. There were now over six million trade-union members and over four million Labour Party members, more than ever before.[1]

The whole political scene was still too unpredictable for an aspiring Labour politician to make specific plans for his political advancement. But Shinwell had no doubt that certain old revolutionary ideas and styles had to be jettisoned in the post-war world. He found the ideological changes easy, for he had always been weak on commitment to ideas beyond the most general aims of the left. And he started to adopt a new style, the new Labour style suited to organised public meetings. The rabble-rousing of Glasgow Green and George Square was an out-of-date technique.

In the 1922 election Shinwell's new style still contained enough of the violence and hatred of the revolutionary period to keep his audience interested. He never lost the ability to exploit the gossipy interest of a personal attack, although he now started to use sarcasm more than name-calling. He also shifted from street orator to political speaker in the way he looked at people, especially at the start of every speech:

He looked you straight in the eye. He could make you feel quite uncomfortable. Why the heck's he looking at me? People who felt themselves stared at started shuffling uneasily in their seats. The nearest thing I ever felt was when one of our school mistresses used to fix me with her eyes – like a fish on a spike. It was a great relief when Manny turned away and looked at someone else.[2]

Shinwell seemed to be honest because he looked his audience in the eye and 'like the Mona Lisa, he always seemed to be concerned with you personally, no matter where you were in the room'. He was very aware of his audience. He always claimed he could sense the mood, when to slow down and tell a story, when to orate and when to stop. Typically, he would start with a comment or story in a conversational style that would seem to have nothing to do with the main subject. Then, just when any audience is at its most receptive, between five and fifteen minutes into the speech, he would push his message across. This was usually the weakest part of his speech; his lack of clear political ideas never afforded him the conviction of a great political speech-maker. Whatever it was he wanted to say, he said loudly, clearly, with emphatic gestures and often several times. At length he would relax again, smile at his audience and re-engage eye contact. He would tell them jokes at the expense of political opponents and appear to be generally sociable and pleasant, and to have some empathy with the people he was addressing, whether they were dockers in Glasgow, miners in his constituency or trade-union delegates at a conference. As Shinwell later explained:

> If you get nerves that's okay; it may even help. Take your time. Don't gabble. Use silence. Breathe deeply, and wait for the words. Let your mouth do the talking.
>
> Sometimes I quite deliberately pause and appear to be searching for a word … It's more interesting that way, gives them time to follow. It's sometimes said of my speeches that my pauses are more eloquent than the speech, because pauses are usually accompanied by gestures – a bit of drama.[3]

In the three years between prison and Parliament, Shinwell became a master of that conversational part of a public speech where a well-timed pause, a rhetorical question, or a little joke could keep an audience expectant. He never seemed to ramble and used the pause most effectively of all if he felt he was losing his way:

> Just occasionally he did lose track – he never used notes – and the silences would get longer and longer. One time – I think it was in the 1922 election or a few months before – he'd been talking about Lloyd George and the coalition and how they had thrown away the opportunities presented

by the peace. The problem was that Manny simply couldn't bring to mind what those opportunities were or where they had been lost – it went something like this – 'why were the opportunities lost?' – pause – 'Every chance was thrown away...' – pause (so long that some of us started to giggle) – 'the chance for improvement, for a better way of living... – even longer pause, almost unbearable, then a complete change of subject, an escape.[4]

He apparently escaped from his dilemma by relaunching the high-volume attack he had made earlier on Lloyd George with slightly different words, and the embarrassing interlude was forgotten. The fact was that, although it could occasionally go wrong, it was an enviable political skill to 'let your mouth do the talking', to speak without a note.

Later, as a minister with civil service briefs, he was mediocre. But from 1919 to his centenary, his speeches without notes were legendary. He was coherent, he got a clear message across in prose which was not necessarily grammatical when transcribed but made perfect sense when combined with the atmosphere and gestures which could not be transcribed: arms spread or brought together as if for a prayer, head scratched or shaken or nodded, finger pointed, fist banged down, chin jutted or relaxed, voice raised or lowered to a whisper. All this not from memory but just from a few ideas in his head before he started. Few of his colleagues had this ability and it could put him at a great advantage at a conference or any meeting where he might not have known in advance the type of audience or what they wanted to hear. Whenever he could, he would mix socially with the audience beforehand and refer to them in his speech. This strategy worked well. They would feel he was concerned with their interests, and this was obviously not possible with a prepared speech.

From his time in prison onwards, encouraged or nagged by Fanny, he learned to dress more smartly too.[5] By 1922 he had combined his talents as a confident political speaker who understood the detail of his subject with the best of his old street-fighter techniques, standing still and upright at the rostrum and tearing an opponent to shreds with words and gestures. It made for a good spectacle. When Shinwell spoke, hundreds – sometimes thousands – now turned out to listen.

Between the end of the war and the 1922 general election, the party on the left had to decide whether it was for the Soviet revolutionary approach or for MacDonald's now firmly constitutional approach, to win government by the ballot and in that way to win as much power as Lenin in Russia.[6] The Labour Party in Parliament and its leaders outside opted against violent revolution and therefore against participation in Lenin's Third International, the world communist organisation. With the founding of the British

Communist Party in July 1920, the few revolutionaries remaining in the Labour Party had an alternative and more suitable home.

Straight out of prison, Shinwell could hardly find a platform soon enough to reject the revolutionary side. At the ceremony where he was presented with a gold watch by the Trades Council (now technically the Glasgow Trades and Labour Council, recognising its political role) he only hinted – 'this important constitutional organisation' – and most of the speech was about the watch and Fanny's present, a gold bangle,[7] but when he was presented the next day with another gold watch by the British Seafarers he presumably ran out of things to say about watches (they later changed it for a wallet) and used the occasion to state his new political position. He said he was prepared to fight the capitalist class by 'all legal and constitutional means' and wanted thorough 'nationalisation instituted by Parliament'.[8]

Nor were these protestations of purely local or of Scottish interest. Bloody Friday had paraded Shinwell before a wider public. He was no household name yet, but his profile within the labour movement was much sharper. This made it all the more important for him to make clear whether he was on the parliamentary or revolutionary wing of the political left. Before Bloody Friday it hardly mattered. As a national figure standing for Parliament, regularly addressing Labour and union gatherings, people asked questions and felt they had a right to know.

There was additional pressure too after the TUC had met in Glasgow on 8 September 1919, a bare fortnight after Shinwell's release. He had been something of a local hero there, cheered to the hilt at his short welcoming address as president of the Trades and Labour Council and receiving general adulation from all sides of the movement.

The central debate at the conference was the political, as opposed to the industrial, activity of the 'Triple Industrial Alliance' of the miners, the transport workers and the railwaymen. In April, the alliance had decided to support 'the right of the working class of each country to decide its own destiny' and therefore to oppose the use of British troops to try to suppress the Russian Revolution.[9] Labour's MPs, the 'Parliamentary Committee', opposed the alliance with strong warnings about the use of the strike weapon for political purposes.[10] The miners' leaders, Bob Smillie and Frank Hodges, proposed a vote of censure on the parliamentarians. Everyone was taking sides.

Ernest Bevin, the powerful leader of the transport workers, opposed the miners; his priority was unity. Shinwell the revolutionary was assumed to be a radical miners' supporter. Smillie spoke with approval about Shinwell's involvement with the miners in Linlithgowshire, all but making Shinwell an honorary member of the Miners' Federation. And a group of delegates, now a small minority, in favour of 'direct action', invited him to speak at a fringe meeting they had organised. Bevin and the executive of the TUC lost and the Parliamentary Committee was duly censured for not taking a stronger political line, but there was no serious debate on direct action or revolutionary activity.[11]

This Glasgow meeting of the TUC was the first chance that Shinwell had had to meet Bevin for more than a passing handshake. His association with Bevin's opponents – Shinwell was not actually a delegate – was Bevin's first concern. He told him that this was no time to be sitting on the fence; he had to come down on the side of 'common sense and the working man' or 'violence and destruction'. Shinwell made it clear to Bevin personally that he was constitutionally-minded now, but said he was still getting over prison and had no desire to take sides at a conference where he wasn't even a delegate.

Then Bevin asked about the situation between the British Seafarers' Union and the Sailors' and Firemen's Union. He had no particular proposals; he seemed simply to be seeking information and was considerably surprised at Shinwell's intention of carrying on the fight in Glasgow. He had been told by Havelock Wilson that Shinwell was finished; in reality, he was told, the Seafarers had lost about a quarter of their Glasgow members since the end of the war, very damaging but not terminal. Feeling, as people often did on meeting Shinwell for the first time, that here was a reliable man he could work with, Bevin said he hoped to see him again and wrote shortly afterwards that they would get a chance to spend some time together to discuss the seamen's unions at the Irish TUC at Cork, where Shinwell was to be the Scottish TUC fraternal delegate and Bevin would be a guest of honour.

In the event, Bevin never turned up. Shinwell thought it was just as well:

> It wouldn't have suited Ernie Bevin. The Black and Tans were everywhere. I remember hearing machine-gun fire in the street outside. The door of our hotel bedroom flew open. I expected a whole regiment to come barging in to shoot us all. But in fact it was the hall porter who ten minutes before had been carrying our luggage. You can imagine our relief.
> It was short-lived.
> The porter calmly walked across to the window, took a revolver out of his jacket pocket and started firing down the street.'

Shinwell dived under the bed and cracked his head. 'It was no place to discuss the finer points of the seamen's troubles.'[12]

By the end of 1919, Shinwell had made it clear on several occasions that he was a radical within the constitutional wing of the labour movement. He was not with Gallacher or MacLean on the revolutionary wing but having opted for the softer line, he was determined to show himself to be tough and unrelenting.

Glasgow Town Council was his chosen forum. It was at least more widely reported, though hardly more effective from the Labour point of view, than the Trades Council.

The day after the TUC conference, Shinwell got his first quick and easy pieces of town council publicity. First, there was the matter of some demobbed soldiers who had lost their jobs issuing ration cards. This brought a clash between Shinwell and John Stewart, a long-standing moderate Labour councillor, who told Shinwell to keep quiet, saying he had been away and was out of touch. Shinwell yelled back at him in the council chamber:

> Let the others lecture us, John. Don't you do it! I have heard Conservative councillors giving lip service to the cause of the soldiers during the war; they had prated about their patriotism, but now when the men came in to see them, limbless, blinded and maimed, what did they do? [Cries of 'Order!', 'Chair' and general row to prevent Shinwell being heard][13]

Minutes later, he formally returned his Council Peace Medal in disgust, along with a letter identical to those of Pat Dollan and three other Labour councillors who had done the same thing. They each insisted it should be read out to the full council:

> I return herewith the gold Peace Medal sent to me without my sanction. I understand that all the members of the Corporation and chief officials have been given similar medals, and as each is estimated to cost £3/8/– the total expense would probably be £500. This unauthorised expenditure on trinkets for adults is a wanton waste of public funds, which is condemned by the majority of the citizens and many members of the Corporation. So far as I can ascertain, the purchase of the gold medals has not been authorised by the Town Council.[14]

With an eye on yet more publicity, Shinwell then attacked the 'fripperies' surrounding the Freedom of the City ceremony for South African war hero General Botha, objected to the expense of the champagne and cigars for the visiting President of France and said it would 'spoil the boy' if 500 knights and baronets wasted money at a banquet planned for the following month for the Prince of Wales.[15]

The serious issue a couple of months later was rents. The council wanted to increase them. The Labour Group opposed. Shinwell suggested delaying tactics to his fellow Labour councillors and was turned down for being only 'semi-constitutional'. He decided to ignore the group's decision. John Wheatley pleaded with him over the necessity for a 'single socialist voice'. John Stewart, still smarting from his telling-off over the dismissal of the ex-soldiers, moved Shinwell's suspension from the Labour Group. Only Pat Dollan now supported Shinwell, who attributed the group's behaviour to their jealousy of his having become a national figure; he was the one who occupied the pages of *Forward* and the *Glasgow Herald*.

> Just a few months after being cheered on my release from prison, I was no longer even welcome at their social gatherings at Kate Cranston's café, but to some extent I had outgrown them anyway. I was becoming better known than most of them.[16]

The night after his suspension, the Trades and Labour Council came down strongly on his side:

> The action of John Stewart in moving the suspension of Emanuel Shinwell is greatly to be deplored, and further, the Trades and Labour Council heartily endorses the militant attitude of Emanuel Shinwell on the question of economic rent, and trusts that in future the Labour Group of the Town Council will as occasion arises consistently adopt a straight militant attitude on all Labour questions.[17]

Glasgow became a microcosm of the TUC's fight to put backbone into Labour MPs in the 1918 Parliament. Shinwell was on the side of the angels and riding high.

Militant in attitude and in action, he soon made the Glasgow Town Council itself – not just the Labour Group – suspend him. On 25 March the proposed increase in rents of 10 per cent (the straw that will break the back of many poor tenants) came up only in the discussion of the accuracy of the minutes of the previous meeting when the matter had been briefly discussed. As he persisted in making debating points at this inappropriate time, the chairman pleaded with him to stop, then ordered him to stop and then moved his suspension. The motion to suspend him was discussed while Shinwell continued to harangue the council. The *Glasgow Herald* reported the scene with relish:

> Mr Shinwell occasionally made himself heard above the din. He continued shouting while the vote was being taken and created laughter by warning 'the capitalist hooligans' that they were adopting tactics which would recoil upon their heads when the workers got into power. 'Suffering' and 'oppression' were words audible in the uproar as he continued to harangue the chamber. Suspension having been carried, Mr Anderson, Council Officer, approached and plucked Mr Shinwell by the sleeve. 'If I go out,' the latter exclaimed, 'it is simply because I have no desire to get into conflict with Mr Anderson.' Derisive laughter greeted this admission. Mr Shinwell angrily retorted, 'I won't go out. This kind of thing may be done today, but it won't be done in the future.' There was a renewed outburst of interruptions, during which Mr Shinwell reminded members that they would have to face their constituents, 'I

am prepared to resign my seat in Fairfield and fight it with any member on the question of rents alone.' He turned to leave the chamber, where Mr Kirkwood said a member had accepted his challenge, but as this apparently was a misapprehension Mr Shinwell left the chamber.

David Kirkwood, in fact, to everyone's surprise, took up Shinwell's arguments 'in a high-pitched voice and with excited gestures' but he soon ran out of steam. The council duly increased their rents and continued with the ordinary business. Shinwell had proved his 'constitutional militancy'. The rest of the Labour Group seethed while he took all the publicity.[18]

Rather less successful was his attempt to support a fading rent strike among private tenants by refusing to pay increases in his own rent. He was eventually evicted, along with Fanny and the four children, but no one took it very seriously because he had in fact already organised a move straight into one of the very council houses where in his previous arguments he had found the rents so objectionable.[19] After this political miscalculation, he was allowed back to Maxton's and Wheatley's table at Cranston's.[20]

As befitted his return to intellectual conversations over tea at Cranston's, Shinwell was now expressing himself in writing more often, and on 18 September 1920 he gave his long-awaited views on Lenin in *Forward*. The gist of his muddled argument was that Lenin's statement about the use of Parliament, as distinct from his diatribes against Henderson and MacDonald, was not much different from the aims of the labour movement, especially the ILP. Lenin had argued that the revolutionaries must enter Parliament to 'vanquish it' and to 'prepare for the success of the Soviets'. That is what he was doing. The criticism in the following week's communist *Worker* that Shinwell had completely failed to understand Lenin and was 'hopelessly up the pole' was probably fair.[21]

Did Shinwell really believe that parliamentary success was simply a precursor to revolution? By the end of 1920 he almost certainly did not. On 18 December, again in *Forward*, he made fun of his would-be revolutionary colleague on the Trades and Labour Council, Walton Newbold, later a Communist MP, who had called for the physical training of his 'comrades' to replace the army under a Labour government. These comrades would defend the revolution. Shinwell retorted that the army would 'make short work of Field Marshal Newbold and his provisionals. Even a knowledge of military tactics derived in the course of comradely conversation in the comfortable cafés of Manchester and Glasgow would be of no avail.'[22]

By the spring of 1921, Shinwell had even shed a good many romantic illusions about what a Labour majority government could do, at least in a short time. He had also apparently convinced himself that the army and police would not be disloyal. 'It is now inconceivable that the ruling class would seek by violence to prevent the workers from using the ballot or to alter the consequences of that ballot.'

His basic idea that the revolution could be left to political and trade-union leaders like himself met with some angry reactions, including a powerful attack from the anti-Semitic communist Tom Jackson, again in the *Worker*, entitled 'Emanuel: God with Us' (a biblical allusion to Shinwell's new-found status in the Labour movement, an 'aspirant to the throne of MacDonald'): 'We fear the Greeks bearing gifts. In like manner, when a member of the Hebrew race looks like a complete idiot, watch out for "the catch".' The catch, Jackson explained, was the complacency in Shinwell's ideas and his failure to grasp how the power of the capitalists went far beyond having the army or the police to defend them. He criticised Shinwell in strong language for forgetting about the press, the schools, the pulpits, the cinema and so on. Jackson ended with a personal jibe:

A rebel Irishman dying with his gun in his fist rather than surrender is a far nobler figure than an elected person who in his new-found respectability has grown ashamed of his ancestry and, seeking to turn himself into an inferior imitation of an Englishman, conceals under the pose of a student the understanding of a sheep, and under the garb of a gladiator the spirit of a poltroon.[23]

Shinwell was now enough of a national figure to be elected to the National Administrative Council of the ILP and he started to take a serious interest in the international socialist movement. Just as in Glasgow, the international left was split between the reformers and the revolutionaries. The reformers had been in the Second International which had disintegrated in the war. The revolutionaries were now in Lenin's Third International and the reformers were refusing to join.

Shinwell was sent as one of the ILP's five delegates to a conference in Vienna designed to set up an alternative successor to the Second International and, if possible – and this was what specially interested Shinwell – to bridge the gap with the communists. Devised by Friedrich Adler of the Austrian Social Democratic Party and attended by more than seventy delegates from twenty parties in thirteen countries, excluding the Bolsheviks of the Soviet Union, it claimed to represent a cross-section of the world proletariat.[24] The conference was soon dubbed the 'Two-and-a-halfth International'.

The journey to Vienna was in itself exciting for Shinwell. Thrilled crowds in German towns waited for hours for passing delegations to address them for a few minutes in railway marshalling yards and on station platforms. Then in Vienna there was the opera – Shinwell saw *Die Meistersinger* – as well as the poverty and starvation, and the staggering inflation.[25] The hotel prices approximately trebled (but were still ridiculously cheap) in the fortnight he was in Vienna.

The idea of bridging the gap between the reformers and the communists was dealt a severe blow on the very day the conference opened, when news seeped in about the Soviet invasion of Georgia. In May 1918, Georgia had declared itself an independent republic and was dominated by Lenin's Menshevik opponents. It was a democratic socialist republic; Ramsay MacDonald and Friedrich Adler were among its most fervent admirers. Now, while the assembly at Vienna was discussing overtures to Lenin, telegrams started arriving from the Georgian capital: 'Russian troops, without previous declaration of war, have now reached us in Tiflis. Our government is overthrown.' After two weeks of heavy fighting, on 25th February 1921, the third day of the Vienna conference, a Bolshevik government was set up in the newly-styled Transcaucasian Soviet Socialist Republic. In a brief war 21,000 Georgians and 10,000 Russians had died.

The conference sought urgent clarification from Moscow. A conciliatory reply came from the Commissar for Nationalities, himself a Georgian, Joseph Stalin:

> This is a question of local risings among the Georgian population, and the Soviet government have offered to arbitrate between the rebels and the Georgian government.
>
> ... the October Revolution confirmed and gave practical effect to the decisions of our Party on the national question. By overthrowing the power of the landlords and capitalists, to whom national oppression was chiefly due, and by putting the proletariat in power, the October Revolution at one blow smashed the fetters of national oppression ... cleared the way for the collaboration of peoples and won for the Russian proletariat the confidence of its brothers of other nationalities ... in Europe, in Asia and in the states of the Caucasus such as Georgia.

Stalin's telegram went on for eighteen pages in a similar style. In the custom of such conferences, it was read out and translated in full in three languages. Shinwell spoke in the debate on the situation in Georgia after the French socialist, Jean Longuet, had denounced the invasion and declared Lenin and Stalin to be criminals beyond the pale of civilisation.

Shinwell introduced himself as a novice in international politics but 'somewhat experienced in revolutionary affairs'. He said how much he admired the Georgian experiment: land redistribution, mines nationalisation, state export monopolies and state transport monopolies. But 'in Russia this would not have been possible without the violent establish-

ment of the dictatorship of the proletariat'. Georgians and Russians were
two working-class states established in the way appropriate to each of them:

> We must have some degree of confidence in the fraternity of these two
> states. If there is a dispute between them, can we mediate? Let us inves-
> tigate and not prejudge. Monsieur Stalin has sent us a full explanation
> from his point of view.

Not perhaps Shinwell's sharpest and most perspicacious speech. Of
course at that time Stalin was little known, and it was widely held that the
Bolshevik leadership was benevolent but maligned in the capitalist press.
Shinwell's theme that there was little to choose between the two workers'
states met with general approval. The new delegate was thought diplomatic
and competent and he was proposed by his colleagues in the ILP, supported
by the Lithuanian Socialist Party (heavily infiltrated by Bolsheviks), for a
place on the executive which would continue the work of the conference
after it had broken up.[26]
In the event, the bloody Kronstadt rebellion against the Bolsheviks and
the increasingly obvious centralisation of power in the Soviet Union left
the possibility of overtures, Adler's original hope, out in the cold. Shinwell
did attend a further meeting at The Hague later in the year, but was little
more than a message bearer from the ILP and Labour Party conferences
in Brighton, protesting about political prisoners and the absence of
democratic freedoms in Russia. Even then, Shinwell strained to look for
some good in the Soviet Union:

> Lenin's new slogan 'Go out to the masses' should find a good reception
> among socialists in the capitalist world. It is what we have been doing.
> We must be seen to be on the side of the working man to gain his
> confidence.[27]

It was too late. The Communist Third International met in July 1921,
and marked the Soviet retreat towards 'Socialism in One Country'. At the
ninth Soviet Congress in December 1921, Lenin made it clear to his own
people that that the 'Vienna process' was irrelevant; Soviet Russia and
capitalist states could coexist for the time being, 'both militarily and politically it is already a fact'.[28]

Lenin and Stalin had a good deal less influence on Shinwell than the police
sergeant in charge of the day-to-day activities of the constables who con-
trolling the docks in Glasgow. While Shinwell had been in prison, the Sailors'
and Firemen's Union had reached 'sweetheart' deals, by which only that
union had access to ships belonging to certain companies. His own leaderless
union had not been able to stop them. When he returned to take charge,
he realised he had no choice but to take his life in his hands, yet again, and

approach men from the 'closed ships'. He had to try to board these ships with a gang of his own supporters, which nearly always caused trouble. The police were constantly being called by the ship-owners and they then had to sort out the 'bad characters', invariably Shinwell's men.

Before long the police were sending officials of the British Seafarers' Union away from the quayside as soon as they saw them, leading to absurd cat-and-mouse chases among the cranes and gantries.[29] Shinwell fought tirelessly for the British Seafarers' Union, against the police, against the rival union and in the council chamber. The defence of the shipping companies against his union, he argued in council, was being paid for out of the rates for the police. He was also convinced, though he never said so publicly, that the sergeant in charge on the quayside was in the pay of his rivals.

By now he was tired of it all and wished he was not so committed as he could see no long-term future in this kind of work. The British Seafarers' Union was in danger of again becoming the minority union – its membership was now down to about 60 per cent of that of its peak – after ten years on Clydeside, and it remained the representative of only about 20 per cent of all unionised seamen nationally. Shinwell managed to keep the union in existence with a reasonable number of members in the years after prison, but he distanced himself from it and it became a smaller part of his life.

His intention now was to become an MP and possibly a minister, and he attached himself firmly to Ramsay MacDonald. At the time, the diminished parliamentary party was in fact being led by J R Clynes; but like many in the ILP, Shinwell knew that Clynes would have to go if Labour was to succeed after the next election, and he backed MacDonald to take over right away once he was back in Parliament. Friend and foe alike recognised the Labour parliamentary opposition to Lloyd George's Coalition government as ineffective and divided. Shinwell was devastated, however, when MacDonald's first attempt to get back at Woolwich in 1921, was a crushing failure even though the seat had been Labour since 1903.

Woolwich was a hard-fought campaign marred by rowdy meetings but launched too late to win the seat against the Coalition's candidate. When Shinwell, in London for an ILP meeting, dined with him privately for the first time on 3 March, MacDonald was still feeling the Woolwich failure bitterly. The night before, miserable, lonely and missing his dead wife, MacDonald had written in his diary: 'It was a great and strenuous fight but the filth used was absolutely disgusting. Hope never to go through another such racking hour as when the votes were being counted.'[30]

Also at dinner were MacDonald's son Malcolm, a twenty-year-old keenly interested in politics who joined his father in persuading Shinwell to fight to keep Snowden and Maxton out of office in the ILP, and his daughters Ishbel, eighteen, and Sheila, eleven. Over the mutton and onion sauce in the MacDonalds' semi-detached house in Hampstead, they talked about the personalities of the day, especially those ostensibly on MacDonald's own side. To Shinwell, it seemed a shockingly gossipy session. 'Snowden was this. Maxton was that. Henderson had done this. Lansbury had done that. He was a man surrounded by ghosts. Malcolm spoke more sense, constantly bringing his father back to the ILP.'[31]

The ILP was, after all, MacDonald's mainstay. Without it during the war years he would have been even more isolated. Now he needed it to get back into power, and there was a real risk of it becoming an exclusive class party of the far left without the broad public appeal needed to bring about Labour's success in the general election. Despite Shinwell's flirtation with revolutionary politics, MacDonald, who had met him several times in Glasgow and at various conferences, knew him as a pragmatist and populist. He saw Shinwell as an ally in the constant fight against sectarianism.

In his attic study after dinner, MacDonald showed a grasp of the practical political requirements of the period leading up to the next general election, which he had certainly not shown downstairs with his family. The change of atmosphere in the workroom seemed to bring about a change of gear; the introspective family man became a practical politician aiming for office.

The first practical move, however, came from Shinwell. He had no chance at that time of gaining any further influence on the National Administrative Committee of the ILP. He made it clear to MacDonald that he was not yet sufficiently well known and he would have no chance of being elected to the chairmanship or any official position. With this out of the way, the two men got down to discussing preparations for winning substantially more seats in the general election. They mulled over the lessons of Woolwich, the disruption and the violence, the appearance of the 'patriotic' Horatio Bottomley in support of the Coalition candidate and the short preparation time. Shinwell compared this with the relative peace of Bathgate and Linlithgow and helped persuade MacDonald to return to Aberavon, the working-class South Wales seat he was to win in 1922, and to leave London well behind.

The most useful outcome of the meeting, as far as Shinwell was concerned, was new ideas of what to say to his constituents. Unemployment had trebled in the three months between December 1920 and March 1921. Now he was able to tell them what would be done by a potential Labour government. MacDonald agreed to promote policies to facilitate the purchase of small-holdings, especially by miners who were also ex-servicemen. This simple idea was to become a recurring theme in Shinwell's constituency speeches over the next few years. It was just the kind of positive work which appealed to Shinwell and which made MacDonald stand out among his party colleagues. It was politically effective because it attracted floating voters looking for solutions to economic and social problems.

MacDonald and Shinwell were never intimates. MacDonald regarded Shinwell as a promising young politician of the middle rank, not an outstanding Clydesider like Wheatley but not a poisonous one like Maxton or a crazy one like Kirkwood; Shinwell was still green enough to be excited by dinner with the MacDonalds or with 'Philip Snowden and his charming aristocratic wife Ethel – the Snowdens spent most of the evening criticising MacDonald'.[32] MacDonald did accept return hospitality from the Shinwells a few months later in Glasgow. It was a brief visit on a busy tour. The main business on this occasion seems to have been MacDonald's many apologies for not visiting Shinwell's constituency, although he may have also talked about the potential importance of the National Joint Council co-ordinating the work of the party and the TUC which both he and Shinwell would be joining as ILP delegates.

The visit was altogether more memorable on account of the numbers turning up at the Shinwells' tiny council house, including Francis Johnson, the ILP National Secretary, and various English and Scottish officials in MacDonald's entourage. They ran out of chairs and glasses. Lucy drank her tea out of a vase while Fanny, preparing soup and cakes, was more concerned about who was going to pay for it all; no one offered so it came out of Shinwell's wage which had now risen to £4 but had still not kept pace with inflation.[33]

MacDonald's visit to Glasgow took place at a time of great political uncertainty. A minor post-war boom had ended abruptly. Coalmining was especially badly hit. A Royal Commission in 1919 had recommended nationalisation of the mines, but in 1921 the industry, which was still under government control from the war, lost £15 million. Lloyd George wanted it off the government books so, in spite of pledges to the contrary, the Coalition government removed controls and handed the mines back to the private owners. Decontrol was sudden, violent and brutal. Three months were allowed for the whole process. Overseas competition was unbeatable, and wages were halved. A long strike resulted in victory for the owners as miners were forced back to work on breadline wages and the Triple Industrial Alliance fell apart as the railwaymen and transport workers failed to come to the miners' aid.[34]

MacDonald's constitutional Labour Party now had the opportunity to be an alternative to the failed direct action typified by the Triple Industrial Alliance, an alternative to the last vestiges of the revolutionary idea. It was the only realistic option for those who felt there must be a better way to run the country's affairs than impoverishing millions for little or no obvious benefit. By the time the 1922 election was called, when the Conservatives withdrew support from the Lloyd George Coalition, MacDonald was talking of 'something remarkable in the atmosphere, a sense of relief, of hope' in the Labour movement.[35]

Vote, vote, vote for Mr Shinwell,
Vote, vote, vote for a' his men.
Oh we'll buy a penny gun,
And we'll shoot Kidd up the bum,
And we'll never see the likes o' him again.

Largely thanks to the skilful organisation – and extraordinarily hard work which had led to a nervous breakdown in 1921 – by Arthur Henderson, Labour candidates such as Shinwell contested seats like Linlithgow with much more co-ordination than in 1918 or before. Agreed policy was circulated to candidates in time for the election addresses to be printed, and realistic appeals were made in good time to unions and trades councils for funds. Shinwell squeezed a few pounds from his own Glasgow Trades and Labour Council[36] and a valuable grant of £50 from the British Seafarers' Union which enabled him to rent a car and driver for the whole campaign to get around the villages of his spread-out constituency much more easily than before.[37]

In the months leading up to the election, he had been planning and canvassing hard, visiting the constituency weekly and making a wide circle of friends there going well beyond the labour movement. The campaign of 1922 was much more like a modern election campaign than that of 1918. Shinwell was presenting a clear set of alternative policies, not an attitude and a few ideas. His speeches were no longer the 1918 revolutionary tirades but long, well-developed lectures on Labour's alternatives. His speeches may have been long but they were never boring. The need for investment in the local shale oil industry was colourfully compared with expensive military adventures to secure oil in Mesopotamia: 'the nation's wealth squandered by decaying generals in the dust of the east.' Sometimes the metaphors were rather confused; the taxes on tea, sugar and tobacco should be used to 'grease the slippery pole down which Lloyd George and Bonar Law will slowly, painfully and inevitably slide'.[38] But there was a clear message.

The many differences between Labour in 1918 and Labour in 1922 were summed up in Shinwell's election address: 'Labour has a definite policy on all questions affecting our national life.' Unpopular policies, such as pro-hibition, had been dropped or modified. Blatant appeals to the middle class on taxes and value for money in public services were added.[39]

It worked. Conservative scares about Bolshevism and revolutionary socialism rang hollow. The broken Coalition split the opposition to Labour in many constituencies, including Shinwell's. Updated electoral rolls emphasised the swing. Labour won one hundred and forty-two seats, including twenty-nine in Scotland. MacDonald was elected comfortably. So were Maxton, Kirkwood and Johnston among the Clydesiders. Snowden was back and Clement Attlee was elected for the first time. Ironically, only Henderson among the leaders failed to secure re-election. Shinwell's majority was comfortable:

Emanuel Shinwell (Labour)	12,625 (46%)
James Kidd (Conservative-Unionist)	8,993 (33%)
Fraser Orr (Independent Liberal)	5,605 (21%)
Majority	3,632

The early announcement at County Hall, Linlithgow, took the crowd by surprise. News of the votes piling up for Shinwell on 16 November, the day after the election when the count was taking place, had spread around the constituency by lunchtime, and victories in neighbouring seats boosted expectations. At 3.30 p.m. a large crowd, mainly of Labour supporters, cheered as they saw Shinwell take his place immediately to the right of the bewigged deputy returning officer. The yelled result was barely audible above the racket. Shinwell made a rather lame acceptance speech ('arduous campaign … overtaxed my strength'), but had recovered considerably half an hour later when Fanny, who was accompanying him on a victory tour, passed on the news of Churchill's defeat at Dundee. After a rousing speech, they carried him shoulder-high up the village street, and so it went on across the constituency well into the night: cheering, flowers for Fanny, lighting of bonfires, 'For he's a jolly good fellow', the 'Red Flag' …

One young woman declared in the local newspaper that she was 'ashamed that Linlithgowshire should be represented by a Jew' and the editorial sourly commented that 'if the electors who voted Labour think that their representative will be able to solve our constituency's problems better than the men who have been rejected, we are afraid they are destined to be sadly disappointed'.[40] From Linlithgow, the celebration moved to Glasgow. The victors of twenty-nine Scottish seats met for their evening meal at the Blytheswood Hotel next to the station where they were all to catch the night train to London. A crowd of fifty thousand gathered to cheer them off, singing the 24th Psalm ('If it had not been the Lord who was on our side …') and the 'Red Flag'. David Kirkwood screamed above the cheering and chanting: 'We're going to change everything.' He reckoned he was the boss of the show, deciding who was going into which compartments and who was going to discuss what with whom on the way to London. Fanny and the children came to see Shinwell off and they all had to fight through the crowd, Shinwell clutching his suitcase and a new pillow for the journey. Most people remembered it as a great celebration, which of course it was, but to his credit Shinwell also recognised in it the certainty of thwarted expectations:

I think that all of us who had been dubbed the 'Wild Men of the Clyde' were chastened by that demonstration. We had been elected because it was believed we could perform miracles ... but miracles and politics do not mix.[41]

Elated and humbled by the belief of the crowd, the new MPs planned and plotted far into the night. In the freezing fog of London's early morning lay reality.

Shinwell knew of some digs in a dingy corner of Pimlico, where there were also some cheap restaurants, which he shared with George Hardie, one of Keir Hardie's brothers. His MP's salary of £400 had to provide for Fanny and four children as well as his own food and lodgings.[42]

On Monday 20 November, the ILP group of MPs met at Johnson's Court, off Fleet Street. The leadership question came up and Shinwell proposed that MacDonald should be backed to replace Clynes, but Maxton and Wheatley opposed this, preferring to continue with the lame-duck leadership until better people had emerged from the new intake – themselves for instance. They regarded MacDonald's leadership as likely to be all hot air and living off a reputation made in the previous decade.[43] They took no vote but it was clear that Shinwell had little support. His first real break with the Clyde group was therefore when he spoke for the first time to the Parliamentary Labour Party as a whole: 'With great respect to J R Clynes we want ... an outstanding personality. We want someone who's an orator and somebody who understands the Party and is ready to give service to the Party.'[44] MacDonald won with a majority of just five.

Quickly and deliberately, Shinwell pulled away from the Clyde group. He was not going to be led by Maxton or marshalled by Wheatley, and he found Kirkwood embarrassing with his infantile comments about 'the sweeping changes which would immediately and inevitably follow Davie's election to Parliament – he was the least effective of all'.[45]

In the debate on the King's Speech, Shinwell's maiden speech was a world apart from the glorified election addresses given by the other new Clyde MPs. It was not particularly good, but it was a surprise for the press since it was a debating speech rather than a declamatory one. Shinwell was wordy – 'I regard the reasoning of the Right Honourable Member as most fallacious and his argument as not being productive of information nor of satisfaction of any kind' – but he dealt quite neatly with his old theme of the expenditure on the military expedition in Mesopotamia (where the British were, among other things, bombing the Kurds with poison gas) compared with the need to put up old age pensions.

It was not a speech for the hustings or for the revolution; it was a parliamentary debating speech. Without a single note, Shinwell ranged from the need to end the taxation of food to the extravagant claims for a 'whole

new world' which Lloyd George had made in 1918, 'a very revolutionary proposal' compared with the so-called revolutionary ideas of the Labour
Party. In his peroration he replied to an earlier speech by Lady Astor, who
had claimed that immorality was rife among Russian children under
Bolshevism, by accusing British military intervention in Russia of being
responsible for starving little children through siege tactics. 'I suggest that,
in any case, before Honourable Members opposite attack Russia, they should
try and clean up the somewhat dirty stable at home.'[46]

The *Glasgow Citizen* said how much it wished other Clyde MPs could
be like Shinwell. *The Times*, after several such contributions from Shinwell,
rather disappointed by the lack of fireworks, said he was 'explosives yet to
be detonated'.[47] He even failed to explode when four Clyde MPs led by
Maxton and Wheatley were suspended because they refused to withdraw
the word 'murderers' from their description of Conservative MPs supporting
a bill to cut milk from the list of entitlements for mothers with infants.
Shinwell refused to join in the 'murderers' furore, although even his
modestly worded intervention brought the (presumably) intended insult
'Jew' from the egregious Lady Astor.

It seemed to Shinwell like histrionics to get knowingly thrown out of
the House of Commons for an indefinite period and it infuriated Ramsay
MacDonald. Nevertheless, it did gain a good deal of publicity for an
important cause, just as Shinwell had found using a similar technique in
the council a few years earlier. It displayed an understanding of how to
use what Wheatley had called 'the best broadcasting station in the world'.[48]
It certainly got a good deal more coverage than Shinwell's well-prepared
and worthy contribution to the debate on new rents legislation, concentrating on the important question of dwellings left empty by landlords.
Shinwell's speech was admired in the House of Commons and it dealt effectively with the minister responsible, Neville Chamberlain, but to little avail.[49]
He got more publicity a week later when he signed Wheatley's pledge not
to have dinner with Lady Astor to meet the Prince of Wales and to refuse
all similar invitations.

In 1923, to eighteen-year-old Lucy's disgust but the rest of the family's
excitement, Shinwell moved Fanny and the children to London, at first
to Forest Gate and then to Becontree in the Essex suburbs. No sooner had
he done so than his mother became ill in Glasgow and died after he had
rushed to her bedside in an isolation hospital, abandoning a constituency
meeting. She was just fifty-nine. Grief-stricken after Rose's funeral, Shinwell
returned to the parliamentary fray just in time for Baldwin, now Prime
Minister, to call a surprise election on tariff reform. An apathetic public
felt the election unnecessary and turned out in relatively small numbers.
In Linlithgowshire, Shinwell fought on the familiar issues of unemployment, the need to nationalise coal and shale oil and a capital levy for the

rich to pay off the war debt. He increased his majority by one thousand on a smaller turnout than 1922.

With one hundred and ninety-one seats, and backed by the Liberals, Labour formed the new government. Shinwell was to be Minister of Mines in the first British Labour government. Jamie Lamond, his agent, a fireman and amateur poet, sent him a verse from Matthew Arnold:

Thundering and bursting
In torrents, in waves –
Carolling and shouting
Over tombs, amid graves –
See! on the cumber'd plain
Clearing a stage,
Scattering the past about,
Comes the new age.

CHAPTER 9

In the Shadow of Ramsay MacDonald

Shinwell was handicapped as Minister of Mines by his two bosses. Prime Minister Ramsay MacDonald was openly doubtful about Shinwell's ability but reluctantly gave him a chance on the strength of his loyalty and his affinity with the Clyde Group on the powerful left of the ILP. Both the Clyde Group and the ILP were heavily underrepresented in the new Cabinet and the junior appointments would have to compensate.[1] Shinwell's immediate boss was Sidney Webb, President of the Board of Trade, a job not as important as the great Fabian would have liked, made up, he claimed, 'of many bits and pieces'. On the one hand, Webb distanced himself from Shinwell's negotiations to avoid a miners' strike and attempts at legislation in case they failed, but on the other hand he resented Shinwell's 'empire-building' and 'failure to consult'.[2]

On top of this unpromising set-up came the complaints of the miners. One of the miners' MPs, James Wilson, wrote personally to the Prime minister to complain:

> Your selection for the Mines Department is bound to, and has already, led to some heartbreaking. No one appreciates Mr Shinwell's abilities more than I … but it has revolted the miners to place a man in that position who knows nothing about the industry. That has been our chief complaint for years against Liberal and Conservative administrations: that they selected men for that work, who knew nothing of our industry. With the coming of Labour to office, it was expected that we'd be able to get an intelligent discussion on mining questions, with the Chief of the Department, instead of listening to permanent officials speaking through the figurehead of the government. For years we've kept this before our men in the coalfield, and I must say that I am disappointed at the selection you have made; for it will create indignation among what I always feel, is that section of the movement that forms its real back-bone, the miners. Shinwell's abilities could have been utilised in other directions.

MacDonald simply replied: 'I feel quite sure that Shinwell will justify himself at the Ministry of Mines. If he does not, we shall have to make a change.'[3]

Even the commissionaire at the Board of Trade refused to let him in, soaked by a sudden shower, to take up his new position. Webb himself had to make the identification. Still, an engine-driver was Colonial Secretary, a foundry-hand was Foreign Secretary, a weaver's son was Chancellor of the Exchequer, a miner was Minister of War and Manny Shinwell was Minister of Mines.[4] Labour had one hundred and ninety-one MPs compared with the Conservatives' two hundred and fifty-nine and the Liberals' one hundred and fifty-nine, and Labour now had to prove it could govern the country.

For a few weeks a Lib–Lab pact had seemed possible. Asquith made overtures for the Liberals, but they came to nothing. MacDonald was determined to show Labour could rule just as naturally as the other two parties. To do so he had to perform a delicate balancing act between ensuring Liberal or Conservative support for government legislation and avoiding the alienation of the Clyde left. Most of the left would have preferred more obvious socialism followed by a quick appeal to the country if necessary. Whatever his instinctive feelings, Shinwell's strong and increasing devotion to MacDonald (an 'orator of natural magnetism and impeccable technique' with 'incomparable international prestige', 'the most handsome man I have ever known … his face and bearing can best be described as 'princely'), stopped him even thinking of rebelling. Although Shinwell admitted MacDonald's powers had now deteriorated due to overwork, he still considered him capable of greatness and worthy of the trust of his followers.[5]

Shinwell found he wanted desperately to please MacDonald. He echoed his views in his speeches. He insisted that a whole list of institutions, the defence of the State, the continuation of the Empire and the parliamentary constitution were national interests and also legitimate interests of a working-class party. Capitalism was indeed the cause of Britain's problems but the gradual and democratic introduction of socialism was the cure. As MacDonald put it at the Albert Hall rally following his appointment as Prime Minister:

> We are a Party that, away in the dreamland of imagination, dwells in a social organisation fairer and more perfect than any organisation that mankind has ever known. That is true, but we are not to jump there. We are going to walk there.[6]

The view of the *Patriotic Magazine* that the Party of Revolution now had 'their hands to the helm of the State' putting the 'war of classes above the safety of the Empire'[7] was obvious nonsense, as MacDonald appointed some

Liberals and even Conservatives to his government. Shinwell may have had his doubts about the detail but had no doubt at all that the task of the government, as MacDonald had said, was to put on a good show and to make Labour a natural home for the four and a quarter million who had just voted Liberal, to win a majority in a future House of Commons. The faithful had nowhere else to go and the revolutionary alternative had faded into insignificance. Constitutional power for socialism would involve a long process of persuasion starting with this minority Labour government.

The split between the government and the left wing, which the Liberals had banked on bringing down the government, never came. MacDonald's appointment of Wheatley to the Ministry of Health (which at that time also included Housing) was a diplomatic master-stroke, albeit after the blunder of first offering him a junior post which he turned down. Wheatley's Housing Act was a major achievement which gave councils the financial backing to build cheap but acceptable houses. And there were specific projects, such as the diplomatic recognition of the Soviet Union and an attempt to diminish the landlord's right to evict unemployed tenants, which appealed strongly to the left.

Shinwell also played a part in appeasing the left. Except among the miners – or at least the miners' MPs – his appointment itself was welcomed, but more important was the question of nationalising the mines. Shinwell's position on this, more than anything else, helped him to gain the confidence of the fast-rising star of the left, Arthur Cook, the new Secretary of the Miners' Federation of Great Britain.

Cook was a preacher as well as a union leader, imprisoned twice during strikes in South Wales, he was an agitator with a gift for revivalist oratory. Shinwell won praise from him by arranging for a miners' MP to introduce a symbolic Bill to nationalise the mines, which the government then supported. This was a long-standing key aim of the Miners' Federation.[8] It would not be a government Bill – the government would not survive or fall on it – but it would have the government's weight behind it. The Bill was flawed and quite easily attacked by the opposition parties, but it gave Shinwell a chance to make all the right noises:

> It is equitable, wise and judicious in the interests of the nation to own both the minerals and the machinery which brings the minerals to the surface. Members who are more intimately acquainted with those who derive the greater part of their large incomes from mining royalties must face the facts. The principle cannot be ignored. Sooner or later it will be accepted by the nation as a whole.

One of the flaws in the Bill was the idea of running the industry through a managing board dominated by the Miners' Federation's nominees.

Shinwell reached an understanding with Cook on the make-up of this Board before the Second Reading debate:

> There is no proposal for a great State Department running the industry. Our nationalisation proposals involve the establishment of a body scientific, technical, able, efficient, a body not of amateurs, not of those who have never been associated with the industry, but through people who, because of their knowledge of the industry, are capable of administering it.

He went on to argue that nationalisation would mean streamlining. The cost of having lots of small firms in the industry was pushing up the price of coal and holding back development. In his peroration, Shinwell expanded the three basic principles which would carry him through to the actual achievement of nationalisation nearly a quarter of a century later. An industry 'vital to our national life' should 'not remain in private hands'; 'fullest use of our national resources' can only be secured by 'such co-ordination of ability and energy as the whole community, operating in a collective capacity, can provide'; and 'the workers' maximum efficiency cannot be expressed without the incentive which is based on true partnership in industry'.[9]

The Bill was lost, opposed by Liberals and Conservatives, but it went down in a blaze of glory. For Shinwell there were plaudits from Maxton and the left and from the miners' MPs whose confidence he was winning.

The commitment to nationalisation went hand in hand with such visible improvements as could be brought about by a minister for an industry in private hands. Safety regulations were tightened. He increased the size of his inspectorate and tightened regulations on water levels and winding gear. At the same time he set up inquiries into the costs of distribution with a view to lowering the price of coal in London and he also set up an enquiry into the apportionment of liability in cases of negligence. Legislation to introduce compulsory pit-head baths failed only because it ran out of time.[10] He eagerly brought all this to the attention of the Prime Minister who would send back a stream of notes back saying well done. MacDonald clearly realised Shinwell needed a good deal of patting on the back.

Shinwell also made a good impression through regular visits to pits all over the country, occasionally addressing groups of miners with Cook or other Miners' Federation officials. It was on these trips that he started to take an interest in pit ponies. He was horrified by the ponies' cruel treatment – '63,000 dumb animals: like human beings, they vary enormously in their powers of work, their intelligence and in the length of their working life, all of which should be taken into account.'[11] He drafted regulations himself to make it a specific responsibility of sub-inspectors to check the working conditions, the harnesses and the general health of pit ponies, and to ensure as far as possible that those with greasy heels, broken wind and other ailments were 'rescued from their hard labours'.

This set him up well with the middle-class National Equine Defence League and other animal protection charities. It was new ground and Shinwell started to feel quite strongly about it. On one occasion, at a mine near Coventry, he infuriated local officials, from the owners and the union alike, by showing a noticeable interest only in the ponies. For the next visit, just down the road, he had told his officials in the ministry to arrange for a photographer to be at the mine. The officials in their best outfits duly lined up with Shinwell and had their photograph taken. Then they watched in amazement as the Minister for Mines had another photograph taken with his arms round the necks of two ponies. He asked the pit manager their names and was annoyed when the the manager replied that he didn't know if they had names at all. The boy who drove them revealed that they had quite distinct (rather bad-tempered) personalities and were in fact called Millicent and Pertwee. Needless to say, the photograph released the next day to the *Daily Herald* was of Shinwell with Millicent and Pertwee.[12] Ultimately, this interest in the fauna of mining led to a dispute with Noel Buxton, Minister of Agriculture. But, as in all the other important details, especially the health and safety of the mine, Shinwell left a considerable improvement at the end of his productive ten and a half months in office.

Less straightforward was the overriding need to avoid a miners' strike. It was never going to be easy. Shinwell had inherited a crisis and needed to find a settlement which satisfied the miners and which the owners could realistically afford to pay. He was lucky: the situation in the Ruhr offered him a chance of success.

It so happened that the victorious allies had fallen out over reparations from Germany at the end of 1922. In the previous year, the allies had jointly agreed some revisions of the Versailles Treaty which included reparations in the form of Ruhr coal payable to France, Belgium and Italy, instead of money. Unfortunately, this glutted the market, leaving spare stocks of British coal. On 18 January 1923 the Reparations Commission, by a majority vote, stopped the coal reparations. On 23 January, Belgian and French troops occupied the Ruhr, reversed the commission's decision by force and started to take back the coal. The Ruhr miners then went on strike, along with millions of other German industrial workers. With industrial production severely reduced, Germany was soon hit by hyperinflation. However, just as Shinwell came to office, with the Ruhr out of production there was a booming export opportunity for British coal.

The miners saw their opportunity. On the day the Labour government took office, the Miners' Federation told the owners they wanted a substantial rise. The owners were reluctant to make any offer on the strength of what they considered to be windfall profits arising from a temporary situation. Shinwell claimed later that he had bluffed the owners with threats of unspecified drastic measures,[13] but it is unlikely that they were so naïve. On the contrary, the 13 per cent on miners' basic wages which Shinwell finally got both sides to agree to, actually worked out at an increase of little more than 2 per cent on the average earned each shift. Nevertheless, there were a number of adjustments to help the low-paid which contrasted with Noel Buxton's neglect, much criticised by the left, when dealing with agricultural wages a few months later. Shinwell tried to intervene but merely got a retort that, as with pit ponies' welfare, he was interfering where he did not belong. He wanted no trouble and he did not press the point.[14]

Indeed, throughout the first Labour government, Shinwell was in the business of keeping in with government leaders. He was even received by King George V. Fortunately he was not required to wear court dress, a great relief since MacDonald was very particular about ministers obeying the rules of dress. In fact, the first thing that Shinwell asked his civil servants when MacDonald told him the King wanted to see him was what should he wear. They went to see the Lord Chamberlain and came back with the answer, 'black clothes'. Shinwell had no black clothes and the civil servants advised him to hire them: 'Hired clothes! I have had trouble in my time but I've never needed to hire clothes.' After considerable negotiations, they agreed on a dark lounge suit. Shinwell walked down Buckingham Palace and said to the policeman on duty: 'I've come to see the King.' After a hurried telephone call, an equerry showed him in and the King shook his hand. He started booming '*Daily Mail* stuff' about strikes and the seamen, nothing to do with the mines. Shinwell got only one or two words in at the end and complained when he got home that he was never even offered a cup of tea or a cigarette. He realised that all he was expected to do was listen.[15]

Respectability was a very important aspect of the 1924 government. Shinwell always considered that MacDonald revelled in it, which may have been true, but at the same time he considered it necessary. Labour, in MacDonald's opinion, had to be seen to be doing what the public expected from its government, and arguing about petty matters such as the correct dress for the occasion was a foolish way to use up public sympathy. Only once did Shinwell rebel on the issue of clothes. Invited to dine with the Speaker, he drew the line at court dress and finally, to MacDonald's indignation, compromised with a dinner jacket. Fanny bought him a second-hand one which was too short in the arms and showed all his cuffs:

> To us, a formal and pleasurable opportunity to meet colleagues and opponents 'off duty' was turned into a hilariously comic occasion by the sight of our fellow ministers. Ramsay MacDonald stood looking very

nautical in a blue uniform which I believe had something to do with
the cinque ports. He at least was tall enough to wear his shining sword
with some semblance of fitness. Unfortunately he was standing next to
the small and rotund Stephen Walsh, Minister for War, whose weapon
touched the floor and continually got between his legs. Tom Shaw
(Minister of Labour) was doing his best to look as if the breeches and
stockings of court dress were his normal attire, but he was extremely
self-conscious. Not so Sidney Webb who was entirely oblivious of the
ridiculous appearance he presented with spindly legs and a short little
body. It was perhaps very childish to burst into guffaws.[16]

Fanny was content to stay out of the way much of the time with her
two younger children, although she would never have put up with the
patronising way that Wheatley deprived his wife of the right to move from
Glasgow, saying. 'She is a very quiet domesticated working-class woman
and I doubt whether she will feel equal to social life in London.'[17] Fanny
certainly had little interest in Beatrice Webb's well-meaning semi-intel-
lectual picnics arranged for ministers' wives, the Half-Circle Club, although
she enjoyed occasional dinners with the Webbs, as well as the Haldanes
and the Snowdens. The Snowdens spent much of the time talking down
MacDonald, but the other two Fanny enjoyed 'in a social way'.[18]

Shinwell took care to keep in with MacDonald, meeting up with him
whenever he could, but MacDonald was overworking, sowing the seeds
of his own destruction and that of his government.

One Glasgow socialist who had chosen a revolutionary path was the editor
of the communist *Workers' Weekly*, the ebullient J.R. Campbell. A good
journalist in search of improved circulation figures, he published an article
on 25 July, just before the House of Commons was due to go into recess,
directly appealing to soldiers in the British Army – he had been a war-
hero himself – to mutiny if called upon to fire on fellow workers. The
abstract idea that soldiers and sailors would not fire to put down strikers
or revolutionaries was common enough, but such a direct appeal was
unusual, so Patrick Hastings, MacDonald's Attorney-General, decided to
prosecute Campbell under the 1795 Incitement to Mutiny Act.

Shinwell had just answered questions on mines in Board of Trade
questions in the House of Commons, when Hastings made his statement
that he intended to prosecute. The line-up on the front bench was
MacDonald, Webb, Shinwell, then Hastings.

Remembering his own speeches five years earlier in George Square,
Shinwell winced when George Buchanan, one of the Clyde Group,
shouted from behind him that 'the article expressed opinions held by
several members of the Front Bench ... if MPs were to be prosecuted for

expressing the same views, half the Labour members would be in prison.'[19] MacDonald looked like thunder; the flabbergasted Hastings whined softly in Shinwell's ear that he had anyway been 'unhappy to take the advice to prosecute'. Shinwell agreed that it was 'obviously politically inept, even if it was legally right' and whispered back to Hastings, unhelpfully, that he was a 'typical lawyer – people like you never get on very well in politics'.[20]

That evening, MacDonald ordered the prosecution to be withdrawn, but in doing so he left himself wide open to the accusation of being a prisoner of the left, especially of the Red Clydesiders. Asquith, furious about the lack of Labour support for the Liberals' Proportional Representation Bill, demanded that a Select Committee to look into the Campbell case should be set up as soon as possible after the House of Commons had reassembled in the autumn. It was a good political move because it kept the debate going through the summer, giving Buchanan, Kirkwood and Maxton repeated chances to make the same hustings-style speeches about the use of troops in industrial disputes and the importance of strikes.

Shinwell, who had been summoned in early August to see MacDonald at 10 Downing Street to discuss mines legislation, found the Prime Minister actually wanting to talk about the sniping from the back benches. 'I can't stand it any longer. Not from old colleagues.' Shinwell suggested that he play the whole thing down, go along with a Select Committee and ignore dramatic speeches from his old enemies on the left. 'Don't bother about it,' he advised.[21] MacDonald ignored Shinwell's advice and acted on Snowden's, opposing the Select Committee. The House of Commons decided against him by 364 to 198. MacDonald went straight to the King and told him the government had fallen.

The general election campaign that followed was one of the hardest and most vigorous MacDonald had fought. His motorcade took him to over a hundred constituencies, including Shinwell's, where he stressed the main theme of the first Labour government, indeed the main point of the first Labour government, Labour's fitness to govern: 'the extraordinary phenomenon of a Labour government that has met Kings and rulers of the earth, that has sat by them, that has conducted itself with distinction and with dignity.'[22]

It was 24 October, five days before election day, when MacDonald made that speech. It was also the day the Foreign Office published, without first checking its authenticity, as MacDonald had demanded, the Zinoviev Letter. This letter, almost certainly a forgery, purported to come from the Communist Third International to the British Communist Party Central Committee urging them to do everything possible to expedite the loan and treaties which MacDonald had been trying to arrange with the Soviet government, while at the same time exposing the true capitalist nature of the Labour Party. MacDonald gave it too much credibility by attacking the civil servants at the Foreign Office for publishing it and at the same time himself denouncing it in the strongest terms.

The *Linlithgowshire Gazette* talked of the 'Communist Bombshell' which had hit Shinwell's campaign.[23] But the true bombshell in Shinwell's case, as in many others', was that there was no Liberal candidate. The *Linlithgowshire Gazette* had anyway always confused Labour with communism, rowdiness with revolution: 'The display of Party fervour was marred by vulgar Socialist protests', it reported, 'in which several Conservative supporters were dipped in a muddy ditch at the village of Carriden.'[24]

James Kidd's Conservative campaign was well organised by his formidable lawyer daughter, Margaret, with many cars, buses and lorries to take supporters to the polls, the first election in which these had featured. As a local paper put it: 'on a day of rain and deluge, Labour had too few mechanical lifts for their supporters.'[25]

Along with his new friend, Herbert Morrison, and other ministers including the first woman minister, Margaret Bondfield, Shinwell lost in Linlithgowshire:

James Kidd (Conservative)   14,765 (51%)
Emanuel Shinwell (Labour)   14,123 (49%)

Majority   642

It was agonisingly close. What next for Manny Shinwell?

In the election, Labour increased its vote by over a million but the Conservatives gained two and a half million. Above all, it was a terminal Liberal defeat with Asquith at Paisley among the casualties. The red scare no doubt played a part in persuading Liberals who were deserting anyway to switch to Conservative rather than Labour.

Shinwell immediately began writing a testament to his time at the Ministry of Mines which he gave as a speech to the ILP 1925 annual conference and then published. He claimed it was a blueprint for nationalisation; it was not, but he did put some flesh on the generalities he had used in welcoming the nationalisation Bill a year before. He would set up a Coal Council, answerable to Parliament, consisting of miners, technical experts and consumers; it was to have considerable powers, moving whole communities when pits had to close and setting up new industries to convert coal to oil and chemicals. He did not say how all this would be paid for. What he did say, more controversially as far as the ILP was concerned, was that mine-owners should be bought out generously to stop them sabotaging their pits in the run-up to nationalisation 'vesting' day.

Whatever they thought of this apparent shift to the right of the former revolutionary, the ILP also lost no time in re-adopting him as candidate in Linlithgowshire. MacDonald was doubtful about his re-adoption, hoping to get him in at an earlier by-election: 'You were doing so well and there were such fine opportunities for you in the Opposition. I hope that the Party will be more alive than it has been up to now, in taking steps to get essential men back.'[26]

Philip Snowden wrote to Shinwell in a similar vein: 'Your loss to the Parliamentary Labour Party is irreparable and the serious aspect is that I see no immediate prospect of your return. But I do hope some accident will soon bring you back again.' He was also still unable to resist a jibe at MacDonald: 'This General Election ... only throws into great prominence the magnificent opportunities we have wantonly and recklessly thrown away by the most incompetent political leadership which ever brought a government to disaster.'[27] Shinwell was certainly not persuaded that Snowden could have done any better, and he remained a loyal MacDonald man.

Shinwell had to ignore the bickering at the top of the Labour Party to lead his union's serious struggle to survive. The British Seafarers had joined up with the Cooks' and Stewards' Union led by Joe Cotter to create the Amalgamated Marine Workers' Union in 1920. It had infuriated Havelock Wilson because this let the Seafarers into the TUC indirectly, since the Cooks and Stewards were already members. Cotter became president of the Amalgamated Marine Workers and, as soon as Shinwell applied after losing his seat, he became the national organiser.

Between 1920 and 1924, Wilson had severely damaged the Amalgamated Marine Workers. He had persuaded his own members to accept a series of pay cuts to help the employers through a difficult time. In return, the employers joined with him to exclude the Amalgamated Marine Workers' Union from the crucial Maritime Board which decided who could and who could not serve on board a ship. The board had created a form called a PC5 which a recognised union – in this case only Wilson's Sailors and Firemen – had to sign before employment on board ship could be offered. Apart from in Southampton, where they were very strong and could override the PC5 requirement, the Marine Workers lost out heavily by being excluded.[28]

A further and nearly fatal blow for the Marine Workers occurred when Cotter, in response to a bribe by Wilson, decided to defect to the Sailors and Firemen within days of Shinwell starting as national organiser. Wilson was delighted. 'The Jew's finished before he can start again,' he told Tupper in 1925, 'but he may not give up without spilling blood.'[29]

Shinwell made straight for the heart of the enemy, Liverpool docks, where the PC5 system had just about destroyed his union, and announced he was spending six weeks there. He was going to raise hell. It went wrong from the start.

As soon as he arrived in Liverpool, he heard that Cotter in London had announced the dissolution of the Marine Workers' Union. Of course he had no such right, but Wilson had made it a quid pro quo that, if Cotter were to be given a well-paid sinecure (his bribe) in the Sailors' and Firemen's Union, he would have at least to disrupt the union he was leaving, and if possible destroy it. Among other things, there were suddenly no more salary cheques since Cotter, who had never technically resigned as president of the Marine Workers, had to sign them, and an advertisement appeared offering Shinwell's Lower Street office 'to let'. Mad with rage, Shinwell had to spend his first week in Liverpool righting this situation as best he could by telegram and telephone, including arranging for his own wages to be paid.

The only local official of the Marine Workers known to Shinwell was a certain Ben Mollan who had apparently refused to defect with Cotter, although he was a steward. Unknown to Shinwell, however, assisted by a dwarf called Kirtley Green, he was also acting as Cotter's agent and secretly circulated a letter in Cotter's name telling seamen that the Marine Workers had now become part of the Sailors' and Firemen's Union. Without realising Mollan's double role, Shinwell started on one of his energetic rounds of practical negotiations that had made him such a successful trade unionist in Glasgow.

He took one case at a time, starting with Coast Line Steamers and then moving on to White Star's *SS Lancastria*. For each ship, he got together a group of men, negotiated individually pay and conditions based on national agreements but tailor-made for the particular circumstances of the next voyage. He then had to arrange locally for his signature on a PC5 to be sufficient. Mollan and Green seemed to be willing accomplices in this fight-back, but actually Mollan was cabling to Wilson each night the alarming news of Shinwell's increasing popularity and success.

Wilson thought of confronting Shinwell personally, but settled for bribery instead: 'either way, we must never allow it to be said that we were beaten by a Scottish Jew.' He told Mollan to go slow on collecting sub-scriptions from the men, to allow another official, William Hales, enough time to offer them completely free membership of the Sailors' and Firemen's Union and free admission – normally there was a ten-shilling fee – to the Maritime Board scheme. It finally dawned on Shinwell at the end of nearly two weeks of exhausting negotiations with ship-owners that something was wrong with his team. Hales cabled the following report of Shinwell's last meeting in Liverpool:

In the evening a special meeting of officials was held which amounted
to a cross-examination by Shinwell. First he started on Mollan. Shinwell
asked him why it was that he was only able to take so little money. Mollan
replied by asking the same question back. Shinwell was wild – said 'look
here, Mollan, I haven't come down here to take off my coat to fight,
but if that becomes necessary I shall do so.' Mollan replied that he didn't
care if he took his shirt off. Hot words followed and Mollan told Shinwell
that he didn't give a —— for any of them from the highest to the lowest
and that they could do what they liked. Green was the next victim.
Shinwell asked him if he thought it useless to carry on in Liverpool. Green
replied that he did and he didn't. Shinwell pressed the question and Green
said he did not wish to comment any further. Murray, another part-timer
whose takings last week were 9d, was next. He said he couldn't take
money out of men's pockets and the men were fed up to the hilt now
that the scheme for amalgamation had fallen through. Shinwell then sacked
each official saying it was hopeless to carry on. Then he made a violent
attack on me. Said I was a worthless fellow ... a danger to be avoided
by all officials. He said he would give me the biggest chewing up I'd
ever had in my life.[30]

Shinwell abandoned Liverpool to its fate. Wilson had wanted to torment
him further by getting more of Cotter's supporters to a public meeting he
had planned. He quickly found urgent legal business in London leaving
only Green behind. A few weeks later he heard that 'the dwarf Green has
gone on the beer and has not been sober since a week last Tuesday'.[31]

Almost as soon as Wilson was back in London, the TUC stepped in to
encourage the 'amalgamation' of Marine Workers with the Sailors and
Firemen, realistically a takeover, which Shinwell had been trying desperately to resist. Ernest Bevin, in particular, hated internecine divisions
between unions and arranged for Fred Bramley, General Secretary of the
TUC, to call on Shinwell and offer him and his two general secretaries a
thousand pounds each (later, it turned out, put up by Wilson) to get out
and allow amalgamation to go ahead.

Shinwell was indignant. He told Bramley: 'you're asking me to take a
thousand pounds to give up my principles and resign from the union. Is
that what you call trade unionism?'[32] Shinwell of course refused, but one
of the general secretaries accepted. The Amalgamated Marine Workers'
Union was being chipped away.

In July 1925, the Sailors' and Firemen's Union agreed to a further cut
in seamen's wages of a pound a month. A number of men refused to sign
on at the Maritime Board offices and ships were delayed. An outcry in
Liverpool led to the men making the whole PC5 system there inoperable,
but there was little the Marine Workers could do to take advantage because

legal action by Cotter had again blocked the use of their funds. Green was still drunk, and by the time Shinwell got to Liverpool, paying for himself, he found a new alternative registration scheme had been set up which still excluded his union.

He decided that the best thing to do would be to call a strike of the Marine Workers against the pay cut, once the proper groundwork had been laid. He arranged for one of his general secretaries, Arthur Cannon, to send telegrams to seamen abroad somewhat exaggerating the militancy at home. Wilson was livid, this time with some justification. He complained to the international seamen's organisation:

> Lying and misleading cablegrams were sent by Arthur Cannon informing the men on the ships in South Africa that the whole of the seamen of Great Britain were on strike. Similar cables were sent to Australia and New Zealand, and one cable even went so far as to state that the dockers, shipyard men and others had joined the fight.[33]

Shinwell then waited a month before calling his members out, telling them in turn great news about strike action across the Empire. Southampton came to a standstill but few ships from any other port were affected. Attempts at getting financial support for the men on strike also landed Shinwell in difficulties:

> They issued an appeal for the women and children and had collecting boxes out everywhere, but only a very mild attempt has been made to account for the collection as will be seen in the January issue of the *Marine Worker*. This only deals with Southampton whilst all the other districts are ignored. The unofficial Strike Committee have failed to publish a balance sheet of what they have done with the money they collected, which will have a very detrimental effect on any future appeals.[34]

In the middle of all this came the September annual conference of the TUC, and Scarborough soon resounded to the arguments. Shinwell acutely embarrassed Bevin and Bramley by mentioning the thousand pounds bribe in his speech, which moved Bevin to call him a 'bloody fool of an oriental' as he pushed past him in the lobby outside the conference hall.[35] The TUC decided to leave the Marine Workers to die a natural death. Shinwell himself had already quietly decided there was no future in it and had applied unsuccessfully to be general secretary of the National Union of Corporation Workers.

As it happened, the impending General Strike gained the Marine Workers' Union a stay of execution. They supported the miners and the General Strike while Wilson actually gave money to a breakaway union from the Miners' Federation and opposed the TUC.

Since he left office, Shinwell had kept in close touch with Arthur Cook. They had even toured parts of Scotland together and it was Cook who persuaded Shinwell of the rightness of the miners' cause. Cook's oratory made even Shinwell look pedestrian, and the miners and their families loved him, sometimes even leaning forward to touch his clothes as if he was a passing Messiah. Nevertheless, Shinwell recognised, along with MacDonald and the rest of the political leadership, that feelings of injustice, righteousness and hatred for capitalists who owned coalmines, along with a willingness to die at the last ditch, needed a good deal of organisation if they were to become an effective policy.[36]

The dramatic leadership of the miners coincided with a move to the left on the council of the TUC and the consequent threat of a general strike when the coal-owners wanted to reduce pay and lengthen hours in August 1925. 'Not a penny off the pay, not a minute off the day,' was the familiar cry. Prime Minister Baldwin was so concerned that he agreed to subsidise miners' pay for nine months until a commission, headed by Sir Herbert Samuel, reported. It was time well spent by the government in planning and building up coal stocks. The TUC, by contrast, did no planning at all. When the commission reported it predictably recommended a wage cut and, at the end of April 1926, negotiations broke down. The General Strike began at 11.59 p.m. on 3 May and collapsed nine days later.

As a Labour politician, Shinwell was annoyed by the way the Labour Party had been taken for granted by Cook and the miners. He sympathised with MacDonald's misgivings. But he also worked hard for the nine days the strike lasted to keep the London docks idle. The Amalgamated Marine Workers' Union strongly supported the strike. Havelock Wilson spoke against it, and his Sailors and Firemen were suspended from the TUC, leaving Shinwell's union as the sole representative of the seamen.

By now, though, the Amalgamated Marine Workers could not survive. A series of injunctions from infiltrators funded by Cotter and Wilson prevented access to funds for long periods. Shinwell was paid for only seven months in 1927. In the spring and summer, increasingly gloomy, Shinwell toured all the main ports and came to the conclusion that there was no alternative but to wind up the union. On this tour alone, he was prosecuted in both Bridgend and Hull for assaults on various officials of the Sailors' and Firemen's Union; in Hull he demolished a door by throwing William Hales right through it, and in Bridgend he was charged for obstructing the police:

It was stated by a police witness that Mr Shinwell was standing on a chair and addressing a crowd of about a hundred. The policeman elbowed his way to the front and asked him if he had permission to hold the meeting. Mr Shinwell replied, 'I have no permission; I am not causing any obstruction, and I won't move for any policeman.' He then proceeded to lead the crowd in the singing of the Red Flag.[37]

These were desperate times.

In October the Amalgamated Marine Workers' Union ceased to exist and Shinwell was without a job. Ironically, the following year, Wilson's new single seamen's union was finally expelled from the TUC and Bevin's Transport and General Workers' Union set up branches for recruiting seamen.

In 1926 Lucy was twenty-one and she received a piano from her parents. They held a big party and the Shinwell family seemed remarkably normal and happy considering the stresses and strains of Manny's long absences and the move from the family home in Glasgow.

Lucy turned down Manny's offer of a pound a week to be his secretary, an offer he had been saving up as a wonderful surprise. Encouraged by one of Manny's younger sisters, Julia, whom Manny never quite forgave, she got a job helping to design fashionable clothes in Knightsbridge. At the same time, Rose at thirteen was sarcastic with Fanny and doted on by Manny; she would slam doors and refuse to kiss the people she was supposed to kiss – in fact, she was a normal thirteen-year-old girl.

Manny was always fastidious about making sure the children were clean and well-dressed and none of them showed any signs of being anything other than relatively well-off, normal, working-class children. Manny being a government minister had not affected them very much, since by the time they had arrived and resettled he was again a union organiser on a low wage, as he had been in Glasgow. When he got back into Parliament in 1928, it was as much a financial relief as a political one.[38]

As far as the left was concerned, Shinwell had done well in 1926, supporting the General Strike, opposing Havelock Wilson and speaking for the miners. Like David Kirkwood, he got into trouble under the Emergency Powers Act which prevented 'inflammatory' political meetings in mining areas but, unlike Kirkwood who carried his political case to court, Shinwell got off with a caution.

James Maxton was now Chairman of the ILP. He had been out of action throughout most of 1926, including the General Strike, because of illness, but by 1927 he was back on top form, encouraging Shinwell's re-election to the National Administrative Committee of the ILP as a valuable link between the MacDonald leadership of the Parliamentary Labour Party and the left-wing Clyde-dominated ILP. More than this, even out of Parliament, Shinwell would be a reassuring figure for the eighty or so nominally ILP

MPs who never bothered with the ILP because they saw it as too far to the left under Maxton's leadership.

Accordingly, Maxton was neither surprised nor irritated when Shinwell described MacDonald to the ILP's 1926 conference, as 'a giant who deserves the support of the whole nation, a socialist who shares and shapes our vision of the new age'. It was all peroration, one of Shinwell's poorest conference speeches. He was immediately upstaged by the young Jennie Lee:

> A young dark girl took the rostrum, a puckish figure with a mop of thick black hair thrown impatiently aside, brown eyes flashing, body and arms moving in rapid gestures, words pouring from her mouth in a Scottish accent and vigorous phrases, sometimes with a sarcasm which equalled Shinwell's. It was Jennie Lee making her first speech at an ILP Conference. And what a speech it was! Shinwell was regarded as a Goliath in debate, but he met his match in this girl David.[39]

There was not really a great deal of distance between Shinwell's and Maxton's views of what a majority Labour government should do. Both included higher working-class wages to create economic demand and greater involvement of the government in the economy through planning and nationalisation. The difference was in the framework: Maxton saw politics in the context of an uncompromising class party in a hurry to achieve proletarian power for 'Socialism in our Time'. It was a difference of more than rhetoric; it affected the view taken by left politicians of their very role, especially in a minority government.

Was it really possible to use all the paraphernalia of private ownership of capital, the House of Lords, the courts, the Empire and so on without being inveigled into loving them? Maxton thought not, and cited the first MacDonald government as evidence. Shinwell thought it the only practical and electorally possible way to work. He felt that advocating the removal of cherished institutions was the sure way to electoral defeat, just when the party looked like a real party of government, and he was hungry for office.

The idea of a link, as envisaged by Maxton, between these two points of view was naïve. Shinwell certainly never fulfilled that role. Instead, by hard work, regular attendance and careful advance preparation for meetings, Shinwell – with Oswald Mosley – simply strengthened the minority of MacDonald supporters on the National Administrative Committee.

The MacDonaldites' plan for each meeting was to try to use the agenda to concentrate on areas of agreement with the official policy being developed for the 1929 election. But in the end they were still in the minority and there was less and less compromise with official Labour policy. Instead, the Cook–Maxton manifesto, a document widely promoted in the ILP in 1928, insisted that 'the Labour Party should scrap its existing programme and develop a vigorous socialist programme'. MacDonald urged Shinwell to stay on the National Administrative Committee, although it was beginning to lose its relevance and power in the Labour movement. The organised use of union block votes at the party's annual conference and the increasing political sophistication of Labour MPs were pushing the ILP into history.

At the 1928 Labour Party Conference, the ILP line was soundly defeated. A reformist statement, 'Labour and the Nation', was passed by a huge majority. Shinwell expressed the hope that Maxton, his 'dear and extravagant friend' – he was the most likeable of men with no personal enemies – 'may not put me in difficulty in my constituency'.[40]

Shinwell won back Linlithgowshire in a by-election in 1928. James Kidd had died suddenly, and his daughter Margaret became Shinwell's opponent. This time there was also a Liberal, Douglas Young, whose only policy seemed to be to say how dangerous Shinwell was, a theme followed enthusiastically by Lloyd George on a campaigning visit. This line soon began to sound defensive and ineffective.

Following Lloyd George's speech, the Liberal candidate got into such a muddle over the Liberal policy of nationalising mining royalties, but not mines, that he had to be rescued by Lloyd George himself.[41] It created a very poor impression in a constituency where two coalmines and five shale oil mines had closed in the previous twelve months.[42] It was an impossible task to defend the government under such circumstances, and Miss Kidd proved to be a much less effective candidate than she had been organiser in a previous election. She found it impossible to defend effectively the Mines Eight Hours Act, increasing the number of hours miners would have to work, and even her admirers were reduced to reporting: 'And then Miss Kidd began to speak, her eyes shining brightly and her voice, contralto and musical, fell pleasantly upon the ear.'[43]

Only Shinwell, and the speakers who supported him, including Philip Snowden, seemed to have positive ideas about training, social conditions, the future of the oil and coal industries and so on. He was duly elected.

Emanuel Shinwell (Labour)	14,446 (49%)	
Margaret Kidd (Conservative)	9,268 (32%)	
Douglas Young (Liberal)	5,690 (19%)	
Majority	5,178	

Shinwell carried on the persuasive practical Labour arguments of the late 1920s in Parliament. He became an advocate of the policies which ordinary people in ordinary jobs – or the unemployed – knew instinctively was right for them at the time. He spoke for a programme for the reconstruction of roads and railways, on training for the unemployed, on assistance for local authorities in difficulties, on land reclamation schemes, on programmes to alleviate the suffering of single unemployed young men in places like Bathgate and Bo'ness and Linlithgow and all the towns and villages where people like his constituents lived. He concluded his first major speech after his return to Parliament with the accusation 'that the government who are responsible for this distress, the government who are responsible for the continuance of the employment problem as we see it, ought themselves to be rendered unemployed'.[44]

They soon were. After an election where Shinwell increased his majority to a record 8,822 (52 per cent of the vote) in another three-cornered fight, Ramsay MacDonald was back in Downing Street.

CHAPTER 10

A Stiletto in the Back

As he came to the end of his speech to the Glasgow ILP, Shinwell knew he had done himself harm. Could a would-be Labour minister's career recover from an attack on the way the General Strike had been run? It was January 1927, seven months after the disaster. The strike leaders knew very well it had been a disaster and they hated to be reminded about it. Walter Citrine, General Secretary of the TUC, and Ernest Bevin, the Transport Workers' leader, took criticisms very personally. *The Times* headline 'Sickness of Trade Unionism: Mr Shinwell on the General Strike' was hardly likely to please. The text was worse:

> Although the General Council have whitewashed themselves, nothing can blind working people to the fact that they entered the General Strike without adequate preparation. They tried foolishly and obviously to bluff the government ... The General Council can never again be entrusted with the conduct of an industrial dispute.[1]

Coming a few months after Shinwell's public exposure of Bevin's involvement in an attempt to bribe him to abandon the Amalgamated Marine Workers' Union, the speech could most charitably be described as a bad career move.

Safely back in Parliament, Shinwell compounded his error eighteen months later by saying that the repeal of Conservative legislation against trade unions should be put well down the list of Labour legislation. Shinwell's explanation to MacDonald and Clynes, who were asked by Bevin to 'investigate' him with regard to his suitability as a Labour candidate, was that under a Labour government there would be no urgency for trade-union legislation because there would be no need for any strikes. MacDonald liked it, Bevin did not, muttering that it was his experience that there were often strikes under a Labour government. He made it very clear to MacDonald that, as far as the unions were concerned, Shinwell should not be in any Labour government.

Shinwell let rip at an ILP conference on democracy just a few weeks before the 1929 election: 'If you go into a fight you must prepare yourself for it. The TUC General Council did not. You must be prepared to carry it through. They were not.' It was a hard time for Shinwell, and his style and behaviour were becoming more consistently aggressive. He was 'a shrieking, vituperative, snarling figure' in the late 1920s, according to W.J. Brown of the Civil Service Union: 'He exuded a quality snake-like and cold, under the violence of his language, which at once impressed and repelled.'[2]

When the time came for forming a government, Shinwell stayed behind in his constituency taking a few days to share with Fanny the adulation of his supporters, rather than sitting back and watching his younger colleagues – Dalton undoubtedly, Attlee probably, Mosley certainly – join the government. But forty-eight hours passed and a letter came from Downing Street asking him to return to London at once.

At 10 Downing Street, MacDonald told him: 'I'm having trouble with you joining the Cabinet.' He explained about the unions' position, and Shinwell sulkily replied: 'Well, just don't bother about me.' He had originally hoped for the Admiralty – Jim Thomas had actually told him as much – but now there was evidently no chance of it. 'I was only talking about industrial democracy; I wasn't condemning them,' he told MacDonald, and provoked a surprisingly robust reaction: 'Oh, that's their attitude. They want to run the show. They want to run my show, but I'm going to have you in somewhere.'[3]

The next day, 'somewhere' seemed to Shinwell to be about as menial as you could get and still be in the government: Financial Secretary at the War Office. Meanwhile the other appointments were out. The old guard was back except for Shinwell's friend Haldane who had died in 1928; and among the new faces, as he feared, were Hugh Dalton, whom Shinwell considered to be an upper-class intellectual nonentity desperate for power, as Parliamentary Secretary at the Foreign Office under Henderson, and Wedgwood Benn, whom Shinwell considered to be a first-class opportunist, having ratted on the sinking Liberal Party only two years before, as Secretary of State for India. Among his friends, though, he was pleased to see Herbert Morrison as Minister of Transport. He had reservations about the appointment of Oswald Mosley, his ILP colleague, as Chancellor of the Duchy of Lancaster to help out Jim Thomas on unemployment policy. If he were to accept the post on offer, his boss would be the Secretary for War, Tom Shaw, an old friend of Shinwell's and a leader of the cotton-workers' union, who had been a moderately successful Minister of Labour in the 1924 government; he had also played quite an important part this time, along with Snowden and Webb, in drawing up plans for Labour in government.

Shinwell immediately turned down MacDonald's offer. His criticism of the TUC had, he accepted, blown up in his face. He told MacDonald frankly it had not been accidental, it had been a conscious expression of views which he knew were held, but could not possibly be given publicity, by MacDonald. At the time of the first outburst, he had been out of office and even off the National Administrative Council of the ILP. At that time, also, he was quite determined not to be out of mind. What better way could there be to stay on the political map than to seize the opportunity to play a role in a major debate, on the side of the man likely to be Prime Minister again, and to escape for a moment from the sordid death throes of the breakaway seamen's union?

MacDonald agreed that when Shinwell launched his first salvo in 1927, he was irritating but not important enough for the TUC to worry about. By 1929, though, at the time of his second outburst, he was a likely future Cabinet minister talking about legislation and standing for chairman of the ILP (albeit without much chance) against Maxton.

MacDonald made it very clear to Shinwell that he was not at all displeased with what he had said about trade-union legislation.[4] He may well have explained to Shinwell that a Cabinet post would have to wait, but was inevitable at the first reshuffle. What Shinwell had definitely not expected, though, was the offer of a post effectively junior, although technically at the same level, as the one he had held in 1924. It seemed frankly insulting. MacDonald pressed Shinwell to accept: 'Now, don't refuse an old friend, Manny. I want some people in the government on whom I can depend.'[5]

The two men finally agreed that Shinwell should consult with the leaders of the ILP meeting that afternoon at Westminster. Although it was much less influential than before, MacDonald still greatly preferred to have the support of the majority of the ILP as a counter-balance to the trade unions, and greatly regretted their move to what he considered the far left. For this he blamed Maxton; as he had written a few months earlier to Shinwell: 'Maxton's chairmanship is scandalous, but there is no lack of pure artfulness in him. Vanity unsupported by capacity for work is at the root of his trouble.'[6] Now was a chance for him and his closest supporter on the National Administrative Committee to split their opponents over MacDonald's offer. It was really only a minor issue but it worked.

Shinwell put the proposal that he should take the War Office post to the committee. Most were in favour, isolating Maxton who pleaded for a 'real fight'. No one else in the ILP had been offered any post in the government, not even Wheatley or Jowett who had both been in the 1924 Cabinet. Shinwell's acceptance threatened to split the already marginalised ILP. He didn't care. It held no interest for him now. It had little political power and he had failed to get into a strong enough position to change its political stance. In the event, the leadership of the ILP agreed by a majority that he should accept the post of Financial Secretary at the War Office.

Despite this shaky start, Shinwell and Shaw developed quite a productive working relationship. Specific commitments in Labour's manifesto, especially £12 million of improvements to unemployment benefit, combined with the generally accepted need, in those pre-Keynesian days, for a balanced budget, meant cuts in the army. This was the responsibility of the War Office. Shinwell and Shaw were entirely sympathetic although neither went anything like so far as some on the left who wanted to abolish the army altogether. Shinwell accused them of 'a bad attack of inverted national-ism', ignoring the needs of the international system; 'there will be no further cuts in the size of the Army without international agreement.'[7] Shaw put the government's position succinctly in the House of Commons: 'The government, who are wishing not merely to take part in international arrangements for drastic reductions in armaments, but to take the lead in negotiations, is not prepared to take unilateral action.'[8]

Shinwell was left to find ways of saving money in an army of one hundred and fifty thousand men, active in China, India, Bermuda, Jamaica, Gibraltar, Malta, Cyprus, Egypt, the Sudan, Palestine, Aden, Mauritius, Ceylon and Malaya, and costing £40 million a year, without reducing its size. This was at a time also when pay was increasing as more specialised units were established and new laws on pensions were enforced. Rhineland troops previously maintained by Germany were transferred back to Catterick and new mechanised equipment was more than ever demanded. Shinwell found it surprisingly easy.

Working closely with the Chief of the Imperial General Staff, Sir George Milne, he called in the heads of the Army Service Department and the Ordnance Department who theoretically shared responsibility for mech-anisation but in practice competed for it. In a matter of weeks Shinwell and Milne had imposed a new system for the supply and maintenance of mechanised equipment. This unlikely committee of two also reorganised the system of storage, a process which included spot inspections which terrified the officers locally in command. (At one store in Pimlico, the minister and the general arrived on foot from Westminster. There, in a sort of drill hall, they discovered a mountain of boots with the brass eyelets missing – they had all been sold off by a civilian storeman in 1918!)[9]

The best moment was when Shinwell got Shaw to revoke Baldwin's 'British Fresh Meat' order. The previous Prime Minister, having visited some farmers a few months before the 1929 general election, had announced that the army would in future be fed on home-killed beef. This meant in practice that herds of cattle were driven across the frontier from the Irish Free State into Northern Ireland to be slaughtered for the army. It cost the army an extra £200,000 in its first year of operation and at the same time badly damaged part of the Dominions' trade in cheaper frozen meat. As Shinwell said of Baldwin: 'Sometimes electoral questions and possibilities do concern members of governments, even Prime Ministers, to the detriment of good practice.'[10] It prompted Sir George Milne to call Shinwell 'the first breath of fresh air we've had from the politicians in the War Office for a long time'.[11]

Inevitably, not all of Shinwell's fifteen months at the War Office were such fun or so successful. Maxton's constant sniping at him and the government as a whole led to a row at the ILP Scottish conference with the passing of a resolution condemning Maxton's behaviour. A War Minister in a Labour government unwilling to cut the size of the army was always vulnerable to attack from the left.

On a personal note, there was also what Shinwell considered to be a great humiliation when his Private Secretary found a reminder in his post of a debt of £100 which Fanny had run up for children's clothes in Glasgow. Manny paid it off but it caused a row, not so much because of Fanny's expensive tastes – it was a lot for clothes in 1929 – but because she evidently obtained credit on the strength of his job as a minister. It didn't last long because the whole family was taken up a couple of days later with celebrating Lucy's engagement to a likeable but confirmed Tory, 'Young Manny' Stern.

By the middle of 1930, Shinwell had had enough. He had quite enjoyed the War Office but he was keen to play a bigger part now; he felt ready for the Cabinet. He was not at all pleased when MacDonald merely gave him back the Ministry of Mines.

Once again Arthur Cook announced that the Miners' Federation was thoroughly dissatisfied with Shinwell's appointment. He had previously asked MacDonald to appoint a miner and now he had been ignored again. He said he had nothing against Shinwell personally, but he doubted very much whether he could cope with the complex issues to be discussed at the International Labour Conference at Geneva. In fact, MacDonald had appointed Shinwell specifically because he was convinced he was one of the few men who could cope with representing the British government in Geneva. Within a few days of his appointment, Shinwell was on the boat-train.

Willie Graham, the dynamic President of the Board of Trade and Shinwell's new Cabinet boss, had pointed out to MacDonald the importance, and the possibility, of getting an international agreement on coal. Ben Turner, Shinwell's predecessor at the Ministry of Mines, had introduced a Coal Mines Bill aimed at reducing the miners' working day to seven and a half hours. Turner had simply overlooked the loss of international competitiveness that could have resulted from the reduction. It was soon pointed out that this, along with the question of subsidising exports and allocating production quotas, would all have to await international agreement. The Geneva Conference was vital to the Coal Mines Bill. Without the agreement, the Bill had no chance of getting through the House of Commons.[12]

The background to the International Labour Conference in Geneva was one of gloom and disaster in Britain and abroad. The Wall Street Crash had destabilised the world economy. Investment was cut and unemployment was soaring. By January 1930 there were one and a half million out of work in Britain and by June nearly two million. This was a disaster for a government whose philosophical and practical commitment was, above all, to cure unemployment.

Jimmy Thomas, the ex-leader of the Railwaymen, was put in charge of policy on unemployment by MacDonald. He was an old friend of Shinwell's and admired him for his combination of 'brain and brawn'.[13] While Shinwell was at the War Office, Thomas had been keeping him up-to-date with the work of MacDonald's new Economic Advisory Council, the first real predecessor of the modern National Economic Development Council. He met Shinwell regularly in the House of Commons tea room or at the Privy Council office, and the meetings had become increasingly depressing. Eschewing anything approaching radical economics, Thomas had come to rely on the reactionary civil servant, Sir Horace Wilson. He called him 'My 'Orris', and it was well into their first meeting before Shinwell realised he was a man and not a horse or an oracle.[14]

In fact, Wilson was an extremely cautious and conventional economic adviser and was firmly against even Shinwell's mild suggestions about gathering economic information for the mildest sort of indicative planning. On the other hand, any initiative which might cut the number out of work, especially some kind of international agreement on coal which Shinwell might now obtain, was desperately sought-after. Otherwise, even the government's promise to improve unemployment benefit would turn out to be too expensive to implement because of the number of its possible recipients. The government were running out of ideas.[15]

The International Labour Conference included delegates from all over Europe. Most countries had sent one representative from the owners, one from the miners' unions and a government minister. Britain was no exception, but all the serious work was done by Shinwell. The owners' delegate was completely predictable in opposing all suggestions for a reduction in hours, which was the main bone of contention. Cook for the Miners' Federation produced his usual bombast. Shinwell made the unprepared speech of his life after a night of rich food and wine, arguing about Stalin's purges with Albert Thomas the French communist founder of the International Labour Organisation. He persuaded the majority to accept the objective of seven and three-quarters hours 'surface to surface':

with the British system of a half-hour winding time – effectively a seven-and-a-quarter-hour working day:

> The workers require it as a modest measure of social justice; the employers, whatever might be their view, require it on democratic grounds; and the governments, as part of public welfare, are compelled to obtain some measure of stability and unification in this vital industry.[16]

Shinwell's proposal was accepted 73:33 (69 per cent) as an agreed medium-term objective. Then, at the final session, when it came to formal resolutions to send the agreement to the various governments for ratification, it was accepted only 70:40 (64 per cent), a majority of less than two-thirds. The Germans had abstained on a technical question to do with overtime. With the ink on MacDonald's congratulatory telegram barely dry, Shinwell made no effort to disguise his disappointment:

> Every attempt was made to make concessions to the views of the Germans, even at the risk of the convention itself. The responsibility is now on their shoulders. The question must be settled not only in the interests of the miners throughout the coal-producing countries of Europe, but in the interests of every nation.[17]

MacDonald had told Shinwell when he appointed him that the task was likely to be impossible. In fact, a seven-and-a-half-hour deal was made the following year under a new government (which Shinwell misleadingly refers to in his memoirs, muddling the two conferences and claiming a conference triumph).[18] The fact was that Shinwell felt he had been a failure when he got back from Geneva in July 1930.

The rest of his time at the Ministry of Mines was largely taken up with trying to reach local agreements on hours and promoting exports, travelling extensively. It was a classic Shinwell grind. Even despite his efforts, and occasional personal interventions by MacDonald, exports grew painfully slowly and there were short-lived strikes in most coalfields.[19] He was constantly dousing emotional fires and banging the heads of warring parties together; important but basically negative work.

The one piece of positive planning associated with a highly modified and limited Coal Mines Act, planned amalgamations, were taken over, to his great annoyance, by Willie Graham. As MacDonald wrote in a letter, which explains at the same time why Shinwell was frustrated and why his colleagues found him so annoying:

> I was very glad to see at last in the *Daily Herald* a paragraph which appreciated the work you are doing, and I am just dropping you this note to assure you that it expressed my sentiments.

It has been reported to me, however, that you had an interview with Norman [the Governor of the Bank of England] regarding the Mines Amalgamation Committee, during which you stated you had been approaching people and had received their consent, and also that you had made up your mind regarding the duties of the chairman! I hope this has been done after consultation with Graham. The rule is that all committees of such importance are appointed only after a Cabinet Minister has submitted his proposals to me and has talked over his intentions. I was put in a fix today because I knew nothing about it.[20]

This reprimand so depressed Shinwell that he cancelled his appointments for the rest of the day and went home to Tooting where the family now lived. He took the two youngest children straight out to Bertram Mills' Circus. The rest of the day evaporated in a haze of the Fabulous Fabrinis and Leinert the Human Cannon.

What with the captive lions and tame bears and no longer wild horses, he decided he had better not tell the serious-minded Pit Ponies' Protection Society, whom he was due to meet the next day, where he had been. However, he still sympathised with the pit ponies' plight and was successful in getting the Mines Inspectorate to take their welfare seriously again.[21]

All in all, Shinwell's second term at the Ministry of Mines cannot be counted a success, despite a few highlights. Unlike that of Attlee, Dalton and Morrison, among his contemporaries, his performance did not attract much attention.

When hostilities in the Labour Party flared up, MacDonald could still, as always, count on Shinwell as a loyal supporter. And MacDonald was still capable of rewarding his followers with a political tour de force. Shinwell knew at once why he remained a loyal follower when MacDonald delivered one of the greatest speeches of his life to the Labour Party Conference at Llandudno in October 1930.

The omens for the speech were bad. The R101 Airship had crashed at Beauvais on the Monday of the conference, and, two hours before he was due to make his speech on the Tuesday, MacDonald was handed a report blaming Lord Thomson, the Minister of Aviation and also a great personal friend, for the whole disaster. Thomson himself had also been incinerated in the crash. MacDonald gave Shinwell the report to read that evening and Shinwell gave the opinion that if the terms of reference of the forthcoming Board of Trade Inquiry could be carefully worded, then blame could be put on the technical advisers rather than on Lord Thomson himself. He knew this was exactly what MacDonald wanted to hear. He desperately wanted to save Thomson's reputation; Thomson had been very enthusiastic for this technical marvel of Labour Britain and, at first sight, had quite blatantly ignored some technical advice. Shinwell advised that it was arguable where the final blame for the decision to fly would lie, and the inquiry could focus on that. Confidential correspondence about the inquiry followed between MacDonald and Shinwell and Willie Graham was asked to leave the matter to Shinwell. The inquiry duly blamed two Aviation Ministry officials and exonerated the dead minister. Shinwell wrote triumphantly to MacDonald in April 1931,

> I am sending you a copy of the R101 Report, thinking that you may care to glance through it during your well-earned holiday. I hope very much that you will feel that we have dealt fairly and considerately with the subject of poor Thomson's responsibility: he was clearly relying on technical advice which he had no means of checking.

Shinwell was probably the only person in the government at that time whom Macdonald felt he could completely trust with such a delicate matter. He was not too far to the left, he was not too pure and he was loyal.

But as he got up to make his speech at Llandudno, MacDonald knew only that his friend was dead and probably also responsible for the whole R101 disaster, killing forty-six people, injuring many others and humiliating British technology, the absolute reverse of all his plans.

His speech began full of human emotion and grief, and he created an atmosphere in which criticism would have sounded like blasphemy. He even publicly condoled with Maxton over the death of his wife a few weeks previously: 'Oh, the bastard, the bloody bastard,' Maxton wept. Then MacDonald claimed that the foundations of socialism were being laid: 'The temple will rise and rise until at last it is complete, and the genius of humanity will find within it an appropriate resting place.'[22] Everybody stood and cheered. It was followed by a censure motion, sponsored by Maxton, which lost heavily, and MacDonald returned to Downing Street in triumph.

The Conference was far from over, however. Two days after MacDonald's speech came one from Oswald Mosley. It was one that Shinwell and other ILP leaders had heard before. Mosley said that there should be a massive programme of public works, state ownership of the banks, a huge-scale reorganisation of industry and agriculture, detailed planning of international trade and substantial improvements in social services, all of which would require big changes in the structure of government, including a much more autocratic executive leader. Shinwell was among the minority who did not give a standing ovation to Mosley. Instead, he gave no ovation at all. Mosley's memorandum, on which the speech was based, narrowly missed on a card vote being referred for consideration by the National Executive Committee of the party. Mosley himself, however, was swept on to the National Executive.

Shinwell already knew Mosley well. He had worked with him, an ex-Conservative and ex-Independent, on the National Administrative Council of the ILP, in the group supporting MacDonald. On one occasion the leadership of the ILP had all been invited to the Mosleys' country house at Denham. Fanny had come too and, although Mosley's brusque dealings with his own wife had rather shocked her, she had regarded the whole thing as quite a pleasant day out. The Shinwells changed their minds about Mosley over the months ahead when they heard about his electioneering style – the provision of a car here, a meal there, an introduction here, a little favour there. Nor was Shinwell happy about Mosley's subsequent election to the constituency section of the party's National Executive. For probably the only time in his life, Shinwell agreed with Hugh Dalton's assessment: 'The fellow stinks of money and insincerity.'[23]

In January 1930 Shinwell had received a copy of Mosley's memorandum, which contained most of the ideas in his later conference speech, probably even before the Prime Minister. By February most Labour MPs had read it and eighty of them were demanding its consideration by the Cabinet. It seemed at that time to be a real innovation. Even MacDonald, although he was angry at the way the normal channels had been by-passed – Mosley should have first discussed his ideas with his superior, Jimmy Thomas – liked Mosley personally and gave some of the ideas serious attention.[24]

Arthur Cook was soon an enthusiastic Mosley supporter too. Shinwell noted that 'it appealed to his type with its sweeping solutions and do-or-die mentality'; and the young Aneurin Bevan also acclaimed its divergence from the arid orthodoxies of Thomas, Wilson and the Chancellor of the Exchequer, Philip Snowden, an alternative to free trade, the gold standard and the balanced budget. Even Ernest Bevin only really disagreed with the way Mosley was putting his ideas around, 'rocking the boat in a most unwelcome way'.[25]

Frustrated as he was by the failure of the government to solve the unemployment problem, Mosley never appealed to Shinwell:

> I knew it was an international slump. I agreed with MacDonald that the world system of capitalism was collapsing. All we could do was our best to hold the line for ordinary people. I was all for more planning and controls, but Mosley was all wrong in saying that it was Parliament that needed restructuring. Not a bit of it. It was more constituencies voting Labour that we wanted so we wouldn't be hamstrung by the Liberals. It was all MacDonald could do to resist their demands for proportional representation, which would have put us in the position of never being able to form a Labour majority government. Men like Mosley who have nothing to do with the working class – and other intellectuals and very rich people in the Labour Party – are dangerous because they think

ordinary people are stupid. Some of them even think I'm stupid because I am not their type. They think I don't have a vision. I do. And at that time I did. But I understood the limitations. I wanted Macdonald's government to say openly 'this is what we'd like to do but these are our limitations; now let's achieve what we can', and that's pretty well what MacDonald did at Llandudno. The ILP, at least Maxton's supporters in it, had some good ideas ahead of their time, increasing demand and so on, but politically they faded because they had no concept of how to work in a minority government. Mosley got a lot of support at first but when our MPs listened to their constituency members and then looked at the alternative to MacDonald – Chamberlain, Baldwin and the rest of them – they knew MacDonald was right.[26]

As soon as his memorandum was defeated at conference, Mosley decided to leave the Labour Party and form a new party. He still needed more money, more press support and to get the timing right.[27] In fact, he misjudged the situation. The New Party, set up on 28 February 1931, had too few supporters, too little money and was led too autocratically by Mosley who became increasingly attracted by fascism. It fought the by-election at Ashton-under-Lyne on 30 April. Shinwell spoke for Labour and came away convinced that Mosley had not made a significant impact. But the impact was big enough, as it turned out, to give the seat which had been Labour with a majority of 3,407 in 1929, back to the Conservatives with a majority of 1,415. The New Party won 4,472 votes. 'What's new about the New Party?' raged Shinwell. 'Didn't Brutus stick his knife into Caesar? The stiletto in the back is as old as the hills.'[28]

In August 1931, governments throughout the West were entering uncharted waters. For Britain the banking collapse which started in Vienna was now causing an unparalleled run on the pound as investors sought liquidity. Snowden and MacDonald were convinced that the only answer was to introduce the most stringent measures to save money and restore confidence.

Estimates of the cuts needed ranged from £70 million to £170 million.[29] The government-appointed May Committee on the Economy had recommmended that this should include substantial cuts in unemployment benefit, around 20 per cent. Henderson and Graham argued for more taxes and fewer if any cuts. But on 22 August the government was told that a vital American loan would not be made available without at least a 10 per cent cut specifically in unemployment benefit. Henderson said this was unacceptable as a policy and unacceptable as interference, but MacDonald went to the King who asked, to the Prime Minister's surprise, if he should send for Henderson now to form a government. MacDonald instead entered into discussions with the Conservatives and Liberals, at first actually authorised by the Cabinet. But he soon went beyond his brief of discussing policy on to the formation of a new non-party government. On 24 August, Ramsay MacDonald tendered the resignation of the second Labour government and the National government was formed.

MacDonald's meeting with all his junior ministers the next day in the Cabinet Room at 10 Downing Street – Shinwell sat opposite him – was well described by Attlee:

> The Prime Minister told us that he had hoped merely to tell us that our salaries were to be cut, but now he must ask for our resignation. He made us a long and insincere speech in which he begged us to remain with the Party out of regard for our careers, but really because he had all the appointments fixed up and any adhesions would have gravely embarrassed him. Except for a question by Dalton and one by me, we received his speech in silence and left without a word.[30]

Although Attlee certainly seems to portray the frosty atmosphere of the meeting very accurately, it is not strictly true that MacDonald would have been embarrassed by junior ministers staying with him. On the contrary, he would have been very pleasantly surprised. He certainly offered Shinwell the chance to stay, in a telephone conversation the same evening, remembered some years later perhaps with a certain amount of 'esprit d'escalier':

> 'I want you to remain where you are at the Ministry of Mines.'
> 'I can't do that –'
> 'Oh yes, you can carry out your policy. I'll see that nobody interferes with you.'
> 'No. You needn't have done this. You could have gone into Opposition and the Party would have stood by you. Many a time Mac, I've stood by you when I didn't understand you. This time I must stand by the Party.'[31]

Even if some of this is exaggerated, there is no reason to doubt that MacDonald did genuinely want Shinwell to stay on in the National government, as he did with Cripps and Morrison who were the only junior ministers seriously to consider it. He wrote Shinwell a long rambling letter of regret:

> I need not say how deeply I regret the necessity for the resignation of the government, but I wish to thank you most sincerely ... It is a very painful decision that has had to be taken ... We were on the verge of a financial crisis which if not dealt with within the space of days, would have meant not cuts of ten per cent, or anything of that kind, in unemployment pay, but would have disorganised the whole of our financial

system, with the most dire results to the mass of the working classes. It may take a little time for people to understand ... Having failed to meet the immediate situation we should have been swept away in ignominy before the end of this week by popular clamour, so that it can be proved later on, whatever offence we have caused at this moment, we have created the conditions under which the Party can continue as an Opposition and allow the public, saved from panic, to consider a return of our general policy when things have become more normal.[32]

Shinwell did not reply.

In September, the National government introduced its National Economy Bill containing the proposed cuts. With the rest of the Labour Party away at the annual conference at Scarborough, Attlee and Shinwell had agreed to hold the fort in the House of Commons. It was the first time they had worked together and, considering the empty benches behind them, they both gave competent performances. Attlee concentrated on general economic policy and Shinwell on unemployment benefit.[33]

Despite its economies, however, the new government could not save the pound, and Britain went off the gold standard on 21 September. Soon the cuts brought about marches of the unemployed and a mutiny in the navy. Foreign confidence wilted. An election, to give the non-party government legitimacy and authority in the eyes of the world, seemed more than ever necessary. Yet MacDonald had promised his colleagues in the Labour Party that there would be no 'coupon' election.

The die was cast when the Labour Party expelled MacDonald, along with Snowden and Thomas who had followed him; MacDonald's wild dream of returning to the party evaporated. On 5 October he called a general election in which each of the parties participating in his coalition would present its own manifesto, but seek an overall 'Doctor's Mandate'. Furthermore, the coalition parties would not oppose each other. It was a 'coupon' election in all but name.

On the evening the election was called, MacDonald broadcast to the nation over the BBC, the first time the wireless had ever been used in this way. The Labour Party failed to realise its importance. Instead, the next to take the air was Snowden, who launched a vitriolic attack on Labour's manifesto, 'Labour's Call to Action':

The Labour policy will destroy our national credit, the currency will collapse, and your incomes and wages and pensions and unemployment pay will have their purchasing value reduced enormously. The Labour Party programme is Bolshevism gone mad and the issue of this election is between prosperity and ruin.[34]

Snowden also claimed inside information when he put the Liberal, Lord Runciman, up to claiming publicly that Labour would rob the Post Office Savings Bank of depositors' money. It had no basis in truth at all and Snowden knew it; but Shinwell, like many of his fellow Labour candidates, found it coming up again and again on the hustings.[35]

Mosley's New Party had meanwhile run out of steam. It had promised four hundred candidates but had found only twenty-four, and all of them, including Mosley, were to come bottom of the poll. They even had difficulty in finding the twenty-four; Harold Nicolson, then a journalist and supporter of Mosley, reported going to interview potential candidates and finding them antique or adolescent, illiterate or mad. Mosley had said he wanted young men 'with the minds of philosophers and the bodies of athletes' in his party; Nicolson feared they were ending up with middle-aged men 'with the minds of athletes and the bodies of philosophers'.[36]

Shinwell was pleased to find there were no Mosleyites around his constituency; Mosley had gone to Scotland only once, to Glasgow, and had been attacked with razor blades. The New Party was now almost irrelevant. It was a more serious matter that Shinwell was in a straight fight with a Conservative, Sir Adrian Baillie, who had Liberal endorsement under the 'Doctor's Mandate'.

At the last minute MacDonald made a final attempt to persuade Shinwell to go with him. The Conservative agent was sent to visit Shinwell's agent, Angus Livingstone, an upright Presbyterian schoolteacher and a personal friend of Shinwell's. The Conservative said that if Shinwell supported MacDonald, Baillie would not oppose him. Apparently Livingstone diverged from the normal language of a Scots Presbyterian schoolteacher when he gave Shinwell's firm 'no'. It was the last time that Shinwell heard anything about joining the National government. Electorally it did him no good at all:

Sir Adrian Baillie (Conservative)	20,475 (55%)
Emanuel Shinwell (Labour)	16,956 (45%)
Majority	3,519

The whole Labour Cabinet, except those who had joined MacDonald and the elderly pacifist Lansbury, lost their seats along with most junior ministers except for Clement Attlee and Sir Stafford Cripps. Political power for Labour was once again a distant dream.

Shinwell found himself with no union job, no more government job and not even an MP's £400 a year. There was not realistically the slightest chance of a Labour government for at least ten years. He was getting on for fifty.

What on earth had it all been for?

Part 4

CHAPTER 11

Squalid Rotten Years

Professor Selig Brodetsky, one of British Jewry's leading lights, waited for Shinwell in the Kenilworth Hotel lobby. He knew Shinwell had been proud of being the first Jewish Labour MP and he also knew that the Zionist Federation could use a man like that. Brodetsky invited him to speak for Zionism.

The idea of a Jewish national home in Palestine had not yet received its terrible boost from the Nazi Holocaust. Even many Jews needed persuading. Shinwell seemed a good man to do it. He had a reputation as a speaker and his socialism accorded well with the principles of the inter-war Zionists, many of whom envisaged a workers' state based on the Kibbutz. Jewish migration to Palestine was increasing fast from Europe and from the Arab world, and there were expensive schemes for which the Zionist Federation now wanted to raise money, which were to increase the number of migrants from three thousand five hundred in 1930 to nine thousand five hundred in 1932 and over thirty thousand in 1933. Speakers would need to persuade Jewish and Gentile audiences alike that the Jews were entitled to their own homeland, that they had been promised it by the British government in 1917 (and, prior to that, by God) and that they could build their own country and make it safe. Pitched battles between Jews and Arabs at the Wailing Wall and on the Temple Mount showed the ineptitude of British colonial administration in the territory held under a League of Nations mandate. Shinwell could talk, orate, cajole and persuade. He was someone the Zionist Federation needed, Brodetsky told him.

Shinwell told Brodetsky that he would give his suggestion very serious consideration but, as he knew, he was unemployed now and he had only enjoyed a ministerial wage of £1,500 a year for two years. He couldn't live on it for ever. How much did Brodetsky propose to pay him? Now came the surprise: it was all to be voluntary. Shinwell exploded with rage. How could this millionaire come to a man with a family to support, knowing he was out of a job, and ask him to work for no pay? They parted in bitterness, and Shinwell, who had started to take some interest in

Zionism, thought of it no more until news of Nazi persecutions forced many ambivalent Jews and Gentiles to change their minds.

Shinwell left the Kenilworth Hotel with the same problem as he had when entering it. He had taken out a mortgage with the Co-op on his house in Balham and he would soon be unable to make the repayments. He had hoped to send Sam and Lucy to university, but now it looked as though the family would need their earnings. Even Fanny might have to go out to work, but then there would be the problem of looking after the two younger children. It was a familiar enough story of a man suddenly sacked from a moderately well-paid job, whose life had been built up around the money coming in, who had hardly any savings and a fair number of commitments and a bad headache.

Shinwell contacted Lord Hyndley who immediately offered to lend him money. Hyndley and Shinwell had been friends since they first worked together in the 1924 government, when Hyndley had been Honorary Industrial Adviser at the Ministry of Mines. Shinwell would accept neither gifts nor loans but he did accept an introduction to the chairman of the International Nickel Company of Canada. They met at the company headquarters in Millbank, and apparently Shinwell was about to be offered a job when he was asked whether he intended to carry on in politics, to remain a candidate, to make speeches and so on. He was taken aback. He replied that he would never give up politics and they parted, saying that they would both 'consider' their positions. As he walked away from that interview, Shinwell realised that if he was going to provide for himself and his family in a decent way, he might well have to give up politics.

It was hardly an auspicious time to be a Labour politician anyway. A mere forty-nine seats in the House of Commons, a failed government just fallen, and no love lost between him and the most powerful people left in the labour movement, the union bosses. He was nearly fifty years old. If he gave up political ambition, he could at least have a comfortable life-style and no worries about his own security or his family's future. He had experienced the thrills and spills of the political stage, so perhaps it was time for something else.

A couple of days and he would almost certainly have given up politics and taken that job in the International Nickel Company. In the event he got a telephone call from Arthur Henderson, who had also lost his seat in the election, asking him to come and see him at his office in Transport House, Labour's headquarters. Henderson explained that he had heard about Shinwell's problem and he wanted to offer him a job. It would not be much of a job as far as money went, but it would be in politics. Henderson offered Shinwell £250 a year to go round the country, eight days on and four days off, making public speeches. It spelt poverty but it was neither starvation nor the dole. The defeated MP and ex-minister accepted.[1]

The political outlook for Labour was bleak, slaughtered by the right and now sniped at by the left. Not satisfied with attacking the Conservatives, the Communist Party saw in the apparent collapse of Labour a chance for rich pickings. They used the failure of the two MacDonald Labour administrations as proof that compromise socialism was dead. Gradualism must be impossible. Not only that, you had only to look at the Soviet Union, the one country that had gone in for real socialism, to see a budding paradise. (Never mind the purges, never mind Stalin's dictatorship and the centralisation.)

The communists were helped by the Webbs who apparently felt they had witnessed in the Soviet Union the birth of a New Man and by Hugh Dalton who used columns in the *Daily Herald* to sing the praises of the parks and concerts of Stalingrad. Shinwell was sceptical:

> Of course Dr Dalton was a very clever man and so were the Fabians who went with him to Stalingrad, all very clever men. But did they have judgement? I understand that in Stalingrad they had a workers' palace where men and women could sunbathe on the roof and shoot pistols in the basement, and Dr Dalton told us that they sometimes fired at an effigy of Sir Austen Chamberlain. That showed good judgement by those people in Stalingrad. I too admired this when I heard about it and I was also willing to believe that the miners there were better off than the Durham miners. I believed in planning, and Stalin and his Gosplan people made it work. But how could they just ignore the trials and the shootings? These great intellectuals like Dr Dalton should have known better before giving ammunition to our Communists – who were a serious threat to us at that time when I was out touring the country for the Party.[2]

These recollections, quite apart from showing up the early stages of what was later to be a hearty mutual dislike between Shinwell and Dalton, demonstrated the frustration with many of his party colleagues at the centre which Shinwell developed while he was going round the constituencies. He found himself, like many local party leaders and officials, constantly urging more electioneering effort and less philosophical self-indulgence from head office.

The truth was that party organisation was in disarray. There had been very few defections to MacDonald's National Labour Party, but the sheer weight of the 1931 defeat and the uncertainty and recriminations that went with it had demoralised the party at all levels.

The ILP soon quit the Labour Party altogether in a shower of acid comments and bitterness, taking a small group of Labour's depleted parliamentary opposition with them. Shinwell had resigned from the National Administrative Council of the ILP in 1930 when it looked like withdrawing support from the Labour government but, along with Dollan and Kirkwood, he had still fought to keep the ILP within the Labour Party, at least up to the 1931 general election. Afterwards, the younger Labour Party leaders, such as Attlee and Morrison, talked openly of ILP withdrawal from the party as inevitable, and Maxton, who was still the ILP's leader, retorted that it was only the ILP that was keeping socialism alive and if that was a job which had to be done outside the party, then so be it. Compromisers like Shinwell were few and far between after 1931 and the split was inevitable. It turned into a disaster for the ILP rather than the Labour Party. Within two years of breaking away, ILP membership withered to just four thousand across the country.

Shinwell soon realised that the local Labour parties he visited would need to rely on their own resources rather than anything likely to come from the top. He helped to set up local conferences of parties and unions which would get publicity and help to galvanise organisation and thinking about new policy for the 1930s. He also thought hard about new ways of selling policy to potential Labour voters who had defected at the last election or who had never voted Labour. He told listeners to

be conscious of the need for effective and constructive propaganda without lavish promises of what we're going to do in the direction of extending our social services, until the foundations of a new economic order have been laid. The voters are suspicious of the swing of the pendulum.[3]

There was plenty to attack in MacDonald's National government that would show Labour in a favourable light, and much of Shinwell's propaganda concentrated on it. Unemployment benefit was cut at the same time as the increasingly powerful Neville Chamberlain declared that a million unemployed was a reasonable figure and the 'minimum for the foreseeable future'. Poverty was intensified by a new, strict and humiliating Household Means Test. Benefit was now refused to the unemployed unless they could prove that there was no one in their family capable of supporting them in even the most humble way.

When he visited the mining areas, Shinwell still argued, as he always had done, for nationalisation as not only being fairer but also economically preferable, facilitating planning in what was then the British economy's most basic industry. As ex-Minister of Mines, these speeches about nationalisation usually attracted the attention of the local press.

Visiting Durham in May 1932, it was just such a speech which impressed delegates from constituencies all over North-East England. Shinwell had spoken in Durham before, as long ago as 1920 when he was already senior in the ILP, but now he spoke with new authority on coal policy and he was prepared to talk about nationalisation in the context of the thorny issue of wages:

How are miners' wages to be stabilised at a reasonably high level? How are miners to be given an assurance of more employment, of more congenial employment, and of greater safety? How are consumers of coal to be given an assurance of just and fair prices? How is the nation to be guaranteed the satisfactory and scientific development of their coal resources in the national interest?

These questions, Shinwell argued, could be answered properly only with a Bill to take the mines into democratic control and national ownership.

It is not so much workers' control we require as democratic control, in which both producers and consumers can exercise their proper functions in relation to the needs of the community. Nationalisation of industry means what it says: it means that industry should be owned and managed in the interests of the national community, and not in the interests of any one section.

The coal-owners were claiming that they could not afford to pay higher wages, but there were no statistics to support their case. All anyone knew was that there was a large gap between the pit-head price and the price paid by the consumer:

A great national asset is being abused. Where does all the money, earned by the sweat of every miner, go? Under the present system, the pit-head price for coal is too little to give the miner a living wage. But if wages were determined by the price paid by consumers, the miners would amass considerable fortunes! It may or may not be true about the fabulous profits of coal owners and coal merchants. It is certain that we have a right to know.[4]

The speech was reported all over the North-East, and it should certainly be seen in the light of Shinwell's new ambition to fight a safe Durham coalfield seat. After his defeat at Linlithgowshire, Shinwell had told his local party that he was going to think about his future as a free agent and that they should choose another candidate without considering him. Nevertheless, he was rather surprised when they got on with their selection process so quickly that it would have been hard for him to get back.

Before Shinwell's Durham speech, Ebby Edwards, MP for Morpeth, who was then thinking of retiring from his safe Labour mining constituency, urged him to put his name forward as his successor. Now, after the speech, he was invited to put his name forward for the far more interesting seat of Seaham. The present incumbent, none other than the Prime Minister Ramsay MacDonald, had been offered the seat in 1929 by Sidney Webb who had called it 'safe and cheap'.[5] MacDonald wrote:

They offer me a constituency which I need not visit more than once a year and where, at a General Election, three or four speeches at the outside will be all they would ask for ... they guarantee that no subscriptions would be asked for and that the whole organisation is maintained from local sources.[6]

Shinwell's reputation for serious campaigning and his knowledge of the coalmining industry made him a very serious contender among the twenty-four nominees. Several local miners stood against him and there was some whispering opposition from the local unions, but they could hardly claim as they had in 1924 that he was too inexperienced. Shinwell was selected to fight the Prime Minister on 10 September 1932. The news received national coverage and Shinwell challenged MacDonald publicly to resign there and then. MacDonald ignored the challenge – and also continued ignoring his impoverished constituents.[7]

Shinwell still had to earn his crust. It was arduous and, although there were amusing incidents, it was rarely enjoyable. Away from his family for much of his time, his occasional letters to 'My Dear Fay' were either factual notes about the trains he hoped to catch or a few lines of affection. As a minister he had saved a little, and his eldest son Sammy and eldest daughter Lucy could both pay their own way now. At least Fanny would not have to work, he could give her just about enough to survive with Rose and Ernie.

As he scrimped and saved, he also watched with envy the rise of Attlee and Cripps in Parliament, and the supremacy of Bevin in the union movement. Shinwell's day-to-day contact with constituency members made him aware of the low regard in which these leaders were held. Cripps struck out indiscriminately at the House of Lords and then the Royal Family. Attlee was still largely unknown. Lansbury, although a more effective leader in Parliament than expected, was given to extreme views on pacifism; so much so that he even opposed the League of Nations as a club for rich states. Shinwell tended to Bevin's view in favour of the League as at least a stab at collective security.

The truth was that Shinwell was out and no one really cared what he thought. In 1932, he was still years away from being an MP again, even if he ever climbed the mountain of MacDonald's 28,978 votes which had given him a majority of nearly six thousand.

The real power in the party now lay with a nominally consultative National Council of Labour, 50 per cent of which was made up of the General Council of the TUC (dominated by Bevin and the Transport and General Workers' Union) with 25 per cent each from the NEC and the Parliamentary Labour Party. It was this body which laid down the fundamentals of new Labour policy, still gradualist but rather clearer than in MacDonald's time. It could take all the decisions because it held the majority of votes at the party's annual conference. It decided on how best to approach fascism and it refused to collaborate with the communists; it made moves towards nationalisation of many basic industries, various social reforms and the beginnings of economic planning.

Shinwell, as a mere junior employee of the party, had no say in making any of this policy, but equally there is no indication that he disagreed with any of it. Indeed, on two occasions, in Lanark and Durham, he was asked to appear on a platform with Lansbury, the parliamentary leader, specifically to give the official line on collective military security involving the League of Nations, because Lansbury could not be relied upon to do so.[8]

In the constituencies, things were not always so clear-cut. The ordinary members were not employees of the party, just volunteers, so they were not bound by the National Council of Labour. In South Wales Shinwell came across Workers' Freedom Groups, a joint Labour and communist youth movement designed specifically to fight against fascism or Nazism if either should take root in Wales. Shinwell said that it reminded him of Clarion when he first saw it, but he soon realised it was more sinister, a kind of fascism to fight fascism. A number of South Wales party members, including Aneurin Bevan, associated themselves with the movement. Its declared aims included:

> To promote all forms of working class resistance to a lower standard of life ... to encourage and organise physical training among the workers in readiness to meet any demands that would be put upon them ... to organise working class resistance to war ... to encourage the dignity and self-reliance of all workers.[9]

They were preparing for class war in the full belief that fascism or Nazism in Britain was inevitable as the capitalist class defended itself from catastrophe.

In other parts of the country, the National Unemployed Workers' Movement, also led by communists, attracted a far larger and more militant following in many areas, even in parts of Durham, than the Labour Party. Shinwell reported all this to the party officials at Transport House, but they guessed, or hoped, that these alternative movements would fade.

At party headquarters, Shinwell was considered mainly useful as a link between them and new candidates. He was usually introduced by the local parliamentary candidate when he visited a constituency. The general pattern was then that the candidate would speak for about ten minutes and share a question time with his visitor afterwards. Shinwell found that candidates sometimes knew staggeringly little about party policy and were terrified of making speeches. One young candidate in Bristol stood up before three hundred people and, after a minute's silence which Shinwell thought was commemorating something, laughed nervously and said rather too loudly, 'I don't know what the hell to say,' and sat down blushing furiously. Shinwell stepped in with an hour-long speech without notes and received ten minutes' solid applause when he finished. Another candidate told an audience of independent-minded fishermen in Cornwall that he wanted to nationalise the whole fishing industry and, when he had said that, it was too late for Shinwell to rescue him. Not surprisingly, neither of those two candidates had any luck at the general election. Fortunately, most candidates were reasonably competent, or at least not beyond rescue.[10]

Nevertheless Shinwell, was soon heartily sick of his jobs: 'I never experienced anything comparable with the misery, depression, frustration and occasionally agonising feelings endured during those years. They were squalid rotten years.'[11] He was, after all, an ex-minister and fifty years old, and it was humiliating to climb into children's alcoves in miners' cottages, the children having been turfed out of their beds by their parents to fulfil the requirement on the local party to provide hospitality to their visitor. Unable to sleep and with three more exhausting bookings to go, he could only look forward to a tiresome train ride back to London for a couple of days, where he would probably have to sit down and write articles for general-interest magazines like *John Bull* or *Tit-Bits* to pay off family debts.

At least the miners' cottages were preferable to the rich socialists' houses where he frequently had to sleep on the top floor and eat in the back-kitchen like a servant. He also found some local parties incredibly mean. He charged twenty-five shillings for an evening, but Wakefield Labour Party had bargained him down – after he had talked and answered questions for three hours – to a guinea, 'the same as Mr Wedgwood Benn' (who was a millionaire). Sometimes they would put him up at the most disgusting boarding houses where he would have to share a bed with another guest, not to mention the primitive toilet facilities. Indeed he claimed afterwards to have become an authority on Britain's public toilets and public libraries.

There were compensations, such as hours spent in local libraries giving him an excellent opportunity to update himself on local issues and to discover new literature, but they were small compensations for the drudgery.

Insult and injury combined in Newport in South Wales where the local party apparently decided, since Shinwell was from party headquarters and also a Jew, that he would undoubtedly be able to meet his own expenses. They booked him into the West Gate Hotel and he was faced with a bill for £2. No one had come to settle it and the local secretary was nowhere to be found. The receptionist started to look less and less sympathetic as Shinwell waited with his suitcase in the lobby tapping his fingers. Finally he decided on drastic action. Although it was January, he would pawn his overcoat. Leaving his suitcase behind, he went out wearing his overcoat for what he thought might be the last time, but he was too embarrassed to ask the way to the pawn-brokers in case he asked one of his audience from the night before. After all, he had been addressing them on the judicious planning of the national economy. This complete failure to plan his personal economy would not look good. In the end, after a long and acutely awkward wait, Fanny wired him £2 which she scraped together from Sam and Lucy.[12]

The sheer grind of this period of his life stopped Shinwell from participating very much in national Labour politics. Sometimes he was away from home for fifty days out of sixty, either on party work generally or in Seaham constituency. He had neither the time nor the inclination for more conferences.

It was not until 1933 that he even made a contribution to the annual conference, this time speaking on a resolution against persecution in Germany where Hitler had now been in power for eight months. It was expected to be one of those occasions when no one opposes an obviously worthy resolution and everyone listens patiently and waits for more controversial business. This particular resolution was made more memorable by both the proposing and seconding speeches. The proposer, a certain H. Elvin from Spen Valley Divisional Labour Party, started off with an insensitive and inappropriate remark, describing the German government as consisting of 'ex-lunatics, drug addicts and homosexuals', just when the mentally retarded were being gassed and homosexuals were putting on the pink star in Germany. Elvin failed to mention the persecuted Jews at all. Then Shinwell's speech, given at a time when the SA already had a free hand against any Jewish man, woman or child in Germany that it wished to torment, started with a cringing apology:

> I must not stress, at any rate unduly, any special aspect of this problem and yet I crave the indulgence of the Conference so that I may say just a few words on behalf of a race which in recent months has been humiliated and tortured beyond endurance. To that race I belong, and I have never sought in my long experience of the Labour Movement to conceal it. It is no doubt true that members of the Jewish race are guilty from time to time of acts which incur the displeasure of others, but that fact is by no means peculiar to the members of that race, and whether we be of Nordic or Oriental origin, neither can be regarded as a pretext for persecution.

But his speech improved, specifying horrifying acts of brutality and appealing to the tradition of a socialist party:

> To us of the Labour Movement there can be no race distinctions. The very existence and purpose of the Movement ensure the utmost

antagonism and hostility to any effort to create dissensions among the people of any land, race or creed.

Shinwell warned about growing anti-Semitism in Britain, saying that even the Labour Party was not immune. It was the party from which Oswald Mosley, now parading his fascist Blackshirts, had sprung; it was a party where the visiting Jew was deliberately left to pay his own expenses in an unaffordable hotel; and it was the recent Labour Colonial Secretary who had said that it was wrong for a Jew from Poland, Lithuania or the Yemen to be admitted to Palestine.

It was one of the very few occasions when Shinwell spoke at a Labour Party gathering on Jewish affairs. He had re-entered Labour's national life at this 1933 annual conference with a typical Shinwell contribution – controversial and hard-hitting, a speech of curate's-egg quality. He earned a long ovation.[13]

The wedding of Shinwell's elder son Sammy in November 1933 was a poignant affair. Most of the family were there, including Manny's young sister Clara and her deaf and dumb three-year-old daughter Joan; it was the first time that Manny had seen her and in later years he would do all he could to help her. Considering the state of the Shinwell finances, it was quite a lavish affair. But Manny felt a bit let down by Sammy. He had wanted him to go into politics but he had insisted on being an accountant; and for the time being he was working as a tea-taster for the Co-op because of the financial situation. As for politics, Sammy said, he had no inclination for that kind of life, he had seen too much of it close up.[14]

Sammy's complaints were justified when his father slipped away after the wedding breakfast for another session with Herbert Morrison. He was helping Morrison on his nationalisation proposals for the next meeting of the NEC. His ideas on transport nationalisation were in danger of being thrown out because they proposed too little union involvement on the boards which would run the industries. Shinwell had been closer to what the party wanted in his proposals for the mines. Together they were working on the early drafts of what was later to be known as the 'Morrisonian' model for nationalisation.[15]

Shinwell was becoming noticeably more loyal to the party line in general. Although he still liked to think of himself as a rebel, in truth he was a reliable party employee and a middle-of-the-road parliamentary candidate.

In 1934, he was rewarded with two months off with pay to campaign in his own constituency. The miners were moving towards him, partly because the MacDonald National government had simply failed to deliver. There were still half a million unemployed in the North-East and the new means test had exacerbated the resulting poverty. It also impressed the voters of Seaham that Shinwell was bothering; he spoke in pit village after pit village, on street corner after street corner, he met the miners at all times of the night when they went on and off shifts. He was a tireless campaigner in a seat which the current MP hardly ever visited. MacDonald said afterwards: 'I talked to people whose minds had been poisoned by a previously conducted campaign of lies and calumny to regard me as the author of all their hardships.'[16] To some extent this accusation was true of Shinwell's campaign, but MacDonald, with all the resources available to a Prime Minister, had made the serious mistake of leaving Shinwell all the ground to himself.

At the 1934 and 1935 conferences, Shinwell again showed his loyalty to the party mainstream. In 1934 he backed Bevin's attack on the rebellious Aneurin Bevan, saying he should get out of the party if he found party policy too insipid. And in 1935 he again backed Bevin in his famous attack on Lansbury: 'you hawk your conscience around from body to body asking to be told what you ought to do with it.' Shinwell knew only too well from his own constituents that Lansbury's pacifism was out of date in 1935. He backed Bevin's successful call for Lansbury's resignation and it was Attlee who led Labour in the 1935 election campaign. Bevin now backed Shinwell wholeheartedly, writing the following letter:

All the trade unionists in the country are particularly anxious that you should be returned to the House from Seaham Harbour with an overwhelming majority.

No organised body of men ever gave to a Prime Minister more loyal and whole-hearted support and help than we gave during the regime of the Labour government, and nobody was more wickedly treated afterwards. When the crisis arose he did not even call the Party together to advise them of the facts or to place the situation before them and give them a chance to help. Any suggestions that were made by trade unionists were turned down without any serious consideration having been given to them ...

We all hope that the miners, their wives and families and every working man and woman in your division will vote solidly for you and say to the world – 'We will not be intimidated by the threats of Mr Neville Chamberlain and the great City Interests, neither will we be deluded by the last-minute promises of your opponent.'[17]

The formal campaign in the 1935 general election opened on 29 October when Ramsay MacDonald arrived in Seaham Harbour to be adopted as the National Labour candidate. Shinwell was officially adopted to fight for Labour the next day. While Shinwell was spoiling for a fight, MacDonald was completely exhausted before he started. He was looking older than his sixty nine years and his mind was prone to wandering. Short spurts of coherence could be followed by rambling, and he was no longer able to cope with interruptions and found mocking laughter particularly difficult.[18] Shinwell had no need to encourage the heckling and the hatred: there was plenty around without him joining in and so he was able to keep his hands clean in the campaign itself. He had laid the groundwork effectively and the National government's performance had done the rest in this impoverished constituency.

Shinwell and MacDonald never met face to face on the campaign trail and MacDonald never referred to his old supporter in his speeches. He might have intended to, but so many of his speeches were shouted down – even when Jimmy Thomas came to share his platform – and the meetings were abandoned one after the other. The second week of the campaign was worse; not once was MacDonald given the chance of being heard. His own diary records the atmosphere:

> There developed a wild and hysterical rowdyism, the persistent inter-ruption of meetings which prevented connected and built-up speeches and the actual breakup of meetings. Some of the displays were absolutely bestial. Many of the faces of the women were lined with destitution; their eyes flamed and gleamed with hate and passion; their hair was dishev-elled; their language filthy with oaths and obscenity; they filled one with loathing and fear just like French Revolution studies.[19]

Shinwell stood back and made a series of quite staid speeches on Labour's mining nationalisation policy and on foreign affairs, correcting any impression that a Labour government would be pacifist: 'Can we allow dictators like Hitler and Mussolini to go on the rampage, to brandish their weapons in the faces of all other nations? We prefer economic sanctions but even military sanctions could be considered if all else fails.'[20]

Ramsay MacDonald himself was mentioned very little; in a speech at Murton Colliery which effectively closed his campaign, Shinwell declared: 'We are not concerned with Ramsay MacDonald and I will not waste words on him. The most generous thing we could say is that we dislike the company he keeps.'[21]

MacDonald left Seaham the night before the count. He knew he had only a remote chance of keeping the seat. He had been howled down at meetings, miners had literally turned their backs on him and his posters were hard to find while row upon row of cottages displayed a head-and-shoulders shot of a misleadingly young Shinwell. The children sang:

Vote, vote, vote for Mr Shinwell;
Who's that knocking at the door?
If it's Shinwell, let him in;
If it's Ramsay, kick his shin,
And he won't come a-knocking any more.

At a press conference when polls closed, Shinwell was asked if he thought he would win. 'Fifteen thousand majority,' he bombasted. A journalist shouted back, 'Don't make us laugh.' The *Manchester Guardian* correspondent, whom Shinwell knew, sought him out to warn him that he could only expect a couple of thousand majority at most, and he hoped that the press conference had simply been a show of bravado or he was in for a big disappointment.

As the counting started, bets were laid and MacDonald was soon the clear favourite. Ishbel and Alister MacDonald stayed at the count on their father's behalf. Shinwell knew them of old and they exchanged a few tense courtesies.

At lunchtime on 15 November, MacDonald's friend, agent and host, Dr Grant of Easington, spoke in a broken voice to MacDonald over the telephone, telling him that he should expect to lose by fifteen thousand. Shortly afterwards, they proclaimed the result to an enormous crowd which had assembled in the school playground at Easington Colliery.

Shinwell emerged from the school with a staggering majority of 20,498. He was hoisted shoulder-high and carried across the road to the Miners' Hall. The Labour vote had gone up by 49 per cent:

Ramsay MacDonald (National Labour)   17,882 (32%)
Emanuel Shinwell (Labour)   38,380 (68%)

Majority   20,498

For Shinwell it was the end of a nightmare. It was also sweet revenge by the Labour Party on the man who, after years of serving the cause of British socialism, had nearly destroyed it.

CHAPTER 12

Civil War and the End of the Peace

As Shinwell returned for the third time to the familiar halls and corridors of the House of Commons (MPs had no offices in those days), he must have been struck by the amount of catching-up he would have to do. Fifteen years earlier he had committed himself irrevocably to parliamentary rather than revolutionary socialism, yet he had managed to spend only five of those years in Parliament.

There were new faces and as well as familiar ones of his own generation who had overtaken him. Herbert Morrison and Hugh Dalton were both on Labour's National Executive and were now back in Parliament with an agreement that if Morrison became leader and then Prime Minister, Dalton would become Foreign Secretary or Chancellor. They made a powerful team, the London party boss and the socialist intellectual. When the challenge was made, they openly canvassed support for the first time ever in such a contest, which annoyed Shinwell and others of his generation intensely. The bitterness grew worse when Dalton openly criticised the performance of the two men who had been the main spokesmen for the party for the previous four years, Clement Attlee and Arthur Greenwood. He called them, respectively, a nonentity and a drunk.[1]

Shinwell's first objective was to try to get the looming leadership election put off, arguing that Attlee's leadership was quite adequate for at least another few months, and that they should see how the candidates actually performed in Parliament before they voted one way or the other. After all, he insisted, out of Labour's one hundred and fifty-four MPs, over one hundred were new to the House. But he mustered hardly any support, eventually winning only three votes when he proposed his idea formally to the Parliamentary Labour Party at its first meeting.[2] So, along with everyone else, Shinwell was faced with the choice between Attlee, Greenwood and Morrison.

In many ways the most immediately appealing candidate was Morrison. Of the three, he was certainly the closest to Shinwell, having worked with him on his transport nationalisation proposals. Shinwell, though, was unhappy with Morrison's strong anti-left stance. He had little time nowadays for.far left divisiveness, but he was equally unhappy with Morrison's constant attacks at conferences on fellow members of the party and his apparent right-wing zeal when it came to reassuring capitalists about compensation if there should happen to be any nationalisation. Not only this, in common with many MPs, Shinwell could not see how Morrison could be an effective party leader in the House of Commons and also continue to be leader of the London County Council, which he wanted to do.

So Shinwell voted for Attlee. After all, Dalton had been right about one thing: Bevin's man Arthur Greenwood was usually drunk and, although Shinwell was no longer teetotal himself, he strongly disapproved of the way Greenwood was so often befuddled by drink. He had also worked briefly with Attlee in 1931, when the two of them were left behind to mind the House of Commons during the party conference, and anyway voting for Attlee seemed at the time the next best thing to putting off the election. Few thought him anything more than a stopgap. If he lasted two or three years, who knows what would then happen? Morrison would be away running the London County Council, Greenwood's chances would have evaporated completely in a mist of alcohol and the field would be wide open – maybe even he himself would have a chance. Attlee scraped home.

It was rather a blow to Shinwell's self-esteem when he failed by a wide margin to get a place on the Parliamentary Labour Party Administrative Committee, the elected part of what later became the Shadow Cabinet. Far from being a possible leadership candidate, he would have to prove his mettle again from the back benches. He was left wondering why, in the light of his parliamentary experience going back to 1922, he got so few votes in 1935. The simplest explanation was that he had become out of touch with the leaders and decision-makers in the party. In retrospect he might actually have fared better, from the point of view of his career, had he sought work outside politics but in London. He could then have met regularly with his former colleagues and kept up with what they were doing and thinking. He might not have secured any formal position, particularly as he had lost his union base as well as his parliamentary seat, but he would not have lost the respect of his colleagues to the extent that he did. His employment by the party as a poorly paid itinerant preacher was hardly a launch-pad for the Shadow Cabinet. His frequent financial difficulties, requiring advances from party funds, were almost certainly better known among the people who mattered when it came to choosing the party leadership than his equally frequent successes in local newspapers and with regional party organisations. Additionally, the man who appointed him to do the party's work and who might have spoken up for him, Arthur Henderson, was now dead.

Shinwell also expected that just by defeating MacDonald personally he would automatically gain some stature, but he was soon forced to admit that 'they aren't interested in that kind of thing. I was just the instrument of the party to teach MacDonald a lesson.'[3] In fact, the defeat of MacDonald was very rarely mentioned. When MacDonald returned to the Commons as MP for the Scottish Universities in February 1936, there was some booing on Labour benches in a half-empty House, but Shinwell didn't join in. MacDonald was so obviously the beaten underdog by now. In fact, Shinwell was almost moved to say how sorry he was when he saw MacDonald alone in the Lobby a few days' later, but in the end they passed each other in silence.[4] The whole situation became rather embarrassing. MacDonald was now worn out and almost unintelligible, a million miles from the near-heroic figure of Shinwell's early political life and a shadow of the more recent wise political master.

Shinwell was horror-struck when Winston Churchill, irritated by a new MP's reference to his own loss of the parliamentary seat of Leicester some years before, remembered that MacDonald had also lost that seat once. Churchill snarled: 'They also refrained from electing the Right Honourable Member for the Scottish Universities.' At this, the Labour Party 'let forth a hoot of triumph' breaking the solemnity of the new Leicester MP's maiden speech. The new MP, Harold Nicolson, one of MacDonald's few National Labour supporters, then tried a eulogy of MacDonald. Nicholson recalled: 'They yelled. They hooted. Our people shouted "Order! Order!" On I went, heaping on Ramsay's head, which was exactly below me and bowed in acute misery, the compliments which I had prepared.'[5]

Before the end, Shinwell left the Chamber to vomit.

If somebody is the underdog who's been in trouble – cases of colleagues or members on the other side of the fence – I've always a feeling that that sort of thing shouldn't happen. MacDonald was broken then. He was in a daze, a shocking condition. I dealt him the final blow in the election, the knockout, but it was a duty to be done. Nothing more was needed. This new attack was unnecessary. It served no useful purpose.[6]

A year later, MacDonald was dead.

Meanwhile, Shinwell, the new Member for Seaham Harbour, was making himself a fresh reputation for short sharp attacks on government policy in and out of Parliament and also for a sustained interest in economic policy. It would be a few years before he developed fully his ideas on economic planning which he was to publish during the Second World War, but it was in this field that he was soon specially impressing his fellow MPs with his careful and sometimes original arguments.

A long-standing advocate of coal nationalisation, he now extended his interest to the public control of all basic industries including shipbuilding, steel and transport. Unimpressed with the Soviet experiment of complete central control – a view reinforced by a long discussion with Attlee who visited Moscow in 1936 – he explicitly recognised a role for private capital. When he said as much in the 1936 King's Speech debate, a number of Conservatives guffawed mercilessly at such unexpected moderation.

More important, perhaps, for the impression he sought to make as a serious contender for a senior role in the Parliamentary Labour Party, and eventually in government, was his development of constructive policy ideas for the depressed regions. It was on this subject that Attlee asked him to speak for the Labour front bench as early as April 1936, using the leader's prerogative to appoint front bench spokesmen from outside the elected committee.

When Shinwell spoke on the regions, he was highly effective. He was ready to admit that there had been some improvements in the general economy since the slump years of 1930 and 1931, but there were parts of the country that these improvements had yet to reach. National unemployment was 14 per cent. In Durham, including Seaham Harbour, it was 34 per cent. In Wales and Scotland it was 28 per cent. In some black spots it was much higher, for instance in Bishop Auckland it was 52 per cent, in parts of Glamorgan 60 per cent and in Jarrow 70 per cent. To all this the government had reacted feebly. All it did was to pass a Special Areas Act in 1934 setting up non-profit-making companies to build industrial estates. Shinwell welcomed this as far as it went. It was a good idea to have factories ready in Team Valley and Treforest, but the scale was pitifully small next to the glaring problem.

He proposed instead not just a change of ownership in the basic industry on which most of these depressed areas depended, the coal industry, but also proposed its development into the focus of a modern industrial complex. He argued for a national investment authority to direct funds into the depressed areas to take advantage of the coal from which gas and perhaps eventually oil could also be derived. He saw exactly the fundamental problem of regions dependent on one commodity and proposed what was for those days a rather stunning solution, a planned industrial complex.[7] After a series of powerful speeches, Attlee encouraged Shinwell to develop his ideas on regional policy, and some of them eventually found their way into party documents, although never quite in the form of Shinwell's idea of the planned industrial complex.

At the same time Attlee also started to use Shinwell's expertise on defence, dating from the time he spent as Financial Secretary at the War Office, and he invited him on to his new unofficial Labour Party Defence Committee. It was certainly time for Labour to clarify its stance on defence with the world looking more dangerous by the day.

The Italian invasion of Abyssinia had caused great indignation across the political spectrum from Maxton to Chamberlain. Despite Churchill's unfortunate comment that 'no one can keep up the pretence that Abyssinia is a fit, worthy and equal member of a league of civilised nations',[8] there was almost unanimous support for sanctions against Italy. But they excluded vital oil sanctions at the insistence of the French because they feared that Italy might declare war on France if they went ahead. Labour pressed for oil sanctions and later proposed a vote of censure on the government for its weakness in the enforcement of other sanctions. As he pressed the government, Attlee found Labour views moving with the tide of opinion. The Italians were soon occupying chunks of Abyssinia and the British press was indulging in a tanks-against-spears image of the war.

Then, Hitler's army occupied the demilitarised Rhineland. The Italian fascists and the German Nazis suddenly appeared as a far greater threat together than they had been individually a few months before. Attlee spoke up against the government's inclination to accept a German offer of a non-aggression pact in return for being left alone in the Rhineland, but he spoke from a position of weakness as Neville Chamberlain called Hitler 'a mad dictator' for the first time and then taunted Labour with its refusal to support any increase in defence expenditure.[9] This indeed did set Attlee a problem and he called on Shinwell personally to see if he, with his particular experience of saving money on defence, had any ideas about how to make Labour look more credible.[10]

If he could make robust proposals, Shinwell would certainly earn Attlee's gratitude for pulling him off the horns of a very tricky dilemma. It was a time when the Opposition should have been making a powerful attack on defence and foreign affairs. The Foreign Secretary, Sir Samuel Hoare, had been forced to resign after making unauthorised concessions to Italy in the so-called 'Hoare–Laval Pact'. Baldwin had put up a poor defence of a dithering policy and the government looked vulnerable. Yet Labour was split between the bullish supporters of rearmament, such as Dalton and Bevin, who saw the Nazis as a threat to the labour movement as a whole, and a large body of pacifism and near-pacifism in the party's membership. Attlee and Shinwell had to find a middle line which they could defend as a sensible policy in order to be in a position to attack effectively.

Shinwell's experience at the War Office had taught him that the army was wasteful. Savings could be made, for example, in stores and transport, mechanised services and training methods, by challenging traditional methods without threatening efficiency. At the same time, Shinwell backed Attlee's call for a unified Ministry of Defence to avoid the duplication of three separate service ministries, a logical suggestion supported by a number of Conservatives as well, which eventually resulted in the government conceding a 'Minister for the Co-ordination of Defence' with special responsibility for procurement. Shinwell had something to say about this too. Labour, he argued, would support increases in defence expenditure only when 'proper controls' on procurement – which he never specified – could be introduced to avoid the disgraceful examples of profiteering at the expense of the workers that he had seen in the 1914–18 war.[11] Labour was therefore able to enter the 1936 defence debates with something like a coherent policy. They could oppose Neville Chamberlain's Tea Tax of twopence in the pound because simply throwing new money at defence would dislocate the economy and scarcely improve defences.

This compromise approach, neither appeasement nor rearmament, was effective until November when a dramatic warning by Churchill of the German threat, followed by an extraordinarily weak response from Baldwin, started to shift even Attlee towards support for rearmament. If necessary, the changes which Shinwell proposed would have to come later.

Shinwell himself was less sure. It was only the Spanish Civil War that eventually convinced him that rearmament was essential, even without the improvements in efficiency. In July 1937, along with all but six Labour MPs, Shinwell voted for the government's defence estimates. Later, at the 1937 conference, the Labour Party as a whole gave its support to this new stance. At the Administrative Committee elections later that year, Shinwell's reward for devising an effective temporary policy was to win him a place on the front bench.

Ironically, this took him away from defence. He became the party's spokesman on trade where he continued to develop his ideas on economic planning and regional policy. The government was a relatively easy target; it had no answer to unemployment. Indeed, even after a year of the Second World War, there would be a million unemployed and a 20 per cent unemployment rate in Seaham.

Like many of his colleagues, Shinwell's attention was now drawn to Spain. With increasing horror, Labour watched the slow agonising death of socialism in Spain at the hands of Franco and the fascist generals.

The good was not all on one side. About a thousand men had been executed by the Servicio de Investigacion Militar, the Spanish Republican equivalent of the KGB, and they held about three thousand political prisoners in various conditions, mostly horrific. Yet this was a government whose coming to power Labour had celebrated, a democratic socialist government in Spain. Even now, as Attlee said when he visited Spain a month before Shinwell, in December 1937, it would have been wrong to have described the Spanish government as communist, but they had been forced to adopt communist methods as the price for Stalin's support. They had wanted the support of the democracies. After all, Mussolini's Italy and Hitler's Germany were aiding Franco's fascists, but France had again been fearful of reprisals from Italy, and Britain had insisted on 'neutrality' while actively wooing Italy to tempt it away from an alliance with Germany.

Despite their glaring faults, however, Labour still strongly supported the Republicans. As Shinwell himself had pointed out when raising money to help the dependents of British soldiers who had gone to fight for the Republicans, in war atrocities on both sides had to be expected.[12] But he had never actually seen a war, so he was more than a little horrified on his visit with seven other Labour MPs when a jovial member of the Servicio welcomed him and fellow MP Sydney Silverman to Madrid and took them straight to the infamous 'Tunnel of Death' dug from a suburban house in the direction of Franco's Nationalist lines. Sixty seven Nationalist sympathisers had been lured from hiding and paid the people who were helping them to escape; they had entered the tunnel equipped with torches and clutching a few valuables and keepsakes; then the Servicio had opened up with machine guns and had mown down every one of them.

The Nationalist side was quite capable of even more extreme brutality, their model being the Gestapo rather than the KGB. The scenes in some of the towns they had captured in the Basque part of Spain were early warnings of fascist or Nazi conquests elsewhere. A similar precedent set by the Nationalists was the bombing of civilian targets, an early taste of Blitzkrieg, which left a profound impression on Shinwell and his colleagues as they were driven along vulnerable open roads, delayed by snow, sitting targets for the 'Black Raiders' from Franco's air bases a few miles across the Mediterranean on Majorca.

Once in Madrid, Shinwell felt comfortable only when he was entertained to dinner by the Commander-in-Chief, General Miaja, deep underground. Elsewhere in the surrounded city you could be hit by a shell without any warning. Nationalist artillery bombarded the centre of Madrid every night from about six o'clock onwards. The front was so near that it could be reached by tram. Shinwell actually went in a car, but he noticed that soldiers coming off duty merely walked a few hundred yards back from the front and went home for tea. The front-line trenches were so quiet when he visited that he could hear Nationalist soldiers talking in their trenches, but on their way back to their hotel, Shinwell and Silverman saw small boys collecting hot shrapnel in the street a few yards from a man lying with his head blown to pieces. Women hung out their washing on barbed wire defences and their hungry children went to school in air-raid shelters.

Indeed, it was not just the shelling but the hunger too that was so horrifying. Shinwell and Silverman were provided with an interpreter who explained at great length about the lack of vitamins in the diet of the people living in Madrid. The interpreter himself suffered from boils on his neck and chilblains on his hands as a result. Even distinguished foreign guests did little better. Shinwell had been horrified by the food which he had hardly managed to eat; usually paella cooked in rancid oil or mashed lentils with bread.

Despite major setbacks for the Republicans, Shinwell found an air of optimism arising from the great victory at Teruel – one of the few Republican successes of the war – a week before. But it was possible to sustain the advantage only very briefly. There were not enough arms or any other supplies getting through. Shinwell's other companions, including Aneurin Bevan and George Strauss, went to Teruel instead of Madrid. They reported back that the massive propaganda campaign associated with the victory was hollow. Already it was obvious that a counter-offensive by the Nationalists was gaining ground. The anarchist-led 25th Division, which had been badly mauled in the initial offensive, was ordered back into line. At first the division's political commissar refused to counter-sign the order, saying that it was inhuman to send men into battle without proper equipment and arms. The Divisional Commander, however, insisted that the order be carried out.

Both the Teruel party and the Madrid parties saw well-fed, well-dressed Italian prisoners, and both were bombed by Italian Savoias. Shinwell was horror-struck to see a building collapse and the people in it blasted or buried. Three years later in London, of course, it would be no less horrifying but much more familiar.

They all met at the port of Valencia for a farewell dinner. It was another awful paella, and Shinwell gave the last of his many speeches of the visit. Despite his many misgivings about the way the war was going, he delivered an encouraging preroration: 'Comrades, we return to our country in a new spirit disposed to give you every aid and to exert extraordinary pressure on the British government in order to terminate once and for all the "non-intervention" farce.'

The final act of the group Labour MPs in Spain was unfortunately petty. Attlee had got into trouble with the press for making a clenched-fist salute on his visit; he had been accused of indulging in a Bolshevik ritual. Shinwell was determined to avoid his group falling into the same trap. When it came to their departure, he found a guard of honour was drawn up and there was a band. He had to ask specifically for the band not to play any national anthems because none of them would know how to salute for the benefit of the press. They would all have different ideas, for example Bevan would certainly use a clenched fist, and he himself wouldn't know what to do. The band settled for 'It's a Long Way to Tipperary' and no one saluted.

His fortnight in Spain was one of the most memorable of Shinwell's life. He had seen a new dimension of suffering. The poverty of Valencia and Madrid was every bit as great as that of Glasgow at the turn of the century, and it was compounded by war. He had also been duly impressed by the scale and efficiency of the fascist war machine and, if he hadn't been before, he was now genuinely horrified by the British government's policy of appeasement. As for 'non-intervention' in Spain, the refusal to allow any. British arms to be supplied to the side fighting for democracy was impossible to justify next to the full panoply of assistance given by the Italians and Germans to the Nationalists.[13]

Back in Parliament, he did as he had said he would. Whenever possible along with his colleagues he brought up the subject of Spain. He even angled trade questions to Spain, drawing attention for example to the consequences of German and Italian exclusive access to Spanish minerals. But supporters of the Republicans were hitting their heads against a brick wall.

On 4 April 1938, Question Time in the House of Commons went like this.

> ARTHUR HENDERSON ['junior', Labour MP for Kingswinford] asked the Prime Minister whether he was aware of the establishment of an Italian airbase at Palma, Majorca, and of a German airbase at Pollensa, Majorca; and whether he would draw the attention of the Non-Intervention Committee to this breach of the Non-Intervention Agreement?
>
> THE UNDER-SECRETARY OF STATE FOR FOREIGN AFFAIRS ['Rab' Butler on behalf of the Prime Minister]: I am aware that there have been reports that German and Italian aircraft are present in Majorca. The Hon. Member will recall that under Section 6 of the British Plan of 14th July last, provision is made for the examination of methods of controlling by observation the arrival of foreign aircraft in Spain. It is not, therefore, considered that any useful purpose would be served by raising this matter with the Non-Intervention Committee in the absence of such a scheme of control being agreed upon and being put into force.
>
> MR HENDERSON: Is the Hon. Gentleman aware that the Spanish government officially stated that the facts contained in this question are correct?
>
> MR BUTLER: I have answered the Hon. Gentleman's question by saying that I am aware that there are reports to this effect.

The government at this time were moving towards recognising the Franco regime as part of their policy of appeasing Mussolini. An agent, the Duke of Alba, with semi-diplomatic status was already in London. Shinwell, Willie Gallacher, now a Communist MP, and two other Labour MPs, George Ridley and George Strauss, had planned an assault – only to be met with stonewalling.

> MR GALLACHER asked why, in a communication from the Foreign Office to the London County Council Motor Licence Department, dated 4th March, reference is made to the Spanish Nationalist government, as this conflicts with assurances that the reception of an Agent of General Franco in London in no way constituted recognition by His Majesty's

government of the authorities of the territories at present under his control; and he asked why diplomatic privileges have been extended to the Duke of Alba, contrary to the assurances that were given by His Majesty's government when an agreement to exchange representatives was made with General Franco?

MR RIDLEY asked what privileges and facilities normally accorded to duly accredited diplomatic representatives are now being accorded to the Duke of Alba and his staff; and what privileges and facilities are not being so accorded; and he asked what reply had been returned to the request from the secretary to the Duke of Alba for a driving licence with a further request that he should be exempted [as a diplomat] from the obligation of passing a driving test and of paying the fee of five shillings normally chargeable?

MR STRAUSS asked whether, in view of the fact that the letter of 4th March from the Foreign Office to the London County Council Motor Licensing Department, stating that the Duke of Alba and his staff are regarded officially as diplomats in all but name, goes beyond the agreement between His Majesty's government and General Franco. According to that agreement, neither party will accord or expect to receive diplomatic status for their Agent, so will he say why Parliament was not informed of this further step towards the recognition of General Franco?

MR BUTLER replied: My attention has been called to the letter sent from the Foreign Office to the Licensing Department of the London County Council, and I am glad to have the opportunity of removing the misapprehensions to which its unauthorised publication has obviously given rise. The use of the phrase 'Spanish Nationalist government' in this letter, which was in fact only of a semi-official character, implies no sort of modification of the attitude of His Majesty's government in regard to the recognition of General Franco's administration. It was, however, felt desirable to secure for the British Agent and his staff certain privileges of a kind which are commonly enjoyed by diplomatic officials in order to facilitate the discharge of their duties. It was thus found necessary to concede corresponding privileges such as the one in question to General Franco's Agent and his staff. Such concessions made by either side involve no admission that the recipients possess diplomatic status. The privileges accorded to them are of a limited character.

All further questions – even an attempt by Attlee to get some sort of admission from Butler of the subtle change in policy which had really taken place – were met with 'the views taken in the Foreign Office are those which I have just read out'.

At length, Shinwell, who had been seething on the front bench, exploded: 'Is not the Honourable Gentleman's answer just a piece of humbug, and will he stop this hypocrisy? Why doesn't the Honourable Member answer?'

The Speaker intervened: 'The Honourable Member knows quite well that that is not a proper way to put a supplementary question.'

Shinwell's political anger became a genuine loss of temper. He persisted: 'On a point of Order, if the Honourable Member persists in indulging in half truths, it is the only way to address him.'

Shinwell was still standing on the point of Order when Commander Bower, Conservative MP for Cleveland, shouted loudly and clearly above the din: 'Go back to Poland!'

An old Glasgow colleague, John McGovern, saw what was about to happen and tried quickly to make light of the implicit anti-Semitism: 'On a point of Order. Is it in order for an Honourable Member of this House to suggest to another Honourable Member' (by this time Shinwell was halfway across the gangway, storming towards Bower) that he should return to another country instead of this country, to Poland, suggesting that he belongs to Poland?'

Hansard blandly states: 'At this juncture the Hon. Member for Seaham (Mr Shinwell) crossed the Floor of the House and struck the Hon and Gallant Member for Cleveland (Commander Bower) a blow on the face.'[14]

Shinwell had made his way from the Opposition front bench to the second row of the government seats below the gangway, where Bower sat, as McGovern was speaking, and just as he finished, he smacked the offender very hard with the palm of his right hand across his left ear.

Sir Henry 'Chips' Channon, Butler's PPS, took Shinwell's side:

> The crack resounded in the Chamber – there was consternation, but the Speaker acting from either cowardice or tact, seemed to ignore the incident and when pressed, refused to rebuke Shinwell, who made an apology, as did Bower who had taken the blow with apparent unconcern. He is a big fellow and could have retaliated effectively. The incident passed; but everyone was shocked. Bower is a pompous ass, self-opinionated, and narrow, who walks like a pregnant turkey. I always disliked him.'

But he added wisely: 'The incident does not raise Parliamentary prestige, especially now, when it is at a discount throughout the world.'[15]

Shinwell started shaking. He had now retreated to the Speaker's chair and found Willie Gallacher had also jumped up and was holding his arm. Ignoring Gallacher, he recovered his poise and beckoned Bower to meet him outside where, he gestured, he would roll up his sleeves and deal with him properly. Bower sat, transfixed and, as it turned out, with a burst eardrum.

Attlee signalled to Shinwell to return and apologise, realising what a meal the press could make of it. Meanwhile a Conservative, Sir William Davison, was lumbering to Bower's defence:

Is it in order in this House for a Member sitting on any bench, let alone the Front Opposition Bench, to go across the House and assault a Member and, may I ask you to order the Honourable Member to get out of the House?

Shinwell tried to explain but was ordered by the Speaker not to explain but to apologise. Eventually he had the presence of mind to do so – before storming out. Bower also apologised before going for hospital treatment on his ear.

It was one of those moments when reputations are made or broken. When he found out later that the well-built Bower had been heavyweight champion of the navy and still packed a powerful punch, he was inclined to blanch. But he was really a little pleased by his new reputation for principled ferocity. The Bower incident would live with him right through to his obituary. He had done something which, in truth, many men wish they had the courage to do. There is no verbal retort to some insults. Bower had insulted a socialist just back from Spain where children were dying in the streets because of British 'non-intervention'. In the same phrase he had also insulted a Jew at a time when Hitler was torturing hundreds of thousands of his race. In his half-hearted apology, Bower said that he thought Shinwell's conduct would harm his reputation. That was a misjudgement. Shinwell did himself, his beliefs and his race no harm at all by being seen to fight back, hard.

To intellectuals like Hugh Dalton, changing one's mind was part of an honest searching after the truth. To a more instinctive politician like Shinwell, it smacked of skulduggery. To complicate matters, Dalton was so clever that he could make the worst skulduggery look intellectual. Shinwell and Dalton hated each other.

Dalton, the son of a royal tutor, seemed to Shinwell to weave from one extreme to the other in dealing with the two most crucial issues for Labour of the late 1930s. As a frequent spokesman on foreign affairs in Parliament, Dalton was called on to oppose the slide of the Chamberlain government into closer agreement with Mussolini and Hitler. So far so good. Shinwell had no problems with this, as his line was as anti-fascist as Dalton's. The problem was that Dalton was always trying to make secret deals with rebel Conservatives who were also opposed to appeasement. Shinwell considered this to be playing with fire for the sake of a short-lived parliamentary victory, ignoring the needs of the general election due within eighteen months. He was convinced that collaboration would cost the party dear. Dalton, he felt, was out of touch, wanting to look like a hero in Parliament, regardless of the wider consequences.

To some extent Shinwell was vindicated by the victory of Vernon Bartlett, the Popular Front candidate at a by-election in Bridgwater in November 1938. The Popular Front was a creation of Sir Stafford Cripps who now, as earlier in the 1930s, had tried to set up an alliance of the left, consisting of Labour, the ILP and the communists. The victory of this left alliance candidate, according to Shinwell, showed how wrong Dalton was in trying to fix up a deal with Conservatives. Labour looked weak and compromising.

Dalton and Shinwell also clashed over what to do about Cripps. The issue was straightforward for Shinwell. In January 1939, Cripps issued a memorandum calling for combined youth organisations – again, Labour, the ILP and the communists. This was in direct opposition to the fragile official Labour Party youth movement and would damage the party's credibility at election time by tying the party to the unpopular communists and tiny ILP. Even worse as far as Shinwell was concerned, the intellectual trickery didn't stop there. Cripps supported Dalton's idea of an alliance with rebel Conservatives in October, but in January publicly referred to Churchill, the leading rebel, as a reactionary imperialist. Then suddenly, after much equivocating, to Shinwell's amazement, Dalton bowed with the wind and backed the 1939 conference decision to expel Cripps and his supporters from the party.

It was not just a question of jealousy. No doubt Shinwell did envy Cripps's dazzling left-wing gymnastics and Dalton's remarkable debating skills and economic insights. Both men had slipped away from Shinwell and would be contenders for the leadership if Attlee went, whereas Shinwell, although he had made considerable progress since 1935, was no longer in that league. Attlee was still seen as more likely to be replaced than not; Morrison was now preoccupied with the London County Council; so Dalton was one of his most likely successors. It was not that he had been left behind that made Shinwell dislike Dalton, Cripps and many other middle-class Labour intellectuals, and it went beyond the feeling that some of them were untrustworthy; it was more a feeling that these people were somehow usurpers in the working-class movement. Attlee was different; he had worked his way through London's East End. Dalton and Cripps (and years later Gaitskell and Crossman) had built careers in the labour movement without ever putting down roots.

Fanny was also an influence in this. Shinwell's home life was frankly uneventful. His emotional and physical relationship with Fanny was quite ordinary, and there was never any gossip to the contrary. It was much the same for the puritan Cripps, although Fanny, who was given to singing and dancing and risque jokes, found the disapproving Lady Cripps, always knitting and talking politics, hard work. Dalton's distant wife, Ruth, was widely unpopular and Dalton himself had homosexual tendencies – the Shinwells never associated with the Daltons. But Fanny and Vi Attlee got on well.

Who can measure the effect of these likes or dislikes? Probably they count for little in themselves, but they each pull lightly in one direction or another. Fanny was never directly involved in politics after the Glasgow rent strike, but she had a supporting role, travelling to Seaham, and attending conferences and dinners as the children grew older.

Cripps would always receive political guests in his living-room where Lady Cripps was listening and knitting. Margaret Morrison steered clear of all political meetings. Fanny was at neither extreme. She had no airs or graces, and she said what she liked to whom she liked, and she had no hesitation in telling Manny afterwards whom she loved and whom she loathed. Above all, Fanny and Manny, everyone agreed, were a devoted and thoroughly uncomplicated couple.[16]

In March 1938 Nazi troops marched into Austria and the Anschluss was declared, forcibly including Austria in the German Reich. Labour's response, urged on the front bench by Shinwell, backed by Aneurin Bevan and Chuter Ede, was to identify Spain as the one place where Britain could respond to the dictators. It was all the more frustrating, therefore, when Chamberlain refused even to consider a relaxation of non-intervention.

By September, the threat of war was imminent because of the German threat to Czechoslovakia, and Chamberlain flew to see Hitler at Berchtesgarten and later at Munich. Attlee equivocated when Chamberlain flew to Munich: 'I am sure every Member of this House is desirous of neglecting no chance of preserving the peace without sacrificing principles.' Shinwell agreed publicly, but privately supported Gallacher's more critical approach to doing any deal with the Nazis, telling his old communist friend: 'You're the only Member who had the intelligence to know what was happening and the courage to get up and say it.'[17] But at least Attlee opposed the outcome, the Munich Agreement – in the teeth of public opinion at the time – as a diplomatic defeat that could have been averted if a serious attempt had been made to reach an understanding with Stalin. Shinwell agreed with Attlee's stance and added his criticisms of the Munich Agreement when speaking on trade:

Before the Munich Agreement, Germany was pursuing a policy of self-sufficiency. Now, because of her domination over the agriculture and industry of Europe, she can afford to abandon the self-sufficiency and embark on a policy of exporting goods, and she may well export raw materials, including coal, at prices which will place the industry of this country at a serious disadvantage.[18]

He became one of the strongest advocates on the Labour front bench of an agreement with the Soviet Union to stop German expansion. The purges and terror in the Soviet Union were still softened, in the eyes of many Labour politicians, not only by contrast with the Nazis but also by the very social and economic aims of a revolutionary state. It is doubtful if Shinwell harboured many such illusions but, unlike the Conservatives, he did not see communism as a threat. Anglo-Soviet co-operation became his greatest enthusiasm. He told his constituency party that he was increasingly gloomy about any prospect of the Chamberlain government agreeing anything with the Soviet Union, and appealed to the romance of communism felt still by many of his rank-and-file members:

> I am convinced that Anglo-Soviet co-operation will always be impossible while the government of this country is in the hands of the party that in the early days of the Russian Revolution refused any contact with that resurrected nation, and parroted their determination never to be accused of 'shaking hands with murder'. We know that some of them have done quite a lot of shaking hands with murder. They have not been Russian hands. They have been German and Italian hands.'[19]

Chamberlain formally dropped appeasement when Hitler invaded Czechoslovakia on 15 March 1939. On 18 March he proposed a more constructive approach to Stalin and the Balkan states to limit German aggression. On 20 March he proposed joint consultation with the French, Soviet and Polish governments about 'Joint Resistance' in the event of any action threatening the independence of any of those three states. On 22 March the Poles made it clear they would have nothing to do with a pact involving the Soviet Union.

On 23 March Dalton and Shinwell, with four other Labour delegates, met Chamberlain, at their own request, at 10 Downing Street. They had also wanted to meet with the Foreign Secretary, Lord Halifax, but according to Dalton, 'it had been impossible to get Halifax there so early in the morning'[20] so his senior civil servant, Sir Alexander Cadogan, came instead and recorded the meeting briefly in his diary: 'Friday 24 March. Had to be at No. 10 at 9.45 – P.M. talking to Labour. He explained quite frankly that we weren't cold-shouldering Russia – it was the misgivings of Poland and others.'[21]

Sir Horace Wilson, now Chamberlain's special foreign affairs adviser, was also present. But Chamberlain, after a brief introduction from Dalton, did practically all the talking. The Labour delegation came away from Downing Street convinced that appeasement really had been abandoned at last. Chamberlain now seemed resolved to give specific guarantees to stop Hitler making further progress.

On 28 March Chamberlain ordered a doubling in the size of the Territorial Army and other minor rearmament measures. On 31 March the Soviet problem was circumvented by Britain giving a guarantee directly to Poland; war would be declared on Germany if Poland were attacked. Labour supported the guarantee with the proviso that efforts should continue to be made to bring in the Soviets; both Shinwell and Dalton pushing this line hard as the best way of getting support in the Labour movement. But Polish fears of the Red Army on their territory proved insuperable (and justified).

On 22 August the newspapers carried stories of an impending German–Soviet pact, which was followed immediately by Chamberlain's reminder to Hitler that the obligation to Poland would stand. A formal Anglo-Polish Treaty was signed the very next afternoon, and the French were also now guaranteeing the Poles. On 1 September Germany invaded Poland. That same afternoon, Shinwell, who had previously opposed conscription, now supported it along with the vast majority of the Parliamentary Labour Party. In the early evening, it was agreed that the party would not join the Chamberlain government even in the event of war but that they would support a declaration of war or an ultimatum.

At 7.40 p.m. Chamberlain made a hesitant statement, saying an ultimatum with no time limit had been sent to Hitler; MPs on all sides were appalled. When Greenwood rose, speaking for Attlee who was ill, he was told to 'Speak for England' and 'Speak for the workers'. By the following evening, the government was still finding it difficult to co-ordinate with the French.

Labour's parliamentary leadership met at 9.30 p.m. on 2 September, and two members, Shinwell and the agriculture spokesman Tom Williams, expressed some sympathy with Chamberlain, pointing out that a declaration of war without the French, though doubtless honourable, would be relatively unhelpful to the Poles and could break up a powerful alliance before it started. Dalton said afterwards that Shinwell and Williams were 'inclined to the view that, if France wouldn't fight, we shouldn't either, no matter what the terms of our Treaty with the Poles might be'.[22] Dalton's interpretation is unlikely to be true, since it would have been out of character with Shinwell's earlier stance on guarantees to Poland. There is no reason to think that he was equivocal about war at this late stage.

The argument proceeded no further because an ultimatum was sent to Hitler later in the evening and war was declared the next day, in the knowledge that the French would follow suit, at 11 a.m. At 11.15 a.m. on 3 September, Chamberlain told the nation it was at war with Germany. At 11.30, the PLP Administrative Committee met. Shinwell had just started to speak when the sirens sounded for the first time.

CHAPTER 13

A Barnacle on the Ship of State

Britain came close to losing the war in 1942, its third full year. Disaster followed disaster; there was political turmoil at home and military bungling overseas. Singapore fell in February, Burma in March and Tobruk in June, and there were other disasters in all the main theatres of war, including the escape of German war ships sailing up the English Channel from Brest, record sinkings in the Atlantic and the Far East and the fiasco of the Dieppe raid. The effect of these events was traumatic on British armed forces around the world and on British civilians at home.

No one could have denied that by the start of the year, Britain was hopelessly overstretched. At home, low morale was sapping people's willingness to help the war effort; there were strikes, a by-election defeat for the government and widespread dissatisfaction with the conduct of the war. By the end of October, El Alamein, Guadalcanal and Stalingrad had changed the outlook. This shift from imminent defeat to certain victory was not luck; it was the result of filling every intervening day with hard military decisions and ruthless political change.

Shinwell was active in pushing for political change. Having controversially refused a place in the government in 1940, his main political mission was to stop Labour coalition ministers becoming crypto-Conservatives. His constant barrage reminded them of Labour causes. He pushed hard in Parliament and behind the scenes for improved living conditions in the army, better working conditions in the mines and in shipping and for better planning for reconstruction after the war. He kept in touch with Labour's electorate when ministers simply could not and, in doing so, secured his own position on Labour's National Executive and contributed to Labour's victory in the 1945 general election.

He certainly came to regret refusing a post in the government. His anomalous position as a sort of unofficial leader of the opposition caused him to clash again and again with senior Labour Party colleagues. For Bevin and Dalton he varied from a flea-bite to a bête noire. He was always causing trouble, storming out of meetings and refusing to toe the line. One fellow

MP told him to his face that it seemed to him that he was a Walter Mitty. Sometimes he saw himself as Sir Francis Drake, sometimes as Elisha and sometimes as Ananias.[1] To be sure, by the time they heard this assessment of Shinwell, a fair number of colleagues would have fancied the same quick end for Shinwell as for Ananias, the Biblical teller of half-truths: 'the young men rose and wrapped him up and carried him out and buried him.'[2]

In the early days of the war, the so-called 'Phoney War', Shinwell learned how to fire a rifle in the Home Guard. He also went along with Labour's electoral pact with the government for the war period and Labour's general support for the war effort. When unemployment, six months into the war, still stood at one and a half million, at a time when every brain and muscle was so obviously needed, he could attack the government effectively without the risk of appearing unpatriotic. The idea of planning industry so that the right people and the right amounts of the right products were where they were needed became increasingly popular.

To economic chaos and mass unemployment the Chamberlain government added military disaster in Norway in April 1940. It was no way to run a war. Norway had been neutral but iron ore had reached Germany through the port of Narvik, so Britain had laid mines there. In response, Germany had invaded and conquered Norway and Denmark in a few days. A British and French counter-invasion, inadequately thought-out and supplied, had been a fiasco. Labour demanded a debate.

Attlee's opening speech of the two-day Norway debate widened the issue to the whole conduct of the war, covering unemployment, inefficiency and lack of leadership. It was a crippling indictment. There was so much support for Labour's motion in the House of Commons and in the country as a whole that, after the first day's debate, Attlee recommended to Labour MPs that the debate should be seen as a 'motion of censure' so that if the government lost,it would have to resign.

To the annoyance of most of the Labour leadership, Herbert Morrison saw his chance for promotion. The London Labour leader had developed a burning desire to replace Attlee. He calculated that if Labour wounded Chamberlain but failed to bring him down, then it would be asked to join him in government. Morrison knew that he was much more acceptable than the more outspoken Attlee to most Conservatives. The Norway debate would wound. A motion of censure would kill. He tried, but in the end was unable to muster enough support to prevent the death-blow. The motion of censure went ahead.

Chamberlain won, but only by eighty-one votes instead of by the government's usual two hundred and fifty. He would have to resign and was to be replaced by either Winston Churchill or Lord Halifax, who would in all probability lead a coalition with Labour ministers led by Attlee. The decision fell on Churchill, and within a few hours Hitler invaded Holland

and Belgium. Labour's decision on whether to join Churchill was suddenly desperately urgent.

When Attlee met the Labour National Executive in Bournemouth, where the 1940 annual conference was being held, he did not yet actually know whether Churchill or Halifax was to be Prime Minister. Shinwell reminded everyone that Churchill had been a fierce opponent of Labour all his life. At his most virulent he had called striking miners 'rats' and ordered them 'back to their holes'. Many trade unionists and ordinary members of the Labour Party hated him. Altogether, Shinwell and Attlee expected Halifax to be chosen because of his wider support among Conservative MPs and Shinwell at least made his preference for Halifax clear.[3] But it was not Labour's decision. Attlee had told Chamberlain to his face at 10 Downing Street that Labour would serve under almost anyone but him and the rest was up to the Conservatives.

With news of blitz, invasion and disaster now pouring in, the National Executive agreed a resolution that Labour should take its 'share of responsibility, as a full partner, in a new government which, under a new Prime Minister, commands the confidence of the nation'. It was agreed by the conference by over two million to a hundred and seventy thousand votes.

Soon the choice of Churchill was known and Labour joined him without further hesitation. Within hours of his appointment, Churchill invited Attlee to what they both later called 'a pleasant chat' at the Admiralty to talk about ministerial jobs; Attlee and Greenwood were to be in the War Cabinet without portfolios along with Churchill himself, Chamberlain and Halifax. Ernest Bevin was to be invited in from the Transport and General Workers' Union to be Minister of Labour and National Service. Labour also provided the Minister of Supply, Herbert Morrison, the first Lord of the Admiralty, Albert Alexander, the Minister of Economic Warfare, Hugh Dalton, and the Solicitor-General, Sir William Jowitt. Seven senior ministers overrepresented Labour's tally of MPs but was no more than a fair reflection of Labour support in the country. Labour also managed to secure from a willing Churchill the dismissal of Sir Samuel Hoare whom some considered a potential quisling, and Sir John Simon's elevation out of the way to be Lord Chancellor. Hoare and Simon were the worst examples of the recent past. They were now out, and Labour was in and playing its full part.

Shinwell was offered only a bit-part and he refused it. Churchill, after some difficulty, got in touch with Shinwell in Bournemouth by telephone. 'I want you to join my government. I want you to take charge of the Ministry of Food – in the Commons.'

By this time Shinwell knew that Lord Woolton had been appointed Minister of Food and that he was only being offered a second-rate post. Nevertheless he had taken an interest in food supply in the year or two before the war.

'I'm sorry. I am not interested.'

'What? I understand your colleagues want you in.'

'I'm sorry, I can't accept; but I assure you that I don't intend to embarrass the government in the prosecution of the war.'[4]

And that was that.

The post offered was not good enough for him. Just as he had heard that Dalton had announced he was going to be 'no one's bottle-washer', the last thing Shinwell wanted to be was general assistant to a Conservative peer. He himself admitted later he might have taken a more senior post, especially to do with shipping, although at the time he said he simply disliked coalitions.

His refusal should be seen in context. At the time, no one could have predicted the next few months' events. The early days of the German invasion of Holland and Belgium were serious enough but the idea that France would fall in six weeks and Britain would be threatened with invasion in the summer, all politics forgotten for a while, would have seemed ridiculous. It seemed far more likely at that time that ministers, if not the Coalition, would come and go, as a continental war ground on. Shinwell certainly never imagined that the government now being formed would last five years; otherwise he would have given the whole matter far deeper consideration and probably taken the job.

Shinwell's attitude to Dalton at this time was one of particularly withering contempt. He regarded Dalton as hysterical in his desperation for a job high up in the government, trying to keep all the conference hotel phones to himself in case Churchill should happen to ring him. 'He fully expected that he would be asked to join the War Cabinet, and believed that such a position was well within his capabilities, no matter what view was held by his colleagues.' He finally had to settle for the Ministry of Economic Warfare.

As events unfolded over the next few weeks, Shinwell's action in turning down a job to do with the welfare of the Home Front started to look like a bad miscalculation. When Attlee asked him why he hadn't come and told him what Churchill had offered so he could 'wangle' him something better, it took him by surprise. He had been under the mistaken impression that all the appointments had been worked out between Attlee and Churchill in advance. His reply was truculent: 'I didn't want you to wangle anything for me; I didn't expect an appointment. In any event, I was not going to accept an appointment for which I had no obvious competency. I shall do very well outside the government.' But he realised he might have missed a once-in-a-lifetime opportunity. His heart sank as Hitler swept across France, and some of his constituents started to ask him why he had refused to follow his own leader and help Churchill in such an obvious hour of need.[5]

Bombed out of their Balham home, Fanny, Ernie (until he joined the army a few months later) and Rose went to live in Workington, leaving Manny behind to work out what it meant to be in the wartime opposition. It sounded to people who didn't know, rather like a fifth column. On the other hand it was exactly these kinds of democratic rights, now denied to the whole of Europe, that Britain was fighting to defend.

In any case, Shinwell was not technically in opposition. His party, with his support, was in the government. Elderly Labour MPs, H.B. Lees-Smith and then F.W. Pethick-Lawrence, actually performed formal Opposition duties as far as the business of the House of Commons was concerned. Then there was actual opposition from independent Liberals like Clement Davies, from Willie Gallacher and Labour's far left, notably Sydney Silverman and Aneurin Bevan. Shinwell was an elected member of Labour's National Executive and PLP Administrative Committee, both firmly attached to the Churchill–Attlee Coalition. So much so that when he first ventured some criticism of the government, he was accused of disloyalty to his own party which he was reminded had offered the government its 'full support'. He was even threatened with expulsion.[6]

In some ways Shinwell was a symbol of democracy, harassing and haranguing the government and stopping it from becoming complacent. His role was often merely symbolic and nearly always frustrating. He was delighted when, just once, from outside the government he indisputably played a constructive part in the war effort. This was at the beginning of 1942. Sir Stafford Cripps had just arrived back from Moscow, where he had been ambassador, and was determined to be Prime Minister by March. He returned a popular hero and he immediately toured the country stirring up resentment against the government by comparing British efforts with the Soviet war sacrifice. Morale on the Home Front was low. Cripps decided to make it lower.

He made a broadcast on the BBC on 8 February comparing Britain with the Soviet Union, and he could hardly have made a stronger impression. The Soviets had not been prepared, yet they had organised themselves within weeks; their industrial areas had been overrun yet they had rebuilt all they needed safely in the Urals to the east. They were now building aeroplanes and tanks in unimaginable numbers, but they needed more and Britain could do little to help. Why not? He had discussed the answer to this with Shinwell, whom he later said should be in the War Cabinet himself.[7] Because we could not even provide ourselves with enough merchant ships or protect them adequately when we had them. Each month worse shipping losses were announced.[8]

The Cripps assault petered out as he proved himself an incompetent Leader of the House of Commons and eventually he disappeared from centre stage to go on a mission to India and then to become a moderately successful

Minister of Aircraft Production. But the shipping problem did not go away and this was precisely Shinwell's area of expertise.

Right from the start of the war Shinwell had warned about inadequacies of organisation in shipping that could lead the country to early disaster. On the one hand, there was the very nature of the British cargo fleet; it was too slow and reinforced decks were few and far between, which made it too vulnerable. On the other hand, the crews were not properly trained, the appalling living and working conditions led to problems of manpower recruitment and inadequacies of planning often meant taking the risk of having vessels queueing outside ports waiting to load or unload coal and other vital supplies. It was in this area that Shinwell made his contribution, with apparently some help from the future Prime Minister Harold Wilson, then a civil servant aged twenty-five, working in the Cabinet Office.

Wilson had made a name for himself as a statistician and a competent temporary civil servant. Both he and Shinwell (they did not meet until 1942) were lone voices as far as the importance of figures were concerned. Figures for coal bunkerage, figures for training equipment, figures for regional manpower recruitment, figures even for real tonnage were all difficult to come by, making war planning a nightmare. Not just grandiose schemes of national economic planning, but simply planning to avoid keeping ships waiting in the Bristol Channel while U-boats were around.

Shinwell had a large number of contacts among ship-owners and seamen, and he was able to produce a memorandum pinpointing the information that could reasonably quickly be made available to, say, the Minister of Supply, if only he would use it. Shinwell decided to work up his proposal to the point where civil service scepticism would give way. He enlisted the help of a Hungarian economist working in Oxford, Tom Balogh, who in turn brought in Harold Wilson, also an Oxford economist. Together they worked out a method of ensuring that relevant up-to-date statistics on shipping were made available – in a usable and digestable form – to relevant ministries.

Sir Andrew Duncan, the new Minister of Supply, built this new system of reporting into his department before the end of the summer.[9] Inshore shipping losses were greatly reduced as a result. In a small but perhaps significant way, Shinwell contributed positively to the war effort. He did not, as he said he would have liked, 'ride rough-shod over the conservativism which was strangling our life-lines of food and raw materials'. Nor did he, as he claimed, have 'access to much secret information about our shipping'.[10] He did carve out for himself, however, a niche of expertise. People listened to him when he talked about shipping.

For the rest, he was too angry, too bitter, too destructive. Although some of the press, and Beaverbrook personally, thought it useful to have a 'ginger-up' group, to keep ministers on their toes, it is doubtful if it actually made much difference to ministers in reality.[11] Shinwell for the Labour malcontents and Earl Winterton for the Conservatives became known, only half-affectionately, in the light of the play about elderly murderesses, as 'Arsenic and Old Lace'.

Their most famous attack early in the life of the Coalition was on the parliamentary newcomer Ernest Bevin whom Shinwell assailed for inadequate direction of manpower and capital for the war effort. There were only forty thousand people being trained in Britain compared with seven hundred and eighty thousand in Germany. Bevin agreed with the figures and started to explain the problems he faced in the same patient way he might have dealt with a subcommittee of the TUC. Shinwell for once had Bevin, the new MP for Central Wandsworth, at a disadvantage. He could be as rude as he liked to him here on his own familiar ground: 'The Minister of Labour agrees! Then what nonsense is this? How futile, how childish in comparison!' In vain, Bevin tried to explain the difficulties with industrial relations and consultation which had caused Britain to be so far behind Germany. On this and a whole series of parliamentary occasions, he ended by losing his temper and sometimes also his way through his notes as a result of constant interruptions from Shinwell, Earl Winterton, Aneurin Bevan, Leslie Hore-Belisha (a discontented former Conservative minister) and Clement Davies.

This Bevin-baiting was sometimes fun to watch and sometimes embarrassing. Shinwell was undoubtedly best at it – even his opponents recognised his excellent dialectical skills. But did it do any good? The sad fact is that Shinwell for the most part was just wasting his and everybody else's time. Making Bevin angry didn't make him work harder and pointing out the powers of compulsion in the field of employment theoretically available to him didn't make Bevin use any more of them. Even if he had been inclined to do so, in the conditions of the Coalition, that simply wasn't practical, assuming they could have been made acceptable to the public without causing a revolution.

On the whole, the conclusion must be that Shinwell's style of opposition to the Churchill Coalition, apart from his contributions on shipping and occasionally on the coal industry, was based on the outdated First World War model. Then it had been different. The rights and wrongs of fighting the war at all were much more in doubt, especially on the left; Henderson's joining the 1915 Asquith coalition was a more controversial and lonely decision than the massive conference approval given to Attlee and his fellow Labour ministers.

Never in the First World War was the whole nation involved in an active blitzed Home Front and never was a normally imperturbable senior civil servant able to note in his diary, 'Invasion expected tonight'. The same civil servant, the Head of the Foreign Office, Sir Alexander Cadogan, referred to Shinwell as a 'barnacle on the ship of state'.[12] This was a bit harsh! But to many ministers and not a few of the public, Shinwell's and other opposition to the government could easily look unpatriotic. He could very easily be made to seem a traitor by his enemies, having, as Dalton described it, 'turned down responsibility for the nation's food as a bloody insult'.[13]

There was also quite a clear understanding by the general public – at least among potential Labour supporters – of the limitations on Labour when in a wartime Coalition. Most people did not have a long folk-memory of coalitions as did Labour MPs who had personally watched MacDonald and Snowden in 1931. Few would have seen any sense in Shinwell's note to Attlee when the matter of him refusing office came up again: 'I don't like coalitions. My constituents don't like them. I refused to take office in such a government in 1931 ...'

Behind-the scenes work on shipping apart, never was Shinwell's impotence more obvious and never was the futility of his opposition more apparent than when Britain was on its knees in early 1942. On 15 February, Singapore fell. On 19 February, Shinwell chose to launch a personal attack on Attlee, Bevin and Morrison, accusing them of vying for position in a general debate in the Parliamentary Labour Party on the desirability of a War Cabinet without departmental responsibilities. Shinwell was getting a name for these personal attacks (and for storming puce-faced out of meetings) and it meant that the whole argument tended to get lost while people waited for the personal abuse and the stormy behaviour. He never had enough information, he reduced arguments too much to personalities and, frustrated, he worked on too short a fuse.

The PLP Administrative Committee by now had very little influence, and Shinwell, by offensive behaviour, made sure it had none in most of the cases where he was concerned. A few weeks after his unsuccessful attack on Labour members of the War Cabinet, on 11 March, Shinwell supported Bevan's move at a meeting of the PLP to have all ministers thrown off the Administrative Committee, to make it an instrument of opposition. Properly argued, there was some merit in saying that ministers could not reasonably be in a Cabinet and a kind of Shadow Cabinet at the same time, but it came across as a fire-breathing attack on personalities. Shinwell was by now simply misjudging his audience and he was achieving nothing at all.[14]

On 20 June, Tobruk fell to Rommel. A no-confidence motion on 1 July, proposed and seconded by Conservatives, gave Aneurin Bevan a chance to shine, repeating the witticism doing the rounds that in the British Army someone of Rommel's social class would have reached the only rank of sergeant. He accused Churchill of 'mistaking verbal felicities for mental inspirations' and he demanded a second front in Northern Europe.[15] It was more substantial and less bitter than a Shinwell speech. It marked out the younger Bevan rather than Shinwell as the leader of the malcontents for the rest of the war, except for Shinwell's last hurrah just a fortnight later.

At Question Time on 16 July, the Chancellor of the Exchequer, Sir Kingsley Wood, made a statement on old age pensions to the effect that, despite the increase in the cost of living, little could be done to improve pensions – only half-a-crown a week extra was possible. Shinwell actually missed the announcement; he was boycotting the House of Commons that day because it was holding a shipping debate in secret, much to his disgust. But pensions were a big issue between the Coalition parties. There was a great deal of to-ing and fro-ing by Attlee trying to reach a compromise between the PLP and the Chancellor of the Exchequer, but he was unsuccessful and the crunch came at a PLP meeting a week later.

Arthur Greenwood, now sacked as a minister and formally Leader of the Parliamentary party, speaking in his slow slurred way, suggested that an amendment to the pensions motion which was to be put by Ernest Bevin on behalf of the government the next day should be proposed by him, but withdrawn if Bevin promised improvements in the next session. The idea was to allow the Conservatives in the Coalition to give way to avoid a confrontation on a domestic issue at an awkward time. No one wanted to rock the boat further in the aftermath of the no-confidence debate. Everyone agreed with the tactics. Shinwell was sceptical and started to say that he doubted whether Bevin would be allowed to say much, then he was interrupted mid-sentence by Mrs Janet Adamson, a deaf elderly widow and MP for Dartford, 'using her unpleasant voice even more unpleasantly than usual', telling Greenwood not to forget about elderly widows in his amendment.[16]

The House of Commons waited impatiently the next day for Bevin to make the announcement. First, Pethick-Lawrence formally moved the agreed amendment on behalf of the Parliamentary Labour Party. Then, within a few sentences, any MP used to listening to Bevin realised that he had no news for them. Once he started talking about his lifetime of devotion to the Labour movement it was fairly clear he had nothing to say. Shinwell interrupted him, which Bevin hated, to point out that no one on the Labour side was cheering him, just the Conservatives. 'I don't care how much Tories cheer, nor how much you hate it Shinwell,' came the retort. Bevin waffled for another twenty minutes or so, and expressed some hopes that definitely made no promises for the next session. Nevertheless, to everyone's astonishment, Greenwood staggered to his feet and blandly announced that Labour would withdraw the amendment.

Shinwell lambasted him, telling him he was not the whole of the Labour Party. What did he think he was doing speaking for everybody? 'I refuse to allow the amendment to be withdrawn and we shall take it to a Division,' he declared. He took the opportunity to launch into a good old-fashioned attack on the government for forgetting that they had to maintain a society worthy of its fighting men and so on and so forth. Even Dalton gave Shinwell some credit, although he called the speech 'demagogic'. It persuaded forty nine of his fellow Labour MPs that their minister had got no concessions from the Conservative-dominated Coalition.

In fact, the speech was perhaps the last real Shinwell classic, all atmosphere and style, pauses and gestures. His Biblical critic would have been delighted. He started as Sir Francis Drake saving the pensioners and widows of England from all their foes, switching then to Elisha seeking to transform reactionary Coalition social policy into the true blood of socialism and finally descending to Ananias complaining about the sacrifices the party had already made at the altar of consensus.[17]

This was a success for Shinwell and it gave Labour ministers a jolting reminder about the political compromise implicit in their position, a compromise it was easy for them to forget amid the demands of war. It did nothing for pensions, however, and the same row occurred again a year later. Shinwell claimed that it was good for the country, democracy and the party to have this kind of rebellion, but hardly anyone agreed with him at the time. Instead, his reward for an impressive and well-publicised performance was to be threatened with expulsion again and warned by his constituency party to toe the line at such a critical time in the war.

With hindsight it is hard to see what even this relative success achieved, a minor revolt at a time when, outside the narrow confines of Westminster, few seemed interested in party politics. There was a mood for change developing in the country. Two by-elections, at Eddisbury and Maldon, returned radical left 'Commonwealth' candidates, but the kind of politicking involved in the pensions revolt was perhaps not what people wanted.

When the Administrative Committee met again, Shinwell nearly came to blows with the Secretary, Scott Lindsay, who muttered 'Hear! Hear!' when Shinwell was being criticised for leading the revolt. He followed this up by telling Shinwell he was a 'menace to the party'. Shinwell suddenly went calm, pursed his lips and threatened, 'I will expose you.' No one knew what it meant, and no one ever found out, but Scott Lindsay never breathed another word against Shinwell. All in all, it was clear that there was little mileage in this kind of activity in the middle of the war. Shinwell decided, quite consciously, to apply his energy elsewhere. He would go to the House of Commons from time to time, but the main opposition work could be left now to Bevan, Silverman and a few others.[18]

In the autumn, there were more indications that Shinwell was right not to carry on in such an active way in parliamentary opposition. There were complaints from constituents. The Durham Miners' Association, whose secretary, Sam Watson, had never got on with Shinwell,[19] criticised him and started a campaign for the retirement of MPs at sixty five, which would have meant that Shinwell could not have served in a further full Parliament if the election was later than 1944. In September, the association wrote to all Labour MPs in their area with this proposal, which Shinwell recognised at once as a manoeuvre to get him out. In fact, the association contributed very little to Seaham Harbour funds; what little was contributed nearly all came from local pit 'lodges'. Shinwell had been neglecting his constituency lately, though, and he took the Miners' letter as a warning and decided to nurse it more carefully. Sam Watson in particular felt that Shinwell's was a seat that should be held by a miner or at least by an MP sponsored by the Miners' Federation.

On top of constituency warnings came parliamentary warnings. Shinwell came bottom of those elected to the Administrative Committee in October 1942 with just fifty three votes, as against one hundred and four for Jim Griffiths, the popular MP for Llanelli, and one hundred for Dalton. By then good news from the various fronts had started pouring in, from El Alamein, the Pacific and Stalingrad, which would take the heat out of various campaigns in which Shinwell had become involved, such as 'Second Front Now', 'More Help for Russia' and others implicitly critical of the running of the war.

An eventual victory, however far away, now seemed the most likely result. Shinwell therefore set about the task of putting his party and himself in the best possible position to take advantage of it.

Since 1941, Shinwell had been chairing the Labour National Executive's subcommittee on the Social and Economic Transformation of Britain. By February 1943, he reported to the executive that he had thirteen sub-sub-committees and these in turn had numerous sub-sub-subcommittees working on every kind of industrial and social problem.[20] Many of these produced reports, and the result was a vast amount of paper and an even vaster amount of talk, the main thrust being to maintain the central planning and control which contributed to the war effort to ensure the most efficient use of capital and human resources in peacetime. This in turn would allow a socialist government to produce a more humane society with social insurance and a health service. There were few signs of co-ordination in all this work and not even very much that was new. Papers on town planning, for instance, simply adopted the government's 1941 Uthwatt report which rejected land nationalisation in favour of government development rights, and papers on the health service were little different from those coming out of Whitehall.[21]

All in all, Shinwell's committee accumulated a useful body of material on which the new Policy Committee, set up without him in July 1943, could draw. It is doubtful if it achieved much more. It contributed nothing directly, for instance, even to the 1943 conference document, 'The Labour

Party and the Future'.[22] Shinwell was not even involved in the first day
of the conference when that paper was discussed. Instead, he rather surprised
the conference by drawing together the results of his committee's work
the following day in such a way that it drew applause from delegates but
astonished those who had contributed to the committee's work, since they
were unable to recognise any part of it.[23]

Shinwell used his conference slot less to report on the work of his
committee than to describe the ideas contained in *The Britain I Want*, his
first full-length book, published just before the conference. The book and
the speech both owed more to Robert Blatchford than to any committee
papers and they both help to explain Shinwell's attraction for rank-and-
file party members and supporters:

> Those, even some of the leaders of our party, who have never had to
> go knee-deep into the economic quagmire will little appreciate just what
> wages mean to the average workaday family. To them, wages represent
> the means of survival; without the weekly pay envelope life has no
> meaning, except that of despair and destitution. It follows that the pre-
> dominant economic interest of the great bulk of our workers centres
> around the amount of money they collect in return for their labour.[24]

In dealing with housing he also demonstrated his awareness of everyday
problems, referring to detailed specific needs in living-rooms and bedrooms,
bathrooms and kitchens. He rehearsed in some detail the coherent arguments
for the nationalisation of the mines and the railways but reverted to waffle
when talking about economic planning as a whole:

> We cannot in days to come leave the industrial system to the select pursuits
> of private enterprise bent on the securing of profits and yet more profits.
> What is required is the fixing of national responsibility for the complete
> development of all our resources – so that for the first time in history
> we should be able to lay claim to the title of a state planned with the
> great objective of achieving and maintaining the social and economic
> happiness of our people.[25]

This kind of generalisation about economic planning demonstrates the
lesson Shinwell learned from looking at his own committee's papers. While
the nationalisation of particular industries, notably coal, electricity, gas,
railways and iron and steel, was desirable, Gosplan-style planning of the
whole economy was neither possible with private ownership in most
sectors nor compatible with political freedom.

So, in his new 'Charter for Living', in a booklet published in 1944, *When
the Men Come Home*, Shinwell included wide-ranging social security
measures and tough measures on land ('we have no time to waste on futile

and prolonged arguments as to heredity rights, and special pleading'),[26] but he goes in for 'economic democracy' which is altogether milder than the planned economy which he had been specific about before the war and had waffled about during the previous year. 'Economic democracy' included workers' participation in production committees, a national minimum wage, some degree of control over investment, various improvements in education, training and housing and the nationalisation of coal and the railways.

In July 1943, the National Executive Committee restructured all its sub-committees. Dalton and the party's General Secretary, Jim Middleton, set up a new system designed to see the party through to the end of the war. Dalton was to chair the main Policy Committee and made sure that Shinwell was excluded altogether. Shinwell stormed out of the Executive Meeting of 21 July when the decisions were taken and Dalton simply remarked that Shinwell had 'shot his bolt and lost all support on the National Executive'.[27]

His exclusion at this stage had more to do with the feeling, shared by Attlee among others, that it was time for the party's main policy committee to switch from being a general fund of ideas for the peace to a committee that would co-ordinate between ministers in the Coalition who would eventually have to lead an election campaign and the party as a whole. A 'coup' against Shinwell was thus essential, despite the fact that he had come second in the constituency section's voting for the National Executive, a measure of his considerable and growing popularity in the country. Much less popular in Parliament, he lost his seat on the Administrative Committee in 1943. Outside the house, his books and his speeches were liked, and ordinary members of the party saw and heard more of Shinwell in the last three years of the war than they did of Attlee, Bevin, Dalton or any of the rest of the official leadership.

Shinwell's revolts in the House of Commons and his senior position in the party presented opportunities not just to be published but also to be heard on the BBC's opinion programmes, including from time to time 'The Brains Trust' (at £75 a go).[28] He travelled widely towards the end of the war, speaking at Labour meetings all over the country, homing in whenever possible on Seaham Harbour. At public meetings he rarely strayed from the party's official line and was disinclined to criticise the Coalition, emphasising its worthy preparatory work on employment law, social insurance, industrial injuries, regional policy and coal. The war had shown that State control of industry could work. Ownership had stayed private but Labour ministers had enforced centrally-controlled production. They could, he argued time and time again, do it in peacetime too.

He did not neglect the House of Commons altogether. Throughout 1943 he continued to push for an early second front. He fought Bevin over the government's feeble response to the Beveridge report, but he supported him strongly over his new measures for training in the building industry and to improve conditions in the catering trade.

His tone became so moderate that Churchill even considered making him Minister of Fuel and Power when there looked as if there would be a vacancy in 1944, but Attlee after some thought decided that Shinwell would be a bad choice. When Bevin heard about it, he lost his temper and told Attlee he was being far too feeble by even toying with the idea: 'Bloody hell! If that bugger is brought in, I shall go out, and you can tell that to the Prime Minister. I won't stand for it.' Bevin inveighed against Shinwell and said it would put a 'premium on disloyalty' even to consider him and 'discourage all the decent people in the party who had played the game and supported the government in moments of difficulty'. All this could be viewed as the opinion of a crusty trade-union leader with relatively poor House of Commons debating skills, had he not added: 'He is just another nominee of Beaverbrook.'[29]

Beaverbrook, minister, newspaper magnate, millionaire and reactionary 'eminence grise' behind Churchill as Conservative leader in the war, would certainly have been strange company for Shinwell to keep. But Shinwell admitted years later that Bevin had a point. It was perhaps a measure of Shinwell's wartime lack of direction, and discretion, that he found it useful to have regular lunches, every two or three months, with Beaverbrook. Bevin was probably right that Beaverbrook's closeness with Shinwell, whom he befriended for his own amusement as the 'government's most effective opposition', probably did indeed influence Churchill to consider offering him the Ministry of Fuel and Power. But Churchill was also personally fond of Shinwell as 'a man whose heart was in it', in some ways rather like himself, 'but inclined to screw up his face as if he were taking a dose of nasty medicine'.[30]

It was also probably Beaverbrook's opinion of Churchill as electorally undefeatable which led Shinwell to the otherwise incredible suggestion to Attlee that Churchill should have been invited to continue as Minister of Defence in a Labour majority government. Needless to say, Attlee turned the idea down immediately.[31]

There was also more than a touch of Beaverbrook in another half-worked-out idea that Shinwell touched on from time to time. This was that Britain should not have too close connections either with the United States or the Soviet Union, but instead should have close but vague links with the Commonwealth and Western Europe. In some mysterious way, Britain linking itself to economies in a considerably worse state even than its own was to 'preserve her independence and power'.[32]

By 1945, Shinwell had climbed to a higher position in the party than he had ever reached before. In the small Parliamentary Labour party he had the consistent backing of only about fifty MPs. But the party nationally was his real strength; so long as he kept up his clear partisan line and maintained a high profile in the country, he was virtually guaranteed his position on the National Executive.

As ever, the national membership was to the left of the Parliamentary party. Yet what the Parliamentary party was offering in 1945, nationalisation, a national health service, extensive State controls, had all been made possible by the war. It would have seemed an impossibly radical programme in 1939. The party had moved to the left in its official policy and Shinwell had moved to the right to meet it.

He was reminded of this when he sent H. G. Wells a copy of *The Britain I Want*. The aging socialist remembered that Shinwell had been a revolutionary socialist once, virtually a Bolshevik. Nowadays he seemed to think he was Lenin and Marx rolled into one just because he criticised Ernest Bevin. Wells wrote back:

> I'm very pleased that you've sent me your book with which I am in almost complete agreement. I suppose you were asked to write it and you had to write to the title, 'The Britain I Want'. That seems to have prevented your saying as plainly as you might otherwise have done, that there isn't going to be a Britain except as a part of a unified Socialist world. More strength to your elbow.
>
> Yours for the Revolution,
> H. G. Wells.[33]

The irony was completely lost on Shinwell.

CHAPTER 14

Nationalisation: the Great Victory

The continuous, simmering, damaging row between Shinwell and Dalton carried on right through the 1945 election period. 'I walked into the room and there was Hugh Dalton, his eyes blazing with insincerity,' was a popular quip about Dalton which Shinwell liked to repeat.

On the other hand, Shinwell could be unpredictable, muddled in his thinking and utterly bloody-minded. Dalton loathed and despised him, and he hated Dalton.[1] Dalton was incapable of saying anything about Shinwell without adding a rude remark and Shinwell was invariably at his most unpleasantly sardonic whenever Dalton came into the conversation. Bevin also looked down on Shinwell as an undisciplined Jew and Shinwell saw Bevin as an authoritarian bigot and anti-Semite, but Bevin and Shinwell could at least work together. Britain was to suffer in the winter of 1946–7 because Shinwell and Dalton could not stop.

The events surrounding the Labour Party's 1945 conference at Blackpool illustrated the marked defects in both characters. Churchill had already moved, with the Conservative party, into a position strongly opposed to State intervention in industry and, in part for this reason, both parties were agreed that the Coalition could not continue beyond the few months needed to defeat Japan. Morrison and Bevan led the attack against continuation even for that long at the eve-of-conference National Executive meeting. Attlee, Bevin and then Dalton spoke in favour of staying with Churchill for a few more months, a position which Attlee was under the impression Shinwell also shared; after all, he had experienced elections called by Lloyd George and MacDonald in similar electoral circumstances and surely Churchill could expect a similar result.

Shinwell did fear Churchill's popularity, but when the executive met he had not in fact made up his mind. His travels round the country had made him less sure about Churchill; he thought Labour would do well and could even just win. He was intending to make no contribution to the discussion, until Dalton weighed in on Attlee's side. Then Shinwell instinctively let rip. Dalton was out of touch with the party and country and was simply trying to preserve his unimportant little corner in a Conservative-dominated government which he probably suited anyway; there was nothing useful he could do in the Coalition in reality (he was now President of the Board of Trade) that he could not do better in a socialist government, if his colleagues happened to think he was worth such a responsible position... Attlee swiftly brought the matter to a vote. They decided to withdraw from the Coalition to Dalton's fury and Shinwell's delight. The conference strongly approved, and Churchill tendered the Coalition government's resignation.

If Shinwell's vulgar outburst had been typical of him, Dalton's subsequent behaviour was equally typical of him. In the guise of accepting the democratic decision, he gave the strong impression that he had supported pulling out of the Coalition from the start. He told anyone within earshot of his booming voice that it was those who had been ministers – those who had played their part and not thrown away the opportunity to do so – who knew that the Conservative majority was now becoming more obstructive. It was definitely, in his opinion, time to quit.[2]

Both Shinwell and Dalton were re-elected, presumably by a rather confused conference, to the National Executive. Both remained very popular with the party, Shinwell because of his grass-roots campaigning, Dalton because of his long-standing cerebral and ministerial contribution. Attlee would have to bear this in mind if it came to making a government.

Within the party itself, there seemed to be a stronger left-wing commitment. In 1944 at the annual conference, Shinwell had had to defend the executive's watered-down statement on extending national ownership and had lost to a left-wing revolt led by the young Ian Mikardo. But as Mikardo himself said, Shinwell alone on the Executive expected trouble. He knew that the party was worried about Labour ministers simply being too comfortable in Coalition. He knew that ordinary members were increasingly interested in a programme of economic and social trans-formation probably beyond the capacity of any Labour government to deliver. Mikardo's successful amendment made it clear that a full programme of nationalisation was expected from a Labour government as well as a national health service and comprehensive social insurance.

The second change of attitude, which was a good deal more difficult to detect at Westminster than in the provinces, was the shift to the left among the electorate as a whole. The service vote, now known to be about 60 per cent Labour, was probably influenced by the perceived threat to demo-bilisation posed by a 'warrior' Prime Minister. But even without the service vote, opposition successes in a series of by-elections had shown a marked shift on the Home Front to the ideas now proposed by Labour. Comments on the nationalisation of mines and railways, State control of the purchase and distribution of food and a period of planned but fair austerity in the transition to socialism were invariably well received, Shinwell found, at public meetings and not just party meetings.

He also noticed a clear distinction in the public mind between Churchill and the Conservative party. In any case, some Labour voters failed to realise they were voting against Churchill, and certainly never imagined that he would be pushed right off the scene by an actual Labour majority; otherwise they might well have thought again.[3]

Once the campaign was actually under way, internecine hatchets were temporarily buried. Shinwell and Dalton even spoke at the same meeting in the marginal constituency of Stockton-on-Tees held by Harold Macmillan. Shinwell told a heckler who asked him why he had left Scotland that he had come 'to grease the slippery stairs for Mr Macmillan to slide right down'. And Dalton laughed politely when Shinwell reminded his audience that Churchill had called some of his opponents 'mugwumps'. As far as he was concerned, however, certain Conservative MPs should be called 'mugwumps', especially the ones who sat on the fence, like Harold Macmillan, 'with their mugs on one side of it and their wumps on the other'.[4]

Macmillan's son, Maurice, was standing against Shinwell at Seaham Harbour, which he realised from the start was a hopeless task. His father had warned him that Shinwell could be a tiresome and rude opponent, but one who could be goaded into costly indiscretions. Maurice, however, never got close enough to Shinwell to try any goading.

When the results were announced, Labour's George Chetwynd beat Harold Macmillan and Maurice Macmillan lost spectacularly to Shinwell:

Emanuel Shinwell (Labour)	42,942 (80%)
Maurice Macmillan (Conservative)	10,685 (20%)
Majority	32,257

In his acceptance speech, Shinwell mocked the Conservative reliance on the personality of Churchill:

> The so-called magnetic influence of Mr Churchill had no effect in this Labour stronghold. Seaham electors have taken the advice I gave them which was to accept Mr Churchill as a war leader, but to reject him as the man capable of solving our social and economic problems.[5]

The results poured in over two days, revealing a massive Labour victory and a Conservative disaster. Shinwell was childishly pleased by his margin of victory compared with Dalton's, which had shown only a small increase to less than ten thousand just across the Durham coalfield at Bishop Auckland. Of course, the swing at Seaham Harbour was well above average because Maurice Macmillan could hardly be compared with Shinwell's last opponent, Ramsay MacDonald.

By lunchtime on Friday 3 August, Labour had a majority in the House of Commons and Attlee was forming the new government. He made a few senior appointments – Bevin to be Foreign Secretary, Morrison to be Lord President, Dalton to be Chancellor of the Exchequer, Cripps to be President of the Board of Trade, Jowitt to be Lord Chancellor and Greenwood to be Lord Privy Seal – and then rushed back to the Potsdam Conference with Stalin and Truman.

Shinwell's claim on office was based on his experience in the Mines Department and War Office under MacDonald and, more significantly, on his popularity in the party, proved by his high vote from the constituencies when he stood for the National Executive. Attlee in his autobiography said that he appointed him to the Cabinet as Minister of Fuel and Power because he had 'experience of the Department and had plenty of vigour'. It was disingenuous of him not to mention Shinwell's National Executive vote at all. Attlee would also have reckoned that the best place for a potential trouble-maker was in a difficult job. So he told Shinwell in his blunt way: 'I want you in the Cabinet. Nationalise the mines and electricity.' Shinwell said later that Attlee spoke to him as if he were ordering a drink from a waiter. 'But if I'd known what it was going to be like, I'd have asked for something easier!'[6]

They sang the 'Red Flag' when Parliament assembled. In reply the Conservatives managed a half-hearted 'For He's a Jolly Good Fellow' when Churchill appeared. Shinwell was to have responsibility for the key piece of socialist legislation in the first session, the nationalisation of the mines, and they would sing the 'Red Flag' once again when it came to the big Second Reading debate of his Bill. Somewhere at the back of his mind he sensed the same feeling of expectation that could not be fulfilled as he had nearly a quarter of a century before, in 1922, when the train had pulled out of Glasgow with the new Clydeside MPs on board. But the country had decided and Shinwell's opportunity had come. It was his chance to bring the industry on which over a million families depended for their living, on which whole regions of the country depended for their prosperity and on which vast sectors of the British economy depended for supplies, into the ownership of the State.

The whole point of nationalising the coal industry was to clear the way for the economic side of Britain's 'tremendous overhaul' promised in Labour's 1945 general election manifesto. There would be a 'firm constructive hand on our whole productive machinery', including 'drastic policies of replanning'.[7] With these objectives, the largest and most fundamental industry of all could no longer be neglected.

Nationalisation was hardly a new idea, but this was the first time it was to be put into practice on a large scale. Shinwell now had to produce not just a broad plan but a parliamentary Bill that was to become law by the end of 1946. There were no precedents.

There was, however, one new Labour MP who knew the coal industry inside out, because he had spent the last two years studying it and had even written a book on aspects of its control, actually proposing nationalisation. This was Harold Wilson, the new MP for Ormskirk, the former civil servant with whom Shinwell had briefly shared his ideas about shipping in the middle of the war. Wilson's book, *New Deal for Coal*, while not exactly a blueprint, was an invaluable handbook in the nationalisation process, and Wilson was also popular with the leaders of the newly-formed National Union of Mineworkers; indeed, its national president, Will Lawther, specially visited Lancashire to speak for him in his difficult constituency.[8] Shinwell's relationship with the mineworkers on the other hand had sometimes been stormy, especially in the Durham area where he had clashed with Sam Watson. Wilson would clearly be an ideal aide, so he asked him to be his PPS which would have given him time to settle in as an MP but also enable him to contribute formally to the Ministry of Fuel and Power. Wilson was flattered and ready to accept; but it was not to be. Attlee rang him and offered him instead a junior ministerial post at the Board of Works and Shinwell had to look again. The new MP for Dudley, George Wigg, had been recommended to him by Harold Laski, that year's chairman of the Labour Party, and they had also met and liked each other at a pre-war by-election meeting. Shinwell wrote blandly to Wigg, whose main interest was really defence: 'I am convinced that there is a big and difficult task ahead and the next few years will be both important and interesting ...' But when they met, according to Wigg:

> Shinwell resolved my doubts. I found him a man's man, straightforward and excitingly realistic about the magnitude of the problems facing a Labour government. He wanted me at once, but would make no exacting calls upon my time prior to the Second Reading of the Bill to nationalise the coalmines.[9]

Wigg would be a devoted ally for years to come but he had no particular contribution to make to the coal nationalisation process.

Shinwell did get some help from Herbert Morrison's Cabinet committee, the powerful 'Lord President's Committee'. Its first meeting was held on 10 September 1945, chaired by Morrison and attended by Shinwell and Transport Minister Alfred Barnes. They were the men who would be directly responsible for what Morrison called 'Socialisation' schemes.[10] Morrison himself had been responsible for the introduction of the London Passenger Transport Bill in 1931 and he had worked with Shinwell on nationalisation procedures in the early 1930s. He drew together for the committee such work as there was on the subject. The Labour Party itself had not gone into very much detail in its wartime reconstruction work, but the TUC had produced an important paper in 1944 in which the ticklish question of compensation had been addressed in some detail.[11] This had drawn extensively on earlier work by the ILP (in which Shinwell himself had been indirectly involved) as well as publications by Attlee and Morrison.[12] Even the Coalition government had done some research into public ownership and produced a useful paper on financial and administrative problems in its 1944 Report on Public Utility Corporations.[13]

It is extraordinary, then, that Shinwell claimed in his memoirs that:

> I had believed, as other members had, that in the party archives a blueprint was ready. Now, as Minister of Fuel and Power, I found that nothing practical and tangible existed. There were some pamphlets, some memoranda produced for private circulation, and nothing else. I had to start on a clear desk.[14]

This was frankly a lie designed to make his achievements seem greater than they were. There may not have been an actual blueprint, but there were a lot of useful and detailed guidelines. There was also a wide acceptance that nationalisation was desirable. So long as good compensation was paid, Shinwell could expect relatively little resistance from the coal-owners and even from the Conservative opposition. There was a wide acceptance that there were desperate problems of short-term thinking and lack of investment, which needed a national solution sponsored by government, if not actually State ownership.[15] In those first few months of government it was indeed the disastrous economic environment in which his work on the coal industry would be launched that was Shinwell's chief worry, not blueprints and not opposition from any source.

At one stage there seemed no point in nationalising one industry in circumstances where economic planning and the development of social welfare were impossible because the government were hamstrung by commitments to economic liberalism and social austerity. This looked very much like being the case after President Truman unilaterally rescinded Lend–Lease support for Britain just six days after victory over Japan in August 1945. Shinwell was not alone in thinking that this was a deliberate ploy to force Labour Britain to abandon socialist policy. In the Cabinet, Nye Bevan and Albert Alexander openly expressed this opinion which was undoubtedly also the private view of a number of others.[16]

If the government had serious financial problems but still went ahead with nationalisation, it would only end up with all the problems now faced by private coal-owners without any means of solving them. Shinwell accepted Wilson's estimate of £150 – £300 million investment needed to modernise the industry. There was also a demand for immediate improvements in wages and conditions, not just for humane reasons but also to overcome the problems of recruitment and absenteeism running at about 15 per cent. Money was needed to improve management and distribution and to increase mechanisation of the industry which was becoming less competitive year by year; improvements in underground equipment, especially for loading and cutting in an industry still dominated by the pick and shovel, were urgent. No money and no investment would discredit nationalisation. This – along with the fact that it was Dalton who was negotiating it – was the starting point for Shinwell's fierce opposition in Cabinet to the terms of the loan from the United States negotiated to fill the gap left by the withdrawal of Lend–Lease. There would simply not be enough money. The amount asked for, and in the Cabinet's view needed, was $5 billion at 1 per cent. They were finally offered $3.75 billion at 2 per cent.

It was not just the inadequate total amount of money, there was also the problem of British and American trade. The Americans wanted free world trade and to make sterling a fully convertible currency in one year. Britain after the war was not capable of competing effectively on world markets; not just in coal but in manufacturing as well where make-do-and-mend in wartime had meant the goods were often too poor in quality and too unreliable in delivery to be competitive in peace. Even if the United States was really to open up its markets – and many, including Shinwell, doubted whether it would – Britain would be a very weak trading partner.

The Cabinet was split between those who felt that a loan was the only way of avoiding immediate catastrophe and those who believed it possible to hang on for better terms. Shinwell was firmly in the second category. His first broadside came during the Cabinet meeting of 6 November. Dalton had circulated a report on the present state of negotiations. It was clear that the terms were stiffening all the time as Truman was pushed by Congress into resisting anything short of fully commercial terms. Congress tended to see Labour Britain in 1945 as representing the twin evils of socialism and empire, definitely not to be encouraged with American money.

The 6 November Cabinet meeting was a particularly good one for Shinwell to launch his attack on Dalton's negotiations, because it was due to be attended not just by himself and Bevan, who were already co-ordinating their opposition, but also by another Dalton opponent, Albert Alexander who, as First Lord of the Admiralty, was not formally in the Cabinet at the time. Shinwell knew that this meeting was the crucial one. If he failed, the chances were that the loan would go ahead.

At Attlee's request, an exhausted Dalton introduced the item on the negotiations, explaining the American demands for free trade and convertibility as well as the interest rates which were harsher than he had wanted. As soon as he finished, Shinwell struck. Agreement to these terms, he argued, exchanged vague American promises of co-operation in a multilateral system of world trade for the destruction of every kind of protection of

British industry. The day's Cabinet minutes record that when Shinwell next questioned the need to negotiate the loan at all and nearly won the Cabinet over:

> Our whole approach seems to be based on the assumption that we are suppliants for financial assistance. But, while it is true that the borrower is always in difficulties, so often is the lender; and it should not be forgotten that the United States producers will be in a difficult position if it were made impossible for us to take their produce. In fact, the custom of the debtor countries is essential to American prosperity.
>
> If this point had been sufficiently stressed in the negotiations, we should have found ourselves in a position to drive a hard bargain.[17]

Bevan and Alexander followed with embellishments of this same point. If the Americans impoverished the European market, they would soon have to think again. Shaken by the prospect of presiding over a period of austerity even harsher than during the war, Dalton fought off defeat in Cabinet by promising to redouble his efforts to improve the deal. New negotiators did go to Washington but they got almost nowhere. In the end, Dalton had to work on Bevin, Morrison and Cripps to ensure that Shinwell and Bevan faced a brick wall of insistence that Britain could not do without the money. A siege economy and a period of great austerity were too great a risk. In the end, Dalton's arguments just won the day. Above all, Bevin, who had wavered at the start of the negotiations, telling Cripps 'Britain has got to stand up for herself ... we are not down and out', was finally convinced there was no choice. He regretted that the terms 'would leave us subject to economic direction from the United States', but he was not prepared to 'demand further sacrifices from the British people'.[18] So at the Cabinet meeting of 5 December where Dalton presented those final terms, he was in a better position than Shinwell. He played down the problem of convertibility and talked up some minor concessions on trade. Cripps and Bevin criticised Dalton but then weighed in strongly in support of accepting the terms of the loan, saying there was no alternative. By the time Shinwell's turn came to speak, he could see the deal was as good as done.

He said the agreement as a whole was unsatisfactory and bad for this country. The Cabinet had been told about the immediate hardships if there were no loan, but Dalton had not fully explored what the position would be in the long run if the American terms were rejected. We did not need imports from the United States, Shinwell declared, but on the other hand industrial recovery in the United States did depend on us and others buying United States' exports. In these circumstances, the harsh conditions which the Americans were seeking to impose could not be justified. As for Britain's good relations with the United States, these were doomed either way. If we found in due course that we were unable to abide by the terms of repayment, then it would be just as bad as a break now over the terms being offered.

Only Bevan spoke in Shinwell's support. Inevitably the Cabinet then decided to accept the loan on the terms laid down.[19] Shinwell had wanted to put Labour's programme on hold until the Americans saw sense – as he argued later, they did see sense and then they brought in Marshall Aid – but now he had lost. Coal nationalisation would have to go ahead in much more difficult circumstances. Shinwell would have to be much tougher with miners and owners alike. Attlee told him he expected him to do well in a spot which was now even tighter than a few months earlier and he reminded him of a comment he had made when they were working in harness in the first months of MacDonald's desertion of the Labour Party: 'I am not in politics to whisper sweet nothings into the ears of my rival politicians, nor to be always pleasant, affable and courteous to those responsible for the parlous condition of the people of this country.'[20]

Despite the rapidly deteriorating economic background, Shinwell and his Permanent Secretary, Sir Donald Ferguson, prepared for legislation with a will. Shinwell suspected that he was able to get a lot out of his officials because they were feeling guilty about their lack of preparedness.[21] More likely they were responding, like most organisations do, to clear direction and an agreed purpose. Certainly, once the legislation was out of the way, they were to show far less eagerness on other matters.

It was soon agreed that the coal industry would be run by a full-time National Coal Board supervising powerful regional organisations. The TUC's 1944 report had foreseen this kind of arrangement and Wilson had described how it should work. There had also been a Labour Party statement on coal and power which had envisaged one central National Coal and Power Corporation, but Shinwell dropped this quickly as a complicating factor; in any case the minister could co-ordinate between energy boards. Once the basic form of the Coal Board had been agreed, he was quite happy to delegate the rest of the organisation to the 'best possible men' who would sit on it. So, sticking closely to his notes in the Second Reading of his Coal Industry Nationalisation Bill, he refused to be drawn beyond generalisations about the board or on how the industry would be organised.[22]

A trickier question that would soon need answering was, who were to be these 'best possible men'? Shinwell told the House of Commons he wanted: 'An expert Board, of full-time members, chosen because they possess the appropriate qualifications for running an industry of such complexity and magnitude.'

He resisted all pressures from Morrison in the Lord President's Committee and from Macmillan, now back in Parliament and Shadow Spokesman on Fuel and Power, to allow part-timers on the board. It would then become a board, he claimed, 'where a number of gentlemen gather around a table and talk'. So when he appointed an old friend, Ebby Edwards, Secretary of the National Union of Mineworkers, to the board, he left a vacancy in the union which was filled by Arthur Horner. Horner was a communist, and it was a decision Shinwell was much to regret in the following year during a summer and autumn of intermittent strikes. His appointment of Sir Walter Citrine of the TUC was less controversial, and he filled the other seven posts with two senior civil servants, an accountant, three former directors of coal companies and a professor of physics, all under the chairmanship of Lord Hyndley, long-time adviser to the Ministry and 'one of my dearest friends'.[23]

Hyndley was rich and willing to work for a small salary or even for nothing, but not the others. Shinwell soon found that the going rate for top industrial jobs was £10,000 a year or more. Morrison got his committee to overrule anything over £6,000 as 'socially objectionable'. Shinwell then got the Prime Minister to intervene and got £8,500, stinging Morrison by sneering: 'No doubt there are plenty of people of second-rate ability, who are looking for jobs but these are not the men for the National Coal Board.'[24] He also had to wrestle with the NUM to ensure that Ebby Edwards would get his pension – they wanted the whole thing to be taken over by the National Coal Board although he was already sixty-one.[25]

Getting the people, however, was easy compared with getting the money. The terms of the American loan obviously meant that the government was strapped for cash. Yet any borrowing by a State-owned enterprise, such as the National Coal Board, would automatically count as public sector borrowing. It would, in other words, be a public expenditure calculated on the basis that the Board could go bust and all its assets waste, making the whole liability the Treasury's. Not surprisingly, this meant that quite severe restrictions had to be put on the board right from the start, severely limiting what it could do to improve the industry. On money, Shinwell had to give in on most points. At first he had talked about prices being kept under some sort of social control, but he soon had to modify his position: 'The Board, unlike a private concern, has no interest in … maintaining prices at a level which will bring in the largest possible profit.'[26]

One advantage of the Treasury rules was that such borrowing as the board would be allowed to do would be at Treasury rates. This 'cheap money' policy would perhaps allow lower prices in the end. But the basic fact of life was that the board would have to break even. There would have to be commercial profits and losses, not the social control or the basis for economic planning Shinwell and other socialists had been envisaging for years. The only real advantage of nationalisation in financial terms would be the obvious economies of scale and the ability to plan for the long term, using cheaper borrowing to see the industry through more difficult years.

In the event, after 1947, the Coal Board made a profit for the whole of the life of the Labour government, totalling £87.4 million.

Whatever the immediate stringencies, Shinwell knew that by creating Britain's first nationalised industry, he was creating the basis of socialist industrial planning even if the American loan meant the real thing would be some time coming. However little it could achieve in the short term, it was essential for the future of socialism in Britain to get the nationalisation of the coal industry on to the statute book. This conviction, shared by Attlee, explains Shinwell's willingness to move quickly to arbitration over the crucial matter of compensation, and his willingness to tolerate an eventual commitment of £392 million to be paid out over fifty years. It was a serious burden of debt on an industry with an uncertain future but, to get the Act through in months rather than years, Shinwell regarded it as a painful necessity.[27]

The more bitter compromise forced on him was his limited scope for action as far as colliery managers were concerned. His experience of their attitudes and abilities as Minister of Mines in the 1920s and '30s had convinced him of the need for a purge; but this would have meant yet another burden of compensation so he ruled it out. Instead, he made a speech commending colliery managers and the important part they would undoubtedly play in the nationalised industry! A few days later, this double-talk caught up with him with a vengeance. Halfway through a by-election meeting in Durham he heard that a local manager was putting up as the Conservative candidate.

He banged his fist and roared that it was a first-class piece of impertinence. The audience, who were mostly miners, laughed and cheered. For the first time, they were really starting to take to their hearts this Jekyll and Hyde character who moved from merry and witty chaff to bitter and rancorous attack in a matter of seconds. They had great expectations of the work he was doing – they expected real results in terms of their own pay and conditions, and also in terms of getting rid of the worst managers.

Shinwell's reference to a 'first-class piece of impertinence' gave rise to a good deal of pompous correspondence on democracy and civil rights, including questions to the Prime Minister about the rights of managers to support the Conservatives. Attlee let it be known that he had given Shinwell a mild rebuke.[28]

For the sake of speed, Shinwell played only a small part personally in the massively complex question, which had to be settled very quickly, of what was to be included and what was to be left out in the nationalisation process. Distribution and transport were dropped from the start, but he instructed officials to include most coking plants and to take an aggressive attitude with land assets that went with the pits. He feared the hiving-off of profitable subsectors. The Coal Board ended up not just with coking plants and coal briquetting plants, but also with eighty-three brickworks, ten thousand houses, two hundred and twenty-five thousand acres of farmland, a glue factory and an assortment of more or less random small businesses. Some of these assets were to prove more valuable than the coal in years to come.[29]

Shinwell might have expected least trouble from the miners themselves. After all, he was carrying out what had been the miners' policy for a quarter of a century. Until 10 January 1946 they were co-operative. Then, with the legislative process for nationalisation already under way, the NUM came up with a 'Charter of Demands', twelve in all, dealing with improvements in pay and conditions. They argued that these would pay for themselves, because the industry would then recruit more of the high-quality men and boys it needed. Several of the demands were to do with long-term improvements in pit villages, equipment and youth training. These presented no problem. More awkwardly, they demanded a seven-hour day, a five-day week and extra paid holidays which would cost money immediately. Arthur Horner had the additional idea of no income tax for miners, but nobody ran with that.

The importance of the miners in the Labour movement was such that the Labour government had to give these peremptory demands the same sort of attention as a missive from a great foreign power. The charter was submitted in full to Cabinet which in turn referred it to the Lord President's Committee. There Shinwell suggested quite an effective way of dealing with it. The fact was, he pointed out, that the present owners could not be expected to negotiate such fundamental demands, because after all they were to be shortly dispossessed. On the other hand, the National Coal Board was not yet constituted. Therefore it fell in this interregnum to the government to respond to the charter, and the government would ask the miners to wait until vesting day for the improvements to be put into effect.

Once the day had arrived, 1 January 1947, there would be no chance of some private company making off with improvements paid for by the government. Accordingly, the government committed the board in advance not to all the demands but, most importantly, to a five-day week. Shinwell agreed with Morrison when he protested that it would be difficult for the board to implement the government's commitments, but then at least the bulk of the opprobrium would fall on them and not the government. It was devious, but it seemed to have a good chance of working. Shinwell was authorised by the Cabinet to announce the five-day week provided it was 'organised' into five full shifts.[30]

The five-day week has always been regarded as a specially desirable reform for the coalmining industry in view of the conditions under which miners work. A five-day week is also widely regarded by mining engineers as desirable for the efficient working of modern mechanised mining.

Accordingly, I take this opportunity of announcing that the government offer no objection in principle, provided that arrangements and conditions can be established with the full co-operation of the miners to an organised five-day week of a kind which will secure the output of coal which is necessary to meet the country's needs.[31]

The next day at the National Union of Mineworkers' conference at Bridlington, Shinwell was the miners' hero. He had fought for nationalisation and won. He had supported the five-day week. Coal production was rising. There was, as he said, 'an atmosphere of contentment'.

As vesting day approached, it was increasingly obvious that changes in conditions, wages and ownership were still not boosting recruitment. Without the extra miners, the increased demand for exports or for the power stations in the harsh winter weather could bring early disaster. Stocks were barely adequate. Shinwell came on the Home Service and Pathe News to make stilted appeals in a BBC voice for more miners. He was making mining an industry, he said, for a 'decent well-paid and honourable career'.[32]

When the great day of nationalisation came, everything else was forgotten. A formal ceremony in London attended by the whole Cabinet was followed by ceremonies of unfurling flags and making speeches at the two biggest pits in his constituency. In a long euphoric speech at Murton colliery about a century of struggle coming to an end, Shinwell dismissed the industry's labour problems in just one sweeping sentence: 'It's no use people shouting their heads off for more labour in the mines until they can tell me where it is to come from.'[33] He turned away from that painful problem to the real achievement of the day. The industry which was the basis of Britain's industrial revolution and its modern industrial security was now in the hands of the people. The organised working-class movement which he had served for half a century had achieved one of its most prized objectives. He was proud to be the instrument of this unprecedented gain for his people. In the words of one local activist and fervent admirer: 'They cheered and cheered and cheered. For us he had conquered all the powers of darkness.'[34]

This last comment, viewed from six weeks later, was replete with unintended irony.

CHAPTER 15

The Coal Crisis: the Great Catastrophe

No one could remember how it began, but the grin-and-bear-it slogan 'Shiver with Shinwell – Starve with Strachey' was in wide circulation by December 1946. It says something about the mentality of the British in the late 1940s, however, that the implicit failures of the Minister of Fuel and Power and the Minister of Food were attributed to circumstances beyond their control. They were seen as doing their best. The nation's reward one day would surely be the promised land, but for now – England can take it.

On 4 October 1945, the ministerial Coal Committee met for the first time. Shinwell sat grim-faced. The last thing he had wanted was this committee of ministers chaired by Dalton to oversee his work on coal supplies. A month earlier he had sent a memorandum to the Prime Minister warning him that there could be a shortage of coal in the 1945–46 winter and the result had been this committee. Shinwell kicked himself; he ought to have realised.

They set up various campaigns to try to attract more labour into mining and to cut unnecessary domestic and industrial consumption and they tried to plan the transport of coal by rail and road. In the event, there was no crisis in the first post-war winter. The economy's recovery from the war had barely started and the flow of miners from the armed services back to the pits kept up production.

On 25 March 1946, Shinwell told the committee that the purpose for which the committee had come into existence had been successfully fulfilled.

> We had so far got through the winter without a serious interruption in coal supplies, despite the fact that production had been lower than in 1944-45 ... coal production had increased slightly and, while the position was not yet satisfactory, production was now running rather above the danger point and ought to improve. So no further meetings of the Committee at either level were really necessary.[1]

The committee's busy members readily agreed to adjourn until the autumn.

George Wigg, Shinwell's Parliamentary Private Secretary, regarded the committee's agreement to Shinwell's impetuous suggestion as at best an abdication of responsibility by Dalton. As time went on, he became convinced that it was a deliberate set-up for Shinwell.

Wigg must have been born seeking out conspiracies. He had made his way through the Labour movement, starting, 'like Manny, with my arse out of my trousers – if we could think at all, we came to realise that we could only put things right if we did it our bloody selves.' He had worked his way up through the Army to the rank of Colonel and then left to join the Workers' Educational Association. Now an MP, he was sharing a flat in Bloomsbury with two other MPs, 'forever doing petty-cash sums on the backs of envelopes about who has paid how much for what'. Wigg clicked with Shinwell. Now he told him in the bluntest possible terms that he was being taken for a mug: 'Dalton was chairman of the Coal Committee and he did fuck all. The result therefore was, if the whole thing came unstuck, like they knew it probably would, that it had to be Manny.'[2]

Shinwell saw it rather differently. He came back to his office, summoned Wigg and told him that at last he had got the committee off his back. He knew perfectly well that there was still an enormous problem but, as Wigg remembered, he was quite convinced he was up to solving it:

One of the first things he did when I came in – he said 'Look at that'. And he showed me the coal stocks. So there was no coal except for priorities. But he had Mr bloody Cripps [President of the Board of Trade] building up, and in fact he was to start selling electrical equipment abroad – right left and centre – with no generating plant to supply the current over here.'

Wigg advised Shinwell to go to Attlee right away and confront him with the situation and say that he could get through the next winter but only if Cripps's export drive could be slowed right down and other restrictions imposed immediately. 'He didn't take my advice. Why? Vanity. That's his besetting sin. He said, "I can solve this. I can handle the NUM and the mine-owners and the Cabinet".'[3]

It certainly would have meant swallowing a lot of pride to have gone straight back to Attlee after what he had just told the committee. Shinwell seems to have felt that his good relations with some of the miners' leaders and the goodwill he was generating through the nationalisation process would be enough. Extra rations were turned down by the Ministry of Agriculture, lower taxes were turned down by the Chancellor of the Exchequer, the selective demobilisation of miners was turned down by the service ministers and giving priority to the recruitment of miners over building

workers was turned down by the Minister of Labour. Above all, machinery
needed for mechanising the mines was being exported and Shinwell lost
his Cabinet battle with Sir Stafford Cripps, President of the Board of
Trade, to stop it; Britain desperately needed wheat, beef and timber in
exchange and the Cabinet decision was understandable, but it was at that
moment that Shinwell should have seen the writing on the wall.

The euphoria of fulfilling the socialist dream of the nationalisation of
the mines clouded his judgement of his own ability to make bricks without
straw. He should have gone to Attlee or the Cabinet and said in blunt terms
there and then that if policies outside the control of his Ministry – on rations,
subsidies, demobilisation, recruitment and exports – were not changed, then
he alone could not guarantee that there would be enough coal for Britain
the next winter. The problem was that he thought he alone could square
the circle.

One man close to the Prime Minister certainly did understand the
potential gravity of the situation. Douglas Jay, a confidant of Dalton,
doubted Shinwell's ability even to understand the problem let alone solve
it. He blamed Shinwell directly for not being vigorous enough in his
recruitment campaigns but did, reluctantly, admit the need to give him
some help with subsidies to make mining more attractive. It was no good
having a marketing campaign with nothing decent to sell. As Attlee's
economic adviser, Jay urged on him the need for action now, in the spring
of 1946, if there was going to be enough coal in the following winter.

Attlee's response to Shinwell's self-confidence and Jay's warning was swift
but failed to go to the root of the problem, the allocation of resources. He
replaced the Parliamentary Secretary at Fuel and Power, the old miner Will
Foster, with Hugh Gaitskell, an up-and-coming middle-class technocratic
socialist who had worked closely with Dalton in the war. He must have
known that Shinwell would not like the Dalton connection, but felt that
Gaitskell, with his considerable administrative experience and with the
ambitious drive of a forty-year-old, would complement Shinwell very well
and help to solve the problems of coal supply.

When he appointed him, Attlee told Gaitskell none of the problems.
He simply said, 'I want you to go to "Mines". But this doesn't mean going
down mines all the time. There's Gas and Electricity and the Bills coming
along.' He told him to get in touch with Shinwell at once.

Shinwell gave Gaitskell a frosty reception:

> 'I understand you're going to be my new Parliamentary Secretary.'
> 'Yes, I understand so.'
> 'Well, that's all right. We've got this Bill on Monday but you won't
> be able to do much.'
> 'No, I suppose not.'

'There's a meeting this evening with the Attorney General and the Financial Secretary – you can come and listen if you like.'

Gaitskell recorded in his diary that he said that he 'did like'.[4]

Why *did* Attlee appoint Gaitskell? Wigg thought that Dalton was behind it, spying on Shinwell through Gaitskell, possibly even sabotaging him or wanting Gaitskell to outshine him. But Jay's opinion was probably nearer the mark. Shinwell needed someone who could master the detail and understand the statistics.[5]

Shinwell gave Gaitskell a good deal of responsibility for electricity nationalisation, as Attlee had expected. More significantly for the moment, he asked him and George Wigg to help with recruitment to the mines. Wigg disliked Gaitskell from the start. He was more and more convinced that he was part of the conspiracy against Shinwell masterminded by Dalton. If Gaitskell really could help, it could only in his opinion be because other ministers who had not co-operated with Shinwell were now starting to be helpful. If he failed, the blame would no doubt be laid at Shinwell's door as the minister in charge.

A month after Gaitskell started, Shinwell briefly discussed with him a report he was sending to Attlee, in which he admitted that recruitment into mining was bad and getting worse. It was essential to implement as many of the Miners' Charter improvements as possible, or at least to promise to do so to get recruitment and production up to the necessary level.[6] Here there emerged a clear difference between Shinwell and Gaitskell. Gaitskell agreed that the changes in mining conditions were desirable but he declared bluntly that they would not result in a lot more coal production by the coming winter. Shinwell, on the other hand, reckoned he could solve the recruitment problem in double-quick time through incentives and goodwill; he had such good relations with the NUM that they could work together effectively to reduce absenteeism and to increase productivity in just a few months. Gaitskell discussed the matter with his friend Douglas Jay who was Attlee's Private Secretary, and they both agreed that Shinwell's optimism was groundless and based on long-term solutions to immediate problems. Gaitskell, however, apart from speaking to Jay, remained loyal to Shinwell and kept his criticisms within the Ministry, even when he was slapped down in a departmental meeting for suggesting that extra rations for miners and extra provisions in their canteens were really irrelevant to production.[7]

There can be no doubt that Shinwell's faith in the value of improved conditions for miners was touching but misplaced. He greatly overestimated the impact it would have on the recruitment of coalminers and the amount they could actually produce. Perhaps he had to have that faith. After all, he was now, after having been a member since it was founded, chairman of the Labour Party; the miners had been the one group of workers consistently socialist for his whole political life. He simply knew they would not let him down. In a sense they didn't. They co-operated on absenteeism and on the rearrangement of shifts, and miners' leaders did indeed exhort their members to be Stakhanovites in the lead-up to nationalisation. At the TUC in October, however, Arthur Horner, warned the government that the miners were now working as hard as they could and current levels of production were realistically all that could be expected through the winter.[8]

Horner's statement shook Shinwell. He had expected more. His mood now swung firmly to pessimism. He still believed a serious crisis could be averted; indeed, to his lasting regret, he made a statement at a luncheon for coke-oven managers that would be quoted back at him again and again: 'Everybody knows that there is going to be a serious crisis in the coal industry, except for the Minister of Fuel and Power. I want to tell you there is not going to be a crisis in coal.'[9]

Attlee now ordered Shinwell to take on foreign labour if he possibly could. 'More men now,' he said, 'not plans for the future.' Shinwell angrily put Gaitskell in charge of recruiting foreign labour ('They wanted miracles,' said Wigg, 'so Manny put Jesus Christ in charge.)' Of course, Gaitskell came up against all the problems that Shinwell and Wigg already knew about. In particular, there was a great tendency to over-state the significance of a few hundred Polish miners who had escaped during the war and had no wish to return to Stalinised Poland.

When Dalton started criticising him and the NUM about the Poles, Shinwell still felt confident enough to sneer back at Sikorski's old friend: 'There is very widespread dislike of the Poles among British miners who believe that because the Poles do not wish to return to Poland under the benign protection of the glorious Red Army, they must be Fascists.'[10] Where Poles were forced on to the workforce, productivity immediately deteriorated, not so much through industrial action as through a deliberate lack of co-operation on the part of local miners. A campaign to recruit young men for mining in Ireland foundered when the Ministry of Labour suggested better paid work on building sites.

The reconvened Coal Committee, now chaired by Attlee himself, told Shinwell to prepare the administrative machinery necessary to impose cuts on industries and households and he eventually came up with a plan for cutting deliveries by 5 per cent to essential industries and by 10 per cent everywhere else. It took him six weeks to come up with this extraordinarily simple plan, but the Cabinet seemed to be in no hurry either. It was not even to be implemented until 1 January. Shinwell must take a good deal of the blame for this disastrous procrastination. He was failing to heed Wigg's advice, gambling on something turning up, instead of confronting the Cabinet with the fact that the export drive would have to stop, that power stations would have to take absolute priority and that coal trains – a critical shortage of rolling stock was now emerging – would have to get through unhindered, if a really massive crisis were to be avoided.

Gaitskell, meanwhile, toured the Yorkshire, Derbyshire and Lancashire coalfields, and reported back on a number of specific supply bottlenecks. Small-scale power cuts were already affecting textile mills in Lancashire but these seemed to be caused entirely by transport failures rather than production problems.

It was the signal for Shinwell and Wigg to seize on transport problems as an area to which blame could be shifted in a big but unjustified way. There is no doubt that the crisis highlighted fearful inadequacies of transport, but the basic problem remained that there was simply not enough coal being produced as demand started to rise in the winter, and it was the first signs of this, and not a basic problem of transport, that Gaitskell saw on his tour. Wherever there were specially low stocks or perhaps some broken loco- motives, the situation was on such a knife-edge that huge factories could then be stopped for days from working normally.

Yet winter had begun and there was really little more that could be done now to increase supply. Shinwell ought to have realised this. Miners were working hard. There was even very little absenteeism, which prompted Gaitskell to tell his audience of miners in Chesterfield that, because they were essential, their occasional absence from work attracted everyone's attention, whereas if thirty thousand people went to Ascot or the Derby, 'nobody gives a tinker's cuss'.[11]

On 3 January, Shinwell warned Attlee that the cuts now being imposed at his suggestion would not be enough and it would have to be left to Cripps, as President of the Board of Trade, to allocate drastic and immediate cuts in industry. Cripps acted quickly. Coal for iron and steel was to be cut by 20 per cent and to the rest of industry by 50 per cent from 20 January.[12]

At 6 p.m. on 23 January the temperature on the Air Ministry roof dropped below freezing, where it stayed for forty-four days and nights that would gravely damaging Shinwell's reputation and coming close to ending his career. At 9.30 p.m. it began to snow.

A heavy fall of snow, about five inches deep, enveloped London and the South East on the Thursday night and Friday morning. The next forty eight hours were bitterly cold but dry. On Sunday 26th, the whole of Britain experienced, according to *The Times*, 'the wildest day for many years with very low temperatures, snow and a bitter gale. Everywhere in the country has a blanket of snow, in some places four feet deep. In Kent, the tem- perature dropped twenty degrees below freezing point.'[13] The weather was to stay unremittingly snowy, freezing and with stormy east winds until the middle of March.

By late on the Monday, 27 January, the extent of the crisis was clear. Unless the coal which had already been dug out was moved to power stations within three days, there would only be enough power for about a quarter of domestic demand and virtually none for industry. The problem was that the coal in question was buried under ice and snow at inaccessible pit heads, piled up in railway sidings under snowdrifts twenty feet deep, and loaded on to barges stormbound in the Tyne.

Shinwell, Gaitskell, Wigg, Ferguson and their senior officials met every day for the next week, along with Alfred Barnes and his Permanent Secretary in the Ministry of Transport. Despite further heavy snowfalls, strategically important railway lines were reopened and coal reached all the power stations where the need was most critical. Special orders had to be sent to Tyneside for dockers to be diverted from normal duties to unload coal from the stranded barges and shift it back on to railway wagons to be sent south. There were some shutdowns but they were brief and tolerable. Shinwell displayed a certain raw drive and got results by sheer hard work and no doubt the considerable motivation of saving his political skin. He told the Cabinet on 6 February that further power cuts would be unnecessary; by a military-style operation, nearly all the coal available had been distributed to the power stations and production had been resumed in nearly all mines. It looked like a victory for central planning, and for Shinwell, in crisis conditions.[14]

What happened, then, between the success of 6 February and the disaster of 7 February when Shinwell told a grim silent Cabinet and then an astounded House of Commons that all electricity would have to be cut off that very evening from industry in the South-East, the Midlands and the North-West, and from all private homes for five hours a day? On 6 February, Shinwell had been upbeat and confident. On 7 February, he was ashen-faced, and he knew he faced an uphill task to keep his job.[15]

One thing that certainly happened was that Shinwell and his crisis team had had only partial information. The system they seem to have used was based on the most recent available information about shortages when their operation started in earnest on 24 January, the morning after the great storm. They would work back from those known shortages to where the supply stoppage had occurred and concentrate resources on that stoppage; then they repeated the operation as often as necessary for all the other cases. The problem was that their information was unreliable; different power stations demanded different amounts of reserves in relation to their capacity and, additionally, reserves could be stockpiled up to three or four miles away from where they were needed which could leave them inaccessible after heavy snow; different coalmines, recently under various coal-owners, despite Harold Wilson's best efforts in the war, measured output in different ways; most seriously, nearly half of all mines updated their output figures only every two weeks, which meant that there was a good chance that the information available to Shinwell in fact related to the unnaturally warm weather before 23 January and not to the crisis period at all. In other words, in some cases Shinwell was getting information that painted too bleak a picture, but in most cases it was not nearly bleak enough. There is no evidence that the figures he received were ever really questioned.[16]

At the same time, Shinwell had a good political reason for giving himself a few extra days to make his own plans before dealing his blow to the Cabinet and the country. It gave him time to prepare to shift as much as possible of the blame on to his hated rival, Chancellor Hugh Dalton. As Shinwell was telling the bad news to the House of Commons, greeted by low whistles of disbelief, George Wigg was busy telling lobby correspondents, MPs, party officials and anyone he considered worth talking to and who would listen, how Shinwell had been set up as the fall-guy for Hugh Dalton, but now he was doing the decent thing and shouldering the blame:

> The economic plan put an absurd amount of strain on the coal-mining industry. Now the bad weather is having an inevitably serious effect. It is rather dishonourable of Dalton not to admit at least a share in the responsibility. The Minister of Fuel and Power must not be allowed to take all the blame. The Chancellor of the Exchequer has insisted on overstretching industry to meet his demanding targets, none more so than coal production. It is frankly doubtful if any way of running the mines could have produced a much better result.[17]

Shinwell himself did not at that time blame Dalton publicly, although he undoubtedly did so in private and Dalton knew it. 'Shinwell is by far the least attractive member of the government,' Dalton raged, 'always looking round for someone else to whom to pass the blame.' Dalton wrote to the Prime Minister on 14 February suggesting that Shinwell should be sacked: 'If only there was a decent minister in that job, I could talk to him as I do to my other colleagues frankly and constructively. But with Shinwell this is impossible.'[18]

The crisis had broken in earnest. Attlee asked Harold Wilson to join the emergency team now gathered in Shinwell's outer office at the Ministry in Millbank. And it was the turn of the Transport Ministry to make everything worse. Nearly a million tons of coal were stuck in sidings and at pit-heads. Yet on the Saturday, 8 February, after Shinwell had announced draconian power cuts, incredibly, Barnes allowed football excursion trains on the main lines and then went away for the weekend. When Wigg complained, he promised to 'look into the situation on Monday morning', claiming that it was 'Manny's affair'. 'Wigg retorted that it was a transport crisis: 'The bloody coal is there and it can't be brought here.'[19] Unfortunately it was too late, because by that time a good many excursion trains were stuck where they were by more blizzards and ice and there was no question of moving coal anywhere by rail.

Shinwell, Gaitskell and Wilson called in miners' leader Arthur Horner on the Sunday night and told him that unless London had coal in three days, sewerage and water supplies could be in jeopardy and London would have to be evacuated. Shinwell asked Horner to get the lightermen and tugmen to co-operate in moving coal up the Thames from icebound coasters. At a meeting in a pub in Westminster Bridge Road, the men agreed to have a try. They were finally successful and Londoners could rest easy, if cold.

On the Monday, Attlee moved in and took charge personally, setting up a new Cabinet Fuel Committee to manage the crisis and to establish and control fuel policy for the rest of the year. Shinwell was a member of the committee but from now on his role would be marginal. Wigg could only do so much for him. He had certainly had an influence on newspaper and public opinion. Most people still didn't blame Shinwell; they tended to see him as a victim partly of the weather and partly of government policy. Wigg's briefings making him the scapegoat of Dalton's and Cripps's insistence on exports at all costs were largely successful as far as newspaper headlines were concerned. Makeshift trucks sent from London to the Midlands to fetch coal (one hundred and forty-two out of one hundred and fifty broke down) were affectionately labelled 'Shinwell's Shovels', a good illustration of the public perception of Shinwell struggling manfully against every kind of human and natural adversity. Within the government, however the story was very different. Whether he was a fall-guy or not, the powerful combination of Cripps and Dalton was hard for Attlee to resist and they both wrote explicitly demanding Shinwell's sacking. Bevin, another old enemy, was probably also active behind the scenes.[20]

Cripps told Attlee:

I have become even more convinced that it is essential that a change should be made at the Ministry of Fuel and Power. I am sure this view is held almost universally by your colleagues, and certainly it is by the country and the industry in particular.

Then he wrote to 'My Dear Manny':

I want you to know how much I sympathise with all your difficulties in the present critical time. You have had to bear the brunt of a situation that has come upon us all and I know how terribly anxious and worried you have been. I am sure that all your colleagues are anxious to help in every way they can and to share both the responsibility and the kicks. Good luck to you.[21]

Meetings of the Fuel Committee were acrimonious. Attlee was prone to be short with Shinwell and on one occasion reduced him to tears by harping on his inadequacies.[22] He responded to the pressure to sack Shinwell by cutting him out of the decision-making process, preferring to keep the chairman of the Labour Party and the man who nationalised the mines nominally on board.

For Shinwell it was an appalling summer. Much of the day-to-day work of the Ministry was done by Gaitskell who eventually took over in October, while Shinwell devoted himself to party organisation. If ever there was a lame duck minister, he was it.

In April, the severe restrictions on households and industry were lifted with the spring weather. But the Fuel Committee saw to it that coal was more carefully husbanded than before. On the last day of power cuts, some photographers tried to get Fanny to pose with a candle. Shinwell blew his top with the newspaper editor and it never happened again.[23] He often blew his top now, frustrated and impotent. On one occasion he angrily accused all non-unionised workers, using the phrase which Gaitskell had used to such good effect a few months earlier, of not being worth 'a tinker's cuss'. This irritated Attlee and reduced an important House of Commons occasion, the establishment of the powerful Electricity Organising Committee, to a farcical row with Churchill; Shinwell accused Churchill of being 'up a tree' and 'infantile'. Churchill scored a few points because Shinwell could not deny that he had told the vast mass of Britain's working population that they were 'not worth a tinker's cuss'. The newspapers loved the argument and were full of photographs of 'Tinker's Palace' graffiti on the walls and windows of the Shinwell home in Balham. The whole affair, which could hardly have come at a worse time, did him no good at all.

Who was to blame? Gaitskell reckoned Shinwell had taken a gamble with the odds against him and lost, and he also noticed his unwillingness ever to admit he was wrong. His gambling was one thing, but the way he tried to shift the blame Gaitskell found very unattractive:

> 'Passing the buck' is frequent enough between Ministers. But Shinwell did not just pass it. He picked it up and hurled it. He attacked the Minister of Supply (John Wilmot) about mining machinery and the Minister of Transport (Alfred Barnes) over wagons, and in a manner which somehow made them angrier than others would have done. More than one of his colleagues has said to me 'The Cabinet is really a remarkably harmonious affair, except for Shinwell. His presence spoils the atmosphere. He throws apples of discord the whole time'.[24]

There is no doubt that the Ministers of Transport, Labour and Supply were all incompetent at times. None of them saw the crisis in time or reacted appropriately. None of them gave the necessary priority to coal or understood its pivotal role in the economy at the time. Just like the services who refused to release miners, they made things worse but cannot really be accused of causing the crisis. Even the staggeringly inefficient and idle Minister of Transport cannot actually be said to have caused the coal crisis, although he certainly prolonged and intensified it.

Dalton and Cripps cannot escape a share of the blame. They had insisted on an export drive and had gone for growth with hardly a thought for the supply of fuel. Shinwell, in some vague way, was simply expected to keep up and provide all the coal that was necessary, however excessive the demand. Dalton and Cripps were also much more powerful in the Cabinet, so Shinwell even failed at that level to stop the export of electricity generating-equipment as late as November 1946. On the other hand, Shinwell had not in fact told the Cabinet the true situation because he was absurdly over-optimistic about the results of his good relations with the miners.

There was a lack of information and co-ordination only eventually put right by the Cabinet Fuel Committee and the Prime Minister himself. The old Coal Committee had certainly not been up to the job; Shinwell, intentionally or not, had pulled the wool over its eyes. He probably fooled himself too. His vanity prevented him from seeing he was failing. He was called upon to display leadership and drive in the nationalisation of coal, and in this he was conspicuously successful. In the lead-up to the fuel crisis, however, he needed exceptional administrative skills. Gaitskell, whose strength was administration, was sidelined; he nevertheless observed Shinwell's administrative methods at close quarters and had no illusions:

> He has no conception at all of organisation or planning or following up. Everything is done by fits and starts and on impulse. The best you can say is that he contributes at intervals the kind of rugged force and drive which stimulates the officials. He gets worried about something; he calls a meeting; he asks questions and holds forth and perhaps takes some pre-liminary decision. But there is no follow-up and no system.

> Because of his strong personality, free language and love of a fight, one expects first of all to find that he will be a 'strong' Minister. This is not so. He will always try to evade an unpopular decision, procrastinate or find a way round. Of course there often is a case on political grounds for this. But Shinwell's hesitations go beyond natural prudence and amount to sheer weakness and moral cowardice.[25]

Poor administration was part of his downfall. If he had identified exactly what was going on, it would have helped. If he had even told the Cabinet the truth as he saw it, he could certainly have avoided much of the blame and might have prevailed upon Dalton and Cripps to slow industrial growth. Unfortunately he couldn't quite bring himself to tell the whole truth.

In October Attlee sacked Shinwell from Fuel and Power and offered him a job outside the Cabinet. He told him he wanted him to be Secretary of State for War. He might have considered it, but when he learned that Gaitskell was to succeed him at Fuel and Power, according to Wigg, 'his anger knew no bounds'. All at once, he understood he had been a dupe. There was the successful result of the Dalton conspiracy. He felt terribly insulted.

There was no question of going to the War Office now. He rang Fanny, and she backed him to the hilt. Then Laski got in touch with him and tried to encourage him to take the War Office job. He pointed out that he had had experience of the War Office and they needed 'a sensible Labour man' in charge of it.

Wigg was more direct. Who did Shinwell think he was, talking about turning down the job of being the political head of the British Army? It was a vital and honourable job, explaining political decisions to the army and the army's needs to politicians. Shinwell resisted, and in the taxi to 10 Downing Street where Shinwell was to turn down Attlee's offer, Wigg bawled him out:

> I peppered my criticism with appropriate adjectives, emphasising that there had not been a good War Secretary since his old friend Haldane and that he should be honoured to have the chance ... I spoke more violently than I had ever done before.[26]

With Wigg's expletives ringing in his ears, and with terrible misgivings, Shinwell accepted the post of Secretary of State for War.

Part 5

CHAPTER 16

The War Office

His hopes dashed by the coal crisis, Shinwell took some time to adjust to the War Office. Some of the older civil servants had known him in Ramsay MacDonald's government and they found him not just older but fatter and crosser than they remembered. In those early months he became even more of a loner than usual. He seemed to enjoy being miserable. He claimed that he needed periods of reflection to think about life in general and to meditate, but in reality he was just being miserable.

Rarely in political life did Shinwell make close friends, and the events while he was Minister of Fuel and Power confirmed his every suspicion about knives in his back. George Wigg was the only real exception. Together he and Wigg could work each other into a frenzy of suspicion about fellow politicians, risking only a little more trust in Ministry officials who were not obvious rivals. The flaw in this conception, as Gaitskell rightly observed, was that civil servants are in reality just as serious rivals for a minister's power as other politicians are for a minister's position. This tended to make politicians like Shinwell weaker because they became too dependent on official rather than political advice.

Not that Shinwell's relationships with civil servants were always easy. Especially with senior civil servants of the Eton–Oxford school, he could be difficult and truculent. He liked to give them orders and to show who was boss, although he was never as rude and bombastic as Dalton. He resented above all their expectation that he should master all the details of the department that they considered important. He fought the system of swamping the minister with red boxes full of papers; yet, when they reduced the number, he started to worry about what they were leaving out. The eventual solution was to let Wigg, rather than his official Private Secretary, act as a sorter, so that Shinwell would get space to think (or meditate or be miserable) while knowing at the same time that anything that should be handled politically rather than administratively would not go unnoticed; it was in the hands of one of the few people he trusted. His civil servants never showed any particular resentment at what they simply regarded as rather eccentric behaviour.

Shinwell enjoyed being a minister. He liked the sense of power and importance provided by the official papers, the cars, the luxury and the bowing and scraping. Like all politicians, he was occasionally taken in by it but, unlike many middle-class Labour politicians, he never felt guilty about it.

The secret of his success as War Minister was his clear-headed identification of important problems to be solved – army living quarters and pay, recruitment, the development of the Territorials and so on – which he followed through in a generally efficient way. He was a quick thinker not easily taken in by weak arguments and, through lessons learned painfully in the coal crisis, he was becoming a reasonably effective manager. His failure lay in the way he selected the important problems in the first place and sometimes also in his lack of persistence in following them through. The basic reason for this must be his increasing political aimlessness. Once he dropped his Bolshevism, he dropped ideology. His democratic socialism consisted merely of a conviction that certain practical measures would improve society and the economy in such a way that poverty would be greatly reduced. In itself this was enough for a competent minister to do a reasonably good job in a Labour government; but it meant there was no fundamental thinking to provide a framework for policy. In the case of the armed forces, now to be the preoccupation of his political life, no consideration was given to their purpose or structure. Shinwell merely wrapped himself in the Union Jack rather than the Red Flag and talked more about patriotism than socialism.

At the War Office and later at the Ministry of Defence, the questions that really mattered about the Cold War, Berlin, Palestine, NATO, Europe and Korea went unasked or were seen simply as particular problems for the army, navy or air force. Although he was still at the centre of affairs, his lack of ideology meant that he could never be a great minister, just a reliable and quite effective one. There would be no great thoughts at the War Office while Shinwell was a minister, which would mark him out for the history books. On the other hand, he would be a minister who at the very height of the Cold War cared about the soldiers in his charge and still found time to read the Cabinet papers (which Attlee in a unique concession agreed to send him although he was no longer in the Cabinet); and he still found time to make political speeches defending nationalisation – although only as one possible route to 'socialisation'; and he found time to sit in his office late at night alone or with George Wigg, over a modest whisky, and to reflect on events. Wigg noticed that, as people tend to do as they get older, Shinwell talked increasingly about the distant past.[1]

'Welcome to the War Office. I look forward to working with you,'[2] Montgomery of Alamein, Chief of the Imperial General Staff, wrote briefly and politely to the army's new political chief.

There was not a lot of time for the formalities. The Cold War showed every sign of heating and conflict loomed – or was actually under way on a relatively small scale – in the Far East, India, Palestine and Egypt. The greatest risk was what the civil servants called 'unpremeditated war'. They reckoned that Stalin or his successors would not be in a position to start a war deliberately to take over Western Europe until 1957, but in the meantime there was every chance of an accident. If this happened, Shinwell's first hair-raising briefing as minister claimed, the Red Army would concentrate on Denmark because of its strategic importance in relation to the Baltic and on Italy because of its susceptibility to communism. At the same time, there would probably be invasions of Korea, Manchuria and China. There could also be offensives against British sea communications, subversive activities against British interests around the world and aerial bombardment of British cities. The War Office calculated that the Red Army could occupy France (let alone all of Germany and the Low Countries) within two months of the outbreak of war, freeing extra divisions to attack the oil fields of Iraq, south west Persia and Kuwait.

Against all this, the plan was to assist the military rebirth of Western Europe. No one imagined in 1947 that Western Europe could put up a serious resistance to the Red Army. The idea was to try to kill communism wherever possible in other parts of the world, for example in Malaya, and to use the Middle East as an offensive base for bombing the southern regions of the Soviet Union.[3] Britain's 90 per cent conscript army would play a very small part indeed.

Shinwell soon learned that the army chiefs did not consider the government was pursuing the Cold War with enough vigour. But in his early days at the War Office, Shinwell opposed this hawkish view; a long-time campaigner for friendship with the Soviet Union, he now found it hard to see it as a mortal enemy. He had long since ceased to think of the Soviet Union as any kind of socialist model, but he still felt that the new communist governments of Eastern Europe did offer some hope of lasting improvement for their people. In January 1946, Shinwell had actually welcomed the first alliance forged between an East European Social Democratic Party and the communists. They had formed the Socialist Unity Party in Berlin, under the leadership of Wilhelm Pieck, later to be East Germany's first head of State. Shinwell had declared:

In Germany and other countries of Central Europe it is very desirable that communists and social democrats should enter pacts so they are never divided again in the face of a threat from Fascism or Nazism. It is better in those countries if they do not oppose each other.[4]

He explained that such an alliance was 'obviously inappropriate' in the British case.

In the 1946 elections, the communists had been elected in Czechoslovakia and Shinwell had welcomed the result. This was to be the new start longed for by social democrats and their allies, like Jan Masaryk whom Shinwell had met several times in the 1930s. True, the communists would have a very different approach from Masaryk, but so what? 'How could Czechoslovakia be expected to take lessons in politics and democracy from the signatories of the Munich agreement. No, they have to find their own route to Socialism.'

As chairman of the Labour Party in 1947, Shinwell found among the delegates to the annual conference a great deal of sympathy for the 'new workers' states' of Eastern Europe. There was much talk of their progressive laws on national insurance, pensions, land redistribution and nationalisation.

It was not until 1948 that the first signs of real unease emerged and the popularity of the communists started to slump. In February, a communist one-party State was effectively installed in Czechoslovakia and 'Action Committees to Safeguard the Revolution' were set up in every factory and village by the new premier Klement Gottwald. Jan Masaryk 'fell from a window' and died. The social democrats had refused to join the communists the previous November but now they were forced. Later in the year, it was much the same story in Poland as all power was concentrated in the hands of the communists and their General Secretary, Boleslaw Bierut. Again in Poland – and right across Eastern Europe – the democratic left was destroyed, and many personal friends of Shinwell and other Labour leaders, full of hope at the end of the war, were purged, tortured and murdered. It had a very profound effect on the Labour government, making many of its members deeply anti-Soviet.

Within months of Shinwell becoming Secretary for War, the Soviet commanders also started putting pressure on the British, French and American sectors of Berlin, isolated in the Soviet zone of Germany. West Berlin was totally blockaded by 10 July 1948. An airlift began a few days later and lasted for three hundred and twenty-three days. A third European war started to look inevitable.

So it was that on 27 July, Shinwell attended a meeting of the Cabinet Defence Committee under Attlee's chairmanship to discuss the preparation of the army for war. No one thought it absolutely imminent but few thought it could be avoided altogether. Accordingly, Shinwell presented his plans for building up stocks of ammunition, overhauling communications and moving troops on to the Continent. Despite a shortage of money, exacerbated by the high cost of the British contribution to the Berlin airlift, it was decided to stop the rundown of the services. Shinwell warned that there would be resistance in the party if reservists were recalled or if there were a sudden increase in the length of national service. The Cabinet finally agreed in August to leave the half-trained reservists but to ask all existing conscripts to serve an extra three months. It also approved a system devised by Shinwell and Wigg for soldiers to develop skills useful in civilian life in return for slightly longer periods of service.[5] As Shinwell pointed out, garrulous in his first Cabinet meeting for nearly a year, longer service, despite the cost of extra accommodation, would actually result in very little extra cost overall because it meant that training would become more economical. By 1948, training had become so sophisticated that it already cost twice as much in real terms to train every soldier than it had done ten years previously, and economies were urgently needed.

In the middle of these war preparations, a spy scandal threatened Shinwell's job. Ironically, in the light of his later alleged connections with MI5, the scandal involved George Wigg.

Wigg had befriended a pre-war refugee from Czechoslovakia, Frank Ampel. Ampel was openly communist and had become secretary of the British–Czechoslovakia Friendship League. This was acceptable as far as it went. Unfortunately, just before the Berlin blockade started in earnest, Ampel had chosen to visit the Soviet zone of Berlin and he was therefore suspected of being an active Soviet spy. On his return to England he was threatened with immediate deportation. Wigg felt that he knew Ampel well enough to say that he was not a spy and that, anyway, his openness about his communism meant that he was hardly dangerous. He decided to raise his case in an Adjournment debate in the Commons. Within minutes of putting down the relevant motion for the following day he was summoned to Herbert Morrison's office. When he got there, a solemn-looking Lord President told Wigg to sit down and then started to court-martial him in his half-threatening, half-friendly way. Wigg was told that the Ampel business was a matter of national security: 'The PM's given directions that either you drop the Adjournment or you can just resign as Manny's PPS.'

Wigg then asked Morrison innocently if he had told Shinwell, knowing perfectly well he had done no such thing. Morrison had little option but to telephone Shinwell and, after some conversation, passed the phone to Wigg.

Few preliminaries were necessary between the minister and his PPS. Both realised the serious implications. If Ampel really were a spy, then Wigg and Shinwell would have to go in disgrace in the midst of the Berlin crisis. Anti-communist feeling was becoming irresistible: Attlee, for example, had just barred communists from many civil service jobs. Wigg heard lots of huffing and puffing at the other end of the phone as Shinwell tried to pull on the trousers of his evening suit while balancing the telephone receiver on his neck. He asked Wigg what he was going to do. The reply was a sullen, 'What do you think I'm going to do?' Shinwell said it was up to him and he would have to think it over, slammed the phone down and went out to dinner.

Morrison then formally asked Wigg to resign if he went ahead with the adjournment debate. Wigg agreed, saying that he didn't want to embarrass Shinwell.

At five in the morning the scene shifted from national security to Labour politics. Shinwell rang Wigg and it was now Wigg's turn to huff and puff as he stubbed his toe groping for the phone in the dark. Shinwell started:

'I haven't slept a wink, George. Did you tell the press last night?'

'No.'

'It's that little bastard Morrison. They came on to me and asked me all about Ampel. What are you going to do now?'

Once again, they both knew what had happened without having to say so. Morrison, desperate to succeed Attlee who was currently sick, in the midst of economic and foreign crises, reckoned a spy scandal could topple him. If Wigg failed to bring the matter up at all now or resigned, suggesting a possibility of impropriety, then a spy scandal could break over the Secretary for War and, by implication, the Prime Minister. There could hardly be a more sensitive place to be infiltrated by a Soviet spy than the War Office. The only course now was to bring it up publicly and call Morrison's bluff by not resigning. It was a risk but it was the only way of showing that the whole matter was above board.

Wigg duly made his speech. Then he marched up to Morrison in the Lobby, handed him some scraps of paper containing his speech and announced that he was going to stay as Shinwell's PPS.

Ampel stayed in England, and press comment was light. Shinwell and Wigg had defused the time-bomb. Morrison said afterwards that he could not remember ever having asked Wigg to resign! For the moment at least, everyone's job was safe.[6]

The Berlin blockade ground on and the Cabinet agreed in November to put it to the PLP and then Parliament to extend national service to eighteen months. Despite their lack of nuclear weapons, the Soviets seemed prepared now to risk war. Britain's response was to expedite the move towards a treaty for the defence of Western Europe directly involving the Americans. It was when this process started to fall into place – combined with the evident success of the airlift – that the Soviets started to back down, eventually freeing movement to Berlin along the autobahns and railways from the West. The Red Alert was over.

The War Office trio of Shinwell, Montgomery and Wigg was in place for just a year before Montgomery took up his new job in Europe in October 1948. In one way or another they were all oddballs. None of them made friends easily and all were blunt and outspoken. One of Churchill's jibes seemed all too apt. Shinwell is said to have borrowed twopence to phone a friend from a House of Commons callbox. 'Here's fourpence,' Churchill replied. 'Phone them all.' It could have applied to any of the three of them. They all disguised quick minds behind, gruff, bluff, contentious remarks, and all of them were suspicious and critical of political colleagues. Among themselves, the relationships were not quite equal. Wigg found Shinwell's apparent directness a refreshing change from the compromises and conspiracies of politics generally, while Shinwell found Wigg to be a helpful military adviser and understanding companion when the knives were out to get him – which, in his view, they nearly always were. Montgomery found Shinwell and Wigg pleasant to work with and really seems to have played up to Shinwell, on occasions positively ladling out comradeship, pipe tobacco and whisky in response to Shinwell's almost childish delight in being 'Monty's boss'.

Wigg was instrumental in getting Shinwell to see the War Office job as important and worthwhile. In his first weeks in office he helped Shinwell to set himself up as the ordinary soldier's friend. With conscripts and regulars alike, the minister was seen in barracks in Wiltshire, at the Staff College at Camberley and at an army corrective establishment in Colchester where he mixed with administrators, staff and inmates on equal terms. He soon identified a job of work to be done on behalf of an army of 'nearly a million citizens'. He introduced reforms which improved soldiers' lives in many ways, arguing that a good fighting force with high morale was the first duty of any government to provide for its people's defence. He said he could no longer understand 'worthy and well-meaning pacifists', as he took ever greater pride in his soldiers.

The soldiers were certainly easier to work with than the miners had been, and Shinwell soon found the War Office a pleasant contrast to the insoluble (in the financial circumstances) social and economic problems of his previous job. Wigg encouraged him to keep up a hectic round of visits to army camps. It was an astute move. Soldiers sensed that Shinwell was a chief who cared about them in a world which sometimes seemed to abandon them for no apparent reason in God-forsaken places from North Yorkshire to North Africa, so it was good for Shinwell politically to appear to be concerned with their welfare and he inspired genuine affection in the lower ranks. It also took him out of Whitehall and away from Westminster and gave him the human contact which he had missed as he had struggled with civil servants, union bosses and bitter colleagues at the Ministry of Fuel and Power. All in all, pushed by Wigg, Shinwell's attitude

to the army no longer echoed the typical Labour view articulated by John
Strachey, another Labour War Minister, that some unfortunate had to do
the job at the War Office, 'in the same way as someone in the Corporation has to look after a city's sewers'.[7]

The reform of army life was never going to be easy. But if it were to be
attempted at all, the period from 1947 to 1950 was as good a time as any.
Backed by a government committed to social reform generally, retrench-
ing Britain's role in the world, it was a time when the perception of the
army changed from conscripted young men forced into battle to citizens
doing national service. As citizens, they had rights like any others.

Before and after every camp visit by Shinwell, Montgomery or Wigg,
there started to flow tangible improvements. As commanding officers
knew what was expected of them, money was found for cupboards where
soldiers could keep their personal belongings, for improvements to washing
facilities and bedding and regulations were revised, improved and made
less petty. Shinwell insisted that the citizen soldier was entitled to improved
medical care and better educational opportunities, but here he could only
lay down the principles since financial constraints prevented real progress.
It was to be a new kind of intelligent and sophisticated army, capable of
policing cities and fighting communist insurgency.[8]

Shinwell took a personal interest in the treatment of military offenders.
From visiting the cold cells and witnessing the harsh enforcement of hard
labour in Colchester within a week of coming to the War Office, he slowly
shifted the Army Council – in this case, especially after Montgomery had
been replaced by Sir Bill Slim – to agree to abolish the 'hard labour'
provisions altogether. Long hours at physically demanding pointless tasks,
as Shinwell knew from experience, was not an effective punishment; it simply
engendered resentment. But with the death penalty, which he wanted
abolished for many army offences, he was unsuccessful; any changes would
have involved all three services and the Defence Minister, Albert Alexander,
was having none of it; he was a firm believer in capital punishment. By
May 1949, Shinwell had won the Army Council round to the opinion that
the death penalty for service offences in peacetime ought to be 'reconsid-
ered'. On this second approach too, however, Alexander's rebuff was
immediate and final. He wrote to Shinwell:

> I'm of the very strong opinion that in the interest of morale and discipline,
> and for the safety of our Forces in active service and in times of war, the
> death penalty should be retained for the majority of service offences. There
> may be some anomalies between the different services, but tinkering would
> be of little value. There will be no changes at present.

So, for the time being, Shinwell's citizen soldiers could be hanged or
shot. In prison, though, they would be treated less severely, and given better

food, as he had personally insisted, remembering his own diet in Calton gaol thirty years earlier.[9]

Shinwell soon found out that Attlee and the Treasury ministers were much more receptive to requests for extra expenditure on the army than they had been on the mines. Indeed, Attlee, helped by Dalton and Denis Healey, then working at party headquarters, had been responsible for the party's official statement in reply to the 'Keep Left' group of MPs who had complained about defence expenditure. The statement hit back hard: 'A nation which puts domestic comfort before its own security and independence is condemned to a foreign policy of appeasement leading inevitably to capitulation or to war under unfavourable circumstances.'[10]

Shinwell undoubtedly endorsed this view. He had come a long way since his Bolshevik days and even since his more sympathetic attitudes to communism a year or two before. He was prepared to face critics on the left with the argument that heavy defence expenditure was a regrettable necessity as Labour confronted the changing circumstances of the post-war world.

Labour Britain's world-wide responsibilities and limited resources led to an expenditure amounting to 9.5.per cent of GNP on defence when Shinwell took office in 1947, compared with 6.5 per cent in the United States and 5.0 per cent in France. By 1950, it was down to 7.7 per cent in Britain but still only 5.9 per cent in the US and 4.9 per cent in France. Throughout this period, Britain also had double the American and French percentages of the population under arms. How could an old socialist justify such a thing? The answer could be found in an interview Shinwell gave in *Reynolds News* in December 1947. A new social order was being created:

> The worker must be able to feel that he is playing his part in the evolution of a new social order. His status must be raised. He has to feel that he is not just a person to be ordered around.

Labour was creating a new alternative to capitalism, planning and socialising industry and 'restricting the right to capitalists':

> While we are doing this, we have to have at our disposal an army of men – an army of our own citizens and workers – to preserve our independence, making full use of our resources, to ensure we can co-operate with other nations on equal terms. For this, we must have a properly equipped and well-motivated fighting force.'[11]

His opponents on the left were inclined to shake their heads and watch yet another Labour Minister fall into the establishment trap. There were luncheons at Windsor Castle where the King and Queen found Fanny's easy informality and risqué humour 'really quite amusing', and there were the inevitable parades and salutes. Shinwell even accepted a personal invitation to dine with the Lord Mayor of London, against strong advice from Wigg who told him that there would be, among the Lord Mayor's friends, 'some of the most arrogant, hide-bound, class-conscious men' he had ever met.[12] Afterwards, a horrified Shinwell publicly agreed with Wigg and criticised the Lord Mayor, his friends and even the food – all of which provided a the press with a good story and created a favourable political impression in the party.

It was really quite normal and acceptable for Labour ministers to socialise with the establishment. The middle-class intake of 1945 had more problems with it, but Shinwell was neither a snob nor an inverted snob; he had agreed with Ramsay MacDonald's view that it was right for the representatives of the workers to dine with kings. The hidden issue behind all this was the possibility that the first majority Labour government's would transform society to such an extent that the establishment strongholds of monarchy, City, the public school and even the officers' mess might have ceased to exist. This did not happen. In no sense was the government revolutionary, and Shinwell's performance and job have to be seen in that context.

Montgomery's reputation plummeted after the war. He found himself, as Chief of the Imperial General Staff, in conflict with virtually every member of the government with whom he came into contact and he openly despised the chiefs of the other services. He objected to the messy abandonment of Empire in India and Palestine and considered it a disgrace that the government planned to cut the size of the army rather than to build it up to fight the third world war against the 'Russian Empire'. He was impossibly arrogant and difficult to work with. Shinwell wondered later if a number of his former Cabinet colleagues hadn't said to themselves, 'Send him to the War Office with Montgomery. That'll finish him!' The idea of Montgomery working well with a Jew seemed particularly extraordinary since the one-time liberator of Belsen had ordered soldiers in Palestine to 'prepare for all-out war against the fanatical Jews'.[13]

The first time they met, Shinwell was deliberately rude and aggressive. He pointedly remained in his seat when Montgomery entered the room and for some time refused even to look up from his papers. Montgomery stormed out within minutes. But an hour later he came back with a bottle of whisky 'from the NAAFI'. The tension eased, Shinwell called in Wigg and they discussed army reform.[14] As CIGS, Montgomery had been urging a pleasanter social environment for soldiers for some time and he and Shinwell found they thought alike on this matter at least. In his typical way, Montgomery left the meeting to start campaigns for 'bedrooms not barracks', the end of 'lights out' rules and a cutback on the number of parades to be endured by conscripts. Shinwell's more serious reforms could follow later.[15]

The first problem Montgomery and Shinwell had to tackle together was the case of a general whose diary had been found and sent to the CIGS. It revealed the general as an highly active homosexual, which was illegal at the time and certainly sufficient for him to be thrown out of the army. Together Shinwell and Montgomery decided on leniency. 'First-class man', Montgomery had said; later Shinwell discovered that that was how he described nearly all his appointees, but this time he was persuaded. He should be given a warning by Montgomery personally but the matter was to be taken no further.

Having decided on the general's future, the two men settled down to more whisky and informal talk. The conversation started with the two men congratulating themselves on their unsurpassed understanding of man-management (for which the gay general had provided evidence) and Montgomery explained that he was already introducing improved courses on management for officers under training. Then they moved on to government management. Montgomery poured out his heart about Albert Alexander who seemed to be able to take unalterable decisions on trivial matters but had no vision, and Shinwell poured out his heart about Sir Stafford Cripps who had become Chancellor of the Exchequer when Dalton had revealed his budget secrets to the *Evening Standard*; Cripps, he said, now as in the war, saw himself as a potential dictator – indeed, he had made a speech in Edinburgh in which he had actually talked about the likelihood of a totalitarian regime if the social and economic fabric of Britain continued to crumble. Montgomery said that he had to agree with Cripps that some sort of drastic political event of that sort was inevitable.[16]

Shinwell did not know the alarming facts behind what Montgomery was saying. In the haze of comradeship, whisky and pipe-smoke (Churchill and Shinwell were the only people Montgomery allowed to smoke in his presence), Shinwell had no idea that Montgomery had set out in writing only days before a long list of complaints about the decline of post-war Britain, concluding:

> There has got to be a row with those people who are stopping a man doing a full day's work when he really wants to, and with those who put restrictive practices on output. No good will result until this row, or showdown, has taken place and has been won. The Government won't face it; they think they can get through without it; but they can't. If the thing goes sky-high, I may have to play a part: and would do so.

Montgomery saw himself as a kind of military dictator. If Shinwell had known this, he would certainly not have blundered into a half-joking but nearly disastrous comment at the height of the Berlin crisis:

Monty, you have a very big following in the country and so have I, despite [waving his arm towards Downing Street] what they might think over there. You could save this country and I could rouse the workers to follow me. Between us, you and I, we could do anything.

In the context of what Montgomery was thinking, this was an extraordinary and exciting statement. As Shinwell had intended it, even if taken completely seriously, it was just a comment on the political pressure that he and Montgomery could possibly have brought to bear together. He later admitted that he should have realised that he was playing with dynamite. At their meeting Montgomery had actually said that he and Shinwell should 'start a revolution', but 'I confess *my* eyes glazed over with that sort of talk and I didn't notice *his* eyes blazing'.[17]

Blazing-eyed generals were the problem again a couple of weeks later when Shinwell and Wigg visited Germany together and then met up with Montgomery in Berlin. The Soviet Military Governor was piling on the pressure again, services would be cut and roads closed off with startling regularity. It was at this moment that Truman appointed General Lucius Clay as American Military Governor. The British trio were all in agreement that Clay was more dangerous than the Russians:

> General Clay considers that World War Three will begin in six months' time, indeed, he might well bring it on himself by shooting his way up the autobahn to Berlin if the Russians were difficult about things. He's a real 'He-man' and hates the Russians with a deadly hatred; he will never bargain or give an inch if he can help it.'[18]

Shinwell and Montgomery went on to meet Sokolovsky, the Soviet commander, and both had their views confirmed that the Soviets wanted to keep up the pressure but avoid war. Clay was definitely more dangerous than Sokolovsky.

These matters were of course out of Shinwell's and Montgomery's control. They could only run the army and make suggestions about wider policies. In this period, for once, Shinwell was staying below the parapet and it was Montgomery who spoke out about the unpreparedness of the West for a war which they were going to blunder into without realising what they were doing. And it was Shinwell who was given the job of telling Montgomery off for making speeches with which they both knew he was really in complete agreement.

In October 1948, Montgomery was appointed first chairman of the Committee of Commanders-in-Chief of the Western Union, comprising Britain, France and Benelux. Montgomery wanted General Sir John Crocker to succeed him as CIGS, but Attlee decided on General Sir Bill Slim. Attlee preferred Slim because he had been nearer to the centre of

British political life since the war, first as head of the Imperial Defence College in London and then as deputy chairman of the nationalised Railway Executive. Montgomery protested to Attlee that he had already told Crocker. Attlee for once in his life almost shouted and dismissed Montgomery with: 'Untell him!'[19]

Shinwell backed the appointment of Slim and told Montgomery to his face that he was sick and tired of his persistent campaign for Crocker who was based in the Middle East and was out of touch with the political realities in London. Attlee was so annoyed by Montgomery's behaviour that he refused to take telephone calls from him or to meet him for three months.

Shinwell never achieved with Slim the informal rapport he had had with Montgomery. Yet he and Attlee were proved right as Slim turned out to be a calm and effective operator. Shinwell even arranged for him to meet with a number of left-wing Labour MPs opposed to the government's defence strategy, something he would never have risked with Montgomery. These discussions ranged over delicate problems from Berlin to Malaya and were finally steered by Shinwell on to the concept of a high-quality well-trained citizen army. The idea of the citizen army at least meant something real, compared with Montgomery's vague but dangerous 'New Model Army' fighting the Russians on the Rhine.

Shinwell, Slim and Wigg undertook just one major foreign tour together, to the Suez Canal Zone, the first time Shinwell had visited the region. The strategic importance of the bases in the Canal Zone were to do with both the canal itself and the accessibility of the southern part of the Soviet Union to bombers based there. None of this was obvious to most of the soldiers based there.

By the time Shinwell visited, all he found in practice were troops trying to guard immense stores left over from the war against well-organised Egyptian theft. They certainly could not understand what they were doing there in disgusting living conditions at the taxpayers' considerable expense. Shinwell's explanation of the strategy involved caused explosions of mocking laughter from one group of soldiers he addressed. Worse was to follow at a question-and-answer session for officers, when a young lieutenant told Shinwell he had heard he had been a 'Conchie' in the First World War. Shinwell put the matter straight but he found the splash of newspaper publicity back home, which included verbatim reports of precisely what he had said in court about his opposition to the First World War thirty years before, annoying and upsetting.

A courtesy call on the Egyptian government included a bizarre lunch with King Farouk. The obese young monarch expounded at length his claim on the Sudan and talked about the need to speed up the withdrawal of British troops from the Canal Zone. When Shinwell, Slim and Wigg got back to London, however, they found that the same King had secretly offered Britain a Defence Agreement, including keeping large numbers of troops in the Canal Zone. He had apparently not been able to speak freely in front of his Foreign Minister, and he realised he depended for the safety of his throne on the British who had kept him there throughout the war.[20]

The Egyptian visit underlined Shinwell's weakness. His powers were confined to a very limited area and for most of that he depended on a co-operative CIGS and other senior generals on the army Council. The army, however much improved, remained a mere tool of foreign policy and had to do as it was bidden.

There is a sense in which no Jew, however little he might have to do with his own community, can forget the Holy Land. The Palestine conflict, which dogged the first three years of Attlee's government, slowly but surely awakened this folk-memory in Shinwell.

Jews always regarded their exile from the Holy Land as temporary. Throughout the whole history of their two thousand years of exile, religious Jews struggled to the Holy Land to pray, to die and to be buried on the Mount of Olives in Jerusalem. In Shinwell's own lifetime, all other possible havens at times of persecution, such as Uganda and Argentina, were refused. Only the Holy Land would do. The Nazi Holocaust, the death of six million Jews, and subsequent Gentile guilt, made the modern case for return irresistible.

By the the end of the war most Jews were no longer strict in their religion but they still shared an overwhelming feeling of right to possess the Holy Land and to live there if they wished. In Shinwell's case this feeling had been weak before the war and before the Holocaust, but had now been strengthened. The fact that he had no wish to attend a synagogue on Yom Kippur did not alter his feelings about being a Jew. He made no conscious effort to reject his Jewishness, and with that Jewishness went his sense of a need for the Jews to have a homeland. His specific conviction of that need was made easier by the socialist commitment of many of the Zionists he met after the war – not a bit like Brodetsky back in 1932. David ben Gurion and Goldie Myerson (later Golda Meir) were very different from the British Jewish establishment.

Shinwell's identity with his fellow Jews was also strengthened by the crude anti-Semitism and failing policy on Palestine of the Foreign Secretary Ernest Bevin. Bevin had inherited Britain's mandate to govern Palestine, given by the League of Nations when the territory was relinquished by the Turks after the First World War. The British had promised the Jews a 'National Home' there, but clashes between Jews and Arabs and the strategic importance of good relations with emerging Arab states had led Britain to close off Jewish immigration to Palestine just at a time when the only alter-native for most of them was death in concentration camps. By 1946, the

Labour government was again blockading Palestine against the Jews who had survived the Holocaust, and many were left in refugee camps in Cyprus and Northern Europe. Bevin was even having doubts as to whether there should be a national home at all for the Jews in Palestine, declaring: 'We cannot accept the view that the Jews should be driven out of Europe.'

This was too much for Shinwell and he raised in Cabinet the international opprobrium which the government would bring on themselves if they carried on in this way, citing American newspaper reports of British atrocities against Jews in Haifa. He was a Jew and he would not be leaving Europe, but it was a quite different story for the homeless survivors of Auschwitz and Belsen. What did Bevin imagine that Europe offered them? He reminded Bevin that the Mandate actually obliged Britain to facilitate Jewish immigration to Palestine and not to obstruct it. Bevin angrily retorted that there was a provision that the native people shouldn't suffer and Shinwell came back with the claim that the Jews brought industry, intensive agriculture and jobs to the impoverished people of 'that previously barren and neglected land'.[21]

In November 1945, Bevin and James Byrnes, the American Secretary of State, had agreed to appoint a joint Anglo-American Committee of Inquiry, which reported a few months later in favour of the partition of Palestine into homes for the 'Jewish Nation' and the 'Palestinian Arabs'. But this was accepted only by the Jews and opposed vehemently by the Arabs. As 1946 wore on, Bevin and several of his Cabinet colleagues grew less and less inclined to accept the creation of a Jewish State by partition. At one and the same time, they were under pressure from strategic considerations, especially the need to secure oil resources from the Arab world, to abandon the idea of a Jewish State, and under pressure from the United States, partly because Truman depended on the Jewish vote in New York, to establish a Jewish State without delay.

American opinion was impervious to Jewish 'terrorism' against what they tended to see as the cruel British occupying force. The American press was also generally sympathetic to the Jews, who had already suffered under the Nazis, now suffering more at the hands of openly anti-Semitic British generals. The worst terrorist act was the blowing up of the King David Hotel, the British military headquarters, leaving ninety-one dead and forty-five wounded. Any sympathetic comment that it might have earned for Bevin from the Americans was, however, quickly dispersed by the anti-Semitic British Commanding Officer, General Barker, who responded with a recommendation that Jewish shops should be boycotted to 'hit the Jew in the pocket which is all he understands'.

Shinwell joined the Cabinet in condemning the terrorism and distancing himself from Barker's insensitive comments. He also stressed the distinction between his Zionist socialist friends and the terrorists. He deplored

Bevin's inclination to lump all the Jews together while making careful distinctions among the Arabs.[22]

Shinwell pushed Bevin for a quick solution, 'the only realistic one being partition', and he got the support of Nye Bevan in Cabinet who agreed that this would be the only way to avoid chaos and destruction continuing indefinitely.[23] But Bevin still stuck to the impossible idea of a unitary state for Jews and Arabs together, claiming it was just the 'New York Yids' that were preventing it. What he was concerned about was stopping illegal Jewish immigration into Palestine until the whole matter was sorted out.[24]

Within two months of Shinwell taking over as Secretary for War, Bevin had resentfully handed over the whole problem to the United Nations which voted for a Jewish State. Israel finally came into existence in partitioned Palestine on 14 May 1948. Shinwell was relieved to have little to do except formally to take charge of the evacuation of the British Army by August 1948. He was very relieved to have avoided by a few months being embroiled in potential controversy as a Jewish political head of the British Army in Palestine.

Few deny that Bevin was anti-Semitic. He developed a hatred for Jews, according to Ian Mikardo who knew him well, at a by-election in Whitechapel where his favoured candidate was nearly defeated despite his strenuous intervention. Certainly he was angered and in the end humiliated by the Jews of Palestine and failed to grasp the extraordinary emotions engendered by the Holocaust. Foreign Office officials were left in no doubt about his hatred of the 'Yids who try to jump the queue to get to Palestine'.[25]

Bevin's anti-Semitism was, in fact, probably as deeply and unconsciously rooted in his soul as Shinwell's Zionism. Shinwell always denied strong feelings about the establishment of the Jewish State, but time and again, especially now he was becoming an old man, he clearly felt it necessary to intervene on this issue which was far beyond his ministerial interest. Similarly, Bevin, of course, would always have flatly denied the charge of anti-Semitism; his turns of phrase were unfortunate but intellectually he would certainly have denied any kind of racism. Surely, though, somewhere in his roots in Somerset were those long-learned stories of the crucified Christ that would eventually make him react the way he did, in a way all too familiar to Jews in public life throughout the Christian world. Such Jews, like Shinwell, always knew they could never quite trust the Christian world. To some extent, however slight, they would always be outsiders.

The government's term of office came to an end in 1950. The Boundary Commission had been at work and Shinwell was now fighting 'Easington', named after the collection of pit villages south of Seaham, which now formed the heart of his constituency. Although Labour's effective majority in the

House of Commons was right down to six, the size of its vote actually increased. Shinwell cruised to another easy victory:

Emanuel Shinwell (Labour)	38,367 (81.0%)
Charles Macfarlane (Conservative)	8,972 (19.0%)
Majority	29,395

CHAPTER 17

Minister of Defence

Attlee told Shinwell: 'It's obvious you've been a success at the War Office. The military chiefs trust you, so you must go to the Ministry of Defence.'[1]

Shinwell was back in the Cabinet, but for how long? No one expected a government with a very slim majority to last long. Many of its leading lights were fading. Bevin and Cripps would soon be dead. Dalton, who had been forced to resign in 1947 for accidentally giving away budget secrets, was back in the Cabinet but older and slower; and the Prime Minister's health was not all it might have been. Such a narrow majority in those days was anyway thought an inadequate mandate for new policy. Indeed, the nationalisation of steel was the only controversial proposal of any significance.

Shinwell wanted to cut a distinctive figure in his new job. Inevitably he would have to work closely – and in a subordinate role – with his old adversary Ernest Bevin on Britain's international affairs; but he also had a chance to make his own mark on the organisation of all three armed services. His predecessor, Albert Alexander, had altered little, having been overwhelmed by the series of crises that accompanied the change from world war to cold war and an uneasy peace. Shinwell, on the other hand, was now taking a serious interest in military strategy. Wigg had even fixed up for him a series of meetings with the great military analyst Basil Liddell Hart. So within a month of moving from the War Office to Defence, Shinwell was able to make a parliamentary Defence Statement which acknowledged the revolutionary changes in warfare brought about by the nuclear age. It was the first of its kind since the war.

He committed himself unequivocally to atomic research. Stalin now had atomic weapons as well as the Americans and, even under the protective umbrella of the new North Atlantic Treaty Organisation, the government felt that Britain should be able to retaliate with its own version of the world's most terrifying weapon if necessary. Shinwell had also been persuaded – by Liddell Hart – that the most effective type of war preparation would be to prepare small but very highly trained and specialised combat groups which could manoeuvre easily in the face of an overwhelming Red Army conventional attack, always assuming a nuclear stand off. He therefore encouraged research towards fast movement, jet engines for planes to shift airborne divisions and rockets for missiles carrying warheads and supplies.[2]

It was clear that these fast-moving, highly trained services, able to attack specific targets and then withdraw, and able to counter enemy infiltration on the home front, would need well-paid career soldiers and not the current reality of a million conscripts on national service. The army in Germany, the Middle East and the Far East still needed large numbers of people and, since they all had to be trained and shipped out, even eighteen months' service was proving too short a time. Despite the enormous expense involved and despite its irrelevance to his long-term plans for the services, Shinwell found himself having to persuade the Cabinet to agree to a two-year period of national service. Wigg regretted this more than anybody:

> You've got 60 per cent of your budget going on paying allowances. On top of that, it's screechingly funny, you end up with more wives and children on the Ministry of Defence payroll, than you've got soldiers, sailors and airmen. You couldn't knock the skin off a rice pudding. But we had to do it.[3]

There simply wasn't the scope to be radical. The meetings with Liddell Hart became rarer as the realities loomed larger. Shinwell and Wigg both agreed about the way that warfare was likely to go. Indeed, regular army forays against communist infiltration in Malaya had been very effective, compared with the more heavy-handed approach used in Palestine and the expensive and unpopular occupation of Germany. But with NATO just starting to be organised and military aid from the United States on its way, this was not the moment to advertise what would have seemed a reduced commitment to defence by scaling down the number of recruits.

Indeed, although he controlled a quarter of government expenditure and 7.5 per cent of the whole British national income, Shinwell as Minister of Defence was mostly swept along in the wake of foreign policy. The starting-point for this policy was, of course, that Stalin, like a new Hitler, would not be satisfied with consolidating Eastern Europe but would take over Western Europe and much of the Middle East and Far East, either directly or through puppet communists, if he were given a chance. A likely nuclear stand-off would mean a hard-fought conventional war. Only a strong NATO defensive strategy might prevent disaster, but the prevailing thinking was that Britain would indeed have to fight a third world war in Europe within five years. Once again the French were unwilling to join, especially if the Germans were rearmed. Yet, at the same time, the Americans insisted that the Germans should be rearmed virtually as the price of American support. Britain found itself supporting the Americans against the French on this. With its economic and military dependence on the United States, there was no way that Britain could resist American policy even if it had wished to. It could not oppose German rearmament and it could not restructure the army by reducing its size and improving the quality of its equipment, which Shinwell wanted to do. Britain was a beggar and it couldn't be a chooser.

Shinwell's first few months in office were therefore not marked by great changes; but there was a certain amount of practical progress. He made the army, navy and air force collaborate for the first time on specifications for defence contracts for jet engines and missile launchers, and regular and intensive monitoring procedures were worked out to supervise the performance of defence industries still hampered by chronic shortages of skilled labour and capital investment.[4]

Then there was the question of servicemen's pay which caused a clash between Shinwell and the ex-Viceroy of India and now Fourth Sea Lord, Lord Mountbatten. It was the Fourth Sea Lord's responsibility to negotiate pay for the navy and Mountbatten said that he had no intention of leaving Shinwell to negotiate it with the Treasury, as he wished – and was already doing for the army and air force. Mountbatten had developed a low opinion of Shinwell within a week of his taking office, blaming him for the British failure to secure him NATO's Mediterranean Command; in fact, Shinwell had inherited this decision but had treacherously, in Mountbatten's eyes, described it as 'practical in peace time'.[5]

Now Shinwell told Mountbatten that he was putting together a package of pay proposals for all the armed services and intended to include special bonuses for the lowest ranks in their first pay increase since 1930. In his view, he said, the differential between officers and men was too great. Mountbatten was furious and told Shinwell that he lived in an imaginary age when officers had large private incomes. He insisted on his right to attend all the meetings with the Treasury, where he made life as embarrassing as possible, trying to talk over Shinwell and interrupting him, and later describing him as 'the lowest form of Labour life' and a 'poor operator'.

Both Shinwell and Mountbatten later claimed responsibility for the substantial increases paid to regular servicemen. Shinwell got his way on differentials. They both claimed credit for the boost these pay increases would undoubtedly give to recruitment into the regular services. In fact, Mountbatten probably contributed very little. All the background work on the increase with Treasury officials was done through Shinwell who also had a personal discussion with Attlee to ease its passage.[6]

So far so good. Shinwell's first months at the Ministry of Defence fulfilled the promise of his solid performance at the War Office. In May 1951, at a meeting of the military Western European Union in Brussels, Shinwell even showed new diplomatic skills. As the senior Cabinet Minister present, he led Gaitskell (now Chief Secretary and deputising for the Chancellor of the Exchequer) and Kenneth Younger (deputising for the Foreign Secretary) in a more coherent team than any of their European counterparts. It was the first in a series of inconclusive meetings where Britain argued for German rearmament with safeguards against militarism, as a way of inducing further specific commitments on the supply of weapons from the United States without alienating the French. This was the formula that led eventually to systematic American involvement in the defence of Western Europe. It was clear then that Shinwell had mastered both his political and his military brief.[7]

Everything changed in the early evening of 24 June 1951 (London time) and 4 a.m. on 25 June 1951 (Korean time). Kim Il Sung, North Korea's communist leader, ordered his artillery to attack the South. A few weeks earlier he had apparently assured Stalin of a quick and relatively painless victory, unifying his country under communism. Later on the 25th, the United Nations Security Council, in the absence of the Soviet representative, adopted a resolution calling for the withdrawal of North Korean forces to the 38th Parallel from which they were now advancing. There was no reply and, two days later, American forces were ordered into action to support South Korea, and the United Nations called on the backing of all its member states. By 29 August, the British 27th Brigade had arrived from Hong Kong. On 26 September, Seoul fell to the communists. By then, the British had committed another fully equipped brigade, a fleet of thirteen vessels including an aircraft carrier and eight destroyers, and substantial tactical air support.

As soon as the North Koreans attacked, a new sense of urgency on defence matters among Western governments was inevitable. The European threat increased as the French continued to resist German rearmament, while the fledgling German Democratic Republic in the East hosted twenty-seven Soviet divisions and was building up its own paramilitary 'Volkspolizei'. In October, 99.7 per cent of the electorate of this new Republic were said to have voted communist – actually for the Socialist Unity Party which Shinwell had supported in a speech a few years before – and they were making a start on the 'Volksarmee'. The fear was that an attack could be made on Western Europe while American attention was fixed on the Far East. Yet the French continued to insist that no German state could ever be trusted with an army, no matter what the safeguards, and the Americans showed signs of losing patience. The Americans would ask the French how they could even think of stopping the Germans defending themselves against communism on their own soil. The French would retort that the Americans had obviously learned nothing from recent history, had not suffered Nazi occupation, and could never understand.

The Foreign and Defence ministers of Britain, France and the United States met at the fourth NATO Council Meeting in Washington in September. Bevin went a few days ahead of Shinwell and had a very rough sea journey. He was ill when he started and now all those who met him were shocked by his appearance; he was obviously dying. Wigg came with Shinwell but he often had to leave his own boss to steady Bevin's arm as he struggled to climb stairs or walk outside to his car. The Foreign Secretary's concentration span was short and he often dozed off in meetings.[8]

The United States started the conference with a concession for which Bevin had been pressing for several years. It announced that if any of the countries of Western Europe (including France) were attacked, it would consider it to be an attack on the United States and it would be involved from Day One. It was an important reassurance at a time when Stalin might have thought that America was off its guard in Europe.

After this big gesture, it then fell to Shinwell and General George Marshall, the American Secretary for Defense, to discuss the thorny question of Germany with Jules Moch, their French counterpart. Moch stonewalled. Shinwell stressed that no NATO member would ever accept German dominance of a European anti-communist force. Marshall backed this up with a promise that the United States would make it its own responsibility to shadow the German command, which would be regionally based within Germany and not national. Shinwell then insisted – and eventually Moch accepted – that the French proposal of a Rhine defence line against the Red Army could not even be considered; for one thing, what about the Dutch who lived on the far side? But on the main point – a German army – even the modest proposal of a paramilitary gendarmerie to balance the 'Volkspolizei' was absolutely unacceptable to Moch.[9]

It fell to Marshall to remind Moch that American financial support frankly depended on co-operation on this matter. The British could expect help. The French could not. Substantial increases in military aid would depend on all Western Europeans, including Germans, being seen by Americans to pull their weight. If not, he could not see Congress agreeing to an open-ended commitment. Moch finally agreed to take the idea of the gendarmerie back to his government for consideration, and no more.

Marshall asked Shinwell to see Moch alone in the hope of more concessions. It was heavy-going. Moch was a socialist whose family had suffered under the Nazis and an implacable hater of all things German. Shinwell in turn had come to loathe Moch (a capable man, a fact about which he himself has no false modesty), and Moch loathed Shinwell ('*un orateur de carrefour, c'est tout*').[10] Moch was eventually persuaded to allow a German army of less than one brigade's strength, guaranteed smaller than the contribution of any other member of NATO; 'apparently this excluded Iceland,' Shinwell sneered, 'who were contributing no one at all, but included the Portuguese who, though their Defence Minister was the most garrulous in the Western world, planned to contribute one brigade by the end of five years.'[11]

The Moch proposal was not acceptable to the British or Americans, but it was all that Shinwell could get out of him. With the prospects of the French allowing one small brigade and possibly a gendarmerie, the Council Meeting broke up in time for the UN General Assembly in New York on 20 September. It was decided that the Defence ministers alone would try again to reach an agreement back in Washington at the end of October. Shinwell and Bevin then returned to England together from New York, arriving in time for the Labour Party conference at Margate on 2 October.

For the first time, Bevin and Shinwell had worked well together. They shared the same objectives now and in some ways they had both mellowed. Years of bitterness, Bevin's anti-Semitism and Shinwell's opposition to the union establishment, could not just be put behind them, so they were only colleagues never friends. Travelling back to Southampton on the *Queen Mary* together, they did just once go beyond official collaboration and formal courtesy to work together on their approach to the party conference. Bevin would make the main contribution to the debate on the international situation and Shinwell would move the acceptance of the Executive's report on foreign affairs. There would be opponents of both who would want friendly relations with the Soviet Union and sharp reductions in defence expenditure. Bevin agreed to talk on the reality, as he saw it, of the Soviet menace and Shinwell agreed to home in on collective security as a legitimate objective for good socialists. They knew they would have to rely on the support of the big unions; the delegates in the hall would hate it and the atmosphere would be tense.

When it came to it, Bevin's speech was not just unpopular, it flopped. He had attended every conference since 1917 and this was his worst speech by far. In a weak voice he had pitched the whole speech at too low a level, with unsophisticated rhetorical questions such as, 'Do you think we like having to do it?' and, 'Can you lay down your arms and be safe?' The withered and dying Foreign Secretary sat down to a mere smattering of sympathetic applause.

Shinwell's speech was one of the few he ever prepared and memorised, so he could plough on through cat-calls and heckling if necessary to reach the safe haven of the block vote. His theme was that Labour could not just contract out of the moral decisions of the post-war world. Collective security had always been one of the party's legitimate objectives in international affairs and Korea was a striking example.

News was coming in, right through the conference week, of victories by the United Nations, towns and villages liberated: 'We, as internationalists, should not think of Chungsan and Pyongyang in a different way from

Manchester and Dumfries.' People everywhere had the right to democracy. It would also cost money, and that was why the government had had to increase the defence budget by another 20 per cent to £3,600 million, 10 per cent of National income, and might have to increase it still further. Towards the end of the speech, he dealt with the thorniest matters of all for a Labour Party conference, the two-year compulsory national service he had introduced. The booing and heckling rose in volume until he had to shout into the microphone to make himself heard:

> It is not the government's intention to retain national service as a permanent feature of national life. There is nothing inherently unsound in that principle, but as soon as possible, the government will gladly reduce the length of service or abolish national service entirely.
>
> I must repeat with the greatest emphasis that we are not preparing for another war. Our purpose is peace, not war. War is not inevitable, and it is of no service to humanity to say that a third world war is bound to come. But I cannot conceal from the Conference my anxiety about the international situation. We must be on our guard, and any failure to build up our defences would be fatal.

It was a competent, if neither brilliant nor passionate, performance. The block votes of the big trade unions duly defeated most of the delegates in the conference hall by four million, eight hundred thousand to eight hundred thousand.[12]

Shinwell took only a handful of his officials back to Washington. He had to do without Wigg because his votes were needed in the House of Commons but he took with him the three Chiefs of Staff and for the first time he flew the Atlantic rather than wasting five days on an ocean liner. He reckoned Gander aerodrome on Newfoundland where his plane touched down to be the dreariest place he had ever seen.

The British were very much in favour in Washington. They were the Americans' strongest supporters in Korea and their most persistent allies in Europe. General Marshall knew perfectly well that Shinwell was prone to flattery and he laid it on thickly. Shinwell responded equally effusively. It is even possible the two men quite liked each other: 'a great general and a great man,' said Shinwell of Marshall; 'a man who combines competence with charm,' responded Marshall. Marshall even set up for Shinwell the privilege of an intimate dinner including the Trumans who came as guests of the British Ambassador:

> His guests included President and Mrs Truman, General and Mrs Marshall, the Bishop of Washington and his wife, and Anthony Eden, who was in the States on a private visit. My neighbours were Mrs Truman and the Bishop's wife. Mrs Truman struck me as a very womanly

person, concerned with domestic matters more than the problems that beset her husband. She was full of the arrangements for some church in Alabama which was about to receive a banner, and I admired her for telling me all the details rather than attempting conversation on matters which were not so interesting to her. The main conversation at the table centred around Truman and Marshall, who exchanged reminiscences in rare style.[13]

Jules Moch by now had a new plan, the so-called 'Pleven' plan, named after the French Prime Minister. This reverted to an old idea of a single European army, which the French themselves had rejected before because it would be too cumbersome. The new version of the idea was that the Germans would participate in such an army as soldiers but without any national command structure, without any generals and without any Ministry of Defence. The Germans had already heard about the plan and rejected it, and Marshall and Shinwell did not take much longer to do so. The fact was that the French did not really believe in the imminent Soviet threat to Europe, whereas Britain and America did.

Indeed, in Shinwell's absence, the British government voted for yet another substantial increase in defence expenditure. In the end, the best that Marshall and Shinwell could get out of Moch was his signature on an agreement to proceed with the deployment of additional American troops in Europe and a 'decision in principle to involve the Germans in Western European defence'. At Shinwell's suggestion the French could have nine months to decide how to proceed with this agreement.[14]

On this second visit to Washington, Shinwell managed to find time to turn tourist. After years of austerity, his impression was very favourable:

Washington is one of the finest cities I have ever visited, the splendid buildings, beautiful parks and wide roads ... I took the opportunity to walk round the city to see how the ordinary people lived, taking my excellent breakfast of fruit juice, coffee, toast and two fried eggs for half a dollar in the cafes ... Several times I visited the district inhabited by the coloured population. While there is a certain amount of segregation in Washington these people seemed very prosperous and if the housing conditions sometimes contrasted unfavourably with those of white people the American negro in Washington lives at a much higher standard than many Europeans.[15]

Shinwell had at least helped to prise some limited progress from the conference. Attlee sent a telegram congratulating him on his diplomatic success. The Americans would get more involved in Europe; the risk of isolationism apparent a month earlier had all but disappeared and they agreed also to reappoint Eisenhower – whom Shinwell thought arrogant and unreliable but good in terms of public relations – Supreme Commander in Europe.

On 1 November, some Chinese MiGs had been seen from the Yalu River valley which separated China from Korea. Almost immediately, a company of the United States' 8th Cavalry reported itself under fire from unidentified troops. For some three weeks, Chinese 'volunteers' poured into Korea, followed on 26 November by well-equipped Chinese regular troops. China had threatened to intervene if United Nations troops crossed back over the 38th Parallel in pursuit of the defeated Korean communists, but the UN Commander, US General Douglas MacArthur, relished a fight with Mao's Chinese and refused even to slow down his advance.

MacArthur had been given almost plenipotentiary powers in the Far East, commanding US forces there at the end of the Second World War. He had held for five years virtual suzerainty over Japan and the Philippines and much of the non-communist Far East. He had not even visited the United States mainland since the 1930s and he considered the Truman government feeble in its dealings with communist China. He also considered the British and French untrustworthy if not subversive.

Now, with his back against the wall from the surprise Chinese attack, his propaganda office, beyond the control of Washington, started pouring out criticism and blame everywhere except in the direction of MacArthur himself: 'Forces are inadequate'; 'supplies are of a low quality'; 'intelligence gathering has broken down; 'foreign governments are trying to appease the Chinese Communists.'

On 29 November, Secretary of State Dean Acheson, who had returned from visiting MacArthur, described him as being in a 'blue funk'. The next day, a shaky and hesitant Truman gave the impression at a news conference that the general had permission not just to engage forces where and when he wished, but to use the atomic bomb. This caused instant consternation in Europe, especially in Britain where some of the nuclear arsenal was stored. Truman cabled Attlee to correct the 'false impression' that he had given, but Attlee felt he should visit Washington in any case. Bevin was too ill to go with him, but he took the Army Chief of Staff, Sir William Slim. Attlee and Slim were reassured that the President personally controlled all American atomic bombs and had no intention of using one in Korea, and they also agreed joint control of any atomic weapons kept in Britain. Attlee wanted overtures made to the Chinese but, although Truman agreed that Chinese territory should not be bombed or invaded, American public opinion would not tolerate any form of appeasement.[16]

Meanwhile, Shinwell was faced with the need to describe to the House of Commons British losses at the hands of the Chinese and North Koreans:

As a result of the strong enemy attack in the Chosin area it has been necessary to withdraw. At the present time the 10th Corps, including the 41st Independent Commando, Royal Marines, is opposed by at least seven Chinese divisions, and the build-up continues. Our latest report is that the Commandos are engaged in very bitter fighting alongside the American Marines in a determined attempt to extricate themselves from danger of encirclement. Supplies have been dropped and considerable numbers of wounded have been evacuated by air.

He went on to describe the retreat of the British 27th and 29th Brigades from the area around Pyongyang:

I need not stress to the House the severe strain which is put upon the spirit and discipline of troops by battles of withdrawal in the face of an enemy so vastly superior in strength; and these operations are being conducted in conditions of bitter cold and hardship.[17]

In reality, as Shinwell already knew, the situation was even worse. The 'withdrawal' was a rout. The Royal Marines in the Chosin area were equipped with inadequate clothing for night temperatures which could drop to minus twenty degrees and their weapons were often faulty. Under pressure from the scale and ferocity of the Chinese attack, the chain of command had evaporated and young Marines were left in the middle of the Korean mountains to fend for themselves and to surrender if they could.

In the Pyongyang area, the situation was even more serious for the British because of the numbers involved. Millions of pounds' worth of equipment had already been abandoned to make the escape faster. Supplies had broken down and men were collapsing with exhaustion and hunger. Some Argyll and Sutherland Highlanders and men of the Middlesex Regiment were so hungry that they had started stealing rice and potatoes from villagers at gunpoint. Without maps or compasses, young British soldiers simply followed the rout.

On 4 January, Seoul was hastily evacuated and surrendered to the communists and on 13 January the US offered a ceasefire with an armistice along the line of the 38th Parallel. The Chinese and North Koreans turned it down flat. They were now sure they could conquer the whole of Korea. They should have accepted the ceasefire, because from then on the United Nations troops regrouped and started with many fresh men to advance north again.

As the 38th Parallel was approached and crossed by UN troops for the second time, in the early spring, MacArthur wanted desperately to seize the opportunity to declare war on China, to defeat once and for all what he saw as the source of all the evil in the Far East. The Truman administration and its European allies wanted no such thing. To the British government's immense relief, MacArthur, now an American popular hero, was dramatically dismissed by Truman in April. Shinwell told a public meeting in Easington that they could all sigh with relief now that MacArthur had been dismissed. He claimed that it opened the way for peace negotiations. In the House of Commons he at once got into trouble with Churchill. Was he aware that the slight misreporting of his words had shown him, the Minister of Defence, doubting the supreme commander's military competence: 'If anything could at that time have got about fifty million Americans furious with him, and with the Government for whom he spoke, it would have been to use language like that.'[18]

This awkward moment was soon forgotten as MacArthur returned to the United States for ticker-tape welcomes in every city he visited and the more sober General Matthew Ridgway took over command in Korea. The problem from now on would be how to extricate the West from the bloody mess of Korea rather than how to stop the communist Chinese taking over the whole of the Far East or how to stop the Americans bombing Manchuria or Peking.

Serious attention turned back to Europe where Eisenhower was taking up office in Paris as Supreme Commander. Shinwell wrote a welcoming letter:

> I am happy to make available to you the services of all the British officers you asked for. You and they together with all of our allies will, I am sure, do much to ensure the peace of the world.[19]

Thereafter the correspondence quickly became acrimonious. Eisenhower wanted Montgomery to be the Commander in Chief, Central Europe, but Shinwell said he could not release him from his duties at the Western European Union. Eisenhower complained to Attlee about widespread lack of co-operation, and Attlee asked Shinwell to go to Paris to put matters straight:

> I met the General and some members of his staff and had some lunch – hardly up to my expectations at what one would be served in Paris. (I learned later that the General seldom ate more than a little salad.) However, the lunch being over, Eisenhower asked me to go into his room and told me what the trouble was about. He was angry and I learned it was because, according to him, our Ambassador in Paris – Gladwyn Jebb – had complained about excessive expenditure incurred by the Commander's Headquarters. What form this took I never discovered … He walked up and down, waving a golfclub round his head, and in language more suitable to the rank and file than from a General, expressed his opinion of the Ambassador and all and sundry in a fashion which, frankly, amazed me.[20]

Shinwell returned to London with a whole list of Eisenhower's petty complaints from the status of the Ambassador to the allowances of officers for motorcar hire. Although he felt that these should all have been dealt with by civil service clerks, he did the whole thing personally and wrote a long and detailed letter in reply to Eisenhower – also thanking him for the lunch. The future President replied curtly: 'Thank you for your generally satisfactory letter.'[21]

The rearmament programme soon placed serious burdens on industry. Vast orders were placed at inflated prices, and delivery was all too frequently sporadic. Long sessions between Shinwell and Harold Wilson, now President of the Board of Trade, were aimed at making sure that the orders placed could be fulfilled. The shortage of many materials was disastrous and the government's knowledge about local labour markets negligible, so progress was difficult.

Nevertheless, there was a bright side. The vast arms programme brought prosperity to shipbuilding centres, dockyards and weapons factories all over Britain. Sometimes there were big export opportunities too. On one occasion, thinking he had a winner, Shinwell flew to Washington to try to persuade the Pentagon to buy a new automatic rifle; but this particular trip was a failure and Shinwell returned to England earlier than he planned so he could get back to his constituency to judge the annual Coal Queen beauty competition, prompting the mocking American newspaper headline: 'Shinwell prefers legs to arms.'[22]

The spectre of what Shinwell described rather wildly as 'a hundred and seventy-five Red Army divisions threatening European civilisation' helped to maintain the momentum of enormous arms expenditure, rising with the 1951 budget to £4,700 million. Harold Wilson started to oppose the arms programme in Cabinet at the beginning of February 1951. Industry simply could not handle the new orders. The new Chancellor, Hugh Gaitskell, put all this down to Wilson's jealousy of himself and his fears for the political consequences of a failure of his export programme. But by mid-February Nye Bevan, who, according to Shinwell, really was jealous of Gaitskell, had joined him, and there were the makings of a revolt.

The crunch came in March when Gaitskell imposed a cash limit of £400 million on Hilary Marquand, the new Health Minister – Bevan by now was Minister of Labour – who could only keep to it by charging for dental treatment and spectacles, saving approximately £23 million. Bevan, the founder of the free National Health Service, said this was the first pebble in the avalanche that would destroy Labour's social services. Wilson joined his protests. Both threatened to resign if the charges were not withdrawn.

It was the serious consequences of losing Wilson, whom he liked and considered to be an outstanding Minister, rather than Bevan, that prompted

Shinwell to put personal effort into finding a compromise. A separate Health Services Bill would be needed to introduce the charges and this could not happen until after the budget debate which was about to begin, so there were a few days to try to engineer an agreement to avoid the resignations. Shinwell worked out a compromise with Wilson that the proposed charges should be announced as maximum charges and also that they should be specifically stated as temporary, perhaps with a limit of three years. After a good deal of playing with words, Shinwell and the Home Secretary, Chuter Ede, produced a form of words, 'These changes need not necessarily be permanent', which Wilson was prepared to accept; indeed, he had agreed to something similar a year before when Cripps had threatened similar charges. But Bevan described the compromise as a 'bromide'. He had already said publicly that he would not stay in a government that imposed health charges. He had been overlooked as Chancellor and, on Bevin's death, he had not even been considered as Foreign Secretary. The compromise collapsed and Wilson was forced into a decision. With barely a few minutes' hesitation he went with Bevan to see Attlee who was in hospital and they both tendered their resignations.

Shinwell admired Wilson's carefully worded resignation speech in which he went over familiar ground, especially the problems of large-scale procurement which were becoming a nightmare. It was a speech in marked contrast to an ill-judged diatribe by Bevan the day before. In Shinwell's view the government could easily afford to lose Bevan, but it was a tragedy to lose Wilson on account of the obduracy of both Bevan and Gaitskell. Bevan had refused all his face-saving phrases and Gaitskell was prepared to see the Cabinet torn apart by £23 million out of £4,700 million.[23] Shinwell started to wonder whether the government deserved to survive.

Shinwell and Wigg continued to consult with Wilson on the back benches. Sometimes they would just reminisce about their wartime collaboration and Wilson's time reorganising coal. Shinwell was convinced that Wilson was a man to watch. Apart from anything else, he was still only thirty-five years old.

Shinwell was always prepared to jump to Wilson's defence at this time. When Sir Hartley Shawcross, Wilson's lacklustre successor at the Board of Trade, described him as a 'highbrow educated beyond his capacity', Shinwell replied with a lecture about Wilson's qualities and Shawcross's shortcomings. When Dalton coined the insult 'Nye's little dog', Shinwell reminded Dalton (now back in the Cabinet as Minister of Town and Country Planning) that he was merely a second-rate minister in an unimportant job; Shinwell had learned to deal with Dalton's blows below the belt. In the years to come, Dalton would openly back Gaitskell and Shinwell would openly back Wilson. Of the three, only Shinwell would live to see the strange twists of fate in the decades to come.[24]

Wilson's and Bevan's resignations were followed by that of John Freeman, Parliamentary Secretary at the Ministry of Supply, and in June by George Wigg. Wigg remained on the closest terms of friendship with Shinwell but he felt that imposing charges for health services, so the money could be spent on arms – so much money so quickly that it probably could not even be spent at all – was electoral suicide. In Wigg's own words:

> I left him. I resigned from him. Didn't make a song and dance about it. I said, 'Look, no more. You're going to lose the bloody election, mate. I can't stand any more, this is absolute bloody nonsense. It's based upon a completely false analysis.

Wigg explained why Shinwell himself stayed on:

> He wasn't naïve. This is to underestimate Manny. Manny has got a hell of a good brain. He understood the situation perfectly well. Then the moments came – I suspect because of vanity – it obliterated his judgement. He kidded himself.[25]

Bevin switched from Foreign Secretary to Lord Privy Seal just before his death, and Shinwell canvassed for his replacement by Herbert Morrison. Ever since the 1930s, despite occasional political disagreements and the unfortunate Ampel affair, Shinwell and Morrison had been friends and Morrison was also a favourite with Fanny. One fact that neither Fanny nor Manny knew was that Morrison's wife Margaret, was slowly and painfully dying of stomach cancer throughout her husband's distracted tenure of the Foreign Office.

Morrison was soon confronted with Iran's intention to nationalise British oil interests there. The Americans insisted that the British reach a peaceful agreement to avoid giving Stalin an excuse to step in. Diplomacy failed and the Cabinet soon had to decide between offending the Americans by using force or humiliatingly evacuating Abadan and the oil fields. Morrison's advice from Foreign Office officials was that American oil companies were prepared to step in to 'advise' the Iranians if Britain withdrew and that there was no serious Soviet threat. In Cabinet he favoured force and Shinwell supported him enthusiastically, adding a plan for the temporary evacuation of British citizens. Nobody else in the Cabinet agreed.

Shinwell then came up with a half-serious proposal to bribe top Iranians with 'a million pounds in dollar notes'. The Cabinet eventually decided to refer the whole matter to the Security Council. 'They're all too United Nationsy,' declared Morrison. And they were. The Security Council deferred any decision, and all Shinwell could do was to ensure the navy was at hand to assist in what he called the 'scuttle' of Abadan (right in the middle of the general election campaign).[26]

It might have been possible, if the government had been less tired and more imaginative, to have negotiated at least a face-saving agreement with Iran, perhaps with an implied promise of aid or threat of force. Shinwell thought the show of weakness disastrous. He told his Chiefs of Staff: 'If Persia is allowed to get away with it, Egypt and other Middle Eastern countries will be encouraged to think they can try things on; the next thing may be an attempt to nationalise the Suez Canal!' In fact, while Shinwell was away at a pit disaster in Easington, the Cabinet heard that Egypt had unilaterally abrogated the Anglo-Egyptian treaty and Britain's hold on the Suez Canal Zone certainly did seem weaker than ever.

Shinwell's last international conference as a minister turned out to be the NATO Council of Finance, Foreign and Defence Ministers in Ottawa. Shinwell never enjoyed playing second fiddle, let alone third fiddle to both Gaitskell and Morrison. He played only a minor part in the main conference, although he was active behind the scenes in reaching a security agreement for the newly-founded Federal Republic of (West) Germany, once again earning a telegram from Attlee congratulating him on his diplomacy with the French who had finally agreed to German participation in West European defence.

Three days before they were due to sail back together on the *Queen Mary* from New York, Morrison and Shinwell received a telegram from Attlee telling them that he had decided to call a general election. They sent a joint telegram back asking him to delay his announcement until they could talk to him, but to no avail. Shinwell had not particularly expected to be consulted, but Morrison, deputy Prime Minister, was deeply offended and foresaw disaster.

Their last sea journey as ministers was lavish. Two of the *Queen Mary's* state rooms were converted into an office, and Morrison threw several parties. Knowing they had to face a party conference irritated with foreign affairs and the continuing high cost of defence, and then a tough general election, they felt no guilt at enjoying themselves at the government's expense. And they were both secretly pleased that Gaitskell had returned separately by plane.

At the conference, Shinwell lost his seat on the National Executive, which he found deeply depressing. There were big gains for the left: Nye Bevan, Barbara Castle, Tom Driberg and Ian Mikardo were all elected for the first time. Morrison, Dalton and Griffiths clung to their places, but Shinwell carried the extra burden of being the man who brought in the two-year national service. He left the conference as soon as he knew the result. Morrison stayed on and scored a success with his speech which gave Labour's campaign the catchphrase for the peace party against the war party, 'Whose finger on the trigger?'

In the election campaign, Shinwell started to wonder if his style of politics was simply outdated. The party didn't like him, would the country? He had been swept along by events from Bolshevism to one of the world's biggest military spenders opposed to Bolshevism. The hustings soon revived him. The bare-knuckle political fighter, appealing to basic emotions in long speeches, the Clydeside orator, was certainly out of date, but his audiences still loved it. When he spoke in Leeds, the old and the new clashed with a startling effect on one of Labour's local candidates, the Chancellor of the Exchequer, Hugh Gaitskell:

> The last meeting at Leeds Town Hall was a fiasco as far as I was concerned. I was to speak last and the idea had been that there would be some speakers between Shinwell, who was the other main speaker, and myself. However, when I arrived he was still speaking. He was doing a real Music Hall performance. Dora [Gaitskell] told me she almost vomited, but the audience simply loved it – or most of it. Somebody made a very short speech after him and then I got up to finish up the meeting. My voice, as I have said, was already very strained, and I found it completely impossible to get myself across to the audience. They were so drunk by the emotional nonsense that Shinwell had talked that it was impossible to make them think at all. Rather fortunately for me in a way the mike gave out, and this made it obviously essential that I should wind up the speech quickly. But it was a depressing affair.[27]

Shinwell's speech had been a seventy-five-minute harangue against every possible political bogeyman – landlords, factory owners, bankers, Churchill (except as war leader), appeasers – laced with personal recollections about coal-owners, Ramsay MacDonald, the Glasgow docks and David Lloyd George. No wonder poor Gaitskell was pleased when he was forced to stop.

Easington once again gave Shinwell an easy win:

Emanuel Shinwell (Labour)	37,899 (81%)
George W. Rossiter (Conservative)	9,025 (19%)
Majority	28,874

Labour polled more votes than the Conservatives in the general election, but a further sharp Liberal decline cost Labour enough seats for Churchill to be returned as Prime Minister with a Commons majority of seventeen.

CHAPTER 18

More in Hope than Expectation

Fanny had not been well while Manny was Minister of Defence. She had complained of aches and pains and started to run unexplained high temperatures which made her violently sick. She was admitted to hospital just before the 1951 election with 'neuritis', missing election day with Manny for the first time since the First World War.

Her recovery was painfully slow and in retrospect Manny realised it was never complete. She did seem to be back to her old self at the party conference of 1952 when she danced with Hugh Gaitskell and Herbert Morrison, gossiped with Vi Attlee and passed on the best bits of gossip to the Easington delegates always with a firm instruction, 'Whatever you do, don't tell Manny I told you!' It was her last party conference. The changes were soon noticeable. Her plain but animated face seemed to lose not just its colour but its vigour. Her personality had always made up for her small size when in a crowd; in middle age she had lost much of her shapeliness, and even Manny noticed at the time of the Coronation in 1953 that suddenly she was looking withered and old. When she thought no one was looking, her face became a kind of mask.

Lucy was the first to notice that her mother's arms were getting thin. This and the first signs of inflammation on the stomach pointed inexorably to cancer. She was sent for X-rays and to see specialists, all organised by Lucy. Manny seemed suddenly almost incapable of doing anything about his wife. When he visited her in Hampstead General Hospital where she was having yet more tests, they said little to each other, but held hands. They both knew. He took a taxi from Hampstead to Golders Green to have dinner at Lucy's. Fanny's GP had already telephoned. As he walked through the door, Lucy tried to start gently: 'Dr Whitelaw's been on the phone, Dadda ...' Manny looked away and cried.

For the last few agonising months of stomach cancer, Manny and Fanny lived with Lucy and Manny Stern. Thankful that he no longer had the responsibility of being a minister, Manny spent hours by Fanny's bedside. She enjoyed looking out into the garden and occasionally had better days

264

when she cursed her 'inflammation' and longed to be up and about again. As in many cancer cases, there was a slight remission just before the end, but it was short-lived. Manny was walking half a mile to the local bank when he felt – as maybe only those who have been intimate for more than half a century can feel – a terrible premonition. In any event, he ran back to the house and up the stairs two at a time. The doctor had given her a 'strong painkilling injection' and she was fading. She would never wake and talk again.

When she died, Manny turned her room into a shrine. They had been so close. From the earliest days, at the beginning of the century, Fanny had understood Manny's need for support and she had given generously. She had willingly put aside any possibility of a career for herself – she might easily have become a professional dancer – and gave her husband the warmth of a stable home and real friendship, especially when times were hard. She was hardly ever gloomy. Like everybody she could be depressed and she could be hot-tempered. If Manny was cross with her or sulky, her remedy was to take him straight to bed with her and take his mind off it. She claimed it never failed.

Now at seventy-two she had gone. Her husband felt old and lost.[1]

The Ministry of Defence has never been an easy post for a Labour politician. Whatever attention may be given to the lot of the ordinary soldier, the job is tainted with the perception, often quite erroneous, of close association with the most reactionary part of the establishment. More important, the minister is associated with the expenditure of vast amounts of public money that could otherwise have been used for health or pensions.

Already kicked off the National Executive, Shinwell had to fight hard to keep his place on what was now called the Parliamentary Committee and did so only by the skin of his teeth, with one hundred and seven votes, one from last, just below Dalton and the up-and-coming James Callaghan, and sixty four below Gaitskell. He was not in a strong enough position to argue for anything other than to speak regularly on defence. There were still no formal shadow portfolios.

He duly faced his first defence debate as opposition spokesman in December 1951. It was an uncontroversial affair. Both sides agreed on the inadequacies of European defence. The plan had been for sixty divisions in Western Europe by 1952, but twenty now seemed more likely. There were shortages of ships and aircraft, and Britain was hopelessly over-stretched. There were commitments in Korea, in the Near East and in Malaya where the British High Commissioner had just been assassinated by communist terrorists. Shinwell simply reviewed the way in which he had tried to do his best with the massive demand and limited resources. It was a dull and unremarkable speech, which elicited from Churchill the most unexpected and fulsome response:

> I should not like – if the House would permit me – the speech of the late Minister of Defence to go without its due and proper acknowledgement from this side of the House. We have our Party battles and bitterness, and the great balance of the nation is maintained to some extent by our quarrels, but I have always felt and have always testified, even in moments of Party strife, to the Right Honourable Gentleman's sterling patriotism and to the fact that his heart is in the right place where the life and strength of our country are concerned.
>
> We have our differences, and when we were in Opposition it was our duty to point out the things that we thought were not done right, and it is equally his duty, and of those who sit with him, to subject us to an equally searching examination. I am so glad to be able to say tonight, in these very few moments, that the spirit which has animated the Right Honourable Gentleman, in the main discharge of his great duties, was one which has, in peace as well as in war, added to the strength and security of our country.[2]

Shinwell sat open-mouthed. Churchill sat down with tears in his eyes. What astonished Shinwell more than anything else was the last sentence which implied that Churchill understood and admired Shinwell's conduct in the war. He knew perfectly well that Churchill would not have spoken in this way without preparing carefully in advance what he was going to say. Why this speech at this time?

The answer may simply have been a feeling of genuine admiration and warmth towards another man prepared to fight his lonely corner, much like Churchill himself. This explanation is indeed borne out by David Hunt, one of Churchill's private secretaries who drove back with him later that evening to Downing Street. The Prime Minister told him:

> I am glad I said that about Shinwell. He well deserved it. There's a lot of good in that Shinwell. He's a real patriot. During the war he and Bevan were more or less playing the part of the Opposition, but I always said there was a great difference between them. When things were going badly for us that Bevan used to look quite pleased but Shinwell looked miserable. Yes, there's a lot of good in Shinwell, and I'm glad I took the chance of saying something about him.[3]

Shinwell would undoubtedly have been pleased at these personal thoughts and equally pleased by the fury of some of the letters Churchill received. Letters of complaint poured into Downing Street from Conservatives all over the country, reminding Churchill about all of Shinwell's past iniquities. Shinwell himself sent Churchill a graceful thank-you note.

It would have been out of character if Churchill had not basically meant what he said, but one other factor almost certainly entered into his calculations. With a slim majority, the new government was looking for ways to co-operate with the Labour Opposition; they had learned from Labour's experience and were trying to avoid the pitfalls of continuous late-night sittings and acrimonious debates. Defence was one area where they could certainly be avoided. Indeed, Shinwell was soon eagerly supporting Churchill's proposal for co-operation with a European Defence Community, and then in March 1952 he supported the cuts proposed by Churchill in a speech of 'indescribable vulgarity' in which 'his only complaint was that Churchill hadn't given him enough bouquets'.[4]

His speech in the March debate was certainly one of Shinwell's weaker performances. The problem was that he could never bring himself to condemn communism in the way that Gaitskell or later even Wilson were able to do. The Bolsheviks had been part of his youthful struggle for socialism and now he was back in opposition he felt again that there must be some good in them. So he ended up trumpeting his own achievements at the Ministry of Defence and berating foreigners, especially the French, for not contributing enough support for NATO. He tended to sound like a 'little Englander with a predilection for defending the Empire against Johnny Foreigner'. He had nothing to say about the secret development of the British atom bomb recently exploded at Monte Bello (he had known about it as minister but had had no involvement in its development and looked foolish for knowing so little about it), and he had very little to say about the economic effects of the proposed expenditure on conventional weapons. He ended up proposing only a formal amendment to the government's defence estimates, supporting the defence programme and saying merely that the government were incapable of carrying it out because of their general incompetence. After this performance, fifty seven Labour MPs, Bevanite rebels, refused to support Shinwell's official amendment and drafted a more critical one of their own.

In his Easington constituency, they were also talking about defence. Shinwell's Bolshevik dream was fading but this was not the case for some of the rank-and-file members of his constituency party. Anti-Americanism, if not pro-Stalinism, was rife throughout the active party membership. Easington, like many other parties, was moving leftwards. His members were supporting a more neutral stance in the Cold War with a reduction in military commitments in Korea and Malaya, and a much more radical economic policy with nationalisation on a large scale.

Shinwell knew better than to react to this by means of direct confrontation. Instead, he ignored the difficult contentious subjects and spoke in his constituency on social issues, especially housing and employment, and he paid a good deal of attention to the development of Peterlee New

Town. He peddled the themes of new work, a healthy environment and an alternative to the squalor of the pit villages across the constituency and in two consecutive speeches to crowds of upwards of fifty thousand at Crimdon Dene, a local beauty spot, after the annual Coal Queen contest. No one argued about Peterlee. It was a good thing for left wing and right wing, men and women, young and old, even communists and Conservatives, and it had been started by the Labour government.

Shinwell rarely fought the left in his local party. He avoided difficult issues whenever he could and left the micro-politics to local officials, especially to his friend and agent Bob Taylor, a newsagent from the village of Shotton. With the people he trusted, like Taylor, Shinwell gossiped about political personalities rather than talked politics. He would reminisce about the fuel crisis of 1947 and how the hated Dalton had told him when the power cuts were agreed by the Cabinet: 'Now you bastard, you're on your own!' He insisted he had not been jealous of Gaitskell when he succeeded him at Fuel and Power, but he did say that Gaitskell was not to be trusted: 'I shouldn't be telling you this, but he's bought himself shares in a private steel company – the man's a political innocent – no idea about people.' And he used to talk about Wigg, always affectionately, even when he tried to persuade Shinwell to buy 'a bloody great racehorse I don't want – the man's a fool'.[5]

It may not have been Gaitskell's relative success at Fuel and Power; it may just have been Shinwell's reaction against another middle-class intellectual who had gained power through the Labour Party. Whatever it was, Shinwell took against Gaitskell. He never hated him like he hated Dalton, but his fight with Dalton was old hat. Dalton was getting old and was hardly a serious opponent now. When Shinwell talked loudly and excitedly about 'that man' from the table in the tea room where some North-East MPs gathered daily, Dalton could rarely think of anything insulting to boom back. The whole scene was rather pathetic.

Maybe Shinwell simply needed an arch-enemy: Havelock Wilson, Ernest Bevin, Hugh Dalton, Hugh Gaitskell. In any case, Shinwell and Gaitskell in opposition soon clashed. When it came to dealing with the fifty-seven opponents of Shinwell's defence policy, Gaitskell immediately pushed for the reimposition of Standing Orders. The PLP's Standing Orders had been relaxed during the war and had not been reimposed when Labour had a big majority. If they were reimposed, it would be possible to punish rebels by withdrawing the whip from them or expelling them. Shinwell delivered the Parliamentary Committee a long lecture on the importance of freedom within the party, followed by a peroration on his own contribution during the war as admired by Churchill. Gaitskell was furious and asked himself out loud whether this was really the man who had been humiliated in the defence debate. Shinwell retorted that only those who had served in Parliament in the war could understand the importance of parliamentary freedom. Then Shinwell stunned everyone by voting for the reimposition of Standing Orders. His entire speech had been merely a shot across Gaitskell's bows.[6]

At the 1952 party conference, the Bevanites swept the board in the constituency section of the National Executive. Harold Wilson and Richard Crossman joined Bevan himself, Barbara Castle, Tom Driberg, Ian Mikardo and the only non–Bevanite survivor, Jim Griffiths. Morrison and Dalton were defeated, but even they beat Gaitskell, Callaghan and Shinwell. Shinwell was supported by only ninety-two constituencies, Dalton by over two hundred and fifty and Morrison by nearly three hundred and fifty, whereas all the Bevanites were supported by four hundred and fifty or more. It was a bitter conference in a cramped hall at Morecambe with the leadership and the trade unions fighting the constituencies. Gaitskell decided 'the worm must turn' against the Bevanites. In a furious speech immediately after the end of the conference, at Stalybridge, he accused the Bevanites of being virtually communists and called for effective leadership by 'the solid sound sensible majority of the movement' – 'in other words,' said Shinwell, 'himself'.[7]

The fact was that Shinwell cared for neither of the two champions pushing themselves forward as leaders of left and right. His antagonism to Bevan was not as personal as his antagonism to Gaitskell, but it dated back further, to Bevan's initial support for Mosley and then for what Shinwell had seen as a quasi-fascist youth movement in South Wales in the 1930s. He had also disapproved, and possibly been rather jealous, of Bevan's conduct in the later stages of the war. Finally, he always felt that Bevan's resignation in 1951 had done a good deal to undermine the party's chances in the general election that followed – which cost him his job.

Shinwell now sought a potential leader who could unify the party, put him back at the Ministry of Defence and put Gaitskell and Bevan in their places. Attlee seemed to be failing and, at nearly seventy, was in poor health. A leadership election was expected soon. Shinwell's eye fell on his old friend who had long seen himself as Attlee's replacement, Herbert Morrison. If Attlee went soon, Morrison could even benefit from the right-wing crusade started by Gaitskell at Stalybridge. There Gaitskell had described his defeat in the National Executive elections as an act of 'ingratitude' and 'blind stupidity' and a 'heavy if not crippling blow' to the party.[8]

Shinwell went to see Morrison at his home in Eltham. He urged him to stand. To be effective, he would have to appear to be neutral between left and right. There was, it was true, a risk of being isolated in that position. But, especially if Attlee lasted another year or two, Gaitskell would be in such a strong position on the right that Morrison would never be able to oust him. He would end up as Home Secretary in a Gaitskell government. Gaitskell had gone too far in accusing the Bevanites of communist ideas. Morrison could now dissociate himself from the extremism on both sides and appear the statesman, and Shinwell would organise support in Parliament for his stand.

He would start with the Northern group of MPs, chipping away at Gaitskell's support. George Wigg would also help, starting with Wilson, Castle and the younger, softer left. Of course, the reality was much less straightforward, but by April, with Attlee ill, the *Daily Mirror*, heavily briefed by Wigg, if not the Parliamentary Labour Party, was acclaiming Morrison as Attlee's certain successor, a healer and a leader in one.[9]

Morrison stood in for Attlee and saw Shinwell through a difficult defence debate in March 1953, when he tried to push for a one-year rather than two-year period of national service, even though he himself had introduced a two-year period when he was minister. He argued that the recruitment to the regular army was now sufficient to make the reduction, but in reality it was simply that the Labour Party now felt it would be much more popular to cut the period. A compromise, supporting an annual review of the length of national service, was proposed by Morrison, accepted by Shinwell and by the Conservatives. In any case, the whole thing was forgotten very quickly as the debate took place on the same day that Stalin died. Everyone's attention was on Moscow rather than Westminster and so, with luck and Morrison's help, Shinwell avoided possible acute embarrassment.[10]

It fell to Morrison, having saved Shinwell, to embarrass himself. Bevan had made an unsuccessful intervention in a Commons debate on South East Asia with a sharply different line from Attlee. When he was reprimanded, he resigned from the front bench and his place was automatically taken by Harold Wilson who had achieved the highest vote among those not elected. Morrison then wrote an article in the right-wing *Socialist Commentary*, doing what Shinwell had begged him not to do, attacking Bevan in violent terms. It was a disaster.

Morrison had been seen as taking up the right's cudgels. He and Bevan were the old guard at each other's throats. Gone was the statesman. There would be a leadership election soon and very little time to recover the situation. Wilson was too young. Griffiths had faded. To Shinwell's horror, Gaitskell was seen increasingly as the hope of a new generation. This was the message he got from his fellow Labour MPs, especially the younger ones, and it was MPs alone in those days who elected the party leader.

'He's an honorary Jew. Yes. The Jews of the Janner type, their loyalty to this country is subordinate. Manny's is not.'[11]

Wigg assumed that Zionist MPs had an identity crisis which Shinwell avoided. It was a misconception on both counts. First of all, there was no identity crisis. There was no contradiction between patriotic Britishness and support for Israel. MPs like Barnett Janner who supported Jewish causes world-wide tried to point this out to Shinwell when he was at the War Office and Israel declared its independence. Shinwell did not take Wigg's view.

There is no evidence that Shinwell did anything to help the Jews being murdered in riots in British Aden but he had opposed Bevin's Palestine policy, and is known to have urged Britain to recognise Israel diplomatically in the early days of independence. Since he had walked out on Brodetsky in 1931, the British Jewish establishment 'never bothered me and I never bothered them,'[12] but the Israelis were different from the British Jews. 'They know a mug when they see one,' said Wigg. 'Many of them are socialists,' retorted Shinwell.

Several members of the new Israeli government had met Shinwell at Socialist International meetings and they showed more perspicacity than rich British Zionists. Shinwell was a powerful Jew in an increasingly Zionist Labour Party. He was well worth cultivating. Moshe Sharett, Israel's Foreign Minister, who knew Shinwell slightly, guessed that the way to use him was on specific issues within his power where he would operate behind the scenes and achieve results for which he could claim credit if he wished. Sharett felt that Shinwell would help Israel as a Jew but without realising that he was doing it as a Jew, justifying it in his own mind as support for the underdog and the fighter among nations.

Sharett was right. In 1950, Shinwell persuaded the Foreign Office junior minister Kenneth Younger of the importance of exchanging military attachés with Israel and worked in various ways to promote arms exports, intervening directly to speed up the delivery of eight torpedo boats in the teeth of the Admiralty who wanted them for the Royal Navy. Just as important, the links set up when Shinwell was Minister of Defence between MI5 and the new Israeli intelligence service, the Mossad, with its wealth of information from Egypt and the Arab world, were to last up to the Suez affair and beyond.

There is little doubt that Wigg's visit to Israel at Shinwell's instigation in 1950 played a part in this, and he and Shinwell had no difficulty in persuading Morrison as Foreign Secretary to take advantage of the opportunity. Of course, the strange people who work as spies or spymasters are professionally incapable of telling the whole truth to each other or the world. But out of the murk of 1950 and 1951, certain things are clear. It is undoubtedly significant that Wigg was sent to Israel in 1950 in reality to set up co-operation in the intelligence field. Wigg had probably been recruited by MI5 by this time – there is no doubt that he was working for them by the end of the decade – and the opportunities were obvious. Had any notice been taken at the time, Britain could have had good warning about the activities of the KGB among Egyptian officers, about nationalists in Jordan and about the splits among the rebels in Aden and Yemen.[13]

Shinwell's public interest in Israel started only in autumn 1953 when he had been out of office for two years. He was still regarded by Israel as potentially important and so worth inviting and entertaining. After all, at that time, there was some chance of him becoming a Cabinet Minister again in a new Labour government. He was duly given a VIP tour including, to his undisguised delight, being piped on board a frigate of the Israeli Navy and given a tour of Haifa harbour in one of the high-speed motor launches the delivery of which he had ensured.

Red carpets were laid everywhere he went. He was invited to make speeches to the powerful Labour organisation (Histadout) and to the new Kibbutzniks. He was taken out on launches on the Sea of Galilee and the Gulf of Eilat, to the annoyance of the British Commandant in nearby Aqaba in Jordan who feared a British ex-Minister of Defence on an Israeli launch would cause an explosive incident with Egypt.[14]

He was fêted by the Knesset and treated like royalty at the Hebrew University of Jerusalem. Then, just as the visit was coming to an end, sixty-six Jordanians in a border village were killed by Israeli soldiers and the British government sent a strong protest note to Israel. Israel replied – and by now Shinwell was prepared to accept the Israeli line on just about everything – that over four hundred Israelis had been killed by Arabs raiding from that particular part of Jordan over the previous three years.

In a furious speech to the Mapai (the Israeli Labour Party) in Tel Aviv, Shinwell declared that if a murderer killed your family it was only natural to take retaliation, which was what Israel had done. It was exactly what his hosts wanted to hear. His audience's applause was deafening when Shinwell attacked the British government for trying to interfere and assured his audience that 'strongly-worded Protest Notes are very customary' and Israel should not be prevented from pursuing its own interests.

'Monstrous', said the *Daily Express*; 'Irresponsible', said the *Daily Telegraph*; 'Folly', said *The Times*.[15] But Shinwell was at the far end of the Mediterranean, his vanity flattered to the core, 'basking in the sunshine of Israeli smiles'.[16]

Defence was tearing Labour apart by 1955, yet Shinwell, who was the party's main defence spokesman in Parliament, played only a minor part in the debate. Inclined to right-wing views on military matters, he was kept from wholehearted commitment to German rearmament and Britain's possession of the H-bomb by his distaste for the organised right and especially for Gaitskell. When he took up any position at all, it was a compromise; German rearmament with special safeguards or support for a British H-bomb with certain vague restrictions on its deployment.[17] In Parliament, his inability to say anything with conviction on these subjects led him to one unexpected and dramatic success. With the help of an incisive brief from George Wigg, it was to be Shinwell's last, and most surprising, Parliamentary triumph as a member of the Shadow Cabinet, lovingly recorded by Crossman:

> On Wednesday [1 December 1954], the serious Debate on the Address began. Manny Shinwell had been selected to open and to probe Sir Winston on defence. He spent forty-five minutes in his usual unbearable, shifting, vague, semi-bombastic, repetitious style but on this occasion it was perfect. If a really competent person had delivered a competent, incisive attack on Churchill, the effect would have been disastrous. Manny's blurred, vague, questioning promptings were about the most that the House would take. Moreover, on George Wigg's advice, his theme was a series of questions, suggesting that the telegram had never existed.[18]

Indeed, 'the telegram' did not exist, and if it had existed it would already have been ten years old. Shinwell had unwittingly, on the off-chance that Wigg's information was correct, struck Churchill a sharp blow and inflicted considerable embarrassment on his government.

The crisis had begun two weeks earlier. Churchill had told his constituents about an event in 1945 when the Germans were surrendering: 'I telegraphed to Lord Montgomery, directing him to be careful in collecting the Germans' arms, to stack them so they could easily be issued again to the German soldiers whom we should have to work with if the Soviet advance continued.'[19]

From *The Times* ('What on earth made him say it?') to *Pravda* ('Betrayal!'), they raged.[20] At a time when he was advocating closer contact with the Soviet Union, the speech was certainly a blunder. Churchill knew it as soon as he said it and thought about resigning after his eightieth birthday on 30 November. Worse was to come. One of his private secretaries, Anthony Montague Browne, had searched the records and found no trace of the telegram.[21]

Shinwell relished the attack. Either way he was on a winner. If there had been no telegram (as Wigg suggested), Churchill would be forced to retract. If there had been and Churchill stood by the story, bringing it up now was incredible folly for an enthusiastic advocate, as Churchill claimed to be, of a four-power summit which Labour also supported. When his speech at last got round to the telegram, Shinwell started with waffle and then sharpened the attack with questions he had prepared, using as his lead-in Churchill's earlier careless statement that the telegram was in Volume Six of his memoirs:

... but it is not there. I cannot find in his book any reference to the rearming of the surrendered Germans. Why this omission from these memoirs? Why at this late stage – more than nine years after – is that signal disclosed? What was the purpose of the disclosure – that remarkable revelation? What was the intention? Was the intention to seek an understanding with the Russians? Was this the overture or part of the symphony? The Right Honourable Gentleman, no doubt, will give us his version of the matter.[22]

Shinwell sat down abruptly and Churchill had to reply. He explained awkwardly that the telegram might not have been sent, although he had the 'rooted impression' that it had been sent and published in his memoirs. He justified the attitudes in it by saying how untrustworthy the Soviet Union had proved to be in Eastern Europe, and even recovered the embarrassing situation slightly by saying how he hoped the new leadership in Moscow would be more amenable to proposals for peace: 'I believe their interest is in peace and plenty.'[23] It got him through the debate, but the lasting impression was of an old man, uncertain and evasive. 'I made a goose of myself,' he told his doctor, Lord Moran.[24]

On 21 December, Anthony Eden, Churchill's Foreign Secretary and certain successor, did his utmost to persuade him to resign. On 2 February 1955, Attlee was so exhausted that he fainted into Churchill's arms at Buckingham Palace. They were both getting on.

Churchill was the first to go. On 5 April, Anthony Eden took over as Prime Minister and called an immediate general election. Labour, still led by Attlee, saw the Conservative majority increase to thirty and the Labour vote drop by one and a half million. Afterwards, Shinwell reckoned that the party's left–right rivalry, played out in public, had cost it at least a million votes.

In Easington, Shinwell retained a huge majority after an unusually vigorous campaign in the North-East, making a series of wide-ranging speeches advocating better planning, better health and better pensions, and accusing the Conservatives of squandering the nation's resources on the rich. He hammered home the theme he had hammered home a thousand times over half a century: 'All the fine words of the Tories will not blind us to the fact that Toryism stands for power and privilege, for the few against the many.'[25]

Any time up to his *Socialist Commentary* fiasco, Morrison would probably have succeeded Attlee after the general election. Instead, Attlee stayed on until he was sure that Gaitskell had enough support to be almost certain of winning. Bevan would also undoubtedly throw his hat into the ring but had no serious chance.

Attlee's endgame started as soon as the election was over. Dalton arranged for the leak of a letter he wrote to Attlee, saying that the other old guard had to go. Then, in the last meeting of the old Parliamentary Committee, he 'baited the old men' about standing again:

Can you honestly say, any one of you, can you honestly say that you are as fit and quick-witted today as you were when you were invited to join the Cabinet in those wonderful days of 1945? And can you honestly say that in five years' time you will be fit and able to do a better job than any of the younger members of the Party?[26]

Shinwell, now seventy, had no intention of standing again anyway. He had been bitterly disappointed by the results of the election which clearly meant the end of his career in government, so there was no point trying to stay on the Opposition front bench. Of course, he was furious that Dalton was threatening to make his personal decision look like the result of Dalton's persuasion. He replied to Dalton that he was in fact quite confident about his abilities and that, even if Dalton were senile, he was not and he intended to carry on for some years to come. Whether or not that would be as a member of the Parliamentary Committee, he would decide for himself.[27]

Along with Chuter Ede, William Glenvil Hall, Frank Soskice, Will Whiteley and Dalton himself, Shinwell stood down. Only Morrison stayed on. It was the world of Hugh Gaitskell, Harold Wilson, James Callaghan, Alf Robens and George Brown, all of whom now decided to take on specific portfolios, to be a real Shadow Cabinet for the first time. It was unfamiliar territory for Morrison who belonged to the age of Churchill and Bevin.

Attlee's resignation was constantly expected but stubbornly refused. Then, in no time, the 1955 conference had started. Crossman found Shinwell in sparkling form:

... dinner with Manny, George Wigg and Hugh Massingham [a journalist] – far the nicest two hours we had. Manny is completely rejuvenated, looks about fifty and was in such sparkling form that I could understand for the first time why people liked him. He also seems to accept Morrison's succeeding Attlee as a fait accompli. The evening was mainly just nice and good fun.[28]

Shinwell's good form came in good part from Dinah Meyer, his wartime secretary and soon to be his new wife; she was fun, she was rich and she loved political gossip. A few months before, they had quietly holidayed together in her native Denmark and he had proposed, rather romantically, sheltering her from a rain-storm on a small boat in a lake in the Tivoli Gardens.

His good form also came from a growing belief – not quite as complete as he had deliberately led Crossman to think – that Morrison could win. He was particularly pleased with Crossman's story that George Brown, admittedly drunk, had vowed undying support for Morrison a couple of nights before; Brown carried a lot of weight on the right side of the Parliamentary Party.[29]

There was no doubt that Attlee would have to go in the next few months if not weeks. He had barely recovered from a thrombosis and could no longer take the strain. Shinwell and Morrison worked together on a statesmanlike speech suitable for the Crown Prince giving the Parliamentary Report on Attlee's behalf. Then at the last minute, Attlee decided to make the report himself, depriving Morrison of his major platform and leaving him only bit-parts.

In a number of small speeches, Morrison took the opportunity to lay out a platform on the 'modern automated economy' and the 'new Party machine'. Shinwell's only conference contribution was also on the subject of the party machine. He welcomed a report by Harold Wilson on the amateurish organisation of the party, reminiscing about his own job in the early 1930s when 'Herbert Morrison was doing important work on nationalization, on planning and making everyone's life in London better and safer'.[30] He could hardly have been more blatant.

Finally, it was Gaitskell who stole the show at the conference. His speech on why he was a socialist was emotional, personal and highly effective. It compared very favourably with Morrison's performance a couple of weeks later in a debate on the emergency autumn budget of 1955. Attlee announced his retirement on 7 December when Gaitskell was thought to be unbeatable.

Gaitskell, Bevan and Morrison were the three candidates in the ballot of 14 December. Shinwell and Wigg both canvassed for Morrison and soon found he had very little support indeed. Shinwell and Dick Stokes, ex-minister and right-wing MP for Ipswich, played one last card for the Morrison campaign.

They arranged for Bevan and Morrison to dine together and got Bevan to agree to pull out if Gaitskell did so to let Morrison in for a few years of 'stability' with 'time to improve the Party's organisation'.[31] Shinwell denied he had thought up the scheme, but he certainly promoted it. He must have known Bevan would agree because it would have given him a realistic chance of trying again with more support a few years later, whereas if Gaitskell won at the age of forty-nine Bevan would have no more chances. But how did Shinwell ever think Gaitskell would agree? Either it was desperation or a belief, like Morrison's, that the party would really value loyalty and long service, an idea that Morrison deserve some kind of reward, such as a short spell at the top? Naturally, Gaitskell had no intention of withdrawing.

He won one hundred and fifty-seven votes to Bevan's seventy and Morrison's derisory forty. Shinwell, Wigg and Brown all voted for Morrison, and Shinwell himself persuaded Sir Hartley Shawcross and Arthur Bottomley to vote for him. But, all in all, the result was pitiful. Morrison immediately resigned the deputy leadership. The party had been passed on, as Attlee had intended, to the generation born in the twentieth century. Shinwell made a relatively painless transition, assisted by his new wife, to the rank of elder statesman.

It was in this elder statesman role that Shinwell nearly brought a bitter end to his political life. He was selected with the Marquess of Lansdowne to represent Parliament at the Australian centenary celebrations in summer 1956. Just before he was due to go, Nasser nationalised the Suez Canal, and Eden declared this takeover of a 'vital artery of world commerce' to be a threat to the interests of Britain. Gaitskell supported him, saying Nasser wanted to be 'Emperor of the Near East'. The resulting row in the Labour Party, as Eden appeared to be considering military action, was as deafening as it was surprising to Gaitskell who immediately started to back-track. Shinwell agreed with Gaitskell's original position and did not back-track. On the contrary, he was furious with those in the party who wanted to treat Nasser with kid gloves:

> ... a terrible row in the Labour Party, terrible row. I would say the people who caused more trouble in the House, who were more pugnacious than anyone else, were the pacifist section of the Party, and I remember the occasion – it was probably one of the worst scenes I ever saw in the House of Commons, the frenzy, the agitation, they were almost ready for fisticuffs, particularly the pacifists.

The Shadow Cabinet tried to allay fears by proposing a general resolution which criticised Egypt, Britain, France and Israel although nothing about Israel's possible involvement was yet known. It was just meant to be a sop to the Arabs and the Arabists. Alf Robens told Shinwell about it.

> He came and told me. I said, 'Look if they do that before I leave for Australia, I am going to go to the press to condemn the Party,' and he went back and told them and they withdrew the reference to Israel.[32]

Shinwell left for Australia before there were any more developments. He missed the changing mood of the party and missed Gaitskell's broadcast opposing military action; he missed the clumsy military preparations and Israel's hundred-hour 'Operation Sinai'. He took the view that the reported changes in attitude by Gaitskell were simply the temporary result of left-wing pressure and gave a series of speeches in Australia and New Zealand condemning Nasser and also condemning the British and Americans for pushing Nasser into drastic action in the first place by refusing further finance for his Aswan High Dam project. In one speech he went so far as to back explicitly Israel's involvement, saying that they had suffered too many 'attacks from the desert to stand by and miss the opportunity to help friends and to deal the fatal blow to murderers'.

The cable from Easington Labour Party caught up with him in Wellington, New Zealand: 'Return at once. Explanation wanted about the Suez affair.'[33]

He continued with his schedule and phoned Bob Taylor only when he got back to London. Yes, he should come up to Easington as soon as possible. Yes, Sam Watson and the NUM might make more trouble, but at the moment it was just the more militant members of the constituency party's executive, led by two of the women who were local councillors, Reny MacManners and Ivy Spry. The executive was due to meet two days' later, on a Friday evening at Easington Village Workingmen's Club. Shinwell said he would be there.

For Jack Dormand, then a member of the executive (and eventually his successor as MP), 'it was the only time I remember seeing Shinwell shaken'. He actually arrived about halfway through the meeting and, as ever, was invited to make a statement. He made his usual speech covering the whole range of policies, lasting nearly an hour and barely touching on the Suez affair, which was over by now, except in Easington. He was followed by Reny MacManners and then Ivy Spry both demanding his resignation in the most direct and unmistakable terms.

Shinwell responded weakly that his lecture tour of Australia was personal. Luckily for him, Bob Taylor had made some preparations, so a miner, Teddy Cain, moved a vote of confidence saying that the whole matter should be discussed but without the future of the MP hanging over them. After all, he was hardly likely to go on for more than one more election anyway, and this was just one lapse after more than two decades as MP for the area. His friends had done more preparatory work than his enemies and the vote of confidence was easily won. He was exhausted and very much relieved when Taylor dropped him back at the Grand Hotel, Hartlepool, where he always stayed.[34]

Shinwell was really quite a minor figure in politics in the remaining years under Gaitskell. He never disguised his personal dislike of his leader, but remained loyal to the party as it drifted to defeat in 1959. Easington again presented no problems. If anything, Shinwell found that his (and Eden's) line over Suez was a good deal more popular among the ordinary voters than that taken officially by the Labour Party.

Emanuel Shinwell (Labour)	36,552 (80%)
George Rossiter (Conservative)	9,259 (20%)
Majority	27,293

Defence emerged again as a harshly divisive issue in the party after the 1959 election and it gave Shinwell a chance to irritate Gaitskell by opposing him on the issue of whether or not Britain should remain in NATO and therefore rely on the possible use of US nuclear weapons. The party was already opposed to Britain having an independent deterrent and the abolition by the Macmillan government of the Blue Streak project in April 1960 made it practically impossible in the foreseeable future in any case. Now, the party conference passed a motion opposed to any kind of nuclear defence and therefore opposed to continued membership of NATO. Gaitskell vowed to 'fight, fight and fight again' to get the decision changed, and he physically isolated himself at the conference in a separate hotel from the more left-wing National Executive, keeping company with a select band of supporters including, at that time, George Brown, James Callaghan and Sam Watson.[35]

Bevan died in the summer of 1960 and Gaitskell's only powerful opponent was now Harold Wilson who felt that Gaitskell had sabotaged any attempt at compromise and party unity. He was outraged by Gaitskell's insistence on concentrating on divisive issues and claimed to Shinwell that if they got together for an hour (without Gaitskell) they could devise seven defence policies, any one of which would have united the conference.

Wilson, Shinwell, Crossman and Wigg came up in the event with a form of words which Gaitskell merely dismissed as a 'fudge'. This did not prevent Shinwell from using them in a successful conference speech, proposing 'a more viable but conventional contribution to NATO'. George Brown dismissed the idea as 'nuclear dependency without nuclear bombs'.[36]

Wilson decided to challenge Gaitskell for the leadership of the party as soon as Parliament reassembled. It was a contest between Wilson's compromise and Gaitskell's belief that the issue of nuclear weapons had to be clearly defined and decided if the party were to be electable. Shinwell and Wigg campaigned hard for Wilson, emphasising the need for party unity, and using one of Wilson's favourite expressions in their campaigning, describing the party as a 'broad church' needing tolerance and mutual understanding among its members. Wilson got just eighty-one votes to Gaitskell's one hundred and sixty-six. And Gaitskell got his nuclear defence policy at the next conference, in 1961.

When Gaitskell died suddenly in January 1963, aged only fifty-six, Shinwell was a firm supporter of Wilson's succession. George Brown he dismissed as a 'drunk' and Callaghan as 'all instinct and no policy'. Since he had first come across Harold Wilson as a temporary civil servant at one of the worst moments of the Second World War, Shinwell had admired him. He was delighted when Wilson won the leadership on the second ballot.

Shinwell saw in Wilson something of what he would have liked to have been himself. He always felt keenly his own lack of a university education and admired a man who had fought for it and done so well with it. He admired Wilson's powers of organisation and administration as an efficient President of the Board of Trade and his spectacular ability to pull off deals, whether with industrialists or with the Russians. He agreed completely with Wilson's clear vision of democratic socialism; many of the ideas in Wilson's *The Relevance of British Socialism*[37] were nearly identical to those in Shinwell's *The Britain I Want*, a Britain in which the planned application of science to well-organised modern industry would facilitate the provision of good social services and an end to poverty. No doubt he also had a fellow feeling for another man who had ploughed his own furrow in politics, cautious and introverted, hard to categorise on the left or right, living on the periphery of the party's groups and claques. Wilson was never quite committed, never quite reliable, a very private person with a simple and happy home life, understanding the needs and feelings of the vast majority of the population who lived as he did. Shinwell liked him very much.

At the age of eighty, Shinwell never worked harder than in the 1964 general election. He made sixty-two speeches from Brighton to Edinburgh and back to Easington for another comfortable win.

His young champion was Prime Minister at the age of forty-eight. Shinwell had backed the right man and earned for himself a new spell at the centre of political life when most men of his age had been retired for fifteen years.

CHAPTER 19

The Bad-tempered Antique

'Why on earth', asked John Hynd, Shinwell's left-wing opponent in the contest for the chairmanship of the Parliamentary Labour Party 'does Harold want that bad-tempered antique, Shinwell, to be chairman?'[1] In October 1964, the reason mattered little. Such was Harold Wilson's standing that, if he had chosen his candidate with a pin, they would have been guaranteed a majority, like Shinwell's, of over a hundred.

In fact Wilson did have his reasons for asking Shinwell to stand. He wanted to reward his personal loyalty and also put him in a position where he would not cause too much trouble. Furthermore, fearful of rebellion from left or right on a Commons majority of five, who better than an old Clydesider to speak for him in the Commons' Tea Room and bars? Wigg, consulted by Wilson while he was putting his government together, reminded him that Shinwell was itching to play some part in the new Labour administration although he knew he couldn't expect to be a minister. If he had nothing to do at all, he might well cause Wilson trouble – it came naturally to him after sixty-five years in politics. Give him a job and he still had the energy to help keep the government afloat on its tiny majority.

Preventing the government being defeated in the House of Commons was a job Shinwell shared with Ted Short, the Chief Whip, Herbert Bowden, the Leader of the House, and George Wigg, now Paymaster-General and special adviser to Wilson. Bowden and Short joined Shinwell and his two deputies (MPs Arthur Blenkinsop and Malcolm MacPherson) on a Liaison Committee between the government and back-bench Labour MPs.

Shinwell's job was to communicate what was possible and what was impossible to the committee and to Wilson. He soon confirmed, for instance, that it would be impossible to get the nationalisation of steel through in the teeth of opposition from the Labour right, especially Woodrow Wyatt and Desmond Donnelly. He told Wilson bluntly, and he decided that the government could not risk losing face by abandoning it altogether but could avoid confrontation by prolonging the budget debates. Jim Callaghan played along in Cabinet: 'As my Cabinet colleagues know, I am passionately in favour of the Steel Bill, but I must warn them that the Finance Bill will be a long one.'[2] Everyone knew what he meant.

Shinwell had to warn Wilson about trouble from the left as well. His experience of the Korean War had made him more sympathetic than many Labour MPs to Wilson's position on Vietnam when he first came into office. He even felt that Wilson could go further and safely send 'a platoon or two' from the fifty thousand British troops then in Malaysia as token support for the United States.

His tone changed abruptly a few months later when the Americans started to talk about 'no limit to the possible escalation' of the war; he remembered MacArthur and the nuclear threat. So when Wilson made a speech justifying American bombing of North Vietnam and accusing North Vietnam of aggression, Shinwell told him privately in his room at the House of Commons that he ought to be doing something about mediating and not just supporting everything President Johnson wanted. He said he knew there were major financial problems involved in breaking with the Americans and reminisced about the entanglements the Attlee government had got itself into over Korea. Wilson sharply reminded him that he himself had resigned on the issue in 1951 and had no intention of following Shinwell's suggestion of just a few months ago to send a token force to support the Americans any more than he had any intention of following Shinwell's suggestion now of breaking with the Americans. Shinwell sourly and simply replied that the situation had changed, left the room and found Sydney Silverman, whom he encouraged to prepare an anti-American Commons motion, 'with as many signatures as you can, and Harold can make of it what he likes'.[3]

That evening, Wigg invited Shinwell to dine with him in his flat. He had something to confide which, although it was a strict secret, Wilson had allowed him to pass on to Shinwell, as an old friend and ally. It was that Wilson was preparing a grand Commonwealth initiative on Vietnam, a peace plan involving a mission to the warring parties and an eventual conference. When he got home, as Wigg (and presumably Wilson) knew he would, Shinwell rang Silverman to tell him, in strict secrecy of course, that the Prime Minister was preparing a major peace initiative and perhaps he could quieten things down after all. A few days later both Silverman's and Shinwell's names appeared on a vague and innocuous parliamentary motion which 'supported government policy and had Harold's fingerprints all over it'.[4]

Unfortunately, before the Commonwealth mission could get started, the Americans had used napalm on Vietnamese villages and the communist Vietcong had infiltrated Saigon and were blowing up civilians. In any case, the Commonwealth had become completely preoccupied with Rhodesia.

Nevertheless, an unconnected, bizarre, peace mission did get off the ground, which Shinwell played a part in setting up. It was planned as a round-the-world trip by Harold Davies MP, Parliamentary Secretary at the Ministry of Pensions, ostensibly to study the problem of byssinosis in Hong Kong, but really to visit the North Vietnamese communist leader, Ho Chi Minh.

Davies, originally a Midlands school teacher, had been MP for Leek since 1945. When Shinwell was Minister of Defence, Davies had briefed him on communist China and, throughout the 1950s, he had visited communist East Asia, getting to know the leaders of North Korea, North Vietnam and China. He had also become a close friend of the Shinwells, often dining with them and enthralling them with stories of countries in those days very rarely visited by westerners. He had a high regard for Ho Chi Minh. He once spoke of him to Shinwell over dinner as Vietnam's 'dear old Uncle Ho', whereupon Shinwell brought him back to earth by reminding him that 'lovable old Stalin used to be known as dear old Uncle Joe'.

Davies was one of the few westerners still welcome in Hanoi, the North Vietnamese capital. Shinwell tentatively suggested to Wilson that, if the Commonwealth idea failed, he could use Davies to spearhead a new peace initiative. Wilson seized on the idea with enthusiasm. Within a week, Davies was on his way to Hong Kong, China and Vietnam. The Americans supported the idea because they desperately wanted to know more about what Ho Chi Minh was thinking. The Labour Party in Parliament would also certainly be delighted by the initiative when they could be told about it. Sadly, an early press leak about the visit destroyed any chance of it being a real success, but the Parliamentary Labour Party, as Shinwell had predicted, gave Wilson little trouble over Vietnam for the rest of that Parliament.[5]

When there was a threat of a lost vote – Labour's parliamentary majority soon went down to three – Shinwell used every trick in the chairman's manual to keep quiet any opposition from within the PLP. When he was faced with angry MPs complaining about expenditure cuts to defend Sterling, he changed a crucial draft agenda heading from 'Financial Policy' to 'Economic Policy'. Then he started the meeting exactly on time, having first of all made sure that the government's friends were already in their places and eager to put their names forward. And, under the new agenda heading, he encouraged supportive contributions on the National Plan and regional policy, both areas where the government was strong. A potentially stormy, even disastrous, meeting, where the government were expected to be attacked by their own men, was dull and worthy and the press in the Lobby could get little out of it.[6]

Just as serious was a threatened rebellion on Rhodesia. A group of younger MPs, led by Stan Orme and Eric Heffer, wanted a debate at a PLP meeting to push for military intervention to defeat the illegal white minority government of Ian Smith, whereas Wilson hoped for a successful oil embargo and other economic sanctions. Shinwell himself had some sympathy with the militant line but it was a time when the government majority was about to be reduced as the Conservative Speaker had collapsed and died a few days before. The newspapers were sure it was the end: 'Wilson on the edge of the precipice,' screamed the *Daily Mail*; 'New government crisis,' claimed *The Times*.[7]

So Shinwell used delaying tactics. He altered the date of the meeting to the day Wilson was due to leave for the United States, which brought a secretly prearranged request, backed by Ted Short, for a further postponement till he came back because there would be 'sensitive negotiations'. This further delay was skilfully made more palatable for back-benchers by Wilson himself who had arranged secretly – through Shinwell – to be met in Washington by a telegram from sixty-eight Labour MPs asking him to use his influence to stop the bombing of North Vietnam. Eventually the meeting had to be held but, by then, Wilson had announced oil sanctions against Rhodesia and most people felt they deserved a chance. Orme and Heffer looked isolated, and another well-managed meeting, hurrying through a long agenda of accumulated business, effectively silenced back-bench critics of the government's Rhodesia policy.

The only time Shinwell clashed seriously with a significant number of MPs was over his refusal to call weekly meetings. The Liaison Committee had taken the view that regular weekly meetings would just mean a complaints forum with weekly leaks to the press. As a taste of things to come, Richard Crossman, then Minister of Housing, objected. He reckoned that Shinwell, Bowden and Short were all out of touch with the modern Labour MP who, bursting with intellectual energy, needed a regular safety-valve. At the December 1964 meeting, when Shinwell fought off weekly meetings for the first of half a dozen times, Crossman seethed:

> I listen to Emanuel Shinwell in the chair being urged to concede a regular Party meeting, and treating this request in a completely insane way, which does no good for the relations between Parliament and the Cabinet. In Manny Shinwell we have a man of imagination, of enormous vigour, but somehow he has always impressed me as shiftless and unscrupulous. Certainly on Wednesday he convinced none of them – Peter Shore and David Ennals to take two examples – that we shouldn't have regular Party meetings every week. Indeed, there is everything to commend it. If we had a regular meeting every Wednesday people would know it and come along at the regular time. And contact between government and the Party would be maintained. But Manny wouldn't allow it, for fear – as he put it – that the questions raised would be used for trouble-making. I regard

this as one of the weakest aspects of our Government today and I predict it will prove disastrous.[8]

Shinwell's general success, despite Crossman's criticism, arose from meticulous preparation. He consulted widely before speaking to Wilson who, at this early stage in his premiership, was remarkably open and approachable. For any eighty-year-old, Shinwell displayed considerable energy in finding out people's views, planning and organising meetings, and representing to Wilson the views of over two hundred individualists who filled Labour's back benches.

Shinwell was inclined to exaggerate the closeness of the relationship; he fell for Wilson's skill in persuading people he happened to be with that they were the ones he really listened to, the ones who really mattered. Shinwell would say that he was advising Wilson, for example on the appointment of ministers, but there is no evidence that Wilson ever took any notice. On one occasion Shinwell got it completely wrong, telephoning Roy Jenkins to say he was to be made Foreign Secretary in succession to Patrick Gordon Walker, building up his hopes until he was quite disappointed to be made Education Secretary.[9]

Shinwell was listened to on parliamentary detail by Wilson, who afterwards wrote that the very survival of the 1964–66 government was owed in part to this close and very accurate liaison. One small reward he gave Shinwell was to make him a Companion of Honour, of which – rather to Wilson's surprise because he was uncertain he would accept any such honour – he was inordinately proud.

Shinwell was accused of being a 'disciplinarian' by the 1964–66 Parliament, but it was an accusation that meant very little. What discipline could be imposed on an MP on whose vote the government's very existence depended? Once or twice, Shinwell did suggest the possibility of withdrawing the whip from certain members but he was always rebuffed by Ted Short. All he could do was cajole, encourage, tick off and occasionally harangue. He often seemed to be in a shocking temper. On more than one occasion he could be seen, jaw jutting into the face of some young middle-class MP with a troubled conscience, lecturing him about the need for solidarity to keep the Conservatives out. But such formal 'discipline' as there could have been was the responsibility of the whips. Shinwell's only weapon was the chairmanship itself.

He could be an extremely belligerent old man. He had to be restrained on one occasion after punching Peter Doig, the anti-abolitionist Labour MP, for remarks about hanging during the debate which resulted in the end of the death penalty for murder. And on another occasion he nearly came to blows with Humphrey Berkeley, Conservative MP for Lancaster, over some personal remarks about Shinwell's youngest son, now in prison.

There was to be a worse clash with Berkeley's Labour successor, Stanley Henig.

Manny's favourite children were the two rebels. Lucy and Sam were very worthy and conventional. Not so Rose whose stormy relationship with her mother and father as she went through a succession of boyfriends and marriages never diminished the intense love Manny felt for her. And not so Ernie in whose life of adventure in business, Manny saw a reflection of his life in politics. He was fond of all of his children; Manny and Fanny neglected none of them, but outsiders had no doubt that Ernie was the favourite of all. He remained so until his father's dying day.

Ernie had a good war, rising to the rank of Colonel in the Black Watch. So he was less than pleased when his father-in-law, having persuaded him to leave the army, invited him into his family business in 1946 only to treat him like an office boy. This was not the life he had expected.

Manny had just become War Minister at the time and mentioned Ernie's problem to George Wigg who in turn sought the help of Sidney Stanley whose real name was Solomon Wulkan. Stanley − or Wulkan − was gaining a reputation for underhand dealings to avoid post-war Board of Trade controls. Wigg only knew about his reputation as a 'fixer' and reckoned he could get Ernie a good job if anybody could.

It was typical of Stanley's working methods that he rang Ernie at 3 a.m. with an offer of a job in marketing, starting the next day for Swears and Wells who owned Selfridges. It was equally typical that when Ernie got to his new employer's office, the Fraud Squad were camped in the corridor, investigating their links with Stanley and a junior Board of Trade Minister, John Belcher.

Manny soon advised Ernie to get as far away as possible. He knew that he had always been interested in farming and suggested that now might be a good time to start. Ernie bought a farm in Sussex and set about improving it by converting two cottages into one. Unfortunately, the builder, Piper, kept coming back to Ernie for more money beyond the original estimate. Ernie desperately wanted the work finished because his wife Peggy was just about to have a baby; but eventually he found he had no money left, and told Piper to stop work. He himself went to the Building Licence office − in the late 1940s all building work was licensed − to say he was taking over from Piper. He found to his horror that the licence was for just £800 of work, whereas £3,000 had already been spent. A few days later Ernie was summoned and, for the first time, the press started to take an interest in him, sniffing a good story about the minister's son.

Manny quietly approached Hartley Shawcross, the Attorney General, to see if any retrospective action could be taken. Shawcross, no special friend of Manny's, said no. Ernie would have to face the music; he was sure that Manny would not be dragged into it at all.

In court, Shawcross was proved wrong. Quintin Hogg, Counsel for Piper, attacked Ernie unmercifully on political grounds: 'You thought it was because of your father's position that you didn't need a Building Licence?'

'No.'

'You thought – or you were led to think by your father – that you could walk into the Building Licence office and murmur the name of Shinwell and the licence would be conjured up for you?'

'No, but perhaps if I could have murmured a name like Hogg or Hailsham ...'

At this point, the magistrate intervened.

The builder was fined £1,000 and Ernie was fined to pay £2,000 with the alternative of three months in gaol. He announced to the assembled press, who were starting to enjoy it, that he would prefer gaol. After three months he would come out and write his story. But his father-in-law, who bailed him out, thought otherwise. It was a first in a series of scandals which touched on Manny, not by implicating him directly, but because the press was interested in the irony of a leading socialist having a son involved in business scandals with shady characters.

Ernie just wanted to move on. He was all for buying a boat and setting off around the world with his wife and child. But an advertisement on the front page of *Country Life* drew him to a farm in Ayrshire which he was soon agreeing to buy for £57,000 with the promise of a mortgage of £17,000 from the Temperance Building Society, personally approved by Sir Cyril Black, Conservative MP for Wimbledon and chairman of the society. With the proceeds of the farm in Sussex, he had just enough money to complete the purchase but needed an extra £3,000 from Manny as working capital. Manny's money funded a successful new enterprise, delivering day-old chicks to farmers' wives who reared them to ten weeks when they were collected and delivered to Macfisheries to be slaughtered.

Manny and Fanny visited Ernie on this farm. He had really settled now. He would be happy and this £3,000, which Manny had borrowed from a solicitor friend, had set him up for good.

Unfortunately, by this time Ernie had fallen out with his father-in-law and was asking for more time to pay the £2,000 fine. Manny still didn't want him to go to prison but couldn't himself afford another £2,000. The press sensed new stories. So did Sir Cyril Black MP who cancelled the mortgage offer.

With bankruptcy staring him in the face, Ernie sought a quick sale, but the only offer came from a confidence trickster who hid in a hayrick to avoid the police. Without the sale, he was duly made bankrupt, losing all his own money and Manny's too.

Back in London, Ernie at last had some success with a public relations company and started to repay his father. And there were also other ways he compensated. Through Ernie's friend, Jack Solomons, 'King Sol' the boxing promoter, Manny was able to revive an old interest. He was soon a regular at Solomons' professional bouts at the Grosvenor House, featuring all the great names of the 1950s, Brian London, Hogan Bassey, Brian Curvis and, later, Henry Cooper. Father and son were ringside in July 1951 when Solomons got Sugar Ray Robinson – who had arrived with his extraordinary entourage, including a chauffeur, a hairdresser and a dwarf – jabbed and beaten by the little-known British champion, who remained a personal friend of Manny's for years afterwards, Randolph Turpin.

In small ways, Shinwell helped out boxers young and old. He warned Don Cockell about Rocky Marciano's rough tactics and, when he came back battered from San Francisco, he persuaded him to give up and retire. He helped an impoverished heavyweight hero from his Glasgow days, Bombardier Billy Wells, to get the pension payments to which he was entitled, although sadly not before he had had to sell his Lonsdale Belt.

Through another friend of Ernie's, Philip Magonet, a famous hypnotherapist, Manny was introduced to the Variety Club. There he dined with Danny Kaye and Joe Loss and he invited Frank Sinatra to be his guest at the House of Commons. It takes a lot at the House of Commons for people to whisper behind their menu cards and crane their necks to see the rich and famous, but Frank Sinatra in the 1950s was celebrity enough. It was a new world for Manny and, thanks to Ernie, he revelled in it for the rest of his life. Sanctimonious friends and relations objected to this alliance between father and son but it was harmless and it was fun.

Ernie rarely used his father's name or contacts. Rather it was the other way around in the boxing and entertainment worlds. Only when he first started to combine his agricultural and PR interests in Africa did he ask Manny for an introduction to the Governor-General of Ghana, who in turn introduced him to key people responsible for awarding contracts in Nkrumah's government. Ernie was soon out of his depth. He got a big contract for Thompson's for refuse-burning, but they refused to pay the slush money. Instead, they went to complain about it to Manny who stonewalled. After all, Ernie was forty years old and capable of looking after his own affairs – but it was a reminder of how outsiders would always play on his political connection if things looked like going wrong.

Only once after the £3,000 loan did Ernie ask for direct help, other than just a name or an idea, from his father. It happened when he got into real trouble over a deal in 1963. By now, well established in Africa as a promoter of agricultural development projects, Ernie had been offered some securities by an arms dealer called David Jacobs (who eventually made his fortune by selling arms to both sides in the Biafran war). Jacobs offered him securities which in the end he apparently no longer required for a project in Nigeria. Ernie knew there was something odd about them when they suddenly changed from being Woolworth shares to Quaker Oats shares just before they were delivered. But there was another project to do with the development of jet engines in which Ernie had wanted to get involved and these securities gave him just that opportunity. So he asked no questions, took them and used them. They turned out to be forgeries and suddenly, once again, he faced gaol.

It so happened that, while he was working on the jet engine deal, Ernie heard about Scottish Aviation's contract with NATO. Scottish Aviation was one of those companies that got NATO contracts. They always knew exactly what to put in the tender because they were always tipped off. A ring of NATO officials and corrupt co-directors were taking a rake-off. Among them, Ernie found out, was one of the directors of Scottish Aviation, the deputy leader of the Labour Party, George Brown. Ernie had a document in an American NATO officer's handwriting to prove it.

He took the proof to Manny who said that Wigg must be told. Ernie recalled:

> I told him [Wigg] about all of this and said, 'I have a problem,' and told him about the shares business in which I had become involved. He said he would look into it. Nothing happened for another week and he called me up and asked me to come to his flat in George Square, it was a Saturday morning. He was in this dirty dressing gown and white pyjamas that had turned grey, and he looked disreputable. He said, 'Did you bring the papers to do with this NATO business?' I said, 'Maybe.' I said, 'Have you been in touch with the police about me?' He said, 'Yes, we have and you told a load of lies.' I said I had told the exact story ...
>
> I said. 'I am not going to give the papers to you; you said you would help me.' He started to swear in his customary manner and I said, 'Thank you very much,' and I went to the door to let myself out. He was spluttering and dribbling and shouting out, 'Dorothy! Dorothy!' and out came this woman [his secretary and lover] whom I had never met before in her nightdress from the bedroom. 'I want you to hear this,' he said; 'He refuses to give me these papers.' I shrugged my shoulders and went out.
>
> On Tuesday, I was at my mother-in-law's watching the Test Match and they had to go out, and I said I would come out. I walked downstairs straight into the arms of a policewoman and a Detective Sergeant Sewell who became Chief Superintendent and was up on corruption charges.

There can be little doubt that Wigg, in his fury at not being given the ammunition against George Brown whom he hated, wanted to cause Ernie as much trouble as he could. He devised a statement which Ernie called 'a travesty' and, on 9 February 1965, Ernie was sentenced for deception and issuing forged securities.[10] He had needed a deal from Wigg, but Wigg felt he had been spurned. He was furious at not being shown the papers Manny had seen and told him about, but Ernie had no illusions: 'I knew that Wigg would have thrown me to the wolves, once I had given him the evidence against Brown. He was only interested in getting hold of documents I had seen and, at that stage, had access to.'[11]

No deal was struck. So, while Manny was preparing to chair an awkward and rebellious PLP divided on Rhodesia and Vietnam, his favourite son, whom he believed to be foolish but quite innocent, was convicted and taken to Ford Prison. The mirror-image of his own early career was intriguing; but at the moment he just felt miserable. The next evening he nearly bit the head off left-winger William Warbey. Even Barbara Castle said Warbey sounded like 'Ho Chi Minh's PRO'. Manny was less complementary.[12]

Labour's landslide victory in 1966 brought into the House of Commons, more than ever before, young brash intellectuals from middle-class backgrounds. Easington, however, returned Shinwell comfortably again:

Emanuel Shinwell (Labour)	32,097 (81%)
Michael Spicer (Conservative)	7,350 (19%)
Majority	24,747

Re-elected, with Wilson's blessing, to the chairmanship of the PLP, it was not long before Shinwell started to feel uneasy. The new Chief Whip, John Silkin, remembered the atmosphere:

> Liberalisation! Looking back on it, it was something that was coming anyway. Manny didn't understand it. And therefore he fought it. The structure of Parliament had altered and you'd got a much more intellectual, university-oriented group of members. I think the old ones took it from the old basis that you argued like hell, you then settled it by a vote, then everybody went in together. It was a kind of defence mechanism from 1931 to 1945, when our numbers in the House were so small we couldn't really afford splits. Liberalising meant saying: 'Does it really matter, had the end of the world come, if MPs, on matters which they believed to be of fundamental importance – not just questions of religion, temperance, pacifism – want to go their own way?'[13]

The new intake of MPs was certainly different, and the whole atmosphere of the 1960s was difficult for a man of over eighty to understand. The problems for Shinwell worsened during 1966 when Richard Crossman, a convinced liberaliser and close ally of Wilson, was appointed Leader of the House in place of Shinwell's old friend, Herbert Bowden.

Nevertheless, peace broke out. Shinwell, Silkin and Crossman actually signed an agreement, which Crossman called a 'concordat' at the 1966 party conference, agreeing on mutual consultation. The PLP could discipline MPs but only at the Chief Whip's instigation; the PLP would have the right to decide the penalty – maybe nothing, maybe a warning, maybe withdrawal of the whip.[14]

By October, Shinwell showed the first signs that he was losing his touch. The government was pushing through a Prices and Incomes Bill unpopular, on account of the implied wages policy, with much of the PLP. Crossman himself had to wind up the debate and had a bad day. The speech was poor, the circumstances unfavourable and twenty-eight Labour MPs abstained. Labour still won comfortably, but the disciplinarians, like Wigg, saw it as the thin end of the wedge. He told Crossman in the lobby: 'Well, you got through that all right but now we shall have to take action. Unless you enforce discipline I can't guarantee the consequences.'[15]

Crossman stuck to the principle of liberalisation. The next day at the Liaison Committee, now attended by Crossman and Silkin instead of Bowden and Short, Shinwell angrily demanded the withdrawal of the whip from all twenty-eight abstainers or at least from the ringleaders and he was supported by his two deputies, Willie Hamilton and Malcolm MacPherson. Silkin quietly smiled that this was not the PLP's decision. He as a liberal Chief Whip was not going to instigate any discipline, so the PLP was powerless under the terms of their 'concordat'. Shinwell could only fume.

By November, the EEC had become a major issue in the Labour Party for the first time since Wilson had come to power. Wilson and George Brown, now Foreign Secretary, had all but decided to apply for entry and MPs were making up their minds. Shinwell came down firmly against entry; he had a different view, based on NATO and the Commonwealth, of Britain's role in the world; also, from a nationalistic point of view, he feared eventual moves towards political integration. He thought that Wilson was being cajoled into Europe by the Americans, whereas Wilson himself now argued that he could obtain conditions which would protect the Commonwealth and encourage economies of scale for technological development. Passions were not yet anything like as high as they were to become a few years later – when de Gaulle was not around to veto Britain's entry – but the EEC still put Shinwell, for the first time, in opposition to a strategic part of government policy, an uncomfortable position for the chairman of the PLP.

In January, a technical row over the rights of Members of the House of Lords to speak at PLP meetings ended with Shinwell having to make a grudging apology. A feeble attempt at the same meeting to make an anti-

EEC point by encouraging Stan Orme to complain about a pro-EEC meeting set up by George Brown at the Albert Hall ended with an awkward row with Brown and a chaotic meeting. Crossman, sitting on the platform with Shinwell, told him to call next business. Shinwell almost screamed at him: 'Don't you dare talk to me like that. No one's going to tell me what I am doing. I have had enough of you, Crossman.'[16]

Shinwell physically hustled Crossman off the platform and snarled at him as he stormed out of the meeting to complain to Wilson. Stanley Henig, the new twenty-seven-year-old MP for Lancaster, a fervent pro-European and an Oxford-educated lecturer in politics, shouted at Shinwell at the top of his voice: 'Resign!'

Straight after the meeting, Shinwell sought out Henig in the Tea Room, grabbed him by the lapels and shouted in his face: 'What were you saying in there talking about "resign"? Say it again!' Henig refused saying, 'I'm a coward!' Shinwell would certainly have hit him if he had not been physically restrained. Henig left the room without finishing his tea.[17]

Meanwhile, Crossman had reached Wilson's room and was in the process of finding out that the Prime Minister was starting to change his mind on liberalisation. Silkin had warned Crossman not to expect too much:

> Wilson has enormous respect for Manny. I don't know that Manny well understands that, but it's true he does, and I think he is also rather afraid of Manny if the truth be known. Manny is a very formidable chap. Suppose the whole thing disintegrates [as a result of liberalisation]? And there is Manny telling him it will.[18]

Wilson told Crossman he would contact Wigg, who was visiting Stoke-on-Trent, and tell him to calm Shinwell down. Shinwell himself went to see Wilson the next day. After waving under his nose a letter from Attlee saying 'Wilson is not a good judge of men – I would not give office to that clever fool Dick Crossman', he promised to try to quieten down for a few months at least. He agreed to say nothing more about discipline or the EEC though he could give no guarantee on personal violence in the Tea Room.

There was talk in the newspapers about the possibility of heart transplants. Wilson commented to Wigg that if Shinwell were to have a new heart 'it had better be an older one to slow him down a bit'.[19]

It looked like the end of liberalisation after the defence debate on 28 February, when there were sixty Labour abstentions; the rebels were disappointed with the slow rate of cuts. Wilson reacted with a denunciation of the liberal approach. Addressing the PLP, while Shinwell sat self-satisfied in the chair, Wilson spoke the hard truth that the MPs who abstained on various issues were in reality in Parliament not as individuals but because they represented Labour. They should not deviate from the official Labour line. Like dogs, he declared they would be allowed one 'bite' only, otherwise they would lose their 'licence'. It was a speech which hit home hard.

Two days later, Shinwell openly claimed final victory over the 'Crossman–Silkin regime' on the BBC radio programme 'The Week in Westminster'.[20] He invited Wigg to lunch and they prepared a document together over coffee to replace the earlier 'concordat'. The exclusive power of the Chief Whip to instigate discipline would go; the 'conscience' let-out would remain, but would have to be accompanied by an explanation to the Liaison Committee which could, by majority, instigate discipline by the PLP.

Silkin accepted it by telephone, but changed his mind later when he heard that Crossman was preparing to resign on the issue. He then decided to back Crossman and withdraw his support for the Shinwell–Wigg document. If Wilson's speech meant the end of liberalising reforms, he would have to face the fact that neither Crossman nor Silkin was interested in serving. Suddenly the heat was on the Prime Minister. Could he afford to lose his Chief Whip and his Leader of the House at the same time?

Wilson reluctantly allowed Crossman to make a speech 'making it perfectly clear that John [Silkin] and I are really on the side of the back-benchers and that the implicit threat of the dog-licence speech wasn't going to be carried out because Harold hasn't carried [us] with him.'[21] Shinwell released a statement to the press saying that he was 'neither slighted nor impressed by Mr Crossman's speech. I have been accustomed to his speeches for many years.'[22]

The final act was played out when Wilson summoned Shinwell, Crossman, Silkin and Wigg to his room. Despite being exhausted with arguments over the economy, defence, Vietnam and Rhodesia, he had found time to prepare a document for all four of them to sign. There was to be nothing more said in public, and Shinwell was specifically forbidden to use the press as he had after Crossman's speech. In the document, the power to decide on discipline was effectively left with John Silkin. Shinwell and Wigg knew they had been defeated. Wilson had decided that he needed Crossman and Silkin more than them.

Wigg rounded on Wilson: 'I stand by Manny on this.'

'So you would rather be PPS to Manny Shinwell than a member of the Wilson government?'

'That may be meant as a jibe, but I accept it as a compliment and the answer is "yes".'[23]

At the PLP meeting on 15 March, Shinwell announced his resignation, and Wilson made a pleasant speech thanking him for his services. It was a half-hearted speech on a low-key occasion. There was very little emotion. There was a feeling that, at the age of eighty-two, the old man had simply got out of touch. Despite his occasional outbursts of fisticuffs or bonhomie, he was no longer taken seriously by the party and, unlike Crossman and Silkin, no faction supported him. It was Cassandra in the *Daily Mirror* who gave him the best send-off:

When he first entered politics sixty-three years ago, Harold Wilson was minus twelve and Richard Crossman was minus three. Not one of the present Cabinet Ministers, with the sole exception of the Lord High Chancellor, was born, and the vast majority were neither planned nor on the natal drawing-board. When Mr Shinwell first became MP for Linlithgow in 1922, Mr Healey was five and Mr Crossman was four.

In the days of the Labour battles of the general strike and the foibles of Ramsay MacDonald and the flowing furious eloquence of Maxton and the iron poverty of the Twenties, the more seasoned of the present government were shaking their rattles or bowling their hoops.

Age of itself is not a virtue, but the experience gained and learned from it by a man still as bright as a glint of sunshine is.[24]

CHAPTER 20

A Century and Beyond

Age was extremely kind to Manny Shinwell. Men and women twenty years younger looked and felt older than he did. He started to walk with a stick only in his late nineties. He could cook himself porridge, toast and eggs until he was over a hundred and one. And he went on making political speeches well into his hundred and second year.

When he resigned from the chair of the PLP in 1967, aged eighty-two, he was still leading an active public life with a diary full of engagements and a range of political interests. But he was getting disillusioned about what a Labour government could really do. In this Shinwell was not alone; Benn, Castle, Crossman and Wigg and thousands of ordinary Labour Party members felt the same way, as the government seemed to drift without clear direction or principles.[1] Nevertheless, except on the EEC, Shinwell was unfailingly loyal to Wilson.

The first acid test of his loyalty came in the publication of an article in the *Daily Express* on 21 February 1967 by Chapman Pincher suggesting that a Big Brother Labour government was vetting international telegrams. Apart from being untrue, the *Daily Mail*, which had actually had the story first,[2] had been advised that to publish it would have been a breach of a D-notice, a voluntary censorship system by which the Ministry of Defence could issue a D-notice to indicate that it would like a subject suppressed and not discussed. Unfortunately, the man responsible for telling Pincher that his story should be suppressed was a buffoon called Sammy Lohan who had only given Pincher informal advice over lunch. Wilson had not known Lohan's methods when he told the House of Commons that the *Daily Express* had in fact breached the D-notice system. The press accused him of trying to gag and censor them and, to quieten the protests, Wilson agreed with opposition leader Edward Heath's proposal to appoint a committee of Privy Counsellors to look into the D-notice system and into the details of this particular case.

Selwyn Lloyd was appointed for the Conservatives, Shinwell for Labour and Lord Radcliffe, who had chaired a previous committee on security matters, was made chairman. Evidently Radcliffe had never encountered anyone like Shinwell at this level. The most senior officials and editors were cross-examined as if they were in the dock. Lohan's methods were exposed to the full, as was the fact, of which Shinwell tipped off Wilson, that he was never positively vetted despite having access to virtually all Britain's security secrets. At one point in his cross-examination Radcliffe asked Shinwell to stop stubbing his pipe at the witnesses as if they were criminals. Shinwell retorted that he would stub if he wanted to and he didn't agree with the gentlemanly approach. When Selwyn Lloyd joined in on Radcliffe's side, Shinwell asked him if he would take the same approach if he was interviewing striking dustmen or people who hadn't been trained at Sandhurst or schooled at Eton.

On Thursday evening, 23 May, Shinwell went to the annual conference of the Electrical Trades Union to celebrate the anniversary of electricity nationalisation. The next morning Wilson was due to speak. His topic was to be prices and incomes policy. Shinwell was doubtful whether to attend; he thought Wilson was paying far too much attention to wage restrictions. In the end he did go so that he could spend a pre-arranged couple of minutes with the Prime Minister in a side room to warn him about the extent of Lohan's unreliability and sloppy methods. He warned Wilson that this meant that, despite all his bluster and pipe-stubbing, he was going to have to come down against the Prime Minister and say that Pincher was not truthfully served with a D-notice, unlike the *Daily Mail*. Wilson listened carefully but made no comment at all, then he invited Shinwell to stay for his speech which would 'contain an important statement on foreign affairs'.[3]

Shinwell stayed and heard Wilson declare the Straits of Tiran to be an international waterway for all shipping, including Israeli shipping. Nasser's Egyptian government had closed the Straits and restricted access to the Israeli port of Eilat, and he had sent UN peacekeeping troops home from the Israeli–Egyptian border.

The Six-day War broke out on 5 June. Jews all round the world rallied to the Israeli cause. In Britain, mass meetings, demonstrations and fund-raising on a gigantic scale took place wherever there were Jews. On the second morning of the war, when Israeli victory was still far from certain, Shinwell's nephew Roy phoned him from Manchester asking him to address a rally the next evening. Shinwell turned him down – he had a meeting of the Radcliffe committee – then the philanthropist Sidney Hamburger came on the line and persuaded him that this was a moment when, for every Jew, priorities were priorities.

The Radcliffe committee meeting was cancelled and Shinwell's passionate oratory brought a packed Manchester Opera House to its feet. He spoke for an hour – he was scheduled to speak for twenty minutes – and those who attended the meeting have never forgotten it.

A fiery denunciation of Arab aggression followed a panegyric on the State of Israel and the right of the Jews to defend themselves. The mix of personal recollection, sweeping principles and powerful invective makes odd reading. Parentheses were hidden within parentheses and rambling sentences – without a single note – were delivered with the gestures of body and intonation of voice that roused the audience to fury at Egyptian colonels and then, seconds later, had them weeping at the loss of young soldiers' lives. Young men and women he had met personally were giving their lives for their country, for their people, in the deserts, in the mountains, in the orange groves and in the farms and townships they had made their homes. Had they no right to a home? Had they no right to defend themselves?

To read this great speech is to read a rambling and, in places, incoherent text; questions unanswered, themes started and left in mid-air, punctuation almost impossible to place. It is meaningless to see a speech like this as a text. The tone, the crowd, the atmosphere and the voice were as important as the words. After all, it was not the speech of a Prime Minister setting out policies or of academic making an analysis; it was a speech aimed at creating an atmosphere of support for a beleaguered state thousands of miles away, to which most of the audience already felt some strong attachment. The success of the speech was to turn emotions into actions. One result was the huge amount of money donated to Israel by people who could barely afford their donations but were inspired by him. The other result was the army of young volunteers who left the hall determined to fight for the Jewish State.[4] Israel's crushing defeat of all its Arab neighbours within a week meant that few of those young volunteers from Manchester ever left England.

In the House of Commons it was back again to the mundane business of D-notices. Shinwell, as he had warned, delivered a speech supporting the right of the Daily Express to publish. Wilson dissented from this part of the report and he concentrated instead on the recommendation to update and liberalise the whole system of voluntary censorship. The sudden resignation of Colonel Lohan took some of the sting out of the press attacks and Shinwell refused to say anything more in public after his Commons statement.

Shinwell was more interested now in concentrating on the one area where he was genuinely out of sympathy with Wilson. He was particularly keen not to be seen as a general troublemaker for the very reason that he wanted to be listened to on the iniquities of Britain's application to join the European Economic Community. His arguments, repeated at party conferences and in the House of Commons, were increasingly based on the inevitable loss of independence to an unelected commission and on the potential cost of the Common Agricultural Policy. He was less impressed now with his earlier arguments, which had originated when membership had seemed a possibility in the 1950s, about links with the Commonwealth and the United States, but he was not above simple chauvinism. 'The Germans? We can't go in with them. The French? Never trusted them at all,' he told an anti-European audience in 1969.[5] It was a foretaste of his intellectual decline as a very old man.

His decline was obvious to his constituents too. He could have stayed on if he had chosen to fight, but extreme old age was at last taking its toll. He was rambling more than ever at constituency meetings and he would, after all, be well into his nineties by the end of any subsequent Parliament. Still sharp and attentive, however, with key individual members of Easington Labour Party, he came across as quite sound on constituency issues. He made a whole series of competent speeches on regional policy to combat pit closure, on the need for new motorways and the need to attract investment into the North-East. It started to seem to his exasperated opponents in the constituency that his old age was just something with which to taunt them; one moment he seemed on the verge of senility and the next like a vigorous fifty year-old. In the end, there was no doubt that he could choose his own time of going; after thirty-three years he had too many admirers to be pushed.

Councillor Reny MacManners, his consistent opponent from the left and a frequent recipient of sharp invective from her MP, actually made a speech at his constituency general committee in which she said – with Shinwell present – that they would be hard-pressed to fund a by-election if he died. In 1968, after all, constituencies as safe as Easington were being lost. Most members backed Jack Dormand to succeed Shinwell and it was generally agreed that Dormand, a local school teacher, would be a solid, pedestrian, constituency MP, a relief after forty years of Ramsay MacDonald and Manny Shinwell.

At the end of 1968, Shinwell announced his intention not to fight for a seat in the House of Commons in the next general election. It would be the first time since 1918.[6]

Jack Dormand held Easington comfortably but Edward Heath's Conservatives won the 1970 general election. Shinwell was not so interested. His second wife, Dinah, was starting to die of cancer when he was helping out on the hustings. Once again, family matters started to distract him from politics.

Ernie seemed to be getting into hot water again. Manny had admired many of the development schemes his PR company had helped to set up in Africa, but he was worried about his new project in Panama. The scheme was later described by an American crime writer with little knowledge of the Shinwell family as being 'conceived in the fertile brain of Ernest Shinwell, scapegrace son of one of England's most illustrious families ... the blot on the family escutcheon'.

Ernie had got himself a reputation for getting things done in developing countries and he had been introduced to businessmen connected with the Mafia who were interested in setting up a gambling empire offshore from the United States. Panama, at that time under a military dictatorship desperate for investment of any sort, was a favoured site. Ernie was brought in as the man to get it all going.

> Blessed with a politician's charm, the ability to convince with disarming sincerity, and an overweening self-confidence ... in the summer of 1970, Shinwell arrived in Panama. Using his family name and reputation as calling cards, he set about wooing prominent Panamanian lawyers, bankers, businessmen and government officials, spreading out before them a vision of economic development and progress, a vision he was prepared to turn into reality, with their help. He was persuasive indeed.[7]

His Mafia employers really seemed to deliver. Securities worth over two million dollars were given to him to deposit in a Panamanian bank and he borrowed half a million dollars to get the building started, until the bank checked and found that the shares were forgeries. Ernie rushed out of Panama, back to Dinah's funeral in London and never set foot in Central America or North America again. He was a frightened man and it was the end of the Panama project.

From then on, he decided, he would make sure that any securities were genuine. But unfortunately he was taken for a ride, possibly a Mafia revenge, when he was raising money for a project in Nigeria. Manny had been pleased that Ernie was now back on familiar African territory. He was all the more horrified when Ernie was arrested as he walked into a bank in Luxembourg for handling false securities. He found he was carrying forgeries. This time the courier had apparently kept the originals and substituted fakes.[8]

While Ernie was in a Luxembourg prison, Manny married for the third time. Sarah Hurst – from the wealthy Scottish Jewish Stungo family. She had a flat in Oslo Court in St John's Wood, the same block as Manny, and he moved into her flat and took it over. He was eighty-seven and she was seventy-eight, and like many old couples they found each other physically attractive as well as companionable. But she found his life-style hard and his refusal to have any domestic help a burden. Manny later admitted that his third marriage was probably a mistake.[9]

For Sarah, it was the culmination of a sad life. Her former husband, psychiatrist Dr Ellis Hurst, had lived in the George V Hotel in Paris with another woman for most of their marriage; even in the early days she had never really been happy. Her elderly brother, Meir Stungo, had tried to dissuade her from marrying Manny; then, when she insisted, he tied up all her money in covenants so Manny would be unable to benefit from her death, which caused endless and deep offence. Their marriage was never as miserable as her previous one but it never satisfied her emotionally in her old age as she had hoped it would. She was a delicate old lady; Manny was wrong for her and she died unhappy five years later.

A curious postscript was Manny's discovery when she died of intimate diaries describing everything physical between them, which she had left in her will not to Manny but to her family. Manny burned them.

'Where else could I go? I didn't feel the need to retire. I still felt I had things to say. The House of Lords was there. It will be there, probably in some changed form, for many years more.'[10]

It was a simple and honest view, typically involving no ideology or long-term thinking but a practical answer to a practical question. What does an old ex-MP do? Taking a title, Lord Shinwell of Easington, at least guaranteed him a platform and a comfortable front-row seat from which he could watch the political world.

Shinwell had always regarded constitutional matters as relatively unimportant. Although he would have undoubtedly gone along with the reforms of the House of Lords or the monarchy, especially in his earlier days, he saw constitutional change as following on from economic and social change and not as a priority. At the same time, he never took the House of Lords or the paraphernalia of peerage and monarchy too seriously. One interviewer asked him a long and solemn question about republicanism to which he simply replied: 'It doesn't bother me much. Nor does it bother the electorate.'[11]

He did not play down the ceremonial. When the Civil List was discussed a few months before the 1970 election, he told other Labour MPs who wanted to resist paying the Queen more money that 'If we want a monarchy, we have to pay them properly – we can't have them going around in rags.'[12] It was the same with the House of Lords. If there had to be one, he might as well use it and make the best of it. And he did.

Lord Shinwell soon became a House of Lords character. Throughout the 1950s and '60s, he had been cultivating the image of a gruff old man, helped to some extent by right-wing journalist John Junor who loathed Labour MPs in general: 'Manny was quite different. Manny was prepared to rat on his enemies, but by God, he was loyal to his friends.' Junor and Shinwell were close friends. From 1950 to 1986 they met regularly at the restaurant of the Russell Hotel for a light lunch with a glass of beer. Unlike many politicians, Shinwell would never take hospitality without paying for it in his turn. He gave Junor scoops not to pay for his meals but because he liked him. They were usually about people he opposed within the Labour

Party and they were usually trivial, if embarrassing, diary items. Back in the 1950s, for example, Junor told *Sunday Express* readers, courtesy of Shinwell, about Douglas Jay pouring a jug of cold water over Christopher Mayhew's head, and Richard Crossman sitting on George Brown and pummelling him in a House of Commons corridor.[13] Wigg, especially after Junor had criticised him over the Profumo affair, strongly disapproved and told Shinwell so, but Shinwell liked Junor and, for once, had no intention of taking any notice of Wigg.

Shinwell's old-age opinions had a lot to do with Junor. They were both patriotic populists and, in areas on which Shinwell now mostly spoke, they shared the same views. Shinwell in the House of Lords and Junor in the 'Cross-Bencher' column of the *Sunday Express*, made vigorous defences of tobacco and alcohol, and defended boxing to the hilt (Shinwell was now president of the World Sporting Club) especially against Baroness Edith Summerskill who wanted it banned.[14]

They both shared a crude form of British nationalism which finally became distasteful. By 1975, Shinwell's contribution to the EEC referendum campaign was knockabout and anti-continental, full of stories about the German desire to dominate, reminders about Napoleon and the Kaiser, and the untrustworthiness of the French and Italians. By 1982, when the Labour Party was agonising over the launch of the fleet in the Falklands campaign, he exclaimed, 'Let's get on with the fighting and hang the expense.'[15] By the time he was a hundred, he was seriously proposing the transportation of psychopaths to St Kilda and black people to the West Indies.[16]

In the eighties, Shinwell found himself more and more out of line with Labour on defence, eventually resigning the whip in the House of Lords in a fit of pique at the age of ninety-eight shortly before the 1983 general election: 'I'm a zealot as far as defence is concerned; I won't yield an inch ... We must have a nuclear deterrent.'[17] Of course, resigning the whip did not mean leaving the party, which he would never have thought of doing.

He stayed active on defence matters in the House of Lords all-Party Defence Group until he was well over a hundred. Nuclear weapons and the need for a large well-trained Territorial Army were his main hobby-horses. At the time, his colleagues would say it was wonderful he could talk about such a complex and controversial subject at such a great age. But looking back on it, even his contributions to House of Lords debates were usually rambling and banal. And on issues other than defence, they were often simply embarrassing to former Labour colleagues if they were not quite meaningless.

He did have great moments, though. One of the best was when Harold Macmillan, newly elevated to be Earl of Stockton, mildly criticised Con-

servative economic and social policies, and Shinwell stage-whispered that
he had heard the speech before – in 1924.

Only at election time did Shinwell and Junor fight in opposite camps;
never more so than during Shinwell's last foray into electioneering, to speak
for the ill-starred Peter Tatchell in the Bermondsey by-election. Was it
out of party loyalty that a now reactionary old man spoke for a representative of the far left of the party? Perhaps it was a continued shared view
with the left of what was fundamentally important and what was not.

Just occasionally, he could still reveal an underlying radicalism. One
example was the so-called 'Manny-festo' which he and a group of other
former Labour ministers published in the *Daily Mirror* in 1985 when he
was one hundred and one. Of all the contributors, including former
Foreign Secretary Lord Stewart, Lord Ardwick, Lord Jacques and Lord Oram,
Shinwell's contribution was the most radical. He said Labour should be
more concerned about shifting power to workers, came down against the
EEC as a club for the rich and in favour of workers' control and highly
redistributive taxation. His fellow peers ended up having to tone down
both Shinwell's Bennite views on the left and his super-nationalism on the
right.[18]

The only centenarian peer ever to make a speech in the House of Lords
turned up rather late, having been stuck in the traffic diverted to make way
for a State visit by President Mitterrand. He would have liked to have gone
on top of a bus, but a fall affecting his knee when he was ninety-eight meant
he now had to use a minicab. His minicab on this occasion was a Rolls-
Royce, driven by Ernie's new fiancée, Netta, an Irish Catholic, with
whom he became quite close in the last two or three years of his life.

Peers formed a Guard of Honour and sang 'Happy Birthday to You' as
he walked into the Royal Gallery for a reception, followed by a tribute in
the Chamber of the House itself:

> The noble Lord is the first Member of either House of Parliament to
> have sat in Parliament on his hundredth birthday. Indeed, so far as I have
> been able to discover, only two other Peers have lived to be a hundred
> and neither of them ever took their seat in this House.

Lord Whitelaw, the Leader of the House of Lords, finished by saying
he was pleased the ceiling of the House, which had fallen down a year earlier
in Shinwell's place, only moments after he had left it, had not taken him
before his time!

Lord Cledwyn, the Labour leader in the Lords, referred to Shinwell and
the Clydesiders as the 'militant tendency' of their day:

But, notwithstanding their conviction and their crusading zeal, my noble friend and his colleagues developed and retained their respect for parliamentary democracy. I do not think that my noble friend would wish for a greater tribute today than to be called a great parliamentarian.

The Liberals joined 'wholeheartedly in saluting the noble Lord' and the Social Democrats hoped 'that the noble Lord will live for very many years … to contribute honestly, as he always does, to what is probably one of the most important of all our subjects – defence.'

The Bishop of Norwich, speaking for the Church, found out that Shinwell had lived through the reigns of nine Archbishops of Canterbury and ten Archbishops of York but only five Bishops of Norwich, 'A glorious part of the world with its wide skies.'

Shinwell's reply was rambling. Even the Hansard editors could not find the punctuation to make some parts make sense. Nevertheless it was, of course, a big occasion and every word was warmly received with nods of approval and cries of 'Hear! Hear!' In this landmark speech, it was as difficult as ever to find even a hint of ideology, except a general feeling of patriotism and an even vaguer concept of a 'civilised society':

> Now about the future. I look forward, Members of the House of Lords, to a civilised society. When we speak of democracy what do we really mean? Voting, elections, Parties and Governments? Not at all. We speak of a society that is highly civilised and that is well educated; not highly educated but educated in general terms so that people are well informed and so that the average person in society can be well enough informed to understand a Member of Parliament when he states his policy and makes his promises. That is the kind of society I mean – a society where there is no pollution, a society where there is the highest form of sanitation, a society where hygiene counts above all else.

The nicest touches were about the reality of reaching a hundred: 'I have achieved nothing; it just happened.' And he referred to the problems of living alone at a great age, the loss of members of his family, his illness and his poor hearing. But most perceptively he added, looking round him at fellow peers, all younger than himself but several of them looking older: 'No longer having much knowledge, one becomes an "authority" – or believes oneself to have become an "authority".'[19]

Floods of telegrams and letters came from friends, colleagues and political opponents – Margaret Thatcher and Neil Kinnock both wrote personally, and there were cables from Ronald Reagan, the Queen Mother, the Prince and Princess Michael of Kent, the President and Prime Minister of Israel and, of course, from the Queen. There was a new book of interviews published by John Doxat and a launch by the publishers where, to Shinwell's undisguised delight, there were copies of four of his other books which had been reprinted: his history of the Labour Party (*Labour Story*), his personal history of the twentieth century (*I've Lived through it All*) and his two attempts at autobiography (*Conflict without Malice* and *Lead with the Left*).[20] The Parliamentary Labour Party laid on a special reception for him, as did the Board of Deputies of British Jews, especially in honour of his help in fund-raising, mainly through after-dinner speeches, for Soviet Jewry and Jews in Arab lands. There was also a fund-raising dinner in honour of his long-standing help with Jewish deaf children, a commitment going back fifty years, as his sister Clara had had a deaf-mute child herself. There was no family party. Lucy had just died and he saw little of most of the others:

> I found myself worrying last night about what I was going to give all the grandchildren for Christmas. Then I asked myself, 'Why are you worrying? They never give you anything.'
>
> Sometimes I don't know whether I'm alive or dead. I live in a sort of twilight world.[21]

In his speeches and interviews he could still be as malevolent as ever. At every opportunity he would criticise Crossman, now dead ten years, and Gaitskell, now dead twenty-four years. Ever since he was ninety, he had been able to grab attention almost without trying just for being so old. For party conferences, the House of Lords, and for any other gathering he would attend, he was a living part of history. It was sad that the content of his speeches was usually trivial.

He also suffered from a common misapprehension among the very old that he was too old to offend anyone. Telling people whose lives had been devoted to them that 'We've never had an international organisation worth two penn'orth of gin' was just as hard-hitting at ninety-five as it would have been when he was forty-five, and more or less unjustified comments denigrating former colleagues or critical of the new Labour leader, Neil Kinnock, were hurtful, even coming from the oldest man most people had ever met.

Manny Shinwell was not a man of letters. His books are mainly anecdotal and rarely give much insight into what twentieth-century political life was actually like. He was the very best oral, street-corner politician with a cause. He was part of the great reform of capitalist society that transformed Britain from Asquith to Thatcher. His life of agitation, provocation and dedication to the ending of poverty and squalor, both economic and social, is in itself a memorial.

Having ensured for himself a glimmer of immortality by entering the *Guinness Book of Records* as the oldest peer in January 1986,[22] he started to fail noticeably. At a lunch with John Junor and Lord MacAlpine, arranged by Manny to try to enlist MacAlpine's support in making Junor a peer, his mind was still sharp but his body was 'very fragile ... like a frail sparrow'.[23]

By the early spring, the exertion of going outside was almost too much. He preferred to stay at home and talk about the old days – or complain about the present – to his nephew, Labour activist Roger Robinson. Better still, he would let Ernie and his new wife, Netta, look after him while their adopted Indonesian son Jonathan, aged three, who called Manny 'Father', ordered him to smoke his pipe. Manny would duly light up and tell Jonathan to fetch up a stool; then the youngest and the oldest Shinwell would mumble together about the world.[24]

A bad cough turned to bronchial pneumonia and Manny was admitted to the Royal Free Hospital for treatment. He was a grouchy patient, telling the doctors that, if they were not so incompetent, he would have a good chance of reaching a hundred and five, and he had every intention of doing so.

'Lord Shinwell, the hundred-and-one-year-old peer, has come home from hospital to die,'[25] the bulletin said. He fought hard but on 8 May at 12.10 a.m., with his son Ernie by his side, he died.

The cremation the next day at Golders Green was conducted by a Reform rabbi, Hugo Gryn, and was rather a rush to organise before the Jewish Sabbath set in. Junor gave the address, which he knew Manny had asked for in his will, and all three surviving children, along with a huge crowd of friends and colleagues, turned up for the service. The police closed the street and a great many mourners were left standing outside the small crematorium chapel.

Before very long, the inevitable disputes started. The planned memorial service at St Margaret's, Westminster, was felt inappropriate for even a non-practising Jew and was changed to a memorial meeting at the House of Commons. Apparently inept handling of his will caused endless trouble; Ernie objected to the London School of Economics having taken many of his father's papers – admittedly bequeathed to them – before he had even died. How did he know which ones were personal? He himself took away piles of documents which the London School of Economics had left behind and they were soon complaining through their lawyers. There was trouble over the flat too. Ernie said that the Executors told him to sell the flat but they denied it. He was even charged and taken to court for attempted fraud, but the case was dropped halfway through the trial. Even the meaning of Manny's last words were disputed. 'I've had enough' – did it refer to life or the bottle of Chivas Regal by his bedside? Does it matter anyway?[26]

There is a plaque with Manny's name on in the House of Lords library and another on the site of Freeman Street in Spitalfields where he was born. The street itself has gone. There is Shinwell House in Peterlee for training the mentally retarded, and there is the Shinwell Fitness Centre in Tower Hamlets which Manny opened himself, smoking his pipe, when he was a hundred.

He had no illusions about immortality:

I read the philosophers and the scientists and all the great men and their writings and they know little more about it than I do. I know that there are stars and planets, millions and thousands of millions of miles away. I am told so and I believe what the astronomers say, but there is so very little I know, and so very little that other people know about death, except that it happens. But what happens after it, I can't comprehend; I am prepared for the best or the worst and I leave it at that.[27]

Manny Shinwell was tired out after one hundred and one years and two hundred and one days in this world. It was time to go:

When the disaster comes it will not affect me very much. I shall depart, I shall shuffle off this mortal coil with a melancholy reflection that all those who follow me are going to suffer. But I shall have escaped.[28]

References

PART 1

1. GHETTO CHILD

1. Numbers, 6:24.
2. Quoted in Union of Liberal and Progressive Synagogues, *Service of the Heart*, p. 430.
3. Russell and Lewis, *The Jew in London*, map 'Jewish East London'; Booth, *Life and Labour in London*, part 5, descriptive map of London poverty, North-Eastern sheet.
4. Shinwell, *Lead with the Left*, p. 7.
5. White, *Rothschild Buildings*, pp. 42–3.
6. Shinwell, *Lead*, p. 6.
7. Dubnow, *History of the Jews in Russia and Poland*, Vol 2, pp. 191–3 and 366–7; *Congressional Record, 47th Congress, 1st Session*, Appendix, contains a detailed list of anti-Jewish outbreaks.
8. Shinwell, *Conflict without Malice*, p. 15.
9. Family interviews, especially Roger Robinson.
10. Shinwell, *Lead*, p. 5.
11. Ibid., p. 3.
12. Brewer, quoted in Gosden, *How They Were Taught*, pp. 22–3 and 71–2.
13. *Report of the Committee of Council on Education (London) for 1894–5*, Appendix Part 3, pp. 47–8, 'General Report for the Year 1894' by L.D. Smith, H.M. Inspector.
14. Shinwell, *Lead*, p. 9.
15. Shinwell, speech at a luncheon given by the Board of Deputies of British Jews on the occasion of his hundredth birthday.
16. Jews' Free School, *Jews' Free School, Bell Lane, Spitalfields*, pp. 26–7.
17. Quoted in Fishman, *East End Jewish Radicals 1875–1914*, p. 160.
18. Fishman, *East End 1888*, p. 140.

19. Fishman, *East End Jewish Radicals*, p. 143.
20. Gartner, *The Jewish Immigrant in England 1870–1914*, p. 118.
21. Ernest Shinwell, interview, 1990.
22. Kershen, *Trade Unionism amongst the Clothing Workers of London and Leeds 1872–1915*, p. 224.
23. Ernest Shinwell, interview, 1990.
24. Gartner, *Jewish Immigrant*, pp. 117–18; *Polishe Yidl*, 22.8.1884 and 29.8.1884.
25. *East London Observer*, quoted in Fishman, *East End Jewish Radicals*, pp. 171–2.
26. Kershen, *Trade Unionism*, pp. 222–4; *Polishe Yidl*, 22.8.1884.
27. Kershen, *Trade Unionism*, pp. 111–14; Gartner, *Jewish Immigrant*, p. 118.
28. Kershen, *Trade Unionism*, pp. 231–3.
29. Gartner, *Jewish Immigrant*, pp. 122–6; *East End Jewish Radicals*, pp. 169–79.
30. Ernest Shinwell, interview, 1990.
31. Lord Shinwell, interview by Alan Shinwell, 1979, Part 1, p. 3.
32. Shinwell, *Lead*, p. 10; Johnson, *South Shields in Old Picture Postcards*, vol 2, p. 17.

2.   CHILD LABOUR

1.   Lord Shinwell, interview by Alan Shinwell, 1979 (Shinwell interview 1979), Part 1, pp. 3–4.
2.   Shinwell, *Conflict without Malice*, p. 18.
3.   Shinwell interview 1979, Part 1, pp. 4–5.
4.   Johnson, *South Shields in Old Picture Postcards*, vol 2, p. 17; Hodgson, *Borough of South Shields*, pp. 121–3.
5.   Shinwell interview 1979, Part 1, p. 5.
6.   Shinwell, *Lead with the Left*, pp. 10–11.
7.   Shinwell interview 1979, Part 2, p. 1.
8.   Ibid., pp. 7–8.
9.   Lucy Stern, interview by Alan Shinwell, 1979.
10. Shinwell, *Conflict*, p. 20.
11. Ibid., p. 21; Shinwell, *Lead*, p. 21; Shinwell interview 1979; Clegg et al., *A History of the British Trade Unions since 1889, vol 1 1889–1910*, pp. 165–8.
12. Butler, *A History of Boxing in Britain*, pp. 50–7.
13. Shinwell interview 1979, Part 1, p. 7.
14. Ibid., Part 2, pp. 10–11.
15. Ibid., pp. 12–14.

16. Shinwell, *Conflict*, p. 27.
17. Shinwell interview 1979, Part 2, p. 15; ibid., p. 5.
18. Blatchford, *Merrie England*; Blatchford, *Not Guilty*; Marx, *Wage, Labour and Capital*.
19. Blatchford, *Merrie England*, p. 97.
20. Blatchford, *The Scout*, I, p. 1.
21. Shinwell interview 1979, Part 3, pp. 1–2; ibid., Part 3, p. 17.
22. *Clarion*, May 1895, also quoted in Prynn, 'The Clarion Clubs', p. 68.
23. Shinwell interview 1979, Part 2, p. 18; Shinwell, *Lead*, pp. 28–30.
24. Shinwell, 'Jewish Characteristics – by one of them'.
25. Shinwell interview 1979, Part 2, p. 6; ibid., pp. 20–2; Shinwell, *Lead*, pp. 37–8.

3. UNIONS AND VIOLENCE

1. Lord Shinwell, interview by Alan Shinwell, 1979 (Shinwell interview 1979), Part 3, notes.
2. *Clothiers' Operatives' Gazette* (COG), October 1903, p. 6.
3. COG, April 1905, supplement.
4. Glasgow Trades Council minutes (GTCm), 30.1.1918.
5. COG, April 1905, pp. 10–11.
6. GTCm, 15.2.1905.
7. GTCm, 13.2.1907.
8. GTCm, 24.4.1907.
9. COG, November 1906; COG, December 1906; *Glasgow Herald*, 13.12 1906.
10. GTCm, 2.6.1907.
11. Shinwell, *Lead with the Left*, pp. 39–40.
12. Shinwell interview 1979, Part 2, p. 16.
13. Ibid., notes.
14. Shinwell, *Conflict without Malice*, pp. 42–3.
15. GTCm, 30.11.1910.
16. GTCm, 8.2.1911.
17. Sells, *The British Trade Boards System*, Ch. 1; Stewart and Hunter, *The Needle is Threaded*, pp. 144–7.
18. Public Record Office (PRO) LAB 11 162.
19. PRO LAB 11 153.
20. PRO LAB 11 223.
21. Ibid.
22. Shinwell interview 1979, Part 4, pp. 28–9 and 34; Shinwell, *Lead*, p. 46.

23. GTCm, 4.7.1911.
24. Report of the Proceedings of His Majesty's Advocate General for Scotland v Alfred Wade French, August 1913.
25. Shinwell interview 1979, Part 4, pp. 27–9.
26. Report of the Proceedings of His Majesty's Advocate General for Scotland v Alfred Wade French, August 1913; Shinwell, *Conflict*, pp. 48–50.
27. Shinwell interview 1979, Part 4, pp. 30–3.
28. Shinwell, *Conflict*, pp. 51–3.
29. Shinwell interview 1979, Part 3, p. 2; Shinwell, *Conflict*, p. 52.
30. Shinwell interview 1979, Part 4, p. 32.
31. GTCm, 8.11.1911.
32. *Govan Press*, 6.4.1912.
33. Ibid., 13.4.1912.
34. Cooper, *John Wheatley*, pp. 36–41.
35. Report of the Proceedings of His Majesty's Advocate General for Scotland v Alfred Wade French, August 1913; *Glasgow Herald*, 30.10.1911.
36. GTCm, 18.6.1913.
37. Report of the Proceedings of His Majesty's Advocate General for Scotland v Alfred Wade French, August 1913.

PART 2

4.　'SHINBAD THE TAILOR' GOES INTO POLITICS

1. Lord, *The Good Years*, p. 270.
2. *British Seafarer* (BS), January 1913.
3. Report of the Proceedings of His Majesty's Advocate General for Scotland v Alfred Wade French, August 1913.
4. BS, July 1913.
5. Report of the Proceedings of His Majesty's Advocate General for Scotland v Alfred Wade French, August 1913.
6. BS, July 1914; *The Seaman*, June 1914.
7. Hearing before the Court of Session, Edinburgh, 17 February 1914.
8. Glasgow Trades Council minutes (GTCm), 5.9.1912; McKibbin, *Evolution of the Labour Party 1910–1924*, p. 37.
9. Lord Shinwell, interview by Alan Shinwell, 1979 (Shinwell interview 1979).
10. GTCm, 16.6.1914 and 30.6.1914.
11. 'Outlook', *Socialist Review*, December 1911.
12. *Glasgow Herald* (GH), 20.9.1914.

13. Shinwell interview 1979, Part 3, pp. 38–9.
14. BS, August 1914.
15. BS, September 1914.
16. Hopkins, *'National Service' of British Merchant Seamen 1914–1918*, pp. 13–15.
17. Shinwell interview 1979, Part 3, pp. 39–40.
18. Melling, *Rent Strikes*, pp. 46–9.
19. Shinwell interview 1979, Part 3, p. 41.
20. Lucy Stern, interview by Alan Shinwell, 1979.
21. Melling, *Rent Strikes*, p. 65; Shinwell interview 1979, Part 3, p. 42.
22. GTCm, 21.4.1915.
23. GTCm, 5.5.1915.
24. Reported in *Forward,* 12.6.1915.
25. BS, July 1915.
26. Hopkins, *'National Service'*, pp. 116–17.
27. GTCm, 28.8.1915.
28. GTCm, 28.8.1915; Shinwell interview 1979.
29. Lucy Stern, interview by Alan Shinwell, 1979.
30. GH, 18.11.1915; *Forward*, 27.11.1915.
31. Lucy Stern, interview by Alan Shinwell, 1979.
32. McLean, *Legend of Red Clydeside*, pp. 23–7.
33. Shinwell interview 1979.
34. Ibid., Part 2.
35. McLean, *Legend*, p. 35.
36. GTCm, 29.10.1915.
37. *History of the Ministry of Munitions,* Vol. 4, Part 2, pp. 52–4.
38. Public Record Office MUN 5 73.
39. Shinwell interview 1979, Part 4, p. 48.
40. Oxford, *More Memories*, p. 60.
41. Gallacher, *Revolt on the Clyde*, pp. 7–17.
42. GTCm, 22.12.1915.
43. GTCm, 22.12.1915.
44. Gallacher, *Revolt*, pp. 97–102; Shinwell, *Conflict without Malice*, p. 55; McLean, *Legend*, pp. 52–3.
45. *The Worker*, 8.1.1916.

5.   BOLSHEVIK

1. Brotherstone, 'The Suppression of the "Forward"', pp. 5–23.
2. Macassey, *Labour Policy, False and True*, pp. 72–9.; McLean, *Legend of Red Clydeside*, Ch. 7.
3. Macassey, *Labour Policy*, p. 72.

4. Ibid., p. 73.
5. Ibid., pp. 83–4.
6. Glasgow Trades Council minutes (GTCm), 6.3.1916.
7. Lord Shinwell, interview by Alan Shinwell, 1979 (Shinwell interview 1979), Part 7.
8. Hinton, *The First Shop Stewards' Movement*, pp. 158–61.
9. GTCm, 4.4.1916 and 5.4.1916.
10. GTCm, 17.5.1916.
11. McLean, *Legend*, p. 82.
12. GTCm, 17.5.1916.
13. Lucy Stern, interview by Alan Shinwell, 1979; Ernest Shinwell interview, 1990.
14. Julia Robinson, interview.
15. Hannan, *Life of John Wheatley*, pp. 59–60.
16. Shinwell interview 1979, Part 4, pp. 52–4.
17. *The Seaman*, November 1916.
18. Tupper, *Seamen's Torch*, pp. 125–8; *The Seaman*, November 1915.
19. Tupper, *Seamen's*, pp. 150–3; Shinwell interview 1979, notes.
20. Shinwell interview 1979, Part 4, pp. 59–60.
21. *British Seafarer* (BS), April 1917.
22. Ibid.
23. BS, September 1916.
24. GTCm, 24.11.1915; Milton, *John Maclean*, pp. 101–2.
25. *Glasgow Herald* (GH), 24.11.1915.
26. GTCm, 24.11.1915.
27. Shinwell interview 1979, Part 4, p. 40.
28. GTCm, 24.11.1915.
29. GTCm, 3.4.1917.
30. GTCm, 24.4.1917.
31. *Forward*, 26.5.1917.
32. BS, June 1917.
33. Gallacher, *Revolt on the Clyde*, pp. 69–72.
34. BS, June 1917.
35. Public Record Office (papers of J. Ramsay MacDonald), 30 69 1161.
36. Shinwell, *I've Lived Through It All*, p. 39.
37. BS, July 1917; *Daily Herald*, Leeds Conference number, 9.6.1917.
38. Marquand, *Ramsay MacDonald*, pp. 213–14.
39. Tupper, *Seamen's*, pp. 186–95; Marquand, *MacDonald*, pp. 214–5.
40. Marquand, *MacDonald*, p. 215; Shinwell, *I've Lived*, pp. 39–40.
41. Shinwell, *Conflict without Malice*, p. 56; BS, February 1918.
42. BS, May 1917 and July 1917; Shinwell interview 1979, notes; GH, 27.2.1918.
43. BS, February–March 1917.

44. Shinwell interview 1979, Part 4, notes.
45. GTCm, 11.7.1918.
46. Shinwell interview 1979, Part 5, pp. 44–5.
47. Ibid., Part 5, notes.
48. G. Walker, *Thomas Johnston*, pp. 33–4.
49. *Linlithgowshire Gazette*, 6.12.1918.
50. Ibid.
51. Ibid.
52. *West Lothian Courier*, 13.12.1918.
53. *Linlithgowshire Gazette*, 13.12.1918.
54. Ibid.
55. *West Lothian Courier*, 3.1.1919.
56. Ibid.

6. BLOODY FRIDAY

1. *Forward*, 25.1.19, quoted in Marquand, *Ramsay MacDonald*, p. 239.
2. Middlemas, *The Clydesiders*, pp. 87–8.
3. Lord Shinwell, interview by Alan Shinwell, 1979 (Shinwell interview 1979), Part 4, p. 41.
4. Proceedings in Prosecution at the instance of the Lord Advocate against Emanuel Shinwell and others: transcript of Trial, 7–17 April 1919, High Court, Edinburgh (Trial), evidence by Edith Hughes.
5. Trial, evidence by Edith Hughes.
6. Shinwell, *Conflict without Malice*, p. 60.
7. Shinwell interview 1979, notes.
8. Kendall, *The Revolutionary Movement in Britain 1900–1921*, p. 136.
9. Ibid., p. 137.
10. Ernie Shinwell, interview, 1990.
11. Middlemas, *Clydesiders*, p. 89.
12. McLean, *The Legend of Red Clydeside*, pp. 118–19.
13. Shinwell interview 1979, notes.
14. *Glasgow Herald* (GH), 24.1.1919, quoted in Middlemas, *Clydesiders*, p. 92.
15. Glasgow Trades Council minutes (GTCm), 15.1.1919.
16. GTC (Executive) minutes, 20.1.1919.
17. *The Worker*, 5.3.1921, p. 12.
18. GTCm, 19.9.1919.
19. Patrick Dollan, papers.
20. Trial, evidence by the Lord Provost and Harry Hopkins; Gallacher, *Revolt on the Clyde*, p. 222.
21. Trial, evidence by the Lord Provost.

22. Shinwell interview 1979, notes.
23. Ibid.
24. Public Record Office (PRO) CAB 23/9.
25. *Daily Record and Mail*, 30.1.1919.
26. Middlemas, *Clydesiders*, p. 93.
27. PRO CAB 23/9.
28. Middlemas, *Clydesiders*, p. 93.
29. Trial, police evidence.
30. Shinwell interview 1979, notes; Bell, *Pioneering Days*, pp. 168–9.
31. McShane and Smith, *No Mean Fighter*, pp. 106–7.
32. Trial, police evidence; GH, 3.2.1919.
33. McShane and Smith, *Fighter*, p. 107.
34. GH, 16.11.1918.
35. Rowland, *Lloyd George*, pp. 506–7.
36. PRO CAB 23/9, quoted in McLean, *Legend*, p. 125.
37. Shinwell interview 1979, notes; Gallacher, *The Last Memoirs*, p. 120.

7. POLITICAL PRISONER

1. Gallacher, *Last Memoirs*, pp. 19–21; Lucy Stern, interview by Alan Shinwell, 1978.
2. Cooper, *John Wheatley*, pp. 63–4.
3. Lord Shinwell, interview by Alan Shinwell, 1979 (Shinwell interview 1979), 'Prison Notes'.
4. Shinwell interview 1979, Part 3, p. 50.
5. Glasgow Trades Council minutes (GTCm), 26.3.1919.
6. Proceedings in Prosecution at the instance of the Lord Advocate against Emanuel Shinwell and others: transcript of Trial, 7–17 April 1919, High Court, Edinburgh (Trial).

   The defendants were Emanuel Shinwell, William Gallacher, David Kirkwood, Joseph Brennan, George Ebury, Harry Hopkins, David M'Kenzie, Robert Loudon, Neil Alexander, James Murray, Daniel Stewart Oliver and William M'Cartney; the Judge was the Lord Justice Clerk, the Rt Hon Lord Scott Dickson.
7. Lucy Stern, interview by Alan Shinwell, 1979; Shinwell interview 1979, notes.
8. William Gallacher, reminiscences: 'I Remember', BBC, 15.6.1961, National Sound Archive.
9. Trial, evidence by DC Coulter.
10. *Linlithgowshire Gazette*, 7.2.1919.
11. Trial, evidence by Sgt Beaton, Insp. Gillies, Sgt Wark.
12. Trial, summing up by the Rt Hon The Lord Justice Clerk.

13. Shinwell interview 1979, p. 49; Gallacher, *Revolt on the Clyde*, p. 242.
14. *Daily Record,* 18.4.1919.
15. GTCm 22.4.1919.
16. Shinwell interview 1979, 'Prison Notes'.
17. Ibid.
18. Shinwell, *Conflict without Malice*, p. 69.
19. Ibid., p. 70.
20. Shinwell interview 1979, 'Prison Notes'; Ernest Shinwell, interview, 1990.
21. Shinwell interview 1979, 'Prison Notes'.
22. Shinwell, *Lead with the Left*, pp. 65–6.
23. Lucy Stern, interview by Alan Shinwell, 1979; Julia Robinson, interview, 1990.

8.   MOVING FORWARD

1. Marquand, *Ramsay MacDonald*, p. 243.
2. Andrew Livingstone, interview by Alan Shinwell, undated.
3. Berry, *Your Voice*, pp. 158–9.
4. Andrew Livingstone, interview by Alan Shinwell, undated.
5. Lucy Stern, interview by Alan Shinwell, undated.
6. MacDonald, *Parliament and Revolution.*
7. Glasgow Trades and Labour Council minutes (GTLCm), 4.10.1919.
8. *British Seafarer,* November 1919.
9. Triple Industrial Alliance, minutes of the Executive Committee, 16.4.1919.
10. Labour Party, Annual Conference, 1919 Report, pp. 112–17, 160–2.
11. TUC Annual Conference, 8–13.9.1919, minutes.
12. Lord Shinwell, interview by Alan Shinwell, 1979 (Shinwell interview 1979), Part 4, notes.
13. Glasgow Town Council, minutes, 11.9.1919; *Forward,* 20.9.1919.
14. *Forward,* 20.9.1919.
15. Ibid., 25.9.1919.
16. Shinwell interview 1979, Part 2, notes.
17. GTLCm, 24.3.1920.
18. *Glasgow Herald,* 26.3.1920.
19. Ibid., 17.9.1920.
20. Shinwell interview 1979, Part 2, notes.
21. *Forward,* 18.9.1920; *The Worker,* 25.9.1920.
22. *Forward,* 18.12.1920.
23. *Forward* 22.4.1921; *The Worker,* 5.5.1921.
24. Braunthal, *History of the International 1914–1943,* pp. 223–6.

25. Shinwell, *Lead with the Left*, pp. 175–6.
26. Beschusse der Internationalen Konferenz in Wien, Vienna, 1921; Protokoll der Internationalen Konferenz in Wien, Vienna, 1921.
27. Protokoll der Internationalen Konferenz, den Haag, 1921.
28. Carr, *The Bolshevik Revolution 1917–1923,* Vol. 3, p. 350.
29. Shinwell interview 1979, Part 3, notes; ibid., pp. 25–32, 33; *Glasgow Herald*, 22.6.1922.
30. Quoted in Marquand, *Ramsay MacDonald*, p. 275.
31. Shinwell interview 1979, Part 2, notes.
32. Ibid.; MacDonald, *Socialist Review* (editorial), October–December 1921.
33. Lucy Stern, interview by Alan Shinwell, undated; Ernie Shinwell, interview by Alan Shinwell, 1990.
34. *Labour Leader*, 7.7.1921.
35. Armadale Local History Project, *Tales fae the Dale*, p. 18.
36. GTLCm, 17.9.1922.
37. *British Seafarer*, August 1922.
38. *Linlithgowshire Gazette*, 17.11.1922; West Lothian Courier, 17.11.1922.
39. Linlithgowshire Labour Party, *Parliamentary Election: Linlithgowshire, 1922: Councillor Shinwell's Address to the Electorate.*
40. *Linlithgowshire Gazette*, 24.11.1922; *West Lothian Courier*, 24.11.1922.
41. Shinwell, *Conflict without Malice*, p. 77.
42. Ibid., pp. 79–81.
43. Brown, *Maxton*, p. 122.
44. Shinwell interview 1979, Part 2, notes.
45. Ibid., Part 2, p. 15.
46. Hansard, House of Commons, 23.11.1922, cols 118–21.
47. *Glasgow Citizen*, 26.11.1922; *The Times*, 26.3.1943.
48. Brown, *Maxton,* p. 121.
49. Hansard, House of Commons, 9.7.1923, cols 958–95.

9.   IN THE SHADOW OF RAMSEY MACDONALD

1. Public Record Office (PRO) 30 69 179.
2. Cole, *Beatrice Webb Diaries, 1924–32*, pp. 188–92; PRO 30 69 668.
3. PRO 30 69 1169.
4. Clynes, *Memoirs*, p. 17.
5. Shinwell, *Conflict without Malice*, pp. 113–14.
6. *The Times*, 9.1.1924.
7. Quoted in Lyman, *The First Labour Government 1924*, p. 81.
8. Hodges, *Nationalisation of the Mines.*

9. Hansard, House of Commons, 16.5.1924, cols 1755–64; PRO POWE 12 13.

10. PRO POWE 20 15; 10 51; 8 92; *The Times*, 1.2.1924.

11. PRO POWE 20 69 668.

12. PRO POWE 8 11.

13. Shinwell, *Conflict,* p. 93.

14. PRO POWE 10 81.

15. Doxat, *Shinwell Talking*, p. 50.

16. Shinwell, *Conflict*, p. 119.

17. Middlemas, *The Clydesiders: a left-wing bid for parliamentary power*, p. 164.

18. Lucy Stern, interview by Alan Shinwell, undated.

19. Hansard, House of Commons, 6.8.1914, cols 2928–30.

20. Lord Shinwell, interview by Alan Shinwell, 1979 (Shinwell interview 1979), Part 3, notes.

21. Shinwell, *I've Lived Through It All*, p. 88.

22. Quoted in Lyman, *First Labour Government,* p. 261.

23. *Linlithgowshire Gazette*, 31.10.1924.

24. Ibid., 24.10.1924.

25. Ibid., 31.10.1924.

26. Shinwell, *Conflict*, p. 98.

27. Ibid., pp. 98–9.

28. Clegg et al., *A History of British Trade Unions from 1889. Vol. 2, 1911–1953*, pp. 328–9.

29. Tupper, *Seamen's Torch: the life story of Captain Edward C. Tupper*, p. 284.

30. Amalgamated Marine Workers' Union file, Modern Records Centre, University of Warwick.

31. Shinwell interview 1979, Part 3, notes.

32. Ibid., Part 2, p. 16.

33. Records of the International Transport Workers' Federation, Modern Records Centre, University of Warwick.

34. Ibid.

35. *Report of the Proceedings of the 57th Annual Trades Union Conference*, p. 420.

36. Shinwell, *Conflict*, p. 99.

37. *Daily Mail*, 29.3.1927.

38. Lucy Stern, interview by Alan Shinwell, undated.

39. Brockway, *Inside the Left*, pp. 128–9.

40. Shinwell interview 1979, Part 2, p. 21.

41. *West Lothian Courier*, 16.3.1928.

42. Shinwell, *Conflict*, p. 101.

43. *West Lothian Courier*, 16.3.1928.

44. Hansard, House of Commons, 20.4.1928, cols 1350–5.

10. A STILETTO IN THE BACK

1. *The Times*, 24.1.27.
2. Brown, *So Far*, p.133.
3. Lord Shinwell, interview by Alan Shinwell, 1979 (Shinwell interview 1979), Part 3, .p. 63; Minutes: ILP Conference: 'Democracy', November 1928.
4. MacDonald, letters, Public Record Office (PRO) 30 69 1178.
5. Shinwell, *Conflict without Malice*, p. 102.
6. Ibid., p. 103.
7. Hansard, House of Commons, 24.3.1930, cols 198–200.
8. Ibid., 24.3.1930, col. 82.
9. Shinwell interview 1979, Part 2, p. 41; PRO WO 16 831.
10. Hansard, House of Commons, 24.3.1930, col. 201.
11. Shinwell, *Conflict*, p. 105.
12. *The Times*, 8.6.1930.
13. See Thomas, *My Story*.
14. Shinwell interview 1979, Part 3, p. 16.
15. Janeway, *The Economic Policy of the Second Labour Government*, pp. 129–33.
16. *The Times*, 27.6.1930; Shinwell, *Conflict*, p. 106.
17. *The Times*, 30.6.1930.
18. Shinwell, *Conflict*, pp. 106–7; Shinwell, *Lead with the Left*, pp. 89–90.
19. PRO 30 69 677; PRO POWE 16185.
20. Shinwell, *Conflict*, p. 108.
21. PRO POWE 191; *The Times*, 6.4.1931.
22. Marquand, *Ramsey MacDonald*, pp. 534–6.
23. Pimlott, *Hugh Dalton*, p. 153.
24. Skidelsky, *Oswald Mosley*, p. 253.
25. Bullock, *The Life and Times of Ernest Bevin*, Vol. 1, pp. 449–51.
26. Shinwell interview 1979, Part 3, pp. 17–20.
27. Nicolson, *Harold Nicolson: Diaries and Letters, 1930–39*, p. 156.
28. Shinwell, *Conflict*, p. 110; Doxat, *Shinwell Talking*, p. 75.
29. Feiling, *The Life of Neville Chamberlain*, pp. 190–192.
30. Harris, *Attlee*, pp. 95–6.
31. Shinwell, *Conflict*, pp. 110–11.
32. Ibid.
33. Hansard, House of Commons, 28.9.31, cols 43–50.
34. Cross, *Philip Snowden*, p. 146.
35. *Linlithgowshire Gazette*, 16.10.1931.

36. Skidelsky, *Oswald Mosley*, p. 263.

PART FOUR

11. SQUALID ROTTEN YEARS

  1. Shinwell, *Lead with the Left*, pp. 96–7; Shinwell, *Conflict without Malice*, pp. 122–3; Lord Shinwell, interview by Alan Shinwell, 1979 (Shinwell interview 1979), Part 3, pp. 61–6.
  2. National Sound Archive, LP30922.
  3. Shinwell, 'Ain't it Grand to be Temporarily Dead?', *Labour Magazine* 9 (August 1932), pp. 132–3.
  4. *Seaham Weekly News*, 2.6.1932.
  5. Mackenzie, *The Letters of Sidney and Beatrice Webb*, Vol. 3, p. 169.
  6. Quoted in Marquand, *Ramsay MacDonald*, pp. 481–2.
  7. Shinwell, *Conflict*, p. 127.
  8. Shinwell interview 1979, Part 3, p. 7.
  9. Ibid., Part 4, p. 21; Foot, *Aneurin Bevan,* Vol. 1, p. 172.
 10. Shinwell, *Conflict*, pp. 124–5.
 11. Shinwell, *Lead*, p. 97.
 12. Shinwell interview 1979, Part 4, pp. 28–9; Shinwell, *Lead*, pp. 94–101.
 13. Report, Labour Party Annual Conference, 1933.
 14. Sam Shinwell, interview.
 15. Shinwell interview 1979, Part 3, pp. 59–61; Donoughue and Jones, *Herbert Morrison: portrait of a politician*, pp. 185–8.
 16. Quoted in Marquand, p. 780.
 17. Shinwell, *Conflict*, pp. 129–30.
 18. Quoted in Marquand, pp. 779–81.
 19. Ibid., pp. 780–1.
 20. *Seaham Weekly News*, 11.10.1935.
 21. *Durham County Advertiser*, 29.11.1935.

12. CIVIL WAR AND THE END OF THE PEACE

  1. Donoughue and Jones, *Herbert Morrison: portrait of a politician*, p. 238.
  2. Parliamentary Labour Party, minutes, 1935–6.
  3. Lord Shinwell, interview by Alan Shinwell (1979) (Shinwell interview 1979), Part 4.
  4. Ibid., p. 69.
  5. Nicolson, *Harold Nicolson: diaries and letters, 1930–39*, p. 271.

6. Shinwell interview 1979, Part 4, p. 73.
7. Hansard, House of Commons, 28.4.1936, cols 816–27; 4.12.1935, cols 176–85; 29.7.1936, cols 1557–64; 6.12.1936, cols 463–6; *The Times*, 30.7.1936; *Daily Herald*, 12.5.1936; *Daily Herald*, 20.4.1936.
8. Quoted in Feiling, *The Life of Neville Chamberlain*, p. 264.
9. Ibid., p. 279.
10. Shinwell interview 1979, Part 4, p. 81.
11. Report, Labour Party Annual Conference, 1936.
12. Haldane, *Truth Will Out*, p. 106.
13. Shinwell, *Conflict without Malice*, pp. 140–4; *The Times*, 5.1.1938; and 15.1.1938; *Daily Herald*, 22.1.1938.
14. Hansard, House of Commons, 4.4.1938, cols 4–6.
15. Rhodes-James, *Chips: the diaries of Sir Henry Channon*, p. 154.
16. Shinwell interview 1979, Part 2, p. 46; Reny McManners, interview; Lord Glenamara, interview.
17. Gallacher, *Last Memoirs*, p. 62.
18. Harris, *Attlee*, pp. 152–6; Hansard, House of Commons, 1.11.1938, cols 160–70.
19. *Durham County Advertiser*, 24.1.1939.
20. Dalton, *Memoires, 1931–1945: the fateful years*, pp. 230–1.
21. Dilks, *The Diaries of Sir Alexander Cadogan 1938–45*, p. 163.
22. Parliamentary Labour Party, minutes.; Dalton, *Memoires, 1931–1945*, p. 265.

13. A BARNACLE ON THE SHIP OF STATE

1. Jeffreys, *Labour and the Wartime Coalition: from the diary of James Chuter Ede, 1941–1945*, p. 107.
2. Acts 4, 5: 6, Revised Standard Version.
3. Lord Glenamara, interview; Ian Mikardo, interview.
4. Shinwell, *Conflict without Malice*, p. 146.
5. Shinwell, *Lead with the Left*, pp. 109–10.
6. Parliamentary Labour Party Administrative Committee, minutes, 1 42; Pimlott, *Hugh Dalton*, p. 494; National Executive Committee, minutes, 12.10.1942.
7. National Sound Archive, British Home Service, 21758.
8. Ibid.
9. Lord Wilson of Rievaulx, interview, 1979; Lord Shinwell, interview by Alan Shinwell, 1979 (Shinwell interview 1979), Part 3, p. 46.
10. Shinwell, *Conflict*, pp. 147–8.
11. Harrison, 'He is Parliament's No. 1 Ginger-up Man', *Evening News*, 25.10.1941; Taylor, *Beaverbrook*, pp. 183–91.

12. Dilks, *The Diaries of Sir Alexander Cadogan, 1938–45*, p. 325.

13. Pimlott, *Diary of Hugh Dalton*, p. 119.

14. Parliamentary Labour Party, Administrative Committee, minutes, 19.2.1942; 11.3.1942; and 14.10.1942; Pimlott, *Diary of Hugh Dalton*, pp. 372–3.

15. Foot, *Aneurin Bevan*, Vol. 1, pp. 374–9.

16. Jeffreys, *Labour and the Wartime Coalition*, p. 87; Parliamentary Labour Party, Administrative Committee, minutes, 23.7.1942.

17. Jeffreys, *Labour and the Wartime Coalition*, pp. 86–90; Pimlott, *Diary of Hugh Dalton*, p. 470; Shinwell interview 1979, Part 3, pp. 49–50; Parliamentary Labour Party, minutes, 23.7.1942; Hansard, House of Commons, 29.7.1942, cols 1448–60.

18. Jeffrey, *Labour and the Wartime Coalition*, p. 90; Parliamentary Labour Party, Administrative Committee, minutes, 30.7.1942.

19. Shinwell, *Lead with the Left*, p. 107; Pimlott, *Diary of Hugh Dalton*, p. 289.

20. Taylor, *War and the Development of Labour's Domestic Programme, 1939–45*.

21. CMND 6386, 1941; Addison, *The Road to 1945*, pp. 178–80.

22. Report, Labour Party Annual Conference, 1943, report.

23. Ibid.

24. Shinwell, *The Britain I Want*, p. 21.

25. Ibid., p. 94.

26. Shinwell, *When the Men Come Home*, pp. 13–14.

27. Pimlott, *Diary of Hugh Dalton*, pp. 70–1.

28. Shinwell interview 1979, Part 3, pp. 85–6.

29. Pimlott, *Diary of Hugh Dalton*, pp. 73–7.

30. Shinwell interview 1979, Part 3, pp. 80–8.

31. Jeffreys, *Labour and the Wartime Coalition*, p. 194.

32. Hansard, House of Commons, 30.11.1943, cols 390–41.

33. Shinwell interview 1979, Part 3, p. 88; Shinwell, *Conflict*, p. 163.

14. NATIONALISATION: THE GREAT VICTORY

1. Mikardo, *Back-bencher*, p. 128; Lord Shinwell, interview by Alan Shinwell, 1979 (Shinwell interview 1979), Part 5, notes.

2. Labour Party, National Executive Committee, minutes, 21.5.1945; Shinwell interview 1979, Part 5, notes; Ian Mikardo, interview.

3. Addison, *The Road to 1945*, pp. 266–7.

4. Bob Taylor, interview.

5. *Seaham County Advertiser*, 3.8.1945.

6. Shinwell, Notes (1945), in the possession of Alan Shinwell; Attlee, *As It Happened*, p. 154.
7. Labour Party, *Let Us Face the Future* (election manifesto), 1945, p. 2.
8. Foot, *The Politics of Harold Wilson*, p. 47; Wilson, *New Deal for Coal.*
9. Shinwell, Notes (1945), in the possession of Alan Shinwell; Wigg, *George Wigg*, p. 114.
10. Chester, *The Nationalisation of British Industry, 1945–51*, p. 40.
11. Trades Union Congress 1944 Annual Report, pp. 196–201.
12. See Chester, *Nationalisation,* pp. 217–18.
13. Ibid., pp. 228–36.
14. Shinwell, *Conflict without Malice*, pp. 172–3.
15. CMND 6610, 1945, *Report of the Technical Advisory Committee on Coal Mining.*
16. Morgan, *Labour in Power, 1945–1951*, pp. 144–50.
17. Public Record Office (PRO) CAB 128 4, 6.11.1945.
18. Quoted in Bullock, *The Life and Times of Ernest Bevin*, Vol. 3, pp. 123–5.
19. PRO CAB 129 5, 8.12.1945.
20. Shinwell, Notes on Speeches, in the possession of Alan Shinwell.
21. Shinwell interview 1979, Part 4, p. 86.
22. Hansard, House of Commons, 29.1.1946, cols 701–5; Labour Party, Labour's Policy for Coal and Power, 1937.
23. Chester, *Nationalisation,* pp. 494–5; Hansard, House of Commons, 29.1.1946, cols 701–5; Shinwell interview 1979, Part 3, pp. 88–91.
24. PRO POWE 28 24; Chester, *Nationalisation*, p. 509.
25. Horner, *Incorrigible Rebel*, p. 180.
26. Hansard, House of Commons, 29.1.1946, col. 712.
27. Sir Arthur Drew, interview.
28. Reny MacManners, interview; Hansard, House of Commons, 15.5.1946, cols 821–2.
29. National Coal Board, *Annual Report 1947*, pp. 77–84.
30. PRO CAB 129 7, 26.6.1946.
31. Hansard, House of Commons, 26.6.1946, col. 1311.
32. *Manny: The Fighter*, a film for television by Alan Shinwell.
33. *The Times*, 28.6.1946.
34. Reny MacManners, interview.

15. THE COAL CRISIS: THE GREAT CATASTROPHE

1. Quoted in Robertson, *The Bleak Midwinter, 1947*, pp. 39–40.
2. Lord Wigg, interview by Alan Shinwell, 1979.
3. Ibid.

4. Williams, *The Diary of Hugh Gaitskell, 1945–1956*, p. 23.
5. Mikardo, *Back-bencher*, p. 91.
6. Public Record Office (PRO) CAB 129 10.
7. PRO POWE 28 23.
8. Trade Union Congress, *Annual Conference Report 1946*, pp. 103–6.
9. *The Times*, 25.10.1946.
10. Quoted in Robertson, *Bleak Midwinter*, p. 51.
11. Williams, *Gaitskell*, p. 134.
12. PRO CAB 128 9, 7.1.1947; PRO CAB 129 16, 31.1.47.
13. *The Times*, 27.1.1947.
14. Lord Wigg, interview by Alan Shinwell, 1979; Sir Arthur Drew, interview; Lord Shinwell, interview by Alan Shinwell, 1979, Part 4, notes.
15. PRO CAB 128 9, 6.2.1947; PRO CAB 128 9, 7.2.1947.
16. Harold Wilson, interview, 1979; Colliery Guardian, *Guide to the Coalfields*, 1947; Mining Association, *Statistical Yearbook*, 1947.
17. Lord Wigg, interview by Alan Shinwell, 1979.
18. Quoted in Pimlott, *Hugh Dalton*, p. 479.
19. Wigg, *George Wigg*, p. 114; Lord Wigg, interview by Alan Shinwell, 1979.
20. Wigg, *George Wigg*, p. 127; Pimlott, *Hugh Dalton*, p. 479; Mass Observation Archive (University of Sussex), 2483.
21. Shinwell, *Lead with the Left*, pp. 179–80.
22. Lord Wigg, interview by Alan Shinwell, 1979; Williams, *Gaitskell*, p. 29.
23. Lord Wigg, interview by Alan Shinwell, 1979; *Daily Telegraph*, 11.5.1947 and 8.6.1947.
24. Williams, *Gaitskell*, p. 29.
25. Ibid., p. 30.
26. Wigg, *George Wigg*, p. 131.

PART FIVE

16. THE WAR OFFICE

1. Williams, *The Diary of Hugh Gaitskell, 1945–56*, pp. 28–30; Lord Wigg, interview by Alan Shinwell, 1979; Lord Shinwell, interview by Alan Shinwell, 1979 (Shinwell interview 1979).
2. Shinwell, *Lead with the Left*, p. 140.
3. Public Record Office (PRO) WO 32 12324.
4. *Durham County Advertiser*, 12.7.1946.
5. PRO CAB 131 4.

6. Lord Wigg, interview by Alan Shinwell, 1979.
7. Thomas, *John S. Strachey*, p. 259.
8. PRO WO 32 12243; PRO WO 32 14482; PRO WO 32 12367.
9. PRO WO 32 14482; PRO WO 32 13718.
10. Quoted in Gordon, *Conflict and Consensus in Labour's Foreign Policy 1914–1965*, p. 127; Labour Party, *Cards on the Table*, 1949, p. 106.
11. *Reynolds News*, 14.12.1947.
12. Wigg, *George Wigg*, pp. 143–4.
13. Chalfont, *Montgomery of Alamein*, p. 282; Doxat, *Shinwell Talking*, pp. 79–80.
14. Alan Shinwell, notes on discussions with Lord Shinwell; Shinwell, *Conflict without Malice*, pp. 191–2; PRO WO 32 12324 (annexe).
15. Shinwell interview 1979, Part 5, p. 71; Mikardo, *Back-bencher*, pp. 96–7.
16. Quoted in Hamilton, *Monty: the Field Marshal, 1944–1976*, p. 689.
17. Ibid., p. 713.
18. Shinwell interview 1979, Part 5, pp. 21–2; Doxat, *Shinwell*, p. 79.
19. Hamilton, *Monty*, p. 714.
20. PRO WO 32 14428; *Daily Mirror*, 18.3.1949; Wigg, *George Wigg*, p. 144.
21. PRO CM 91 (46) 25.10.1946.
22. PRO FO 371 52560 E10030.
23. PRO CAB (46) 380.
24. Hansard, House of Commons, 18.11.1946, cols 433, 1917–18.
25. Ian Mikardo, interview; Morgan, *Labour People: leaders and lieutenants, Hardie to Kinnock*, p. 158; Mikardo, *Back-bencher*, pp. 98–9; Shinwell interview 1979, 'Notes, 1950'.

17. MINISTER OF DEFENCE

1. Lord Shinwell, interview by Alan Shinwell, 1979 (Shinwell interview 1979), 'Notes 1950'.
2. Public Record Office (PRO) DEFE 7 6.
3. Lord Wigg, interview by Alan Shinwell, 1979.
4. PRO DEFE 7 665.
5. PRO CAB 128 19; PRO CAB 128 20.
6. PRO CAB 128 20; Ziegler, *Mountbatten: the official biography*, p. 468.
7. PRO CAB 128 18; PRO FO 371 81901; Williams, *The Diary of Hugh Gaitskell, 1945–56*, pp. 177–8.
8. Lord Wigg, *George Wigg*, p. 154.
9. PRO FO 800 449 CONF 58.
10. Shinwell, *Conflict without Malice*, p. 219; *Daily Telegraph*, 21.9.1950.

11. Shinwell interview 1979, Part 5, pp. 48–50.
12. Report, Labour Party Annual Conference, 1950.
13. Shinwell, *Conflict*, p. 220.
14. PRO DEFE 7 681.
15. Shinwell, *Conflict*, p. 220.
16. Harris, *Attlee*, p. 461.
17. Hansard, House of Commons, 7.12.1950, cols 545–6.
18. Shinwell, *Lead with the Left*, pp. 149–52.
19. PRO DEFE 13 3.
20. Shinwell, *Lead*, p. 173.
21. PRO DEFE 13 3.
22. Shinwell interview 1979, 'Notes 1950–51'; Shinwell, *Lead*, p. 148.
23. Foot, *Aneurin Bevan*, Vol. 2, p. 302.
24. *Sunday Telegraph*, 30.7.1961; Shinwell interview 1979, 'Notes 1950–51'; Foot, *Bevan*, Vol. 2, pp. 312–26; Smith, *Harold Wilson: the authentic portrait*, p. 164; Williams, *Gaitskell*, pp. 229, 233, 253–5.
25. Shinwell interview 1979, Part 5, pp. 56, 60; Lord Wigg, interview by Alan Shinwell, 1979.
26. Donoughue and Jones, *Herbert Morrison: portrait of a politician*, pp. 501–6.
27. Williams, *Gaitskell*, pp. 292–3.

18. MORE IN HOPE THAN EXPECTATION

1. Lucy Stern, interview by Alan Shinwell.
2. Quoted in Gilbert, *Winston S. Churchill*, Vol. 8, p. 667; *Daily Mail*, 6.12.1951.
3. Hunt, *On the Spot: an ambassador remembers*, pp. 2–3.
4. Morgan, *The Backbench Diaries of Richard Crossman*, pp. 84–5.
5. Reny MacManners, Lord Glenamara, Paddy Kavanagh, Bob Taylor, interviews.
6. Labour Party Parliamentary Committee, minutes, April 1952.
7. Williams, *The Diary of Hugh Gaitskell 1945–1956*, pp. 304–5; Reny MacManners, interview.
8. Donoughue and Jones, *Herbert Morrison: portrait of a politician*, p. 521.
9. Lord Wigg, interview by Alan Shinwell, 1979; Lord Glenamara, interview.
10. Hansard, House of Commons, 5.3.1953, cols 801–4.
11. Lord Wigg, interview by Alan Shinwell, 1979
12. Lord Shinwell, interview by Alan Shinwell, 1979 (Shinwell interview 1979), 'Notes 1953–6'; Lady Janner, interview.
13. Lord Wigg, interview by Alan Shinwell, 1979; Ian Mikardo, interview.
14. Shinwell, *Conflict without Malice*, p. 232.

15. *Daily Express*, 20.10.1953; *The Times*, 20.10.1953; *Daily Telegraph*, 20.10.1953.
16. Lord Wigg, interview by Alan Shinwell, 1979.
17. BBC, 'Any Questions', 24.2.1956.
18. Morgan, *Crossman*, p. 374.
19. Quoted in Gilbert, *Churchill*, Vol. 8, p. 1070.
20. Ibid., pp. 1070–2.
21. Lord Moran, *The Struggle for Survival*, pp. 612–13.
22. Hansard, House of Commons, 1.12.1954, cols 1128–9.
23. Ibid., cols 1139–40.
24. Moran, *Struggle*, pp. 618–19.
25. *Durham County Advertiser*, 20.5.1955.
26. Morgan, *Crossman*, p. 424.
27. Shinwell interview 1979, Part 6, pp. 8–12.
28. Morgan, *Crossman*, p. 448.
29. Ibid., p. 446.
30. Report, Labour Party Annual Conference, 1955.
31. Hunter, *The Road to Brighton Pier*, p. 23.
32. Shinwell interview 1979, 'Notes 1953–56'.
33. Ibid., and Part 6, pp. 25–30.
34. Lord Dormand, Reny MacManners, Bob Taylor, interviews.
35. Wilson, *Memoirs 1916–1964: the making of a Prime Minister*, pp. 180–1.
36. Report, Labour Party Annual Conference, 1960.
37. Wilson, *The Relevance of British Socialism*.

19.   THE BAD-TEMPERED ANTIQUE

1. Ian Mikardo, interview.
2. Castle, *The Castle Diaries, 1964–70*, p. 21.
3. Lord Glenamara, interview; Lord Shinwell, interview by Alan Shinwell, 1979 (Shinwell interview 1979), 'Notes 1964–66'.
4. Glenamara, *Whip to Wilson*, p. 120; Lord Glenamara, interview; Lord Wigg, interview by Alan Shinwell, 1979.
5. Shinwell interview 1979, Part 6, pp. 27–35.
6. Lord Glenamara, Ian Mikardo, interviews.
7. Quoted in Wilson, *The Labour Government, 1964–1970: a personal record*, p. 134.
8. Crossman, *Diaries of a Cabinet Minister*, Vol. 1, pp. 64–7, 77.
9. Lord Jenkins of Hillhead, interview.
10. Ernie Shinwell, interview.
11. Keith Dovkants, 'Manny, the Mafia and Me', *ES Magazine*, 10.1.1990.

12. Castle, *Diaries,* p. 11.
13. John Silkin, interview by Alan Shinwell, 1979.
14. Shinwell interview 1980, pp. 6–7.
15. Crossman, *Diaries,* p. 93.
16. Shinwell interview 1980, pp. 8–11.
17. Crossman, *Diaries,* Vol. 1, p. 214.
18. John Silkin, interview by Alan Shinwell, 1979.
19. Lord Wigg, interview by Alan Shinwell, 1979.
20. BBC, 'The Week in Westminster', 4.3.1967.
21. Crossman, *Diaries,* Vol. 1, p. 267.
22. Shinwell interview (no date).
23. Lord Wigg, interview by Alan Shinwell, 1979; Lord Wigg, *George Wigg*, p. 345.
24. Quoted in Shinwell, *Lead with the Left,* p. 164.

20.   A CENTURY AND BEYOND

1. *Observer,* 14.6.1984.
2. Wigg, *George Wigg,* p. 347.
3. Lord Shinwell, interview by Alan Shinwell, 1979 (Shinwell interview 1979), 'Notes 1967–69'.
4. *Jewish Chronicle,* 16.6.1967; *Jewish Gazette,* 16.6.1967.
5. John Silkin, interview by Alan Shinwell, 1979.
6. Charlie Short, Paddy Kavanagh, Reny MacManners, Bob Taylor, interviews.
7. Hammer, *The Vatican Connection,* pp. 171–2.
8. Ibid., pp. 177–87; Keith Dovkants, 'Manny, the Mafia and Me', *ES Magazine*, 10.1.1990.
9. Shinwell interview, 1980.
10. BBC, 'The Life Peers', 10.10.1973.
11. Doxat, *Shinwell Talking,* p. 78.
12. Wilson, *The Labour Government, 1964–1970: a personal record,* p. 727.
13. *Sunday Express,* 17.11.1957; Junor, *Listening for a Midnight Tram,* p. 41.
14. Hansard, House of Lords, 26.11.1981, cols 425, 887–9.
15. *Observer,* 11.5.1986.
16. Doxat, *Shinwell,* pp. 29–30, 105–6.
17. Ibid., p. 34.
18. Lord Glenamara, Lord Oram, interviews.
19. Hansard, House of Lords, 18.10.1984, cols 1075–87.
20. Junor, *Listening,* p. 46.
21. *The Listener,* 1966, p. 739.

22. *Guinness Book of Records, 1986*, p. 106.
23. Junor, *Listening*, p. 45.
24. Ernie Shinwell, interview.
25. *Manchester Evening News*, 8.5.1986.
26. Angela Raspin, Roger Robinson, Ernie Shinwell, interviews.
27. Shinwell interview 1979.
28. *Daily Mirror*, 6.5.1977.

Select Bibliography

Shinwell, E. (1909), 'Jewish Characteristics – by one of them', *Clothiers' Operatives' Gazette* (September 1909), pp. 9–10.

—— (1913), 'James Martin: an appreciation', *British Seafarer* (July 1913), p. 6.

—— (1915), The American Seamen's Act, *British Seafarer* (December 1915), p. 11.

—— (1920), 'Lenin and parliamentary Tactics', *Forward* (18 September).

—— (1920), 'The Left Wing: what is its policy?', *Forward* (18 December).

—— (1921), 'The ILP and "Arming the Workers"', *Forward* (19 February).

—— (1922), *Address to the Electors* (Bathgate: West Lothian Printing and Publishing Co.).

—— (1925), *The Mines: a practical policy* (London: Independent Labour Party).

—— (1932), 'Ain't it Grand to be Temporarily Dead?', *Labour Magazine* (August 1932) pp. 172–3.

—— (1943), *The Britain I Want* (London: MacDonald).

—— (1944), *When the Men Come Home* (London: Gollancz).

—— (1953), 'Churchill as a Political Opponent', in C. Eade (ed.) *Churchill by His Contemporaries* (London: Hutchinson).

—— (1955), *Conflict without Malice*, (London: Odhams).

—— (1958), Foreword in *A Hundred Years of Progress: centenary brochure 1858–1958* (Glasgow, Glasgow District Trades Council).

—— (1963), The Labour Story (London: Macdonald).

—— (1965), Funeral obituary for Will Gallacher (August), (privately published).

—— (1973), *I've Lived Through It All* (London: Gollancz).

—— (1981), *Lead with the Left: my first ninety-six years* (London: Cassell).

Adams, R.J.Q. (1986), 'Asquith's Choice: the May coalition and the coming of conscription, 1915–1916', *Journal of British Studies*, vol. 25, no. 3, pp. 243–63.

Addison, P. (1977), *The Road to 1945* (London: Quartet).

Alderman, G. (1989), *London Jewry and London Politics 1889–1986* (London: Routledge.)

Armadale Local History Project (1989), *Tales fae the Dale* Linlithgow: Armadale Local History Project.

Attlee, C.R. (1956), *As It Happened* (London: Odhams).

Avon, Earl of (1965), *Memoirs of the Rt Hon Sir Anthony Eden* (3 vols), (London: Cassell).

Bell, Tom (1941), *Pioneering Days* (London: Lawrence and Wishart).

Berry, C. (1975), *Your Voice – and how to use it successfully* (London: Harrap).

Blatchford, R. (1895), *The Scout: a journal for socialist workers* (June 1895), vol. I, no. 3, Introduction.

—— (1896), *Merrie England* (London: Journeyman).

—— (1906), *Not Guilty: a defence of the bottom dog* (London: Clarion Press).

—— (1931), *My Eighty Years* (London: Cassell).

Bond, B. (1976), *Liddell Hart: a study of his military thought* (London: Cassell).

Bondfield, M. (1948), *A Life's Work* (London: Hutchinson).

Booth. C, (1969), *Life and Labour in London* (New York: Augustus M. Kelley).

Braunthal, J. (1967), *History of the International 1914–1943* (London: Nelson).

Brockway, F. (1942), *Inside the Left* (London: Allen and Unwin).

Brotherstone, T. (1969), 'The Suppression of the "Forward"' *Scottish Labour History Society Journal*, vol. 1, pp. 5–23.

Brown, G, (1986), *Maxton* (Edinburgh: Mainstream).

Brown, Lord George- (1972), *In My Way* (Harmondsworth: Penguin).

Brown, W.J. (1943), *So Far* (London: Allen and Unwin).

Buchanan, T. (1991), *The Spanish Civil War and the British Labour Movement* (Cambridge: Cambridge University Press).

Buckman, J. (1980), 'Alien Working-class Response: the Leeds Jewish tailors 1880–1914', in K. Lunn (ed.), *Hosts, Immigrants and Minorities: historical responses to newcomers in British society 1870–1914* (Folkestone: Dawson).

—— (1983), *Immigrants and the Class Struggle: the Jewish immigrant in Leeds 1880–1914* (Manchester: Manchester University Press).

Bullock, A. (1967), *The Life and Times of Ernest Bevin* (3 vols) (London: Heinemann).

Burridge, T.D. (1976), *British Labour and Hitler's War* (London: Deutsch).

Butler, F. (1972), *A History of Boxing in Britain: a survey of the noble art from its origins to the present day* (London: Barker).

Calder, A. (1979), *The People's War: Britain 1939–45* (London: Cape).

Carlton, D. (1970), *MacDonald versus Henderson: the foreign policy of the second Labour government* (London: Macmillan).

Carr, E.H. (1953), *The Bolshevik Revolution 1917–1923*, vol. 3 (London: Macmillan).

Castle, B. (1984), *The Castle Diaries 1964–70* (London: Weidenfeld and Nicolson).

Chalfont, A. (1976), *Montgomery of Alamein* (London: Weidenfeld and Nicolson).

Chester, L., S. Fay and H. Young (1967), *The Zinoviev Letter* (London: Heinemann).

Chester, Sir N (1975), *The Nationalisation of British Industry 1945–51* (London: HMSO).

Citrine, Lord (1967), *Two Careers* (London: Hutchinson).

Clarke, C.W. (1946), *Farewell Squalor: a new town and proposals for the redevelopment of the Easington Rural District* (Easington Rural District Council).

Clegg, H. et al. (1985), *A History of the British Trade Unions from 1889*, (Oxford: Clarendon).

Cline, C.A. (1963), *Recruits to Labour: the British Labour Party 1914–1931* (New York: University of Syracuse Press).

Clyde Munition Workers Inquiry (1915), *Report*, Cmnd 8136 (London: HMSO).

Clynes, J.R. (1937), *Memoirs* (London: Hutchinson).

Cole, G.D.H. (1923), *Trade Unionism and Munitions (Economic and Social History of the World War)*, (Oxford: Oxford University Press).

Cole, M. (ed.) (1949), *Beatrice Webb Diaries 1924–32* (London: Longman Green).

Collins, K. (1990), *Second City Jewry: the Jews of Glasgow in the age of expansion* (Scottish Jewish Archives).

Cooke, C. (1957), *The Life of Sir Richard Stafford Cripps* (London: Hodder and Stoughton).

Cooper, S. (1973), *John Wheatley: a study in labour history*, University of Glasgow, unpublished PhD thesis.

Court, W.H.B. (1951), *Coal* (London: HMSO).

Cross, C. (1986), *Philip Snowden* (London: Barrie and Rockcliff).

Crossman, R.H.S.(1975 and 1976), *The Diaries of a Cabinet Minister* (2 vols) (London: Hamish Hamilton).

Dalton, H. (1953), *Call Back Yesterday: memoirs 1887–1931* (London: Muller).

—— (1957), *The Fateful Years: memoirs 1931–1945* (London: Muller).

—— (1962), *High Tide and After: memoirs 1945–1960* (London: Muller).

Dilks, D. (ed.) (1971), *The Diaries of Sir Alexander Cadogan 1938–45* (London: Cassell).

Donoughue, D. and G.W. Jones (1973), *Herbert Morrison: portrait of a politician* (London: Weidenfeld and Nicolson).

Douglas, N. (1931), *London Street Games* (London: Chatto and Windus).

Doxat, J. (1984), *Shinwell Talking* (London: Quiller).

Dubnow, S. (1918), *History of the Jews in Russia and Poland* (3 vols) (Philadelphia: Philadelphia Press).

Edwards, J. (1979), *The British Government and the Spanish Civil War, 1936–1939* (London: Macmillan).

Feiling, K. (1946), *The Life of Neville Chamberlain* (London: Macmillan).

Fincher, J.A. (1971), *The Clarion Movement: a study of a socialist attempt to implement the co-operative commonwealth in England 1891–1914.* University of Manchester, unpublished MA dissertation.

Fishman, W.J. (1975), *East End Jewish Radicals 1875–1914* (London: Duckworth).

—— (1981), 'Jewish immigrant anarchists in East London, 1870–1914', in A.N. Newman (ed.) *The Jewish East End 1840–1939* (London: Jewish Historical Society of England).

——(1988), *East End 1888* (London: Duckworth).

Foot, M. (1962), *Aneurin Bevan, Vol. 1, 1897–1945* (London: McGibbon and Kee).

—— (1973), *Aneurin Bevan, Vol. 2, 1945–60* (London: Davis-Poynter).

Foot, P. (1968), *The Politics of Harold Wilson* (Harmondsworth: Penguin).

Fraser, R. (1979), *Blood of Spain: the experience of civil war, 1936–1939* (London: Allen Lane).

Fraser, W.H. (1967), *Trades Councils in England and Scotland.* University of Sussex, unpublished PhD thesis.

—— (1979), 'Trades Councils in the Labour Movement in Nineteenth Century Scotland' in I. MacDougall (ed.) *Essays in Scottish Labour History* (Edinburgh: John Donald).

Gallacher W. (1936), *Revolt on the Clyde* (London: Lawrence and Wishart).

—— (1948), *Rolling of the Thunder* (London: Lawrence and Wishart).

—— (1966), *The Last Memoirs* (London: Lawrence and Wishart).

Gartner, L.P. (1960), *The Jewish Immigrant in Scotland 1870–1914* (London: Simon).

Gilbert, M. (1988), *Winston S. Churchill. Vol. 8, 1945–1965, 'Never Despair'* (London: Heinemann).

Glasgow District Trades Council (1958), *A Hundred Years of Progress: centenary brochure 1858–1958* (Glasgow District Trades Council).

Glenamara of Glenridding, Lord (1989), *Whip to Wilson* (London: Macdonald).

Gordon, M.R. (1969), *Conflict and Consensus in Labour's Foreign Policy 1914–1965* (Stanford: Stanford University Press).

Grenfell, D.R.(1947), *Coal* (London: Gollancz).

Griffiths, J. (1969), *Pages from Memory* (London: Dent).

Guinness Book of Records (1986), (London: Guinness Book of Records).

Haldane. C. (1959), *Truth Will Out* (London: Weidenfeld and Nicolson).

Hamilton, M.A. (1938), *Arthur Henderson: a biography* (London: Heinemann).

Hamilton, N. (1986), *Monty: the Field Marshal 1944–1976* (London: Hamish Hamilton).

Hammer, Richard. (1983), *The Vatican Connection* (Harmondsworth: Penguin).

Hannah, L. (1978), *Electricity before Nationalisation* (London: Macmillan).

Hannan, J. (1988), *The Life of John Wheatley* (London: Spokesman).

Harrington, W. and P. Young (1978), *The 1945 Revolution* (London: Davis-Poynter).

Harris, K. (1982), *Attlee* (London: Weidenfeld and Nicolson).

Harrison, R. (1971), 'The War Emergency Workers' National Committee 1914–1922', in A. Briggs and J. Saville, (eds), *Essays in Labour History 1886–1923* (London: Macmillan).

Harvie, C. (1981), *No Gods and Precious Few Heroes: Scotland since 1914* (London: Edward Arnold).

Hastings, M. (1987), *The Korean War* (London: Michael Joseph).

Healey, D. (1989), *The Time of My Life* (London: Michael Joseph).

Henderson, T. (ed.) (1931), *The Scottish Socialists: a gallery of contemporary portraits* (London: Faber and Faber).

Hinton, J. (1971), 'The Clyde Workers' Commitee and the Dilution Struggle', in A. Briggs and J. Saville, (eds), *Essays in Labour History 1886–1923* (London: Macmillan).

—— (1973), *The First Shop Stewards' Movement* (London: Allen and Unwin).

Hodges, F. (1920), *Nationalisation of the Mines* (London: Leonard Parsons).

Hodgson, G.B. (1903), *Borough of South Shields* (South Shields: Andrew Reid).

Hopkins, C.P. (1920), *'National Service' of British Merchant Seamen 1914–1918* (London: Routledge).

Horner, A. (1960), *Incorrigible Rebel* (London: MacGibbon and Kee).

Hunt, D. (1975), *On the Spot: an ambassador remembers* (London: Davies).

Hunter, E.E. (1924), 'Interview with the Minister of Mines: Mr Shinwell's remedy', *New Leader* (3 October), pp. 11–12.

Hunter, L. (1959), *The Road to Brighton Pier* (London: Barker).

Hyndman, H.M. (1913), *Murdering of British Seamen by Mr Lloyd George* (with a statement and two returns prepared by Father Hopkins), (London: British Socialist Party).

Janeway, W.H. *The Economic Policy of the Second Labour Government*. University of Cambridge, unpublished PhD thesis.

Janner, E. (1984), *Barnett Janner: a personal portrait* (London: Robson).

Jay, D. (1980), *Change and Fortune: a political record* (London: Hutchinson).

Jeffreys, K. (ed.) (1987), *Labour and the Wartime Coalition: from the diary of James Chuter Ede 1941–1945* (London: Historians').

Jews' Free School (1917), *A Short History of Jews' Free School, Bell Lane, Spitalfields* (London: Jews' Free School).

Johnson, D. (1985 and 1990), *South Shields in Old Picture Postcards* (2 vols), (Zaltbommel: European Library).

Johnston, T. (1952), *Memories* (London: Collins).

Junor, J. (1990), *Listening for a Midnight Tram* (London: Chapman).

Kendall, W. (1969), *The Revolutionary Movement in Britain 1900–1921* (London: Weidenfeld and Nicolson).

Kershen, Anne (1985), *Trade Unionism amongst the Clothing Workers of London and Leeds 1872–1915: a study of industrial assimilation*. University of Warwick, unpublished MPhil thesis.

—— (1986) *Trade Unionism among the Jewish Tailoring Workers of London 1872–1915* (London: London Museum of Jewish Life).

Kinloch, J.A. (1976), *The Scottish Co-operative Wholesale Society 1868–1918*. University of Strathclyde, unpublished PhD thesis.

Kirkwood, David (1935), *My Life of Revolt* (London: Harrap).

Knox, W. (1987), *James Maxton* (Manchester: Manchester University Press).

Labour Research Department (1926), *The Coal Crisis: facts from the Samuel Commission, 1925–26* (London: Labour Research Department).

Lerner, S. (1961), 'The Impact of Jewish Immigration on the London Clothing Industry and Trade Unions', *Bulletin of the Society for the Study of Labour History*, vol. XII (Summer 1966).

Leventhal, W. (1989), *Arthur Henderson* (Manchester: Manchester University Press).

Levin, N. (1978), *The Jewish Socialist Movement 1871–1917* (London: Routledge and Kegan Paul).

Levitt, I. (1988), *Government and Social Conditions in Scotland 1845–1919* (Edinburgh: Scottish History Society).

Lipman, V.D. (1954), *A Social History of the Jews in England 1850–1950* (London: Watts).

—— (1990), *A History of the Jews in Britain* (London: Pinter).

Lord, W. (1960), *The Good Years: From 1900 to the First World War* (London: Longman).

Lyman, R. (1957), *The First Labour Government 1924* (London: Chapman and Hall).

Macassey, L. (1922), *Labour Policy, False and True* (London: Thornton and Butterworth).

MacDonald, J.R. (1919), *Parliament and Revolution* (Manchester: National Labour Press).

Mackenzie, N. (ed.) (1978), *The Letters of Sidney and Beatrice Webb, Vol 3, Pilgrimage* (Cambridge: Cambridge University Press).

McKibbin, R. (1974), *The Evolution of the Labour Party 1910–1924* (Oxford: Oxford University Press).

Maclean, J. (1978), *In the Rapids of Revolution: essays, articles and letters 1902–23* ed. and with an introduction and commentaries by Nan Milton (London: Allison and Busby).

McLean, I.S. (1972), *The Labour Movement in Clydeside Politics 1914–22* University of Oxford, unpublished DPhil.

—— (1974), 'Red Clydeside 1915–1919' in J. Stevenson and R. Quinault (eds), *Popular Protest and Public Order* (London: Allen and Unwin).

—— (1982), *The Legend of Red Clydeside* (Edinburgh: John Donald).

McShane, H. and J. Smith (1978), *Harry McShane: no mean fighter* (London: Pluto).

Marquand, D. (1977), *Ramsay MacDonald* (London: Jonathan Cape).

Marwick, W.H. (1967), *A Short History of Labour in Scotland* (Edinburgh: Chambers).

Marx, K. (1902), *Wage, Labour and Capital* (London: Martin and Lawrence).

Maurice, General Sir F. (1939), *Haldane 1915–1928: the life of Viscount Haldane of Cloan* (London: Faber and Faber).

Melling, J. (1982), 'Scottish Industrialists and the Changing Character of Class Relations in the Clyde Region c. 1880–1918', in T. Dickson (ed.), *Capital and Class in Scotland* (Edinburgh: John Donald).

—— (1983), *Rent Strikes: people's struggle for housing in West Scotland 1890–1916* (Edinburgh: Polygon).

Middlemas, R.K. (1965), *The Clydesiders: a left-wing bid for parliamentary power* (London: Hutchinson).

Mikardo, I. (1988), *Back-bencher* (London: Weidenfeld and Nicolson).

Miller, W. (1985), 'Politics in the Scottish City 1832–1982', in G. Gordon (ed.) *Perspectives of the Scottish City* (Aberdeen: Aberdeen University Press).

Milton, Nan (1973), *John MacLean* (London: Pluto Press).

Moran, Lord (1966), *Winston Churchill: the struggle for survival 1940–1965* (London: Constable).

Morgan, J. (ed.) (1981), *The Backbench Diaries of Richard Crossman* (London: Hamish Hamilton).

Morgan, K.O. (1984) *Labour in Power 1945–1951* (Oxford: Oxford University Press).

—— (1987), *Labour People: leaders and lieutenants: Hardie to Kinnock* (Oxford: Oxford University Press).

Morrison of Lambeth, Lord (1960), *Herbert Morrison: an autobiography* (London: Odhams).

Morton, D.S. (1919), *The 40 Hours Strike: an historic survey of the first general strike in Scotland* (Glasgow: Clydebank).

Nicolson, N. (ed.) (1966), *Harold Nicolson: diaries and letters 1930–39* (London: Collins).

Noel-Baker P.J. (1958), *Coal* (London: Labour Party).

Olsover, L. (1980), *The Jewish Communities of North East England* (Newcastle: Ashley Mark).

Oxford, M. (1933), *More Memories* (London: Cassell).

Parkinson, H.C. (ed.) (1938), *The Workers' Charter: a translation of the Encyclical on the condition of the working classes* (Catholic Socialist Guild).

Pimlott, B. (1985), *Hugh Dalton* (London: Macmillan).

—— (ed.) (1986), *The Second World War Diary of Hugh Dalton* (London: Cape).

Powell, L.H. (1950), *The Shipping Federation: a history of the first sixty years 1890–1950* (London: The Shipping Federation).

Price, R. (1986), *Labour in British Society: an interpretative history* (London: Croom Helm).

Prynn, D. (1976), 'The Clarion Clubs: rambling and the holiday associations in Britain since the 1890s', *Journal of Contemporary History* (July 1976), vol. 11, pp. 65–7.

Raeburn, W.H. (1913), *Labour Unrest in the Shipping Industry* Proceedings of the Royal Philosophical Society of Glasgow, XLIV.

Report of the Committee on National Policy for the Use of Fuel and Power Resources (the Ridley Report), Cmnd 8647, 1952 (London: HMSO).

Rhodes-James R. (ed.) (1967), *Chips: the diaries of Sir Henry Channon* (London: Weidenfeld and Nicolson).

Ripley, B.J. and J. McHugh (1989), *John Maclean* (Manchester: Manchester University Press).

Robertson, A.J. (1987), *The Bleak Midwinter, 1947* (Manchester: Manchester University Press).

Rogow, A.A. and P. Shore (1955), *The Labour Government and British Industry 1945–1951* (Oxford: Blackwell).

Rowland, P. (1975), *Lloyd George* (London: Barrie and Jenkins).

Russell, C. and H.S. Lewis (1901), *The Jew in London: a study of racial character and present-day conditions* (London: Fisher Unwin).

Scott, J.H. (1896), *Spitalfields Past and Present 1197–1896* (London: Parish of Spitalfields).

Scott, W.R. and J. Cunnison (1924), *The Industries of the Clyde Valley during the War* (Oxford: Clarendon).

Sells, Dorothy (1923), *The British Trade Boards System* (London: P.S. King).

Sennett, R. (1970), *The Uses of Disorder: personal identity and city life* (Harmondsworth: Penguin).

Sheppard, F.H.W. (ed.) (1957), *Survey of London, Vol 27: Spitalfields and Mile End New Town* (London: Athlone).

Shepherd, W.G. (1965), *Economic Performance under Public Ownership: British fuel and power* (New Haven: Yale University Press).

Skidelsky, R. (1975), *Oswald Mosley* (London: Macmillan).

Smith, D. (1964), *Harold Wilson: a critical biography* (London: Robert Hale).

Smith, L. (1964), *Harold Wilson: the authentic portrait* (London: Hodder and Stoughton).

Snowden, P. (1920), *How to Nationalise the Mines* (Manchester: Labour Press).

—— (1934), *An Autobiography* (2 vols), (London: Ivor Nicholson and Watson).

Stewart, M. and L. Hunter (1964), *The Needle is Threaded: the history of an industry* (London: Heinemann).

Tawney, R.H. (1914), *The Establishment of Minimum Rates in the Tailoring Industry under the Trade Boards Act of 1909*, Studies in the Minimum Wage II (London: Ratan Tata Foundation [University of London]/G Bell and Sons).

Taylor, A.J.P. (1972), *Beaverbrook* (London: Hamish Hamilton).

Taylor, I.H. (1978), *War and the Development of Labour's Domestic Programme, 1939–45*. University of London, unpublished PhD thesis.

Thomas, H. (1961), *The Spanish Civil War* (London: Hamish Hamilton).

—— (1973), *John Strachey* (London: Eyre Methuen).

Thomas, J.H. (1937), *My Story* (London: Hutchinson).

Tracey, H. (ed.) (1948), *The British Labour Party: its history, growth, policy and leaders* (3 vols) (London: Caxton).

Trades Union Congress, Labour Party, Miners' Federation of Great Britain (1924), *The Mining Situation: an immediate programme* (London: Trades Union Congress).

Treble, J.H. (1979), 'The market for Unskilled Male Labour in Glasgow, 1891–1914' in I. MacDougall (ed.), *Essays in Scottish Labour History* (Edinburgh: John Donald).

Tupper, E. (1938), *Seamen's Torch: the life story of Captain Edward C. Tupper* (London: Hutchinson).

Union of Liberal and Progressive Synagogues (1967), *Service of the Heart: weekday sabbath and festival prayers for home and synagogue* (London: Union of Liberal and Progressive Synagogues).

Vernon, H.R. (1967), *The Socialist Labour Party and the Working Class Movement on the Clyde*, University of Leeds, unpublished MPhil thesis.

Walker, G. (1988), *Thomas Johnston* (Manchester: Manchester University Press).

Walker, H. (1896), *East London: sketches of Christian work and workers* (London: Religious Tract Society).

White, J. (1980), *Rothschild Buildings: life in an East End tenement block 1887–1920* (London: Routledge and Kegan Paul).

Wigg, Lord (1972), *George Wigg* (London: Michael Joseph).

Williams, B. (1980), 'The Beginnings of Jewish Trade Unionism in Manchester 1889–91', in K. Lunn (ed.) *Hosts, Immigrants and Minorities: historical responses to newcomers in British society 1870–1914* (Folkestone: Dawson).

Williams, P.M. (1979), *Hugh Gaitskell: a political biography* (London: Cape).
—— (ed.) (1983), *The Diary of Hugh Gaitskell 1945–1956* (London: Cape).
Wilson, H. (1945), *New Deal for Coal* (London: Contact).
—— (1964), *The Relevance of British Socialism* (London: Weidenfeld and Nicolson).
—— (1971), *The Labour Government 1964–1970: a personal record* (London: Weidenfeld and Nicolson).
—— (1979), *Final Term: the Labour Government 1974–1976* (London: Weidenfeld and Nicolson).
—— (1986), *Memoirs 1916–1964: the making of a Prime Minister* (London: Weidenfeld and Nicolson).
Winter, J.M. (1972), 'Arthur Henderson, the Russian Revolution and the Reconstruction of the Labour Party', *Historical Journal*, vol. 15, no. 4, pp. 753–73.
Young, K. (ed.) (1973), *The Diaries of Sir Robert Bruce Lockhart, Vol 1. 1915–1938* (London: Macmillan).
Ziegler, P. (1985), *Mountbatten: the official biography* (London: Collins).

Index

Abyssinia, Italian invasion of, 175–6

Adamson, Mrs Janet, 196

Adler, Chief Rabbi Hermann, 9, 10

Adler, Friedrich, 113, 114, 115

Admiralty, and seamen's unions, 49–50, 63

Alba, Duke of, 180–1

Alexander, Albert, 190, 208, 210, 238, 248

Allen, James, 38

Amalgamated Marine Workers' Union, 133–6, 137, 138

Amalgamated Society of Tailors and Tailoresses, 30

Amalgamated Union of Clothing Operatives, 26, 28–9

Ampel, Frank, alleged spy, 235–6

Anchor shipping line, 38, 94

anti-Semitism: ES first meets, 8–9; at French's trial, 45–6; Wheatley's article, 61; and rise of Hitler, 167–8; Bower incident, 182, 183; Bevin's, 244–5, 246; *see also* Jewish community

army reforms, ES at War Office and, 145–6, 232, 233, 237–9, 240, 241

Asquith, H.H., 53, 125, 131, 132

Astor, Nancy, Lady, 122

Attlee, Clement: MP (1922), 120; and National Government (1931), 153, 155; and ILP, 162; rise of, 164; Labour Party leader, 169, 172, 173, 175, 179, 184; and Munich, 185; and wartime coalition, 189, 190, 191, 203–4; Prime Minister (1945), 206; and coal crisis, 218, 223–5; and defence expenditure, 239; and Korean War, 256; and Eisenhower, 258; illness, 269–70, 274, 276; leadership contest, 269–70, 275; retirement, 277

Attlee, Violet, 185

Augustow, Poland, 4, 5

Australian centenary celebrations, 277

Austria, Anschluss, 185

Baillie, Sir Adrian, 155

Baldwin, Stanley, 122, 137, 145–6, 176, 177

Balogh, Tom (later Lord), 193

Barker, General, (Palestine), 245

Barnes, Alfred, 207, 222, 223, 225, 226

Bartlett, Vernon, 184

Beardmore's Engineering Works, 56, 58, 59–60

Beaton, Sergeant, 97

Beaverbrook, Lord, 193, 201

Bell, Tom, 87

Benn, W. Wedgwood, 143, 166

Doig, Peter, punched by ES, 285
Dollan, Pat, 79, 95, 97, 110–11, 161
Donnelly, Desmond, 281
Dormand, Jack, 278, 298
Driberg, Tom, 262, 269
Duncan, Sir Andrew, 193
Durham, ES's speech (1932), 162–3
Durham Miners' Association, 197–8

Easington constituency, 246, 278, 298
East Germany, 233–4
Eastern Europe: Jews in, 4–5;
    communist governments in,
    233–4
Eden, Anthony, 274, 277
Edwards, Ebby, 163, 212
Egypt, 243–4, 262
Eisenhower, General Dwight D.,
    255, 258–9
elections: 1918 'Coupon', 72–4;
    (1922), 117–20; (1923), 122–3;
    (1928) by-election, 140–1;
    (1929), 141; (1931), 155;
    (1935), 168–71, 173–4; (1945),
    204–6; (1950), 246–7; (1951),
    262, 263, 264; (1955), 274;
    (1959), 278; (1964), 280;
    (1966), 290; (1970), 298
Elvin, H., 167
engineering lockout (1897), 21
European Defence Community, 267
European Economic Community:
    Labour Party and, 291–2; ES's
    opposition to, 297–8, 302

Fairfield Shipyard dispute (1915), 54
Farouk, King, of Egypt, 243–4
Ferguson, Sir Donald, 211, 222
Finn, Joseph, 13, 14
First World War, 48–50, 51, 60,
    66–8, 72
Fitzsimmons, Robert, boxer, 21–2
Forward: radical paper, 40, 47; on
    Lloyd George, 58; anti-Semitic

article by Wheatley in, 61; on
    trial of ES and Gallacher, 98; ES
    on Lenin in, 112
Foster, Will, 218
Freedman, Archie, 26
Freedman, Fanny *see* Shinwell,
    Fanny
Freedman, Nat, 26
Freedman family, 26–7
Freeman, John, 261
French, Alfred: National Sailors' and
    Firemen's Union, 36, 37, 38–9;
    murder of Jimmy Martin, 41–2,
    45–6
Fuel Committee (Cabinet), 224, 226

Gaitskell, Dora, 263
Gaitskell, Hugh: ES's Parliamentary
    Secretary, 218–19, 220, 221,
    222, 225; on ES, 226, 231, 263;
    Minister for Fuel and Power,
    227; at Brussels (1951), 251; as
    Chancellor of Exchequer, 259,
    260; ES's dislike of, 268; and
    succession to Attlee, 269–70,
    276–7; on Suez crisis, 277; and
    Labour opposition to NATO,
    279
Gallacher, Willie: friendship with ES,
    40, 55–7; Clyde Workers'
    Committee, 55–6, 57, 76–7;
    and 40-hour week strike, 77–8,
    81, 83, 84, 85, 86, 88; aftermath
    and trial, 93, 95, 96, 98; as MP,
    180–1, 185, 192; and Bower
    incident, 182
General Strike (1926), 136, 137–8,
    142
Geneva, International Labour
    Conference, 146, 147–8
George V, King, 129
Georgia, Soviet invasion of, 114–15
Germany: and end of First World
    War, 73, 75; Ruhr strike, 128;

seat at 1931 election, 155; as Labour Party speaker, 160–9; on Jews in Germany, 167–8; re-elected 1935 (Seaham), 168–71, 172–7; and Bevin, 169, 188, 194, 201, 203, 248, 253; criticism of Morrison, 172–3; in Parliament (1935), 172–7; and Spanish Civil War, 177–81; visits Spain, 178–9; boxes Cdr Bower's ear, 182–3; refuses post in wartime government, 188, 190–1; opposition role in wartime government, xi, 188, 192, 193–5, 196–7; and PLP Administrative Committee, 192, 195–8; and shipping in Second World War, 193; nickname 'Arsenic and Old Lace' with Lord Winterton, 194; and Labour's Committee on Social and Economic Transformation, 198–9; *When the Men Come Home* (1944), 199–200; *The Britain I Want* (1943), 202; 1945 election, 205; Minister of Fuel and Power, xi, 206; and coal crisis, 216–27; friendship with Wigg, 217, 231, 232, 261, 268; vanity, 217–18, 261, 272; lack of administrative ability, 226–7; Secretary of State for War, 227, 231–44; lack of ideology, 232, 303; verdict on as minister, 232; and Montgomery, 233, 241–3; and Slim, 243; visit to Egypt, 243–2; and Jews in Palestine, 244–6, 297; Minister of Defence, 248–63; and Korea, 253–4, 256–8; visits to Washington, 254–5, 259; and Wilson's resignation, xi, 259–60; 1951 election, 262–3; Shadow defence spokesman,

265–6, 272–4; dislike of Gaitskell, 268; dislike of Bevan, 269; supports Morrison for leadership, 269–70, 275–6; visit to Israel, 271–2; attack on Churchill (1954), 273–4; marriage to Dinah Meyer, 275, 298, 299; on Suez, 277; admiration for Wilson, 279–80, 295; chairman of PLP, 281, 283–6, 290–4; Companion of Honour, 285; devotion to Ernie, 286–90; relations with his children, 286; on D-notice inquiry, 295–6; in old age, 295, 297, 301; Manchester speech on Six-day War, 296–7; marriage to Sarah Hurst (nÇe Stungo), 299–300; defends monarchy, 300; friendship with Junor, 300–1, 302, 305; in House of Lords (as Lord Shinwell of Easington), 300–4; speeches, in Lords, 301–3; centenary, 302–4; radicalism, 302; books by, 304; continuing malevolence, 304; death, 305–6

Shinwell, Ernie (son), ix, 95, 100, 164, 192, 305; chequered career of, 285, 286–90, 298–9

Shinwell, Fanny, 40, 49, 79, 146, 167, 192, 261; meets and marries ES, 26–7; ES and, 31, 50, 61–2, 164; and Glasgow rent strike, 52, 53; support for ES during Bloody Friday and aftermath, 93, 95, 96, 100, 104, 108; and MacDonald's visit, 118; and ES's career, 130, 184–5, 227, 239, 265; and Mosleys, 151; illness and death, 264–5

Shinwell, Jonathan (grandson), 305
Shinwell, Julia (sister), 138